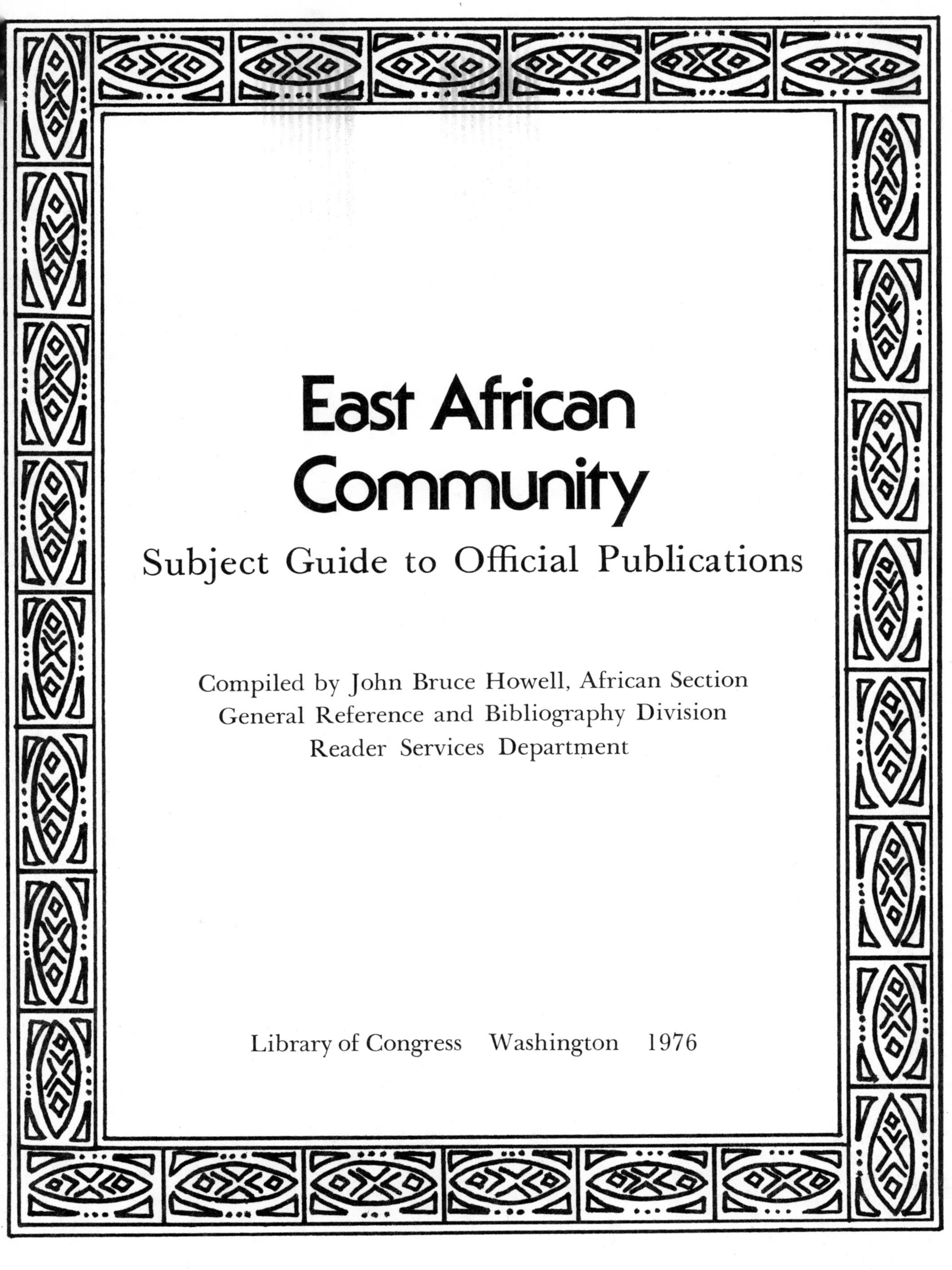

East African Community

Subject Guide to Official Publications

Compiled by John Bruce Howell, African Section
General Reference and Bibliography Division
Reader Services Department

Library of Congress Washington 1976

Library of Congress Cataloging in Publication Data

Howell, John Bruce, 1941–
East African Community.

Includes index.
1. Africa, East–Government publications–Bibliography. 2. East African Community–Bibliography. 3. East African Common Services Organization–Bibliography. 4. East Africa High Commission–Bibliography. I. United States. Library of Congress.
Z3582.H69 [J7301] 015'.67 76–608001
ISBN O–8444–0208–7

For sale by the Superintendent of Documents, U.S. Government Printing Office
Washington, D.C. 20402 - Price $6.65

Stock No. 030–001–00065–6

Contents

Preface vii
Key to Symbols ix
Key to Sources Quoted xi
Historical Note xv
General 1
  Bibliographies 4
  Research 4
Agriculture 5
  Agricultural Education and Extension 12
  Censuses 13
  Coffee 14
  Cooperatives 15
  Cotton 15
  Diseases and Pests 15
  Fisheries 20
  Forestry 23
  Groundnut Scheme 26
  Land Tenure 27
  Livestock 28
  Miscellaneous Crops 28
  Soils 29
  Sorghum 29
  Sugar 30
  Tobacco 30
  Veterinary Medicine 30
The Arts 32
  East African Literature (English) 32
Commerce and Trade 34
  Tourist Trade 41
Communications and Transportation 43
  Air Travel 43
  Posts and Telecommunications 47
  Railroads and Harbors 52
  Roads 73
Description and Travel 74
Economics 78
  Cost of Living 81
  Economic Cooperation 83
  Statistics 84
  Natural Resources 87
    Colonial Concessions 88

Education 91
Adult Education 94
Health Education 94
Higher Education 95
Teacher Education 97
Technical and Vocational Education 98
Home Economics 98
Textbooks 99
Finance 101
Banks and Banking 101
Currency 104
Insurance 105
Public Finance (Including Budget) 106
1890–1947 106
1948–61 108
1962–67 110
1968–74 111
Taxation 111
Geography and Maps 114
History 119
Prehistory 119
Slave Trade 120
Colonial Partition 125
Imperial British East Africa Company 127
Industry 129
Labor 134
Language and Linguistics 135
Swahili Linguistics 136
Swahili Literature 138
Swahili Readers and Textbooks 144
Swahili Study and Teaching 150
Law 151
Law Enforcement 155
Law, Statutes, etc. 156
Libraries 157
Medicine and Health 157
Leprosy 162
Malaria 162
Medical Education 163
Medical Personnel 163
Nutrition 164
Public Health 164
Sleeping Sickness 164
Military 169
Politics and Government 174
Administration, Civil Service, etc. 175
1903–47 175

1948–61 177
1962–66 182
1967–74 183
East African Cooperation 184
1926–47 184
1948–61 186
1961–66 187
1967–74 188
Science and Technology 189
Botany 189
Chemistry 191
Geology 191
Hydrology 192
Meteorology 194
Zoology 209
Entomology 209
Herpetology 211
Ichthyology 211
Ornithology 211
Sociology 212
Population 212
East Africa 212
Kenya 212
Tanganyika 213
Uganda 214
Race Relations 215
South Asians 215
Social Groups 215
Families and Marriage 215
Sports 216
Wildlife Conservation 216
Index 218
Index to Major Series 265
Library of Congress Publications on Africa Since 1960 270

Preface

This is a subject guide to official publications of the East African Community and its predecessors for the period 1926 to 1974, and of the East African region (including Kenya, Tanzania, and Uganda) for the period 1859 to 1974 issued by Great Britain or one of the three partner states. This bibliography includes citations to documents of the East African Common Services Organization, the East Africa High Commission, and the Conference of Governors of British East African Territories.[1] British Government publications have been listed when mention was made of at least two of the three partner states.

The guide is arranged by subjects similar to those found in *Africa South of the Sahara; Index to Periodical Literature, 1900-1970* (Boston, G. K. Hall, 1971. 4 v.) and its *First Supplement* (1973. 521 p.) compiled in the African Section by H. Dwight Beers.

This guide is based on the holdings of the Library of Congress, of other federal libraries of the United States, and of other North American libraries reporting to the National Union Catalog and to *New Serial Titles.* Material in the Library of Congress is indicated by call numbers for cataloged works, and by the symbols DLC–G&M, DLC–LL, and DLC–Micro for publications held by the Geography and Map Division, the Law Library, and the Microform Reading Room respectively. The symbol DLC is used for uncataloged items in the Library of Congress. National Union Catalog symbols (see "Key to Symbols," below) indicate material not in the Library of Congress but held by other North American libraries. Additional sources used in the compilation of this guide are the book catalogs of the Colonial Office Library (Foreign and Commonwealth Office), and the Library of the Royal Commonwealth Society, both in London. Also, the *Library Bulletin and Accessions List* of Makerere University Library, Kampala, and a publication with the same title of the University of Dar es Salaam Library were profitably consulted (see "Key to Sources Quoted," below). Jean E. Meeh Gosebrink, a former staff member of the African Section, compiled many of the East African Literature Bureau entries for the guide.

Entries are arranged within each subject by author (corporate or personal) and then by title. The index lists authors (personal or corporate); references to material on the history of an organization are preceded by the word "about." Literary and other important titles have been indexed. In addition there is an Index to Major Series, which includes British command papers, and microfilmed series such as the *Colonial Office Library East Africa pamphlet* and African confidential print *C.O. 879.*

Later publications of the East African Community may be identified by consulting the *Accessions List: Eastern Africa,* May/July 1975 and subsequent issues.[2]

John Bruce Howell

April 1975

---

[1] Helen F. Conover compiled an earlier guide entitled *Official Publications of British East Africa,* part 1, *The East Africa High Commission and Other Regional Documents* (Washington, 1960) issued by the Africana Section of the Library of Congress.

[2] Correspondence concerning the *Accessions List: Eastern Africa* should be addressed to the Field Director, Library of Congress Office, P.O. Box 30598, Nairobi, Kenya.

Key to Symbols

CLL	Los Angeles County Law Library, Los Angeles, Calif.
CLU	University of California, Los Angeles, Calif.
CSt	Stanford University Libraries, Stanford, Calif.
CSt-H	Stanford University Libraries, Hoover Institution on War, Revolution and Peace, Stanford, Calif.
CU	University of California, Berkeley, Calif.
CaBVaU	University of British Columbia, Vancouver, British Columbia
CaQML	Loyola College, Montreal, Quebec
CtHC	Hartford Seminary Foundation, Hartford, Conn.
CtY	Yale University, New Haven, Conn.
CtY-E	Yale University, Economic Growth Center Library, New Haven, Conn.
DAS	United States, Department of Commerce, National Oceanic and Atmospheric Administration, Atmospheric Sciences Library, Silver Spring, Md.
DBRE	Association of American Railroads Library, Washington, D.C.
DHU	Howard University, Washington, D.C.
DI-GS	United States, Geological Survey Library, Washington, D.C.
DJBF	Joint Bank-Fund Library, International Monetary Fund and International Bank for Reconstruction and Development, Washington, D.C.
DLC	United States, Library of Congress, Washington, D.C.
DLC-G&M	United States, Library of Congress, Geography and Map Division, Washington, D.C.
DLC-LL	United States, Library of Congress, Law Library, Washington, D.C.
DLC-Micro	United States, Library of Congress, Microform Reading Room, Washington, D.C.
DNAL	United States, National Agricultural Library, Beltsville, Md.
DNLM	United States, National Library of Medicine, Bethesda, Md.
DS	United States, Department of State Library, Washington, D.C.
ICJ	John Crerar Library, Chicago, Ill.
ICRL	Center for Research Libraries, Chicago, Ill.
ICU	University of Chicago, Chicago, Ill.
IEN	Northwestern University, Evanston, Ill.
IU	University of Illinois, Urbana, Ill.

IaAS	Iowa State University of Science and Technology, Ames, Iowa
InU	Indiana University, Bloomington, Ind.
MBU	Boston University, Boston, Mass.
MCM	Massachusetts Institute of Technology, Cambridge, Mass.
MH	Harvard University, Cambridge, Mass.
MH-BA	Harvard University, Graduate School of Business Administration, Cambridge, Mass.
MH-L	Harvard University, Law School, Cambridge, Mass.
MdU	University of Maryland, College Park, Md.
MiEM	Michigan State University, East Lansing, Mich.
MiU-L	University of Michigan, Law Library, Ann Arbor, Mich.
MnU	University of Minnesota, Minneapolis, Minn.
NBuG	Buffalo and Erie County Public Library, Grosvenor Reference Division, Buffalo, N.Y.
NIC	Cornell University, Ithaca, N.Y.
NN	New York Public Library, New York, N.Y.
NN-Sc	New York Public Library, Schomburg Collection, New York, N.Y.
NNA	American Geographical Society, New York, N.Y.
NNC	Columbia University, New York, N.Y.
NNC-L	Columbia University, Law Library, New York, N.Y.
NNMR	Missionary Research Library, New York, N.Y.
NNNAM	New York Academy of Medicine, New York, N.Y.
NNUN	United Nations, Dag Hammarskjold Library, New York, N.Y.
NRU	University of Rochester, Rochester, N.Y.
NSyU	Syracuse University, Syracuse, N.Y.
NcD	Duke University, Durham, N.C.
NjP	Princeton University, Princeton, N.J.
OOxM	Miami University, Oxford, Ohio
PPiD	Duquesne University, Pittsburgh, Pa.
PSt	Pennsylvania State University, University Park, Pa.
WU	University of Wisconsin—Madison, Madison, Wisc.
WaU	University of Washington, Seattle, Wash.
WvU	West Virginia University, Morgantown, W.Va.

Key to Sources Quoted

BM Cat., 1965.

British Museum. *Dept. of Printed Books.* General catalogue of printed books. Photolithographic edition to 1955. London, Trustees of the British Museum, 1959–66 [v. 1, 1965] 263 v. **Z921.B87**

BM Cat., 1968.

British museum. *Dept. of Printed Books.* General catalogue of printed books. Ten-year supplement, 1956–1965. London, Trustees of the British Museum, 1968. 50v. **Z921.B8703**

Col. Off. Lib. Cat.

Gt. Brit. *Colonial Office. Library.* Catalogue of the Colonial Office Library, London. Boston, G. K. Hall, 1964. 15 v. **Z921.L388**

_______ _______ First–2d supplement. Boston, G. K. Hall, 1967–72. 2 v.
Contents: [1] 1963–1967.–[2] 1967–1971. **Z921.L388 Suppl.**

Dar es Salaam Lib. Bull. [number]

Library bulletin and accessions list. no. 1+ 1961+ Dar es Salaam, Tanzania, University of Dar es Salaam, The Library. quarterly (irregular) **DLC**

E.A.A.F.R.O. [date]

East African Agriculture and Forestry Research Organization. Record of research; annual report. 1948+ [Nairobi, Printed by the E.A. Community (CPS) Printer] **S338.E3A33**

E.A.C.S.O. debates [date]

East African Common Services Organization. *Central Legislative Assembly.* Proceedings of the debates; official report. v. 1–6, no. 3; May 22, 1962–Nov. 1967. Nairobi. **J730.H24**

E.A.H.C. proceedings [date]

East Africa High Commission. *East Africa Central Legislative Assembly.* Proceedings; official report. v. 1–14, no. 2; Apr. 6/9, 1948–Nov. 8/16, 1961. Nairobi [Govt. Printer] **JQ2945.A75**

Hofmeier.

Hofmeier, Rolf. Transport and economic development in Tanzania; with particular reference to road transport. München, Weltforum Verlag [1973]

363 p. maps. (Afrika-Studien, Nr. 78) HE286.T35H6413 1973
Rev. translation of Der Beitrag des Verkehrswesens für die wirtschaftliche Entwicklung Tanzanias, unter besonderer Berücksichtigung des Strassenverkehrs.

Kenya debates [date]
Kenya Colony and Protectorate. *Legislative Council.* Debates; official report. Feb. 17, 1925–Mar. 21, 1963. [Nairobi, Govt. Printer] J731.K2

Kenya Govt. Press rept. [date]
Kenya Colony and Protectorate. *Government Press.* Annual report. Nairobi, Printed by the Govt. Printer. Z232.K37

Kenya Govt. Print. rept. [date]
Kenya Colony and Protectorate. *Printing and Stationery Dept.* Annual report. 1945?–1960/61. [Nairobi, Printed by the Govt. Printer] Z232.K38A3

London. Univ. Inst. of Educ. Cat.
London. University. *Institute of Education. Library.* Catalogue of the comparative education library, University of London Institute of Education. Boston, Mass., G. K. Hall, 1971. 6 v. Z5814.C76L65

Makerere Lib. Bull. [number]
Library bulletin and accessions list. no. 1+ 1954+ Kampala, Makerere University, Main Library. quarterly. Z965.L5

Makerere Lib. Union list
Makerere University. *Library.* Union list of serials: Makerere University libraries. Comprising the Main University Library, the Social Sciences Library, and the Medical Library. Kampala, 1971. 278, ii, 73 p. (*Its* Publications, 10) Z6945.M247

Mascarenhas
Mascarenhas, Ophelia C. Tourism in East Africa; a bibliographical essay. Current bibliography on African affairs, n.s., v. 4, Sept./Oct. 1971: 315–326. Z3501.C87 1971

Oxford Forestry Lib. list.
Oxford. University. *Commonwealth Forestry Institute. Library.* List of periodicals and serials in the Forestry Library, University of Oxford. 3d ed., rev. and edited by J. S. Howse. Oxford, 1968. xvii, 187 p. Z5991.088 1968

Royal Comm. Soc. Cat.
Royal Commonwealth Society. *Library.* Subject catalogue of the Royal Commonwealth Society, London. v. 3. Africa: West Africa, East Africa. Boston, Mass., G. K. Hall, 1971. 559 p. Z7164.C7R83 v. 3

Royal Empire Soc. Cat.
Royal Commonwealth Society. *Library*. Subject catalogue of the Library of the Royal Empire Society, formerly Royal Colonial Institute, by Evans Lewin. v. 1. The British Empire generally, and Africa. [London] 1930. 582, cxxiii p. Z7164.C7R82 v. 1

SCOLMA [date]
Library materials on Africa; newsletter of the Standing Conference on Library Materials on Africa. v. 1–10; 1967–72. [London, etc.] Standing Conference on Library Materials on Africa. 3 no. a year. DLC
A bibliographic supplement, *Periodicals published in Africa*, compiled by Miriam Alman, accompanies some issues.

SOAS Cat.
London. University. *School of Oriental and African Studies. Library*. Library catalogue. v. 15. Subject catalogue: Africa. Boston, G. K. Hall, 1963. 618 p. Z3009.L63 v. 15

SOAS Cat. (suppl.)
London. University. *School of Oriental and African Studies. Library*. Library catalogue. First supplement. v. 8. Subject catalogue: Africa. Boston, G. K. Hall, 1968. 540 p. Z3009.L63 Suppl. v. 8

Tang. Lib. Ser. East Africana.
Tanganyika Library Service. East Africana collection; a select booklist. [Compiled by Mrs. A. S. Murunga] [Dar es Salaam, 1971?] 46 p. DLC

Tanganyika Blue book [date]
Tanganyika. Blue book. 1921–48. Dar es Salaam, Govt. Printer. annual. J801.R2

Suspended 1939–44.

Tanganyika debates [date]
Tanganyika. *Legislative Council*. Council debates (Hansard) Official report. 1st–36th session; Dec. 7, 1926/Mar. 19, 1929–Feb. 14/16, 1961. Dar es Salaam, Printed and published by the Govt. Printer. J801.H3

Uganda debates [date]
Uganda. *Legislative Council*. Proceedings; official report. 1st–41st session (3rd meeting, pts. 1–3) ; Mar. 23/24, 1921–Feb. 23/28, 1962. [Entebbe, Printed by the Govt. Printer] J732.J47

UNECA, New Acq. [date]
United Nations. *Economic Commission for Africa. Library*. New acquisitions in the UNECA Library. v. 1+ Oct. 1962+ Addis Ababa. monthly. (United nations. [Document] E/CN.14/LIB/ser. B) JX1977.A2

War Off. Cat.

Gt. Brit. *War Office. Library.* Catalogue. pt. 8. Official publications (not including Parliamentary papers), annuals, and periodicals. [London, H.M. Stationery Off., 1910] 559 p. Z6726.G92 1906

Žumer

Žumer, Majda. Natural resources research in East Africa; a report on research services, development and organization of research activity in East Africa. [Stockholm, Swedish Natural Science Research Council, 1971] 87 p. (Ecological Research Committee. Bulletins, 12) HC517.E2Z85

Historical Note

The nations of East Africa—Kenya, Tanzania, and Uganda—are unique among the countries on the African continent in having a history of cooperation dating back to the turn of the century. In 1902 the British government began building the Uganda Railway from the Indian Ocean port of Mombasa across the East Africa Protectorate (now Kenya) to Lake Victoria and Uganda. The railway's administration was composed of officials from both the East Africa Protectorate and Uganda. Today the railroad is called the East African Railways Corporation. In 1911 a postal union was established between the East Africa Protectorate and Uganda that continues today as the East African Posts and Telecommunications Corporation. A customs union was effected between the East Africa Protectorate and Uganda in 1917, with Tanganyika joining in 1933. It was not until after World War I, however, that regional federation became a possibility when Great Britain was granted a mandate over Tanganyika. A British parliamentary commission, the Ormsby-Gore Commission, visited East Africa in 1924 but found little support for political federation. The commission did recommend closer coordination in the areas of trade and research. Also at the commission's recommendation the governor of Kenya convened the first Conference of Governors of British East African Territories in Nairobi, Kenya, on January 26, 1926. Initially the conference was composed of the governors of Kenya, Uganda, Tangayika, Northern Rhodesia, and Nyasaland and the British Resident of Zanzibar, with a permanent secretariat under the governor of Kenya. Many proposals were put forward during the period 1928–31 for political federation. Finally, after much debate and the advent of the economic depression of the 1930's, Northern Rhodesia and Nyasaland gravitated toward Central Africa, leaving Kenya, Tanganyika, Uganda, and Zanzibar to continue their own cooperation, especially in the fields of transportation, postal service, taxation, and, to a lesser degree, trade.

For a variety of reasons, chief of which was African mistrust of European settler domination of any East African federation, a political union was never consummated. Nonetheless, cooperation continued at a pragmatic level. After World War II, another attempt was made to bring about closer regional interdependence. By British Order in Council, the East Africa High Commission was established as the successor to the Conference of Governors of British East African Territories on January 1, 1948. In addition to the services and organizations administered by the Conference of Governors, a new regional legislature called the East Africa Central Legislative Assembly was created to enact laws according to royal instruction. New organizations were established, among the most important being the East African Customs and Excise Department, the East African Railways and Harbours Administration, the East African Agriculture and Forestry Research Organization (successor to the East African Agricultural Research Institute, Amani, Tanganyika), and the East African Statistical Department. The research organizations are often referred to in official reports as "non-self-contained services," i.e., their budgets are reviewed together and financed from the joint fund. The transportation and communication services are referred to as "self-contained," i.e., self-financing with budgets published separately.

On December 9, 1961, the date of Tanganyika's independence, the East African Common Services Organization—a body without colonial ties to Great Britain—was created to supersede the High Commission. Uganda achieved its independence from Great Britain on October 9, 1962, with Kenya following on December 12, 1963. Zanzibar became independent on December 10, 1963, and joined Tanganyika in forming the United Republic of Tanzania on April 26, 1964. It soon became apparent that the Common Services Organization did not fulfill the needs of the three newly independent countries, however, and by 1965 various trade imbalances existed among the three member states. Soon thereafter each country began to issue its own currency, thus spelling the end of the East African Currency Board. In May 1966 Kjeld Philip, a former minister of trade and finance of Denmark, drafted a report proposing a solution to the trade imbalance. This report, which has never been published, became incorporated within a new basis for agreement, the Treaty for East African Co-operation, signed by the three states June 6, 1967, and becoming effective on December 1, 1967, creating the East African Community. As a partial solution to the problems of trade imbalance and varied patterns of economic growth, the East African Common Market was established within the framework of the community.[1] The Common Market provides for a transfer tax on goods as a means of correcting an interregional trade deficit for individual partner states. The community is governed by "The East African Authority," often referred to simply as "The Authority," consisting of the presidents of the three partner states. Within the community, councils consider research proposals submitted to them by the organizations under their advisory and financial auspices, e.g., the Communications Council oversees the activities of the four corporations of the community: the East African Airways Corporation, the East African Harbours Corporation, the East African Posts and Telecommunications Corporation, and the East African Railways Corporation. There are also three tribunals within the community: the Common Market Tribunal, the Court of Appeal for East Africa, and the East African Industrial Court to mediate disputes between various sectors of labor, management, and government. In addition, the Treaty for East African Co-operation provides for decentralization of certain services, and this process continues up to the present date[2]

[1] An analysis of the functions of the Community and its predecessors with reference to various trade agreement and the European Economic Community is Ingrid Doimi di Delupis' *The East African Community and Common Market* ([London] Longman [1970, c1969] 184 p. Development texts).

[2] A succinct outline of the East African Community's structure is included in *A Year Book of the Commonwealth* (London, H.M. Stationery Off.).

General

1
Colonial empire: Introducing East and Central Africa *(Filmstrip)*. British Colonial Office, 1949. Made by Central Office of Information. Published by H.M. Stationery Off. Released in the U.S. by British Information Services, 1950. 45 fr. b&w 35 mm. DLC–Micro Filmstrip
With lecture notes.
Summary: Describes the countries, people, life, and industries of Kenya, Tanganyika, Uganda, Northern Rhodesia, Nyasaland, and British Somaliland.

2
East Africa information digest. 1960–62. London, East Africa High Commission, East African Office. irregular. WU
Supersedes in part the Report of the East African Commissioner (item 292) issued by the East African Office, London of the East Africa High Commission.
No more published.
WU has 1960, and 1962.

3
Gt. Brit. *Central Office of Information*. East Africa to-day. London, H.M. Stationery Off., 1955. 12 plates. 31 x 38 cm. DT425.A52

4
_______ Introducing East Africa. London, H.M. Stationery Off. [1949] 20 cards. (Colonial Empire [picture sets] 12)
Source: Col. Off. Lib. Cat.

5
Gt. Brit. *Colonial Office*. The British territories in East and Central Africa, 1945–1950. London, H.M. Stationery Off., 1950. 165 p. ([Gt. Brit. Parliament. Papers by command] Cmd. 7987) DT431.G72
Contents: Political progress since the war. —Regional collaboration, and liaison with the United Kingdom.—International relations.—Finance and commerce.—Reconstruction and development.—Research and surveys.—The development of natural resources.—Education and community development.—Living conditions and social services.

6
_______ Introducing East Africa. [Prepared by the Colonial Office and the Central Office of Information] London, H.M. Stationery Off., 1950. 91 p. illus. DT423.A5 1950
Includes information on Kenya, Tanganyika, Uganda, and Zanzibar.

7
_______ _______ Rev. ed. London. H.M. Stationery Off., 1953. 92 p. illus.
Source: Col. Off. Lib. Cat.

8
_______ _______ [Prepared by the Colonial Office and the Central Office of Information. 3d ed.] London, H.M. Stationery Off., 1954. 91 p. illus. DT423.A5 1954

9
_______ _______ 3d. ed. with amendments. London, H.M. Stationery Off., 1956. 92 p.
Source: Col. Off. Lib. Cat.

10
Gt. Brit. *East Africa Commission*. East Africa. Report of the East Africa Commission. London, H.M. Stationery Off., 1925. 195 p. fold. map. ([Gt. Brit. Parliament. Papers by command] Cmd. 2387) DT434.E2G7 1925
W. Ormsby-Gore, chairman.
The Commission suggested "the holding of a Governors' Conference to be attended by the

Governors of Kenya, Uganda, Tanganyika, Nyasaland, and Northern Rhodesia, and by the Resident of Zanzibar. The Governor in whose territory the conference is to be held should make the necessary secretarial arrangements, and be responsible for the collection of subjects for discussion. Such conferences should necessarily deal with matters of common interest to all the territories, such as native administration, communications, taxation, land policy, labour, etc., etc."

Contents: Introduction.—Transport and communications.—Native policy: (a). General. (b). Land. (c). Native production. (d). Labour. (e). Native organisation. (f). Education. (g). Medical services.—Trade and commerce.—Tsetse fly.—Scientific research and Amani Institute.—Northern Rhodesia.—Nyasaland. Tanganyika Territory.—Zanzibar.—Uganda.—Kenya.—Conclusion.

11

Gt. Brit. *East Africa Royal Commission.* Report. London, H.M. Stationery Off. [1955] 482 p. 4 fold. col. maps (in pocket) ([Gt. Brit. Parliament. Papers by command] Cmd. 9475) HN792.5.A55

Hugh Dow, chairman.

L.C. has an additional copy in the collected set of British sessional papers (J301.K6, 1955/56, v. 13)

Includes information on population, land tenure, agriculture, economics, finance, health, education, and transportation for East Africa, Kenya, Tanganyika, and Uganda.

The following entries (items 12–21) are arranged alphabetically and concern the implementation of the recommendations in the commission's report.

12

East Africa High Commission. Despatch from the Administrator, East Africa High Commission, commenting on the East Africa Royal Commission 1953–1955 Report. [Nairobi, 1956] 181–196 p. MiEM

A. M. Bruce Hutt, administrator.

"Appendix . . . Transport. Memorandum by the General Manager, East African Railways and Harbours Administration": p. 189–196.

Reprinted from Despatches from the Governors of Kenya, Uganda and Tanganyika and from the Administrator, East Africa High Commission, commenting on the East Africa Royal Commission (1953–1955) Report (item 14) issued by the Colonial Office of Gt. Brit.

13

Gt. Brit. *Colonial Office.* Commentary on the despatches from the Governors of Kenya, Uganda and Tanganyika and the Administrator, East Africa High Commission, on the East Africa Royal Commission (1953–1955) Report. London, H.M. Stationery Off., 1956. 5 p. ([Gt. Brit. Parliament. Papers by command] Cmd. 9804) HN729.5.A552

14

——— Despatches from the Governors of Kenya, Uganda and Tanganyika and from the Administrator, East Africa High Commission, commenting on the East Africa Royal Commission (1953–1955) Report. London, H.M. Stationery Off., 1956. 196 p. ([Gt. Brit. Parliament. Papers by command] Cmd. 9801) HN792.5.A553

Each despatch was issued also separately.

15

——— Land and population in East Africa; exchange of correspondence between the Secretary of State for the Colonies and the Government of Kenya on the appointment of the Royal Commission. London, H.M. Stationery Off., 1952. 33 p. (*Its* Colonial no. 290) NcD

Includes Sir Philip Mitchell's Despatch no. 193 recommending that a Royal Commission be appointed (p. [1]-24).

16

Kenya Colony and Protectorate. *Governor, 1944–1952 (Mitchell).* Land and population in East Africa. Nairobi, 1952. 30 p. (*His* Despatch no. 193)

Source: Col. Off. Lib. Cat.

17
Kenya Colony and Protectorate. *Governor, 1952–1957 (Sir Evelyn Baring).* Despatch from the Governor of Kenya, commenting on the East Africa Royal Commission (1953–1955) Report. [Nairobi, 1956] 106 p. HN792.5.A565

Included also in Despatches from the Governors of Kenya, Uganda and Tanganyika and from the Administrator, East Africa High Commission (1953–1955) Report (item 14) issued by the Colonial Office of Gt. Brit.

18
Tanganyika. Index to Royal Commission Report. Dar es Salaam, Govt. Printer, 1955. 29 p. NNC

"Prepared primarily for use in Tanganyika."

19
_______ Summary of observations by Tanganyika Government on the major recommendations and conclusions of the Royal Commission Report. Dar es Salaam, Printed by the Govt. Printer, 1956. 61 p. HN800.E13T3

20
Tanganyika. *Governor, 1949–1958 (Twining).* [Report by the Governor on the] Report of the Royal Commission on East Africa. Dar es Salaam, Govt. Printer, 1956. 26 p. DS

"Despatch no. 114 dated 7th February 1956, addressed by the Governor of Tanganyika to the Secretary of State for the Colonies."

Included also in Despatches from the Governors of Kenya, Uganda and Tanganyika and from the Administrator, East Africa High Commission, commenting on the East Africa Royal Commission (1953–1955) Report. (item 14) issued by the Colonial Office of Gt. Brit.

21
Uganda. *Governor, 1952–1957 (Cohen).* Despatch from the Governor of Uganda to the Secretary of State for the Colonies on the subject of the Report of the East Africa Royal Commission, 1953–1955. Entebbe, 1956. 63 p. (Uganda. Legislative Council. Sessional paper no. 4 of 1956/57) CSt-H

Included also in Despatches from the Governors of Kenya, Uganda and Tanganyika and from the Administrator, East Africa High Commission, commenting on the East Africa Royal Commission (1953–1955) Report (item 14) issued by the Colonial Office of Gt. Brit.

22
Gt. Brit. *Foreign Office. Historical Section.* British possessions, II: the Congo. New York, Greenwood Press [1969] 110, 39, 174, 49 p. (*Its* Peace handbooks, v. 16) DT423.G74 1969

Originally published in 1920. Each part also issued separately as vols. 96–99 of the Historical Section's Handbooks.

Includes information on the East Africa Protectorate, Uganda, and Zanzibar.

23
_______ Kenya, Uganda, and Zanzibar. London, H.M. Stationery Off., 1920. 110 p. (*Its* Handbooks . . . no. 96) DT432.A5 1920

Peace handbooks, vol. xvi [no. 1]

"Appendix (p. [97]–100): Extracts from treaties, Anglo-German agreement, October 29, November 1, 1886; Anglo-German agreement, July 1, 1890, articles I, II, XI, XII."

"Authorities": p. [108]–110.

24
Gt. Brit. *War Office. Intelligence Division.* Handbook of British East Africa, including Zanzibar, Uganda, and the territory of the Imperial British East Africa Company [by Capt. Foster]. London, H.M. Stationery Off. by Harrison, 1893. 176 p. 2 fold. maps (in pocket) DT423.G78

Contents: General description of British East Africa.—Ethnology and philology.—Climate.—Zanzibar, with Pemba, its dependency.—Coast of mainland.—Central region.—Kittara, or lake region.—Uganda.—History of Uganda.—Countries adjoining Uganda.—Northern region.—Communications and travel.—History of British East Africa.—Explorations of the interior.—Products and trade.—Works of reference.

25
_______ Précis of information concerning the British East Africa Protectorate and Zanzibar. Rev. in the Intelligence Division, War Office,

December 1900. London, Printed for H.M. Stationery Off. by Harrison, 1901. 133, [1] p. 3 fold. maps. IEN

"Originally issued in 1893, and then included Uganda."

26

Handbook for East Africa, Uganda & Zanzibar. Mombasa, Printed at the Govt. Printing Press. annual. (irregular) DT423.H2

Title varies: 1903, East African and Uganda diary.

Superseded by the East African red book?

Compiled by a committee sanctioned by His Majesty's commissioner.

L.C. has 1903–4; MH has 1906; source for 1904–9: Royal Comm. Soc. Cat.

Bibliographies

27

East African Common Services Organization. Catalogue of publications. Nairobi, Information Division, Office of Secretary General [1965?] 7 p. DLC

28

East African Community. Catalogue of publications, 1970/71. [Arusha, 197-?] 5 leaves. DLC

Research

29

Conference on International Support for Research in East Africa, *Nairobi, 1964*. Report. [Nairobi, Printed by Zenith Print. Works, 1964?] 81 p. Q180.A52C6 1964

Michael Word, chairman.

The conference was sponsored in part by the East African Common Services Organization, and the Governments of Kenya, Tanganyika, Uganda, and Zanzibar.

30

East Africa High Commission. Research and scientific services progress report. 1st-6th; Apr./Aug. 1948–Jan./Sept. 1950. [Nairobi] irregular. DNLM

First Research and scientific services progress report preceded by an issue dated Mar. 1948 called Research services in East Africa (item 34) by Edgar B. Worthington.

Ceased publication with Jan./Sept. 1950.

"To be laid on the table at . . . the meeting of the [East Africa] Central Legislative Assembly."

Each issue includes a survey of agricultural and medical research of the departments of the East Africa High Commission.

DNLM has Aug./Dec. 1948–Jan./Sept. 1950.

31

East Africa High Commission. *Commission on the Most Suitable Structure for the Management, Direction and Financing of Research on an East African Basis.* Report. [Nairobi, Printed by the Govt. Printer, Kenya, 1961] 76 p. map. DLC

A. C. Frazer, chairman.

32

Gt. Brit. *Colonial Office.* Colonial research. 1944/45–1960/61. London, H.M. Stationery Off. annual. JV1027.A32

Vols. for 1944/45, 1946/47–1960/61 issued in the series of Papers by command of the Parliament of Gt. Brit. with the following command numbers: Cmd. 6663, 7151, 7493, 7739, 8063, 8303, 8665, 8971, 9303, 9626, Cmnd. 52, 321, 591, 938, 1215, and 1584; for 1945/46 as Colonial no. 208.

Supersedes the Annual report issued by the Colonial Research Committee of the Colonial Office of Gt. Brit.

Includes summaries of reports of various research committees and councils advisory to the Secretary of State for the Colonies, with detailed information on activities of agricultural, economic, industrial, medical, and scientific research organizations in East Africa.

L.C. has 1945/46–1960/61 (1947/48–1948/49 wanting).

33

Journal of Eastern African research & development. v. 1+ 1971+ [Nairobi] East African Literature Bureau. 2 no. a year. DT365.A2J67

"Its stated policy is to provide an organ for an interdisciplinary approach to the study of society. The range of editorial interest will include economics, history, linguistics, and African languages, literature, political science, sociology and education."

L.C. has 1971+

34
Worthington, Edgar B. Research services in East Africa; progress report, March, 1948. [Nairobi?] East Africa High Commission [1948?] DLG-Micro 23940 reel 14 folio 414

Collation of the original: 16 leaves.

Colonial Office Library East Africa pamphlet folio 414.

"This paper summarises the present arrangement for inter-territorial research in East Africa, with particular reference to those services which are directly responsible to the High Commission. It has been prepared for the information of members of the [East Africa] Central [Legislative] Assembly at their first meeting in April, 1948."

Includes information on the East African Agriculture and Forestry Research Organization, the East African Veterinary Research Organization, the East African Tsetse and Trypanosomiasis Research Organization, fisheries, and the proposed East African Scientific and Industrial Research Organization, which was never established.

Later information on research services is included in Research and scientific services progress report (item 30) issued by the East Africa High Commission.

35
——— A survey of research and scientific services in East Africa, 1947–1956. Nairobi [1952] 79 p. (East Africa High Commission. Paper no. 6) DS

Agriculture

36
Agricultural journal of British East Africa. v. 1–5, pt. 2; Apr. 1908–July 1914. Nairobi, Agricultural Dept. illus. quarterly. DNAL

Each issue includes government notices on agriculture, customs trade returns for imports and exports at Mombasa, and digests of Imperial Institute reports.

DNAL has Apr. 1908–July 1914.

37
Agricultural Research Conference, *Amani, Tanganyika, 1931*. Proceedings of Agricultural Research Conference, held at Amani Research Station, February 2nd to 6th, 1931. Nairobi, Printed by the Govt. Printer, 1931. 169 p. S327.A45 1931

Frank A. Stockdale, chairman.

At the head of title: Technical conferences of the East African dependencies.

Includes agricultural information on East Africa, Kenya, Tanganyika, Uganda, and Nyasaland.

38
Agriculture and Forestry Research Conference, *Nairobi, 1947*. Proceedings of a conference held in Nairobi on the 29th, 30th and 31st July 1947. Nairobi, East African Governors' Conference, 1947.

Sir George Sandford, chairman.

Source: Col. Off. Lib. Cat.

39
Amani Library. Catalogue. Amani, Tanganyika Territory, East African Agricultural Research Station [1934] 102 p. Z5076.A6

40
——— ——— [2d ed.] Amani, Tanganyika Territory, East African Agricultural Research Station, 1941. 118 p. Z5076.A6 1941

41
Archer, C. Kenneth. The East African pavilion; report of the Commissioner [for the East African Pavilion] Nairobi, 1937.

DLC-Micro 23940 reel 4 octavo 228

Collation of the original: 49 p. illus.

At the head of title: The Empire Exhibition (South Africa) 1936.

Colonial Office Library East Africa pamphlet octavo 228.

Includes information on coffee, timber, mining, sisal, cotton, tea, and tourism for Kenya, Tanganyika, Uganda, and Zanzibar, with a list of 11 films shown at the exhibit.

42
Brown, E. S. Report to E.A. Legislative Assembly. Muguga, 1970.

Source: E.A.A.F.R.O., 1970.

43
Conference on Co-ordination of Agricultural Research in the East African Territories. [Proceedings] [1st–2d] 1934–36. Nairobi, Printed and published by the Govt. Printer. irregular. S471.A36C6

At the head of title: Conference of Governors of British East African Territories.

The 1st issued under an earlier name of the conference: Conference on Co-ordination of Agricultural Research (Coffee, Entomological and Mycological) and Plant Protection.

A Research conference of the Conference of Governors of British East African Territories.

L.C. has 2nd, 1936; DNAL has 1st–2d. 1934–36.

44
Conference on Crop Responses to Fertilisers and Manures, *Muguga, 1953*. [Papers of the] crop responses to fertilisers and manures conference. [Muguga?] East African Agriculture and Forestry Research Organization, 1953. 1 v. (various pagings)

Source: Col. Off. Lib. Cat.

45
Conference on Public Policy, *2d, University College, Nairobi, 1963*. Conferences on public policy, 1963/4: East African federation; [papers] [Nairobi? 1964?] HC517.E2C6 1963

The following papers concern agriculture: [no. 1] McKenzie, Bruce. A common East African agricultural policy. 7 leaves.

[no. 8] Belshaw, D. G. R. Agricultural production and trade in the East African Common Market—a survey. 16 leaves.

Later revised as Agricultural production and trade in the East African Common Market, published in Colin Leys' Federation in East Africa; opportunities and problems (Nairobi, London, Oxford University Press, 1965 [i.e. 1966] HC517.E2L4) p. [83]–101.

46
Cooney, Sean. The East African scientific literature service. [Dublin, Printed by An Foras Talúntais] 1968. 66 p. illus., map. S535.A23C66

"Report prepared for the Director, East African Agriculture and Forestry Research Organisation."

Note: The service is operated from the Joint Library of the East African Agriculture and Forestry Research Organization, and the East African Veterinary Research Organization, at Muguga, Kenya.

47
Crop improvement in East Africa, edited by C. L. A. Leakey. Farnham Royal, Commonwealth Agricultural Bureaux, 1970. 280 p. (Commonwealth Bureau of Plant Breeding and Genetics. Technical communication, 19) SB123.C485 no. 19

A series of papers given by plant-breeding experts at the Faculty of Agriculture, Makerere University College, Kampala, Uganda.

Contents: Maize improvement in East Africa [by] M. N. Harrison.—Sorghum improvement in East Africa [by] H. Doggett.—Wheat improvement in East Africa [by] E. J. Gutherie and F. F. Pinto.—The improvement of beans (*Phaseolus vulgaris*) in East Africa [by] C. L. A. Leakey.—Soya bean improvement in East Africa [by] A. K. Auckland.—Sesame improvement in East Africa [by] A. K. Auckland.—Cotton improvement in East Africa [by] M. H. Arnold.—The long fibre agaves and their improvement through breeding in East Africa [by] J. F. Wienk.—The improvement of Arabica coffee in East Africa [by] L. M. Fernie.—The improvement of Robusta coffee in East Africa [by[C. L. A. Leakey.

48
Duckham, Alec N. Provisional report on a visit to Kenya and Uganda in September/October,

1948. Washington, Office of the Agricultural Attaché, British Embassy, 1949.
DLC-Micro 23940 reel 14 folio 425

Collation of the original: 13, 21 leaves.

Colonial Office Library East Africa pamphlet folio 425.

"The primary object of my visit was to gather 'background' on the farming conditions and problems in Kenya and Uganda."

49
EAAFRO newsletter. no. 1?+ Sept. 1966?+ [Muguga, Kenya? East African Agriculture and Forestry Research Organization] monthly.

Source for no. 64–65, Jan.-Feb. 1971: E.A.A.F.R.O., 1971.

50
East Africa High Commission. Agricultural, forestry and veterinary research establishment at Muguga, Kenya Colony; preliminary report [by W. Urquhart] [Nairobi?] 1948. 6 p. 2 maps.

Source: Col. Off. Lib. Cat.

51
_______ Regional research programmes 1958/59: agriculture, animal industry, animal disease, forestry. [Nairobi, Govt. Printer, 1958] 83 p. DNAL

East Africa High Commission. *East African Agricultural and Fisheries Research Council.*

Note: In 1954, the East African Agricultural and Fisheries Research Council replaced the East African Advisory Council on Agriculture, Animal Industry, and Forestry, as the prime body for coordinating research into agriculture, veterinary medicine, and forestry in East Africa. The council reviewed the estimates of budgets presented to it by the East African Agriculture and Forestry Research Organization, the East African Freshwater Fisheries Research Organization, the East African Marine Fisheries Research Organization, the East African Trypanosomiasis Research Organization, and the East African Veterinary Research Organization. In 1962 the council was succeeded by the East African Natural Resources Research Council.

52
Annual report. 1st–7th; 1954/55–1961. [Nairobi, Printed by the Govt. Printer] S338.E3A32

Report year for 1954/55–1955/56 ends June 30; for 1956/57–1961 ends Dec. 31.

Superseded by a publication with the same title (item 765) issued by the East African Natural Resources Research Council.

Each issue includes summary reports in nontechnical language and lists of papers prepared for publication issued by the organizations under the Council's advisory control.

L.C. has 1954/55–1961.

53
East Africa High Commission. *East African Agriculture and Forestry Research Organization.* Basic research in agriculture; a brief history of research at Amani, 1928–1947, by H. H. Storey. [Nairobi, 1950] 24 p. illus. S338.E3A53

54
_______ The East African Agriculture and Forestry Research Organisation; its origin and objects, by B. A. Keen. Nairobi, East African Standard [1951] 12 p. DNAL

55
East Africa High Commission. *East African Statistical Dept. Kenya Unit.* Report on an enquiry into the prices of agricultural machinery, spare parts and servicing in Kenya, prepared by P. M. Rees, Deputy Government Statistician. [Nairobi, Printed by the Govt. Printer, 1959] 32 p. DLC

56
East Africa High Commission. *East African Statistical Dept. Uganda Unit.* Investigation into acreage statistics. [Entebbe] 1959. 31 p. DLC

Caption title: Report on second stage of investigation into acreage statistics.

Issued in cooperation with the Uganda Dept. of Agriculture.

57
East Africa tackles the land problem *(Filmstrip)*. Colonial Office, London, 1952. Made by Cen-

tral Office of Information. Published by H.M. Stationery Off., 1953. 27 fr. b&w 35 mm. DLC-Micro Filmstrip

Film strip no. 316.

Also reproduced in book form with lecture notes with the same title (item 73) issued by the Central Office of Information of Gt. Brit.

Summary: Photographs show the different methods East Africans use to improve the land and its cultivation.

58

East African agricultural and forestry journal. v. 1+ July 1935+ Nairobi, Govt. Printer. illus. S17.E2

Bimonthly, July 1935-May 1940; quarterly, July 1940+.

Title varies: July 1935-Apr. 1960, East African agricultural journal of Kenya, Tanganyika, Uganda, and Zanzibar.

"Issued under the authority" of the Conference of Governors of British East African Territories, 1935–47; of the East Africa High Commission, 1948–61; of the East African Common Services Organization, 1962–67; of the East African Community, 1968+.

Includes 5-year indexes.

Indexed in Biological abstracts; Chemical abstracts; Nutrition abstracts and reviews.

L.C. has July 1936+ (scattered issues wanting).

East African Agricultural Research Institute.

Note: In 1927, Imperial Agricultural Research Conference met in London and recommended the creation of "central research stations" for long-range research. The East African Agricultural Research Station was established in March 1927 on the site of the former Biologisch-Landwirtschaftliches Institut Amani which had been occupied by the Department of Agriculture of Tanganyika since 1920. In 1944, the station was renamed institute. In 1948, the institute was absorbed into the East African Agriculture and Forestry Research Organization of the East Africa High Commission and ceased to exist as an independent agency.

59

Amani memoirs. no. 1–91? [London?] 1929–1949? irregular. **DNAL**

No more published?

Amani memoirs are a series of reprinted periodical articles by the staff of the Institute. There are numbers which are original publications (items 112 and 226). A complete list of Amani memoirs is included in the agency's Report, 1942/45 (item 60), and in the Annual report, 1949 (item 67) issued by the East African Agriculture and Forestry Research Organization.

DNAL has no. 1–81, 1928–45.

60

——— Report. 1st-17th; 1928/29–1947. London, H.M. Stationery Off. annual. ([Gt. Brit.] Colonial Office. Colonial no. 50–51, 69, 78, 86, 100, 110, 119, 144, 151, 167, 180–181, 183, 203, 213, 235) S338.E3E3

Report year for 1928/29–1936/37 ends Mar. 31; for 1937–47 ends Dec. 31.

Vols. for 1942/45 issued in combined form.

Title varies: 1928/29–1941, Annual report.

Vols. for 1928/29 issued by the agency under its earlier name: East African Agricultural Research Station.

Superseded by the Annual report (item 67) issued by the East African Agriculture and Forestry Research Organization.

Each issue includes a list of the agency's publications.

L.C. has 1928/29–1946; DNAL has 1928/29–1947.

61

East African Agricultural Research Station. Food crop varieties available for distribution. Nairobi, Govt. Printer, 1941. 8 p. **DNAL**

62

——— List of food crop varieties available for distribution. 2d ed. Nairobi, Govt. Printer, 1942. 8 p. **DNAL**

63

——— ——— 3d ed. Nairobi, Govt. Printer, 1943. 12 p. **DNAL**

64
_______ Plant and seed list. Dar es Salaam. Printed by the Govt. Printer, 1930. 32 p. SB115.E18

Earlier information on plant and seed lists is included in Seeds available at the Biological and Agricultural Institute, Amani, issued by the Seeds Distribution of the Dept. of Agriculture of Tanganyika.

East African Agriculture and Forestry Research Organization.

Note: The East African Agriculture and Forestry Research Organization was created on January 1, 1948, in Nairobi, with the absorption of the East African Agricultural Research Institute, Amani, Tanganyika. In 1951, the organization moved to Muguga, Kenya, a 1,600-acre estate 17 miles northwest of Nairobi. In 1954, the East African Veterinary Research Organization, also created on January 1, 1948, moved from Kabete, Kenya, where it maintains its address, to Muguga. The two organizations are responsible for the Joint Library, the largest agriculture and forestry library in East Africa. Research projects of the two organizations are discussed initially by "specialist research committees," composed of researchers in agricultural botany, agricultural machinery, pasture and range land research, herbicides, entomology, insecticides, coffee, sugarcane, soil fertility, forestry, wildlife, and animal disease. Recommendations from the specialist research committees are submitted to one of four "research co-ordinating committees" on agriculture, animal husbandry, forestry, or wildlife, convened by the deputy chairman of the East African Natural Resources Research Council. Final approval for any project is then dependent upon financial provision being granted by the East African Authority.

65
A brief guide to the work of E.A.A.F.R.O. in East Africa. [Nairobi? 1966?] 26 leaves. S338.E3B3

66
_______ Information resources and services in East Africa; a pilot project proposal to the Rockefeller Foundation. Nairobi, 1966. 5 leaves. DLC

"The joint EAAFRO-EAVRO Library at Muguga will be recognized as the East African research library for agriculture and related subject matter and will provide a special literature service for a minimum period of two years."

67
_______ Record of research; annual report. 1948+ [Nairobi, Printed by the E.A. Community (CPS) Printer] S338.E3A33

Report year for 1948–53, 1957+ ends Dec. 31; for 1954/55–1955/56 ends June 30.

Supersedes the Report (item 60) issued by the East African Agricultural Research Institute.

Title varies: 1948–53, Annual report.—1954/55–1955/56, Annual report; record of research.

Each issue includes a list of the agency's publications, papers prepared for specialist research committees and conferenes, cyclostyled reports, and reprints.

L.C. catalogs under: East Africa High Commission. *East African Agriculture and Forestry Research Organisation.* Report.

L.C. has 1948+

68
_______ Report on the East African Literature Service. Muguga, 1969. 57 p. map. DLC

At head of title: East African Community.

69
East African Common Services Organization. Research programmes. 1962/63–1966/67. [Nairobi] East African Natural Resources Research Council. S535.A23E18a

Suspended 1964–65.

Vol. for 1962/63 includes projected research programs for East African Agriculture and Forestry Research Organization, East African Trypanosomiasis Research Organization, and East African Veterinary Research Organization (for 1966/67 adds East African Freshwater Fisheries Research Organization, East African Marine Fisheries Research Organization, and Tropical Pesticide Research Institute).

L.C. has 1962/63–1966/67.

70
Eastern African Dependencies Trade and Information Office. [Crop report, Tanganyika Territory] May 1930?-May 1939? [London?] monthly. DNAL

DNAL catalogs under: East African Office, *London.*

DNAL has May 1930-May 1939 (scattered issues wanting).

71
——— [Kenya crop report] London. monthly. DNAL

No reports issued Mar.-June.

Includes abridged statistics for maize, wheat, and coffee, from the Crop report issued by the Statistical Branch of the Dept. of Agriculture of Kenya Colony and Protectorate.

DNAL catalogs under: Gt. Brit. *Eastern African Dependencies' Trade and Information Office.* [Crop report] Kenya Colony.

DNAL has July 1930-Jan. 1936 (scattered issues wanting).

72
Father and son *(Motion picture).* British Colonial Office, 1946. Produced by Crown Film Unit, London. Released in the U.S. by British Information Services. Released in Canada by United Kingdom Information Office, Ottawa. PSt

14 min. sd. b&w. 16 mm.

Summary: Portrays a young African petty officer returning to his East African village on leave. In the face of much opposition, he attempts to introduce new ideas on agriculture and medicine.

Credits: Director and cameraman, Leon Schauder; commentary by John Mortimer; commentator, Norman Shelley, editor, George Sturt.

Available for loan from the Audio-Visual Aids Library, Pennsylvania State University, University Park, Pa., 16802.

73
Gt. Brit. *Central Office of Information.* East Africa tackles the land problem. London, H.M Stationery Off., 1953. [12] p. (chiefly illus.) 31 x 38 cm. S471.A35G72 folio

Reproduced from the filmstrip with the same title (item 57).

Also held by DNAL.

74
Gt. Brit. *Colonial Advisory Council of Agriculture, Animal Health and Forestry.* Report of a survey of problems in the mechanization of native agriculture in tropical African colonies. London, H.M. Stationery Off., 1950. 121 p. illus., 2 maps. (*Its* Publication no. 1) S760.G7A5

Includes comparative information for Tanganyika and Uganda.

75
——— A symposium on the operating costs of machinery in tropical agriculture. London, H.M. Stationery Off., 1957. 59 p. (*Its* Publication no. 4) S567.G73 1957

Partial contents: Analysis of tractor costs on a rice farm in Tanganyika, by N. R. Fuggles-Couchman and H. E. Hubbard.—Economic aspects of contract plowing in Uganda, by R. K. Kerkham, D. Innes, and A. J. Armitage.

76
Gt. Brit. *Colonial Office.* Notes on some agricultural development schemes in Africa. [London, 1951] 89 p. CSt-H

Includes information on development schemes in Kenya, Tanganyika, and Uganda.

77
——— Notes on some agricultural development schemes in Africa and Aden. [2d ed.] [London] 1953. 94 p.

Source: Col. Off. Lib. Cat.

Includes detailed information on the following development schemes: Kenya: planned group farming in Nyanza Province, and the Mikueni settlement scheme; Tanganyika: the Rufiji mechanized cultivation scheme, the Nyamilama pilot mechanization scheme, Lake Province, small-scale tractor ploughing services in Ulanga, Kilosa, Bagamoyo, Kisarawe, Matandu, Ruvuma valley, and Nzega; the Usambara scheme; the Pare District mechanized cultivation scheme; the Ulunguru development scheme; and the Mbulu development scheme; Uganda: Busoga Farms, the Bunyoro development scheme, mechanical cultivation investigations, and the Kigezi resettlement scheme.

78
_______ Notes on some agricultural development schemes in the British colonial territories. [3d ed.] [London] 1955. 210 p. CU

Includes detailed information on the following development schemes: Kenya: coast hinterland development, Gedi settlement, Kitui Yatta grazing, Lambwe valley settlement, Makueni settlement, Nyanza group farms, and Shimba hills settlement; Tanganyika: Irangi development scheme, Lake Province Cotton Committee mechanization scheme, Lupiro food farm, Pare District mechanized cultivation scheme, Rufiji ploughing scheme, Ruvuma valley pilot tractor ploughing scheme, small-scale Native Authority tractor ploughing services, Sukumaland development scheme, Uluguru land usage scheme, and the Usambara development scheme; Uganda: Bunyoro development scheme, Kigezi resettlement scheme, and mechanical cultivation investigations.

79
Gt. Brit. *Foreign Office*. Africa. Report on agricultural prospects of the plateaux of the Uganda Railway. London, Printed for H.M. Stationery Off. by Harrison, 1902. 11 p. (*Its* Diplomatic and consular reports. Miscellaneous series, no. 577) HC4.R6 no. 577

[Gt. Brit. Parliament. Papers by command] Cd. 787–13.

Includes information on the Kikuyu lands in the East Africa Protectorate.

80
Gwynne, Michael D. Current rangeland research projects in East Africa. Nairobi, East African Agriculture and Forestry Research Organization, 1968. 57 leaves. WvU

"This survey was undertaken at the request of the East African Rangeland Committee."

81
_______ Plant characteristics that make them suited to areas of low and erratic rainfall. [Muguga?] 1964.

Paper prepared for the Specialist Meeting on Crops in Areas of Low or Erratic Rainfall, Muguga, Kenya, June 1, 1964.

Source: E.A.A.F.R.O., 1964.

82
Heady, Harold F. Range management in East Africa. Nairobi, Printed by the Govt. Printer, 1960. 125 p. illus., 2 fold. maps. DNAL

On cover: Kenya Department of Agriculture and East African Agriculture and Forestry Research Organization co-operating with the United States Educational Commission in the United Kingdom.

83
[Hill, A. Glendon] Précis of work of the East African agricultural departments on improvement of native food crops carried out during 1941. [Amani, 1942] 14 p. DNAL

At head of title: East African Agricultural Research Station, Amani, Tanganyika Territory. Ref. no. DF/5/2 . . .

84
Livingston, H. G. A guide to pasture evaluation techniques for research workers in East Africa. Muguga, East African Agriculture and Forestry Research Organisation, 1961. 85 leaves. DNAL

An earlier edition was issued by the Agricultural Dept. of Uganda.

85
Mann, I. Bees are wealth. Nyuki ni mali. Illustrated by Erica Mann. Nairobi, Published for the Dept. of Veterinary Services, Colony and Protectorate of Kenya, by the Eagle Press, 1953. 109 p. illus. SF531.M284

Cover title. Nyuki ni mali; maelezo mepesi kwa wafugaji nyuki wa Afrika ya Mashariki. Bees are wealth; a handy guide to bee-keeping in East Africa.

Part of illustrative matter in pocket.

Text in English and Swahili.

86
South & East African Combined Agricultural,

Cotton, Entomological and Mycological Conference, *Nairobi, 1926.* Proceedings of the South & East African Combined Agricultural, Cotton, Entomological and Mycological Conference held at Nairobi, August, 1926. Nairobi [1926] 337 p. DNAL

At head of title: Technical conferences of the East African dependencies.

87

Starnes, O., *and* A. Smith. Floating islands in Lake Victoria. Report to the EAC Minister for Communications, Research and Social Services. [Muguga, Kenya?] 1971.

Source: E.A.A.F.R.O., 1971.

88

Stockdale, *Sir* Frank A. Report on his visit to East Africa, January-March, 1937. [London?] Colonial Office, 1937. ([Gt. Brit.] Colonial Advisory Council of Agriculture and Animal Health. C.A.C. 345)

DLC-Micro 23940 reel 4 octavo 227

Collation of the original: 117 p.

Colonial Office Library East Africa pamphlet octavo 227.

Details a survey of agricuture, including major crops, animal husbandry, and soil erosion, for Kenya, Tanganyika, Uganda, and Zanzibar.

89

______ Report on his visit to South and East Africa, Seychelles, the Sudan, Egypt, and Cyprus, 1930–31. [London?] 1931. 100 p. ([Gt. Brit] Colonial Advisory Council of Agriculture and Animal Health, no. 75)

Source: Royal Comm. Soc. Cat.

90

Tanganyika. Despatches from the Secretary of State regarding the financial provision to be made for the East African Agricultural Research Station at Amani. [Dar es Salaam? 1928?] (Tanganyika. Legislative Council. Sessional paper, session 1927/28, part II)

Source: Tanganyika debates, June 11, 1928, and Tanganyika Blue book, 1934.

Agricultural Education and Extension

91

Cockburn, Helen. Poultry keeping in East Africa. Kampala, East African Literature Bureau, 1962. 83 p. DNAL

92

East African Agricultural Diploma Manpower Survey, *1964/65.* An estimate of the demand for diplomates in agriculture, and allied subjects, during the period of 1965 to 1969, by R. H. Clough. [Njoro? Kenya] 1965. 18 leaves. DLC

At head of title: Egerton College.

No more published.

"The survey on which this report is based was undertaken at the request of the Council for Agricultural Education for East Africa. It was financed jointly by the Council for Agricultural Education and Egerton College."

Includes data for the public and private sector for Kenya, Tanzania (mainland only), and Uganda.

93

East African Agricultural Manpower Survey, *1963.* The short-run demand for agriculture and agricultural science graduates in East Africa; the final report, by D. G. R. Belshaw. [Kampala? 1963?] 7 p., 8 leaves. WvU

"FBA/15/634; FA/18/634."

94

Humphrey, Norman. Je, ng'ombe zako zatunzwa vema? Nairobi, East African Literature Bureau [1971] 11 p. DLC

First published 1950.

Title translated: Are your cattle cared for properly?

Text in Swahili.

95

______ Ngombe zako hatarini. Wanyama wana mahitaji sawasawa na wanadamu. [Translated by D. E. Diva] Nairobi, Eagle Press, 1950. 13 p. (Aim at healthy living series) DHU

Title translated: Your cattle are in danger.

Text in Swahili.

96
Mtwanguo, A. Kufuga kuku. Nairobi, East African Literature Bureau [1972] 23 p. illus. DLC

Title translated: Poultry keeping.
Text in Swahili.

97
Waliaula, E. Mahindi bora. Nairobi, East African Literature Bureau [1973] 23 p. illus. DLC
Title translated: Healthy maize.
Text in Swahili.
"To be used after completing the first primer."

Censuses

The following entries are arranged first by country, then chronologically. This section includes only entries for agricultural censuses for Kenya and Tanganyika issued by the East African Statistical Department of the East Africa High Commission. Earlier censuses for Kenya were carried out by the Department of Agriculture of Kenya Colony and Protectorate under the title: Agricultural census (European areas). Later census for Kenya, Tanganyika (later Tanzania), and Uganda are issued by the various statistical divisions or ministries of agriculture of the three countries. These later censuses and the following items will appear in guides to official publications of Kenya, Tanzania, and Uganda.

Kenya

1954

98
East Africa High Commission. *East African Statistical Dept.* Report on the analysis of the sample census of African agriculture. [Nairobi?] 1954. 1 v. (various pagings)
On cover: "Restricted."
Source: Col. Off. Lib. Cat.

99
East Africa High Commission. *East African Statistical Dept. Kenya Unit.* Kenya agricultural census, 1954, highlands and Asian settled areas. [Nairobi] 1955. 12 p. DLC

1955

100
East Africa High Commission. *East African Statistical Dept.* Kenya agricultural census, 1955. highlands and Asian settled area. [Nairobi] 1957. 19 p. DLC

1957

101
East Africa High Commission. *East African Statistical Dept. Kenya Unit.* Kenya agricultural census, 1957, scheduled areas; summary of results. [Nairobi] 1958. [35] p. S338.K4E3
Includes all areas except Coast Province.

1958

102
_______ Kenya agricultural census, 1958, non-African; summary of results. [Nairobi] 1959. [21] p. S338.K4E3 1958

103
_______ Kenya European and Asian agricultural census, 1958; an economic analysis. [Nairobi, Govt. Printer, 1960] 70 p. DLC

1959

104
_______ Agricultural census, 1959, non-African; summary of results. [Nairobi] 1960. [30] p. S338.K4A55 1959

1960

105
_______ Kenya European and Asian agricultural census, 1960; a statistical analysis incorporating data for the 1960 world census of

agriculture. [Nairobi, Printed by the Govt. Printer] 1961. 88 p. S338.K4A56

Includes data for 1956–60.

Tanganyika

1950

106

East Africa High Commission. *East African Statistical Dept.* Report on the analysis of the sample census of African agriculture, 1950. Rev. [Nairobi?] 1953. 46 p. S338.E3A54 1950a

At head of title: Tanganyika.

1958

107

East Africa High Commission. *East African Statistical Dept. Tanganyika Office.* Tanganyika agricultural census, 1958. Dar es Salaam, Printed by the Govt. Printer, 1959. 29 p. HD2136.A45

"The first general census of agriculture in Tanganyika . . ."

L.C. also has on negative microfilm.

1960

108

——— Census of large scale commercial farming in Tanganyika, October, 1960. [Dar es Salaam?] 1961. 15 p. DLC

"On 31st October the Tanganyika Unit of the Department carried out a second census of agriculture throughout the territory."

Coffee

109

Austin, J. R., *Registrar of Co-operative Societies, Southern Cameroons.* Report on a tour of East African coffee producing areas. Buea, Southern Cameroons Govt. [1956?] 25 p. (Southern Cameroons. House of Assembly. Sessional paper no. 2 of 1956) J805.H63 1956 no. 2

"The object of the visit was to study the methods of culture, processing and marketing of the arabica and robusta crops in . . . Kenya, Uganda and Tanganyika.

110

Eastern African Dependencies Trade and Information Office. Coffee; the purchase and development of 100 acres of coffee land in Kenya by a settler with £5000 capital and a small private income. [London, 1924?] DLC-Micro 23940 reel 2 octavo 120

Collation of the original: [4] p.

Stamped at head of title: His Majesty's Eastern African Dependencies Trade & Information Office.

Colonial Office Library East Africa pamphlet octavo 120.

111

——— East African statistics, raw coffee. Dec. 1931+ [London?] DNAL

112

Kirkpatrick, Thomas W. Studies on the ecology of coffee plantations in East Africa. 1–2? [London?] 1935–37?

No more published?

The following numbers have been identified:

1. The climate and eco-climates of coffee plantations. London, Crown Agents for the Colonies, 1935. 66 p. ([Amani memoirs, 28]) SB269.S8 no. 1

"To be obtained from the East African Agricultural Research Station, Amani [Tanganyika] or from the Crown Agents for the Colonies."

2. The autecology of *Antestia* spp. (Pentatomidae) with a particular account of a Strepsipterous parasite. [London?] 1937. ([Amani memoirs, 56])

Reprinted from Royal Entomological Society of London Transactions, v. 86, 1937, p. 247–343.

Cited in the Annual report, 1938, issued by the East African Agricultural Research Station.

113

Specialist Meeting on Coffee Research in East

Africa, *1st, Nairobi, 1966.* First Specialist Meeting on Coffee Research in East Africa, 9–11th February, 1966. [Nairobi, East African Common Services Organization, 1966?] 394 p. SB269.S73 1966

J. B. D. Robinson, chairman.

At the head of title: East African Agriculture and Forestry Research Organization.

Cooperatives

114
Hydén, Göran. Efficiency versus distribution in East African cooperatives; a study in organizational conflicts. Nairobi, East African Literature Bureau [1973] xix, 254 p. map. HD3561.A6E227

Cotton

115
Eastern African Dependencies Trade and Information Office. [Cotton report, Uganda] [London] monthly. DNAL

DNAL catalogs under: East African Office, *London.*

DNAL has May 1930–Mar. 1932 (June 1930; Apr.-Aug., Oct.-Dec. 1931 wanting).

116
Gt. Brit. *Colonial Office.* Africa, further correspondence, October 20, 1909, to December 22, 1911, relating to botanical and forestry matters in British tropical colonies and protectorates in Africa. [London] Printed for the use of the Colonial Office. 1912. (*Its* African no. 953, confidential) DLC-Micro 03759

Collation of the original: xxiii, 264 p.

[Gt. Brit.] Public Record Office. C.O. 879/105.

"Continued by African no. 993."

Includes information on cotton cultivation in Uganda, and in Jubaland, East Africa Protectorate.

117
______ Africa, further correspondence, 1912–1913, relating to botanical and forestry matters in tropical Africa. [London] Printed for the use of the Colonial Office, 1915. (*Its* African no. 993, confidential) DLC-Micro 03759

Collation of the original: xxviii, 296 p.

[Gt. Brit.] Public Record Office. C.O. 879/111.

"In continuation of African no. 953; continued by African no. 1018."

Includes information on the cotton industry, cotton cultivation and legislation in Uganda, and Jubaland, East Africa Protectorate.

118
______ Africa, further correspondence, 2nd January 1914–3rd May 1915, relating to botanical and forestry matters in British tropical colonies and protectorates in Africa. [London] Printed for the use of the Colonial Office, 1915. (*Its* African no. 1018, confidential) DLC-Micro 03759

Collation of the original: 122 p.

[Gt. Brit.] Public Record Office. C.O. 879/115.

Includes information on the cotton industry in East Africa.

119
______ Memorandum on the subject of government action in encouragement of cotton-growing in crown colonies. London, Printed for H.M. Stationery Off. by Darling, 1910. 8 p. ([Gt. Brit. Parliament. Papers by command] Cd. 5215) HD9081.6.G7

Includes information on the East Africa Protectorate and Uganda.

Diseases and Pests

120
Anti-locust bulletin. no. 1+ London, Centre for Overseas Pest Research, 1948+ illus. irregular. SB945.L7A49

No. 1–48 issued by the Anti-locust Research Centre.

The following bulletins relating directly to East Africa are held by L.C.:

[no.] 4. Gunn, D. L., *and others.* Aircraft spraying against the Desert Locust (*Schistocerca gregaria* Forskål in Kenya, 1945. 1948. 121 p.

[no.] 5. Johnston, H. B., *and* D. R. Buxton.

Field observations on locusts in eastern Africa. 1949. 74 p.

[no.] 9. Rainey, R. C., *and* Z. Waloff. Field studies on factors affecting the displacements of Desert Locust swarms in eastern Africa.—Flying locusts and convection currents. 1951. 72 p.

[no.] 15. Richards, O. W. The study of the numbers of the Red Locust *Nomadacris septemfasciata* (Serville). 1953. 30 p.

Research was conducted in the Rukwa Valley, S. W. Tanganyika, in July-September, 1952.

[no.] 20. Vesey-Fitzgerald, D. F. The vegetation of the outbreak areas of the Red Locust (*Nomadacris septemfasciata* Serv.) in Tanganyika and Northern Rhodesia. 1955. 31 p.

[no.] 25. Ellis, Peggy E., *and* C. Ashall. Field studies on diurnal behaviour, movement and aggregation in the Desert Locust (*Schistocerca gregaria* Forkål. 1957. 94 p.

Observations were made in northern Kenya, and Ethiopia.

[no.] 26. Rainey, R. C., Waloff, Z., *and* G. F. Burnett. The behaviour of the Red Locust (*Nomadacris septemfasciata* Serville) in relation to the topography, meteorology and vegetation of the Rukwa rift valley, Tanganyika. 1957. 96 p.

[no.] 31. Popov, G. B. Ecological studies on oviposition by swarms of the Desert Locust (*Schistocerca gregaria* Forkål) in eastern Africa. 1958. 70 p.

[no.] 33. Chapman, R. F. Field observations on the behaviour of hoppers of the Red Locust (*Nomadacris septemfasciata* Serville). 1959. 51 p.

Observations were made in Rukwa Valley, Tanganyika, 1954–56.

121

Anti-locust memoir. [no.] 1+ London, Centre for Overseas Pest Research, 1946+ illus., maps. irregular. SB945.L7A5

No. 1–11 issued by the Anti-locust Research Centre.

The following memoirs relating directly to East Africa are held by L.C.:

[no.] 1. Waloff, Z. Seasonal breeding and migration of the Desert Locust (*Schistocerca gregaria* Forskål in eastern Africa. 1946. 76 p.

[no.] 2. Morant, V. Migrations and breeding of the Red Locust (*Nomadacris septemfasciata* Serville) in Africa, 1927–1945. 1947. 60 p.

Some other numbers include historical or comparative data for East Africa.

122

Ashall, C. Nzige; kijitabu kidogo kwa skuli. The desert locust. Kimefasiriwa na W. Frank. Dar es Salaam, Eagle Press, 1952. 15 p. illus. (Desert locust survey) DHU

Text in English and Swahili.

Desert Locust Control Organization for Eastern Africa.

Note: On October 1, 1962, Ethiopia, Kenya, Somalia, Tanganyika, and Uganda, with France and the Sudan later signatories, established the Desert Locust Control Organization for Eastern Africa by International Convention. All assets of the former Desert Locust Survey were turned over to the new organization by the East African Common Services Organization, which audited the accounts of the organization until June 30, 1964. In its annual audit, the East African Community continues to maintain financial statements for the Desert Locust Control Organization for Eastern Africa. In 1972 the organization moved its headquarters from Asmara, Ethiopia, to Addis Ababa, Ethiopia.

123

Activities of the Desert Locust Control Organization for Eastern Africa, by Adefris Bellehu. [Asmara, Ethiopia, 1970] [24] p. illus. DLC

Prepared on the occasion of the Anti-locust Research Centre, Ministry of Overseas Development, Silver Jubilee 1945–1970, International Study Conference on the Current and Future Problems of Acridology.

124

——— Annual report of the Director. 1st+ 1962/63+ [Addis Ababa] illus., maps. DLC

Report year ends June 30.

Reports for 1965/67 issued in combined form.

Supersedes the Report (item 131) issued by

the Desert Locust Survey of the East African Common Services Organization.
Title varies slightly.
Most issues include a list of the agency's publications and reports.
L.C. has 1962/63+

125
_______ Desert locust situation report. Addis Ababa. semimonthly.
L.C. received Apr. 1/15, 1973; not retained.

126
_______ Monthly desert locust situation report. [Addis Ababa] DNAL
DNAL catalogs under: London. Anti-locust Research Centre.
DNAL has 1962+ (scattered issues wanting).

127
_______ Technical report. no. 1+ Oct. 1962+ Addis Ababa. irregular. DLC
Technical reports are regularly cited in the agency's Annual report of the Directors (item 124).
L.C. has no. 18+ (scattered issues wanting).

128
East Africa High Commission. Memorandum on the Report of the Commission on the Desert Locust Control Organization. [Nairobi? 1956?] ([East Africa High Commission. East Africa Central Legislative Assembly.] Sessional paper no. 1, 1956)
Source: E.A.H.C. proceedings, Mar. 20, 1956.

129
East Africa High Commission. *Commission on the Desert Locust Control Organization.* Report. [Nairobi?] 1955. 87 p. map. NNC
Sir Francis Mudie, chairman.

130
East African Agriculture and Forestry Research Organization. *Plant Quarantine Station.* Quarterly report. Oct./Dec. 1970?+ [Muguga. Kenya?]
Prepared in cooperation with the U.S. Agency for International Development under contract no. AID/afr-691.
Proj. 618-11-110-644.
Oct./Dec. 1970-Jan./Mar. 1973 (scattered issues) held by the Reference Center, U.S. Agency for International Development (AID), Washington, D.C. (Non-AID personnel may use the Center's collections by arrangement with the Office of Public Affairs or appropriate Agency technical offices in Washington, D.C. The Center does not lend documents to non-AID personnel).

East African Common Services Organization. *Desert Locust Survey.*
Note: The Desert Locust Survey was created on October 1, 1948, as an integral department of the East Africa High Commission to prevent the incipient swarming of the desert locust. The survey acquired the resources and assumed the functions of the Middle East Anti-Locust Directorate, Cairo, and the East African Anti-Locust Directorate, Nairobi. On August 15, 1950, the Desert Locust Control Organization was established as a parallel body, sharing common offices with the survey, to control locust plague. In 1956, the Desert Locust Control Organization was merged into the Desert Locust Survey. The major areas of operation for the survey included the Arabian Peninsula and the Horn of eastern Africa until 1956. Thereafter, activities were concentrated in Ethiopia, Kenya, Somalia, Tanganyika, and Uganda. On October 1, 1962, the survey was succeeded by the Desert Locust Control Organization for Eastern Africa.

131
Report. 1948/50-1961/62. [Nairobi, Printed by the Govt. Printer] illus., maps. irregular. SB945.L7E25
Period covered by reports is irregular.
Vol. for 1961/62 called also Final report.
Title varies: 1950/52-1953/55, Report of the Desert Locust Survey and Control.
Vols. for 1948/50-1953/55 issued by the agency under an earlier name: Desert Locust Survey of the East Africa High Commission.
Superseded by the Annual report of the Di-

rectors (item 124) issued by the Desert Locust Control Organization for Eastern Africa.

Vols. for 1950/52–1953/55 include the Report of the Desert Locust Control.

Each issue contains a list of the agency's publications.

L.C. has 1948/50–1961/62.

132

East African Herbicide Conference, *4th, Arusha, 1970.* Proceedings. Arusha, Tanzania, East African Community, Tropical Pesticides Research Institute [1971?] 1 v. (various pagings) DNAL

133

East African Herbicide Conference on Soil Applied Herbicides in East Africa, *3d, Nairobi, 1964.* Proceedings, reported by D. H. Green. Nairobi, East African Common Services Organization, 1964. 369, [21] p. DLC

J. B. D. Robinson, chairman.

At head of title: East African Agriculture and Forestry Research Organization.

134

Gt. Brit. *Colonial Office. Colonial Insecticide Research Unit.* Aerial spraying against tsetse flies in East Africa. Entebbe, 1949–53. DNAL

Superseded by *Aircraft applications of insecticide in East Africa* in Bulletin of entomological research (QL461.B85).

The following numbers are held by DNAL:

1. Preliminary experiments with emulsions and aerosols against *G. palpalis.* [1949?] 23 leaves. 4 maps.

2. Barrier spraying with an oil solution of D.D.T. [1949?] 9 p.

3. Aerosol applications against *Glossina morsitans* and *Glossina swynnertoni* at Kikore, Central Tanganyika, July-November, 1949. [1949?] 58, 2 p. 3 maps.

4. Aerosol application at Kikore, Central Tanganyika, September 1950–January 1951. [1951?] 24 leaves. map.

5. Aerosol application against *G. swynnertoni* in Atta "Island," Kikore, Central Province, Tanganyika, November 1951–March 1952. [1952?] 10 leaves. 2 maps.

6. An attempt to eradicate *G. morsitans* living in "miombo" at Urambo, Tanganyika. [1952?] 15 p. map.

135

——— Aircraft applications of coarse aerosola against maize stalk borer. [Arusha, 1953] 4 leaves. DNAL

136

——— Application of DDT to vegetation. [Entebbe? 1948? 8 p. DNAL

137

——— The choice of jets for house spraying of residual insecticides. [Arusha, 1954?] 6, [5] leaves. (*Its* T.R. 1/2/17) DNAL

138

——— The deposition of aerosols upon tsetse flies and some screening effects of vegetation, by D. Yeo. [Arusha, 1951] 4 leaves. NNNAM

139

——— An experiment to control the tsetse *Glossina morsitans* and *G. swynnertoni* with D.D.T. treated oxen. Arusha [1952] 17 p. DNAL

140

——— Field trials with DDT and gammexane against testse (*G. Palpalis*). Application to cloth screens by K. S. Hocking, A. B. Hadaway, and K. E. Woodcock. Entebbe [1947?] 26 leaves. DNAL

141

——— Interim report on house spraying experiments at Taveta. [Arusha, 1953] 7 leaves. DNAL

142

——— Maize stalk borer trials, Mbulu, 1955–1956. Arusha, Tanganyika, 1956. 19 p. NIC

143

——— Peripheral vegetation spraying: Ziribanje island, by K. E. Woodcock. Entebbe, 1949. 5 leaves. DNAL

144
_______ Statistical variations in dosage [obtained with aerosols released from aircraft] by D. Yeo. [Arusha, 1951] 3 leaves. NNNAM

145
_______ Surface insecticidal deposits on mud by A. B. Hadaway and F. Barlow. [Entebbe? 1947?] 12 p. DNAL

146
Hocombe, S. D., *and* R. J. Yates. A guide to chemical weed control in East African crops. Nairobi, East African Literature Bureau, 1963. 84 p. illus. MiEM

147
La Pelley, R. H., *comp.* Agricultural insects of East Africa. Nairobi, East Africa High Commission, 1959. 307 p. SB919.E3L4

"A list of East African plant feeding insects and mites, with their host plants, their parasites and predators, giving distribution by territories and references to the literature, together with lists of stored products insects and introduced insects, mainly covering the period 1908 to 1956."

148
Nye, I. W. B. The insect pests of graminaceous crops in East Africa; report of a survey carried out between March 1956 and April 1958. London, H.M. Stationery Off., 1960. 47 p. illus., maps. ([Gt. Brit.] Colonial Office. Colonial research studies, no. 31) JV33.G7A48 no. 31

Includes information on insect pests of cereals in Kenya, Tanganyika, and Uganda.

149
Sayer, H. J., *and* R. C. Rainey. An exhaust-nozzle for ultra-low-volume application of persistent insecticide in locust control. London, Anti-locust Research Centre, 1958. [7] p. DNAL

At head of title: East Africa High Commission. Desert Locust Survey.

150
Sheffield, F. M. L. Protecting local crops from foreign diseases. [Nairobi, Govt. Printer] 1962. 5 p. DNAL

Paper prepared for the British Commonwealth Forestry Conference, *8th, East Africa, 1962.*

151
Tanganyika. Report on locust invasions in Tanganyika, including a note on earlier action taken in Kenya. [Dar es Salaam? 1934?] (Tanganyika. Legislative Council. Sessional paper, 1934, no. 2)

Source: Tanganyika debates, Apr. 10, 1934.

152
Tanganyika. *Tropical Pesticides Research Institute.* Progress report. no. 1–30; 1946–1961/62. Dar es Salaam, Printed by the Govt. Printer. 2 no. a year. SB951.T32

Period covered by report is irregular.

Issued by the agency under earlier names: 1946–1955/56, Colonial Insecticide Research Unit; 1956/57–1960, Colonial Pesticides Research Institute.

No. 22, 24? 26? 28, and 30, called also Annual report.

No. 21, 25, 27, and 29, called also Interim report.

Superseded by the Annual report issued by the Tropical Pesticides Research Institute.

L.C. has no. 11–23, 25, 27–30, 1951/52–1961/62; DNLM has no. 6–28, 1949–60.

Tropical Pesticides Research Institute.

Note: In September 1945 the Tsetse Fly and Trypanosomiasis Committee of the Colonial Office of Great Britain established the Colonial Insecticide Research Unit at Entebbe, Uganda. In 1947, the Colonial Insecticide Committee took over the unit and, in 1950, moved it to Arusha, Tanganyika, where the unit came under the jurisdiction of the Tanganyika Government. In 1956 the Colonial Insecticide Research Unit was merged with the Colonial Agricultural Insecticide Research Unit to create the Colonial Pesticides Research Unit. In April 1961 the unit was renamed the Tropical Pesticides Research Institute. The institute became a department of the East African Common Services Organization on July 1, 1962. Current research is concentrated on insecticides, herbicides, fungicides, and molluscicides.

153
Annual report. 1962+ [Arusha?] illus. DLC

Report for 1962 covers period Apr.-Dec.

At head of title, 1962–66: East African Common Services Organization; 1967+ East African Community.

Supersedes the Progress report issued by the Tropical Pesticides Research Institute of Tanganyika.

Vol. for 1962 called also Progress report no. 31.

Each issue includes information on insecticides, herbicides, fungicides, molluscicides, a list of the agency's publications and miscellaneous reports.

L.C. has 1962+

154
______ Herbicides in East Africa; recommendations to the national governments. [Arusha? 1968?]

Source: Makerere Lib. Bull. no. 76.

155
______ T.P.R.I. miscellaneous report. [Arusha] irregular. DNAL

Supersedes and continues the numbering of Miscellaneous report issued by the Tropical Pesticides Research Institute of Tanganyika.

Each report has a distinct title.

A list of the T.P.R.I. miscellaneous reports issued during the year is included in the agency's Annual report (item 153).

Some reports are not for general distribution.

DNAL has no. 487+ Dec. 1964+ (scattered issues wanting).

Fisheries

156
The African journal of tropical hydrobiology and fisheries. v. 1+ 1971+ Nairobi, Published for the East African Freshwater Fisheries Research Organization, and the East African Marine Fisheries Research Organization, by the East African Literature Bureau. illus. 2 no. a year. SH1.A34

L.C. has 1971+

157
Beverton, R. J. H. Report on the state of the Lake Victoria fisheries. [Lowestoft, Eng.?] Fisheries Laboratory, Lowestoft, 1959. 44, A-E leaves. DLC

158
East Africa High Commission. *East African Fisheries Research Organization.* Annual report. 1948–59. Jinja, Uganda. illus. SH315.E3A33

Report year for 1948–53, 1956/57–1959 ends Dec. 31; for 1954/55–1955/56 ends June 30.

Vols. for 1948–49 issued by the agency under its earlier name: East African Inland Fisheries Research Organization.

Superseded by a publication with the same title (item 163) issued by the East African Freshwater Fisheries Research Organization.

Each issue includes a list of the agency's publications.

L.C. has 1949–59 (1950 wanting).

159
______ Pamphlet. no. 1+ Jinja, 1957+ WaU

The following number is held by WaU:

no. 1. Garrod, D. J. A review of Lake Victoria Fishery Service records, 1951–1956. 10 p.

160
______ Supplementary publication. no. 1–2? Jinja, 1956–1957? irregular. DLC

No more published?

The following numbers are held by L.C.:

no. 1. Lowe, Rosemary H. M. Observations on the biology of *Tilapia* (Pisces-Cichlidae) in Lake Victoria, East Africa. 1956. 72 p. maps.

no. 2. Garrod, D. J. An analysis of records of gillnet fishing in Pilkington Bay, Lake Victoria. 1957. 17 p.

East Africa High Commission. *Lake Victoria Fisheries Service.*

Note: In 1944, the Conference of Governors of British East African Territories established the Lake Victoria Fisheries Board. In 1947, the Lake Victoria Fisheries Service became the secretariat to the board and carried out the board's decisions. On January 1, 1948, the service came under the jurisdiction of the East Africa High Commission, with headquarters at Mwanza, Tanganyika. On June 15, 1951, the service moved to Kisumu, Kenya, but retained offices in Mwanza, Tanganyika, and Entebbe, Uganda. One of the main activities of the service was to collect and maintain statistics on the fishing industry on Lake Victoria. On June 30, 1960, the service was dissolved, and its responsibilities were turned over to the fisheries organizations of Kenya, Tanganyika, and Uganda.

161

Annual report. 1949–1958/59. [Kisumu, Kenya?] illus. SH315.V5E3

Report year for 1949–53 ends Dec. 31; for 1954/55–1958/59 ends June 30.

Printed in Nairobi, Kenya, 1949–1955/56; printed in Kampala, Uganda, 1956/57–1958/59.

Later information on Lake Victoria fisheries is included in the Report on Kenya fisheries issued by the Fisheries Dept. of Kenya.

L.C. has 1950–52, and 1955/56–1958/59.

162

______ Records of meetings held on 4th-6th December, 1948. [Kisumu, Kenya?]

Issued by the agency under its earlier name: Lake Victoria Fisheries Board.

Source: Col. Off. Lib. Cat.

East African Freshwater Fisheries Research Organization.

Note: The East African Inland Fisheries Research Organization was created in Jinja, Uganda, in 1947. On January 1, 1948, the organization came under the jurisdiction of the East Africa High Commission. In 1950, the name of the organization was shortened to East African Fisheries Organization. In 1960, the name was again changed to its present form. Much of the organization's research has been directed toward the analysis of Lake Victoria *Tilapia* fisheries.

163

______ Annual report. 1960+ Jinja, Uganda. illus. SH315.E3E37a

Vol. for 1962/63 covers period Jan. 1962-Dec. 1963.

Supersedes a publication with the same title (item 158) issued by the East African Fisheries Research Organization of the East Africa High Commission.

L.C. has 1960+

164

______ EAFFRO occasionial papers. no. 1+ [Jinja, Uganda? 1966+] irregular.

The following occasional papers are cited in the agency's Annual report, 1971:

no. 1. Elder, H. Y. Report on investigation into Tilapias population of Lake Naivasha, Kenya. 1966.

no. 2. The history and research results of the East African Freshwater Fisheries Research Organization from 1946–1966. 1967.

no. 3. East African Freshwater Fisheries Research Organization Annual report, 1948. Reprinted.

no. 4. East African Freshwater Fisheries Research Organization Complete list of published works. 1967.

no. 5. Gee, J. M., *and* M. P. Gilbert. The establishment of a commercial fishery for Haplochromis in the Uganda waters of Lake Victoria, Part 1. 1967.

no. 6. Mann, M. J. The fisheries of Lake Rukwa, Tanzania. 1967.

no. 8. Gee. J. M., *and* M. P. Gilbert. The establishment of a commercial fishery for Haplochromis in the Uganda waters of Lake Victoria, Part II. 1968.

no. 9. Mathes, H. The fishes and fisheries of the Ruaha river basin, Tanzania. 1968.

no. 10. Mann, M. J. A brief report on a survey of the fish and fishery of the Tana river with special reference to the probable effects of the proposed barrages. 1969.

no. 11. Gee, J. M. The establishment of a commercial fishery for Haplochromis in the Uganda waters of Lake Victoria, Part III. 1969.

no. 12. Mann, M. J. Catalogue of EAFFRO scientific archives. 1969.

no. 13. Chilvers, R. M. Bottom trawl codend mesh selectivity to *Bagrus docmac* (Forskahl) from Lake Vitcoria, with some remarks, on the proposed trawl fishery. 1971.

East African Marine Fisheries Research Organization.

Note: The Inter-territorial Marine Fisheries Research Service was created on July 1, 1949, to implement the conclusion of the Standing Committee of Finance of the East Africa Central Legislative Assembly "that marine fisheries research into fishing methods, and the migration, feeding habits of fish of the East African Coast, including Zanzibar, should be carried out on an inter-territorial basis." Financial support was provided beginning September 1950, with the establishment of the headquarters at Zanzibar. The present name of the organization has been in use since 1952.

165

Annual report. 1952+ [Zanzibar] illus. SH315.E3A32

Report year for 1954/55–1955/56 ends June 30; for 1952–53, and for 1956/57+ ends Dec. 31.

At head of title, 1952–60: East Africa High Commission; 1961–65: East African Common Services Organization; 1972+: East African Community.

Suspended 1966–71.

L.C. has 1952+

166

Garrod, D. J. The fisheries of Lake Victoria, 1954–1959. [Jinja, Uganda?] East African Fisheries Research Organization [1959?]

Cited in the Annual report, 1959, issued by the East African Fisheries Research Organization of the East Africa High Commission.

167

Graham, Michael. The Victoria Nyanza and its fisheries. A report on the fishing survey of Lake Victoria, 1927–1928, and appendices. London, The Crown Agents for the Colonies, 1929. 255 p. illus., maps. SH315.U4G7

A report made "to the Secretary of the Conference of East African Governors, Nairobi."

168

Gt. Brit. *Colonial Office*. Fishery publications. no. 1–21? 1950–1964? London, H. M. Stationery Off. illus., maps. SH69.A32

No more published?

The following numbers held by L.C. concern East Africa:

no. 2. Lowe-McConnell, Rosemary H. Report on the *Tilapia* and other fish and fisheries of Lake Nyasa, 1945–47. 1952. 126 p.

no. 6. Frost, Winifred E. Observations on the biology of eels (*Anguilla spp.*) of Kenya Colony, East Africa. 1954. 28 p.

no. 8. Williams, F. Preliminary survey of the pelagic fishes of East Africa. 1956. [68] p.

no. 9. Newell, B. S. A preliminary survey of the hydrography of the British East African costal waters. 1957. 21 p.

no. 10. Fish, Geoffrey R. A seiche movement and its effect on the hydrology of Lake Victoria. 1957 [68] p.

no. 12. Newell, B. S. The hydrography of British East African coastal waters. Part 2. 1959. 18 p.

no. 14. Van Someren, Vernon D., *and* Peter J. Whitehead. An investigation of the biology and culture of an East African oyster, *Crassistrae cucullata*. 1961. [36] p.

no. 15. Wheller, J. F. G. The genus. *Lethrinus* in the western Indian Ocean. 1961. [51] p.

no. 21. Morgans, J. F. C. A preliminary survey of bottom fishing on the North Kenya Banks. 1964. 91 p.

169

Newell, B. S. The hydrography of the British East African coastal waters. London, H.M. Stationery Off., 1957. (Gt. Brit. Colonial Office. Fishery publications, no. 9 and 12) ICRL

Collation of the original: 2 v. illus.

Pt. 1 has title: A preliminary survey of the hydrography of the British East African coastal waters.

Thesis—London University, 1957.

ICRL and MiEM have positive microfilm made by Micro Methods, Ltd., East Ardsley, Wakefield, Yorkshire, England.

170

Okedi, John. Fishery resources; their exploitation, management and conservation in Africa. Jinja, East African Freshwater Fisheries Research Organization, 1974. 20 p. illus. DLC

Forestry

171
Austaraa, Øystein. Report on a tour of Tanga and coastal provinces of Tanganyika, October 1966, and of Kigezi and Buganda districts of Uganda, November 1966. [Muguga?] 1966.
Describes lepidopterous defoliators in exotic softwood plantations.
Source: E.A.A.F.R.O., 1966.

172
______ Report on a tour to Mbeya and Sao Hill districts of Tanzania, 4th–5th September 1967. [Muguga?] 1967. 6 leaves. DLC
Describes lepidopterous defoliators in exotic softwood plantations.

173
Dyson, W. G. Forest tree breeding division: a five-year programme of research for the period 1968–1973. [Muguga?] East African Agriculture and Forestry Research Organization, 1967. 10 p.
Source: Zumer.

174
______ The need for additional measures to preserve forest types and particular tree species in East Africa. [Nairobi?] 1971.
"Paper presented to 19th meeting of E.A. Specialist Committee for Forest Research, Nairobi, October, 1971."
Source: E.A.A.F.R.O., 1971.

175
East Africa High Commission. *East African Agriculture and Forestry Research Organization.* An East African forest bibliography, compiled by A. L. Griffith and B. E. St. L. Stuart. [Nairobi, 1955] 118 p. Z5991.E3

176
East African Agriculture and Forestry Research Organization. Forestry technical note. no. 1+ [Muguga, Kenya, 1953+] irregular. DNAL
Beginning with no. 23 some issues are designated " (Pathology) " or " (Silviculture) ."
The following numbers are held by DNAL:
no. 1. [May, W. B.] Nursery notes to remember. [1959] 9 leaves. illus.
First published in 1953.
no. 2. [Stuart, B. E. St. L.] Seed weights etc. for tree species commonly grown in East Africa. [1954] [15] leaves.
no. 3. [May, W. B.] Fertilizers and forestry. [1954] 6 leaves.
no. 5. [Stuart, B. E. St. L.] Standard forms and covers for recording and filing experimental data and general information. [1955] 2 leaves.
no. 6. ______ Short term planting-out experiments. [1955] 2 leaves.
no. 7. Gardner, J. C. M. An annotated list of East African forest insects. [1957] 48 p.
no. 8. Howard, P., *and* A. L. Griffith. Muguga Arboretum. [1957] 62, 10 leaves.
Revised edition of Forestry technical note no. 4.
no. 9. [Griffith, A. L.] A list of *Eucalyptus* species known to be attacked by the snout beetle *Gonipterus scutellatus* (Circulionidae). 1958. 3 leaves.
no. 10. ______ The stock mapping to quality classes of an even aged forest. 1958. [4] leaves.
Reprinted in Empire forestry review, v. 38, Sept. 1959, p. 301–303.
no. 11. Griffith, A. L., *and* P. Howland. East African yield tables no. 1. Preliminary yield tables for the cypresses of the *Cupressus lusitanica* group. 1961. [17] leaves.
no. 12. ______ Muguga Arboretum. 1962. [145] leaves.
Revised edition of Forestry technical note no. 8.
no. 13. ______ *Eucalyptus* species attacked by the weevil *Gonipterus scutellatus* in Muguga and South Africa. 1962. 3 leaves.
no. 14. ______ Short term planting-out experiments. 1962. 5 leaves.
Revised edition of Forestry technical note no. 6.
no. 15. Griffith, A. L., W. B. May, *and* P.

Howland. Nursery experiments. 1962. 8 leaves.

no. 16. Dyson, W. G. Wood quality assessment for tree breeding in East African *Pinus radiata* Don. 1965. 5 leaves.

no. 17. Dyson, W. G., *and* D. N. Paterson. The selection and appraisal of plus trees for the East African tree breeding programme. 1966. 19 leaves.

no. 18. Paterson, D. N. Crude estimates of genetic gains from plus trees selected in the East African tree breeding programme. 1966. [15] p.

no. 19. ——— Volume and value yields from East African exotic softwood crops in highland sites and a fresh approach to East African silviculture. 1967. 22 leaves.

no. 20. ——— Volume tables to normal saw-timber mercheantable limits for three important East African exotic softwoods. 1967. [8] leaves.

no. 21. ——— The grading of plus phenotypes, its significance in silviculture and volume yields in East Africa. 1967. 17 leaves.

no. 22. ——— Further studies in wood quality, wood quantity, wood value and rotations from wood core analysis. 1968. 6 p.

no. 23. Gibson, I. A. S. Seed pelleting of *Pinus patula* with *Rhizotol combi* for the control of damping off. 1969. 4 p.

no. 24. ——— Diseases of *Pinus patula*, a review. 1969. 9 leaves.

no. 25. ——— A further note on *Fusicoccum tingens* Goid. *(Botryosphaeria ribis* Grossenb. & Dugg.) as a pine pathogen. 1970. 2 p.

no. 26. Owino, F., *and* W. G. Dyson. A list of East African forestry provenance trrials [sic]. 1970. 3 leaves.

no. 27. ——— The growth of pines at Muguga Arboretum 1952-1969. 1971. 54 leaves.

no. 28. Dyson, W. G. Wood properties of young pines grown at Muguga Arboretum. 1971. 3 leaves.

no. 29. Thogo, S., *and* W. G. Dyson. The growth of African conifers at Muguga Arboretum 1952–73. 1974. 11 leaves.

177

——— Mycological note. no. 32+ [Nairobi] 1966+

Supersedes and continues the numbering of a publication with the same title issued by the Forest Dept. of Kenya.

Source: Oxford Forestry Lib. list.

178

East African Agriculture and Forestry Research Organization. *Forestry Division*. Progress report. [Nairobi?] 1971.

"To 19th meeting of E.A. Specialist Committee for Forest Research, Nairobi, October, 1971."

Source: E.A.A.F.R.O., 1971.

179

——— Progress report and proposed programme of forest entomology research. [Nairobi?] 1971.

"To 15th meeting of E.A. Specialist Entomology and Insecticides Committee, Nairobi, November, 1971."

Source: E.A.A.F.R.O., 1971.

180

——— Proposed programme of research, October 1971–October 1972. [Nairobi?] 1971.

"To 19th meeting of E.A. Specialist Committee for Forest Research, Nairobi, October, 1971."

Source: E.A.A.F.R.O., 1971.

181

East African Literature Bureau. Miti ni mali. Kampala [1972] 15, [15] p. illus. SD242.E27E27

"First published in 1950.

Title translated: Trees are wealth.

Text in Swahili.

182

Gardner, J. C. M. Insects injurious to timber in East Africa. Nairobi, Govt. Printer [1957] 15 p. illus. DNAL

"T.A.B. (57) 7."

"Paper presented to the 14th meeting of the East African Timber Advisory Board, Moshi. March 1957."

183

Griffith, Arthur L. The East African Agriculture and Forestry Research Organisation. Nairobi,

East African Agriculture and Forestry Research Organisation, 1951. 4 p. (British Commonwealth Forestry Conference, 6th, Canada, 1952. Statements and papers. vol. 1, no. 4)
Source: Col. Off. Lib. Cat.

184
_______ Planting exotic softwoods in an area with an unreliable climate. [Nairobi?] 1957.
Paper prepared for the British Commonwealth Forestry Conference, *7th, Australia and New Zealand, 1957.*
Source: E.A.A.F.R.O., 1956/57.

185
_______ Statement on the achievements of the Forestry Division of the East African Agriculture and Forestry Research Organization, 1952–1962. [Nairobi?] 1962.
Paper prepared for the British Commonwealth Forestry Conference, *8th, East Africa, 1962.*
Source: E.A.A.F.R.O., 1962.

186
Jones, Tecwyn. E.A. forest insect reference collection: list of insect species [by] T. Jones, M. K. Karanja, and S. M. Kamiti. 3d ed. [Muguga, Kenya?] 1971.
Source: E.A.A.F.R.O., 1971.

187
_______ The East African forest insect survey, by Tecwyn Jones and W. Wilkinson. Nairobi, Govt. Printer, 1962. DNAL
Paper prepared for the British Commonwealth Forestry Conference, *8th, East Africa, 1962.*

188
_______ Progress in forest research, 1962–1967. Nairobi, East African Agriculture and Forestry Research Organization, 1967. 24 p. illus. WvU
At the head of title: East African Common Services Organization.
Paper prepared for the British Commonwealth Forestry Conference, *9th, New Delhi, India, 1968.*

189
_______ Recent investigations of two new tree-borers in the indigenous forests in East Africa. [Nairobi, Govt. Printer] 1962. 8 p. DNAL
Paper prepared for the British Commonwealth Forestry Conference, *8th, East Africa, 1962.*

190
_______ Report on a tour of the S. Highland Province, Eastern and Tanga regions of Tanganyika. [Muguga?] 1963.
"A review of the entomological situation."
Source: E.A.A.F.R.O., 1963.

191
Kenya Colony and Protectorate. *Public Works Dept.* The kiln drying of East African timbers, by W. D. Arnot. Nairobi, Printed by the Govt. Printer, 1931. 80 p. TS837.K35
L.C. also has on microfilm (23940, reel 10, folio 216).

192
Kerfoot, O., *and* J. S. G. McCulloch. The interception and condensation of atmospheric moisture by forest canopies. Muguga, East African Agriculture and Forestry Research Organisation, 1962. 7 leaves. DNAL
Paper prepared for the British Commonwealth Forestry Conference, *8th, East Africa, 1962.*

193
Kirkpatrick, Thomas W. Notes on insect damage to East African timbers. Nairobi, East African War Supplies Board, Timber Control, 1944. 31 p. illus. SB761.K57

194
McCoy-Hill, M. The protection of timber from marine borer damage in East African waters. Nairobi, Govt. Printer, 1962. 4 p. DNAL

195
McCulloch, J. S. G. Hydrological aspects of production forestry, by J. S. G. McCulloch and M. Dagg. Muguga, 1962. 8 p.

Paper prepared for the British Commonwealth Forestry Conference, *8th, East Africa, 1962.*

Source: E.A.A.F.R.O., 1962.

196

Oliphant, F. M. The commercial possibilities and development of forests in British East Africa. Dar es Salaam, Printed by the Govt. Printer, 1937.

DLC-Micro 23940 reel 11 folio 295

Collation of the original: 52 p.

At head of title: Colonial Forest Resources Development Department, Colonial Office.

Colonial Office Library East Africa pamphlet folio 295.

Includes information on Kenya, Tanganyika, and Uganda.

197

Tack, C. H., *ed.* Nomenclature of East African timbers. Nairobi, East African Timber Advisory Board, 1962. 46 p. DLC

198

Wilkinson, W. The principles of termite control in forestry. [Nairobi, Govt. Printer] 1962. 8 p.

DNAL

Paper prepared for the British Commonwealth Forestry Conference, *8th, East Africa, 1962.*

Groundnut Scheme

199

Gt. Brit. *British Information Services.* Not just peanuts; the story of Britain's great agricultural experiments in East Africa. New York, 1948. 28 p. illus., map. HD9235.P32G7 1948a

Illustrated brochure, prepared for American readers, presents the large-scale East African peanut-growing venture as a pioneering effort in social and economic improvement, as well as a means of increasing world supplies of edible fats.

200

Gt. Brit. *Colonial Office.* The future of the Overseas Food Corporation. London, H.M. Stationery Off., 1954. 10 p. ([Gt. Brit. Parliament. Papers by command] Cmd. 9158)

J301.K6 1953/54 v. 26

Recommended the OFC be taken over by the newly established Tanganyika Agricultural Corporation, thus ending the ill-fated groundnut scheme.

201

Gt. Brit. *Ministry of Food.* East African groundnut scheme; review of progress to the end of November 1947. London, H.M. Stationery Off. [1948] 9 p. ([Gt. Brit. Parliament. Papers by command] Cmd. 7314) HD9235.P32G7 1947a

202

——— The future of the Overseas Food Corporation. London, H.M. Stationery Off., 1951. 18 p. ([Gt. Brit. Parliament. Papers by command] Cmd. 8125)

HD9011.9.08G7 1951

The OFC became responsible for the groundnut scheme on Mar. 1, 1948, and assumed control of operations in Tanganyika a month later. A new seven year plan is set out in the appendix for the period 1950–57.

203

——— A plan for the mechanized production of groundnuts in east and central Africa. Presented by the Minister of Food to Parliament by command of His Majesty, February, 1947. London, H.M. Stationery Off. [1947] 48 p. 3 fold. maps. ([Gt. Brit. Parliament. Papers by command] Cmd. 7030) HD9235.P32G7 1947

"Report of a Mission to investigate the practicability of the mass production of groundnuts in east and central Africa, by A. J. Wakefield . . . D. L. Martin and J. Rosa": p. [11]–48.

"A plan for the production of groundnuts in Tanganyika, Northern Rhodesia and Kenya."

This is the "Wakefield Blue Book," blueprint of the ill-fated East African groundnut scheme.

204

Overseas Food Corporation. Conclusions and recommendations on agricultural development

policy in the Southern Province of Tanganyika. London, 1950. 10 p.
Source: Royal Comm. Soc. Cat.

205
——— Report and statement of accounts. 1948/49–1954/55. London, H.M. Stationery Off. 7 v. in 1. fold. maps. annual.
HD9011.9.08A3
Report year ends Mar. 31.
First report covers period Feb. 1948–Mar. 1949.
Superseded by the Report and accounts issued by the Tanganyika Agricultural Corporation.
Also issued in the series of Sessional papers of Parliament of Gt. Brit.
Each issue is almost entirely devoted to either the groundnut scheme or agricultural schemes for Kongwa, Urambo, and the Nachingwea areas of Tanganyika.
L.C. has 1948/49–1954/55.

206
——— Report of the Kongwa Working Party. Recommendations on future agricultural policy at Kongwa. [n.p., 1950]
Source: London. Univ. Inst. of Educ. Cat.

207
Tanganyika. The groundnut scheme. Dar es Salaam, Govt. Printer [1947?] 55 p. DLC

208
Tanganyika. *Laws, statutes, etc.* The future of the Overseas Food Corporation; Tanganyika Ordinance [no. 15 of 1954] London, H.M. Stationery Off. [1954] 6 p. ([Gt. Brit. Parliament. Papers by command] Cmd. 9198) DLC–LL
At head of title: Colonial Office.
Transferred the property and liabilities of the Overseas Food Corporation to the Tanganyika Agricultural Corporation.

Land Tenure

209
Conference on African Land Tenure in East and Central Africa, *Arusha, Tanganyika, 1956.* African land tenure; report. London, Published for the Secretary of State for the Colonies by H.M. Stationery Off., 1956. 44 p.
JQ1881.AlJ8 1956
A special supplement to the Journal of African administration, Oct. 1956.
Includes information on Kenya, Tanganyika, and Uganda.

210
Great Britain. Government lands in British East Africa and Uganda. Return to an address of the honourable the House of Commons, dated 7 August 1907, for "Return showing with respect to the government lands in British East Africa and Uganda (1) area sold (2) sum realised for the same (3) area leased and average period of lease (4) rent of the same during the five years passed, distinguishing land sold or leased in the railway strip and at Nairobi from the other lands leased or sold." Colonial Office, August 1907, Francis J. S. Hopgood (Mr. Wedgwood). Ordered by the House of Commons to be printed, 19 August 1907. London, Printed for H.M. Stationery Off. by Eyre and Spottiswoode, 1907. 6 p. ([Gt. Brit. Parliament. 1907. House of Commons. Reports and papers] 312)
J301.K6 1907 v. 57

211
Gt. Brit. *Colonial Office.* Bibliography of published sources relating to African land tenure. London, H.M. Stationery Off., 1950. 156 p. (*Its* Colonial no. 258) Z7164.L3G7 1950
Comprehensive guide to official and statutory sources for land tenure in Kenya, Tanganyika, Uganda, and Zanzibar for the period 1894–1948.

212
——— Land in crown colonies and protectorates . . . Gambia, Sierra Leone, Gold Coast, Northern Territories, Lagos, Southern Nigeria, Northern Nigeria, British East Africa, Uganda, Seychelles, Nyasaland, Federated Malay States, Trinidad, Jamaica, British Guiana, and British Honduras. Colonial Office, March 1912, John Anderson, Mr. Wedgwood. Ordered by the House of Commons to be printed, 19 March 1912. London, H.M. Stationery Off.,

printed by Eyre and Spottiswoode, 1912. 41 p. ([Gt. Brit. Parliament. 1912. House of Commons. Reports and papers] 68)
HD599.Z5A5 1912

Livestock

213
Gt. Brit. *Colonial Advisory Council of Agriculture, Animal Health and Forestry.* The improvement of cattle in British colonial territories in Africa. London, H.M. Stationery Off., 1953. 144 p. illus., maps, plates. (*Its* Publication no. 3) SF196.G7A52

Includes data for Kenya, Tanganyika, Uganda, and Zanzibar.

214
——— The indigenous cattle of the British dependent territories in Africa; with material on certain other African countries. London, H.M. Stationery Off., 1957. 185 p. illus., maps, plates. (*Its* Publication no. 5) SF196.A35G7

Includes data for Kenya, Tanganyika, Uganda, and Zanzibar.

215
Mason, Ian L., *and* J. P. Maule. The indigenous livestock of eastern and southern Africa. Farnham Royal, Eng., Commonwealth Agricultural Bureaux [1960] xv, 151 p. illus., maps (2 fold.) plates. (Technical communication of the Commonwealth Bureau of Animal Breeding and Genetics, Edinburgh, no. 14) SF55.A35M3

Includes information and bibliography for Kenya, Tanganyika, Uganda, and Zanzibar.

216
Slater, Isobel. Masomo katika kutunza wanyama wetu; mfuatano wa masomo mepesi kwa kutumiwa katika Afrika ya mashariki. Education in animal welfare; a series of 12 easy lessons for use in East Africa. Kampala, Eagle Press, 1955. 62 p. illus. DHU

Text in English and Swahili.

Miscellaneous Crops

217
East African Agricultural Research Institute. An annotated bibliography of cinchona-growing from 1883–1943, by R. E. Moreau. Nairobi, Printed by the Govt. Printer, 1945. 41 p.
Z5074.C5E3

218
Eastern African Dependencies Trade and Information Office. Maize; short estimate of costs of maize farming, drawn up by a prominent and practical farmer in Kenya (1925). London [1925?] DLC-Micro 23940 reel 2 octavo 115

Collation of the original: [2] p.

Stamped at head of title: His Majesty's Eastern African Dependencies Trade & Information Office.

Colonial Office Library East Africa pamphlet octavo 115.

219
Dowson, W. J. Wheat in East Africa. Nairobi, 1919. 10 p. illus. (Kenya Colony and Protectorate. Dept. of Agriculture. Bulletin. [1st ser.] no. 4) DNAL

DNAL catalogs under: Kenya Colony and Protectorate. *Dept. of Agriculture.* Bulletin.

220
Gt. Brit. *East African Rice Mission.* Report on rice production in East and Central African colonial territories, 1948. By Gerald Lacey and Robert Watson. London, H.M. Stationery Off., 1949. 78 p. 5 fold col. maps (in pocket) ([Gt. Brit.] Colonial Office. Colonial no. 246) NNC

The Report is summarized in *Rice production in East Africa: mission recommends method of increasing output,* published in Commonwealth survey (DA10.A35 1950) no. 39, Jan. 21, 1950, p. 37–38.

221
Kenya Colony and Protectorate. *Dept. of Agriculture.* Commercial production of garden pea seeds in East Africa, by F. Hawkins. Nairobi, Printed by the Govt. Printer, 1946. 8 p.
DNAL

222
Oxley, Thomas A. Grain storage in East and Central Africa; a report of a survey (Oct. 1948 to Jan. 1949). London, H.M. Stationery Off., 1950. 42 p. illus. (Colonial research publications, no. 5) JV33.G7A52 no. 5

At head of title: Colonial Office.

Includes information on Kenya, Tanganyika, and Uganda.

Soils

223
Conference of East African Agricultural and Soil Chemists, *2d, Zanzibar, 1934*. Proceedings of the second conference of East African agricultural and soil chemists held at Zanzibar August 3rd to 9th, 1934. Nairobi, Printed by the Govt. Printer, 1935, 63 p. DNAL

At head of title: Technical conferences of the East African dependencies.

See also item 230.

224
Conference of Governors of British East African Territories. Soil erosion; memoranda by governments of Uganda, Kenya and Tanganyika. Nairobi, Printed by the Govt. Printer, 1938. 11 p. DNAL

225
Gt. Brit. *Directorate of Overseas Surveys*. Soil survey: Nairobi-Machakos. London, Stanford. 1963. map on 2 sheets. (*Its* D.O.S. (L.U.) 3014) G8411.J3 1963S3

"Soil survey carried out by the Soil Survey Division of the East African Agriculture and Forestry Research Organization."

226
Milne, Geoffrey. A provisional soil map of East Africa (Kenya, Uganda, Tanganyika, and Zanzibar) with explanatory memoir. [London, Crown Agents for the Colonies] 1936. 34 p. fold. map (in pocket) (Amani memoirs [no. 36]) S599.A15M5

Map scale 1:2,000,000.

"To be obtained from the East African Agricultural Research Station, Amani, Tanganyika Territory, or from The Crown Agents for the Colonies."

227
———, *comp*. A provisional soil map of East Africa (Kenya, Uganda, Tanganyika & Zanzibar). Southhampton. Printed at the Ordnance Survey Office, 1936. DLC-G&M

Scale 1:2,000,000.

"Issued as a publication of the East African Agricultural Research Station, Amani, Tanganyika Territory, and obtainable, with an accompanying Memoir from the Crown Agents for the Colonies."

228
——— A report on a journey to parts of the West Indies and the United States for the study of soils, February to August 1938. [Dar es Salaam, Printed at the Government Press, 1940] 78 p. DNAL

At head of title: East African Agricultural Research Station, Amani, Tanganyika Territory.

229
——— Report on a soil reconnaisance journey in parts of the Tanga, Eastern, Central, Lake, and Western provinces of Tanganyika Territory, 7th December, 1935 to 4th February 1936. [Dar es Salaam?] 1936. [11] 145 p.

At the head of title: East African Agricultural Research Station, Amani.

Source: Col. Off. Lib. Cat.

230
Proceedings of a conference of East African soil chemists, held at the Agricultural Research Station, Amani, Tanganyika Territory, May 21st to 26th, 1932. Nairobi, Printed by the Govt. Printer, 1932. 25 p. S590.P74

At the head of title: Technical conferences of the East African dependencies.

See also item 223.

Sorghum

231
East African Agriculture and Forestry Research

Organization. *Sorghum and Millet Division.* Sorghum, its improvement and utilization. [Nairobi] East African Literature Bureau [197–?] 11 p. illus. DLC

232
Sorghum Mission to Certain British African Territories. Report. London, H.M. Stationery Off., 1951. 105 p. ([Gt. Brit.] Colonial Advisory Council of Agriculture, Animal Health and Forestry. Publication no. 2) SB235.S6

Includes information for Kenya, Tanganyika, and Uganda, with recommendations for pilot schemes.

Sugar

233
East African Specialist Committee on Sugar Cane Research. Proceedings of the meeting on the yellow wilt condition of sugar cane, Nairobi, June 25th–26th, 1969. Ed. by P. F. Rogers. [Nairobi] East African Community, East African Agriculture and Forestry Research Organisation [1969?] 28, 18 leaves. WvU

234
Robinson, John B. D., M. Dagg, *and* S. Mantsur. Report on a visit to the Kilombero sugar estate, Kilombero valley, United Republic of Tanzania. [Muguga, East African Agriculture and Forestry Research Organization, 1965] 16 leaves. illus. WvU

Tobacco

235
Murray, Stephen S. Report on tobacco with particular reference to the prospects of increased production in Central and East Africa. London, H.M. Stationery Off., 1949. 98 p. (Colonial research publications, no. 4)
JV33.G7A52 no. 4

At head of title: Colonial Office.

Includes information on Kenya, Tanganyika, and Uganda.

Veterinary Medicine

236
Binns, H. R. The East African Veterinary Research Organisation: its development, objects, and scientific activities. [Nairobi, Printed by East African Standard Ltd., 1966?] [32] p. illus.
SF719.E37B56

237
Conference of Governors of British East African Territories. *Standing Veterinary Research Committee.* Minutes of the meeting held in Nairobi on August 23rd, 1945. [Nairobi? 1945?]
DLC-Micro 23940 reel 13 folio 373

Collation of the original: 1 v. (various pagings)

R. Daubney, chairman.

Colonial Office Library East Africa pamphlet folio 373.

238
Conference on Co-ordination of Veterinary Research. [Proceedings] [1st–2d] 1934-36. Nairobi. irregular. SF605.C6

At head of title: Conference of Governors of British East African Territories.

A Research conference of the Conference of Governors of British East African Territories.

Includes information on virus, bacterial, protozoan, and metazoan diseases, animal nutrition, and cooperation in veterinary research in East Africa.

L.C. has 2d, 1936; DNAL has 1st–2d, 1934–36.

239
Conference on Rinderpest, *2d, Nairobi, 1939.* Report of proceedings. Nairobi, Printed by the Govt. Printer, 1939.
DLC-Micro 23940 reel 8 octavo 405

Collation of the original: 52 p. fold. map.

At head of title: Conference of Governors of British East African Territories.

Colonial Office Library East Africa pamphlet octavo 405.

Includes "Report on the special anti-rinderpest campaign in Tanganyika Territory, 1938," by H. E. Hornby.

240
East Africa High Commission. *Committee of Inquiry Appointed to Inquire Into the Causes of the Failure of K.A.G. and Other Vaccines Prepared at Kabete.* Report. Nairobi, Printed by the Govt. Printer [1949]
DLC-Micro 23940 reel 8 octavo 403

Collation of the original: 15 p.

Sir Donald Kingdon, chairman.

Colonial Office Library East Africa pamphlet octavo 403.

The inquiry concerns the breakdown of animal vaccines, namely K.A.G. (Kabete Attenuated Goat) virus vaccine, prepared at the Kabete Laboratory.

241
East Africa High Commission. *East African Veterinary Research Organization.* The East African Veterinary Research Organisation; its development, objects and scientific activities. [Nairobi, 1957] [32] p. DNAL

242
East African Veterinary Research Organization. Annual report. 1948+ Kabete. DNAL

Vol. for 1954/55 incorporates Annual reports, 1952–53.

DNAL has 1948–1956/57, 1966/67+; IaAS has 1970+

243
Gt. Brit. *Foreign Office.* Africa. Report on veterinary work in British East Africa and Uganda protectorate for the years 1898–1900 [by Robert J. Stordy] London, Printed for H.M. Stationery Off. by Harrison, 1901. 5 p. (*Its* Diplomatic and consular reports. Miscellaneous series, no. 551) HC4.R6 no. 551

[Gt. Brit. Parliament. Papers by command] Cd. 430–6.

244
Hornby, H. E. Animal trypanosomiasis in Eastern Africa, 1949. [London] Published for the Colonial Office by H.M. Stationery Off., 1952. 39 p. illus. RC186.T82H6

245
Mettam, R. W. M. Contagious pleuro-pneumonia of goats in East Africa. Nairobi [1929] 6 p. (Kenya Colony and Protectorate. Dept. of Agriculture. Bulletin no. 8E of 1929)
S338.K4A35 no. 8E of 1929

"Communicated to Pan-African Agricultural and Veterinary Conference, held at Pretoria, August, 1929."

L.C. catalogs under: Kenya Colony and Protectorate. *Dept. of Agriculture.* Bulletin.

246
Smith, J. Report on his visit to East Africa, April-July, 1940. [London] Colonial Office, 1941. ([Gt. Brit.] Colonial Advisory Council of Agriculture and Animal Health. C.A.C. 558)
DLC-Micro 23940 reel 6 octavo 287

Collation of the original: 32 p.

Colonial Office Library East Africa pamphlet octavo 287.

Surveys the position of animal disease in Kenya, Tanganyika, and Uganda, with particular reference to an outbreak of rinderpest in southern Tanganyika.

247
Walker, J. *and* S. H. Whitworth. East Coast fever: artificial immunization and immunity in their relation to the control of East Coast fever. Nairobi, Printed by the Govt. Printer, 1929. 18 p. (Kenya Colony and Protectorate. Dept. of Agriculture. Bulletin no. 8F of 1929)
S338.K4A35 no. 8F of 1929

"Communicated to Pan-African [Agricultural and] Veterinary Conference, held at Pretoria, August, 1929."

L.C. catalogs under: Kenya Colony and Protectorate. *Dept. of Agriculture.* Bulletin.

The Arts

East African Literature (English)

248
Blumer, J. A. C. Not guilty; a comedy in one act for African actors. London, New York, Published for the East African Literature Bureau by Longmans, Green, 1953. 26 p. InU

Text in English and Swahili.

249
——— ——— [Kampala] East African Literature Bureau [1972?] 26 p. PN6120.A5B633

Text in English and Swahili.

250
Cook, David J. Literature, the great teaching power of the world. [Nairobi] East African Literature Bureau, 1971. [16] p. DLC

Inaugural lecture given by Professor David Cook, Head of the Dept. of Literature, Makerere University, Kampala, Uganda, on Jan. 28, 1971.

251
Dhana. v. 1+ 1971+ [Nairobi, Kenya, East African Literature Bureau] 2 no. a year PR9799.D53

Supersedes Penpoint.

"A literary journal aiming mainly at the new writers." The title means "thought" or "imagination" in Swahili. Includes prose, poetry, drama, and book reviews.

Text in English.

L.C. has 1971+

252
Green, Robert, *comp.* Just a moment, God! An anthology of verse and prose from East Africa. Nairobi, East African Literature Bureau [1970?] 206 p. illus. (Students' book-writing scheme) PR9345.G7

253
Hinga, E. Out of the jungle. Nairobi, East African Literature Bureau [1973] 77 p. PZ4.H6635Ou

254
——— Sincerity divorced. Kampala, East African Literature Bureau [1970] 112 p. illus. (Students' book-writing scheme) PZ4.H6635Si

255
Imbuga, F. D. The Fourth trial (2 plays). Nairobi, East African Literature Bureau [1972] 75 p. PR9381.9.I4F65

Contents: The fourth trial.—Kisses of fate.

256
Joliso. v. 1+ 1973+ [Nairobi, East African Literature Bureau] semiannual. PL8009.5.J64

"East African journal of literature and society."

L.C. has 1973+

257
Kalimugogo, Godfrey. Dare to die. Nairobi, East African Literature Bureau [1972] 177 p. PZ4.K1453Dar

Contents: Dare to die.—Mind in the tether.—The idolater.—The vanished village.

258
Karimi, Maitai. The arrow poisons. Nairobi, East Africa Literature Bureau [1973] 97 p. illus. DLC

259
Karoki, John. The land is ours. Nairobi, East African Literature Bureau [1970] 255 p. (Students' book-writing scheme) PZ4.K186Lan

260
Liyong, Taban lo. Thirteen offensives against our enemies. [Nairobi, East African Literature Bureau, 1973] 123 p. DLC

261
_______ The uniformed man. Nairobi, East African Literature Bureau [1971] xviii, 68 p. PZ4.L79Un

Short stories.

Contents: Preface.—A prescription for idleness.—Herolette.—The education of Taban lo Liyong.—Project X.—Asu the Great.—It is swallowing.—The uniformed man.

262
Macpherson, Margaret. Let's make a play. With the acted version of Kintu, a play, by E. C. N. Kironde. Kampala, East African Literature Bureau [1960] 44 p. illus. InU

263
Mphahlele, Ezekiel. A guide to creative writing; a short guide to short-story & novel writing. Dar es Salaam, East African Literature Bureau [1966] 85 p. PN3375.M7

264
Mugambi, Jesse N. K. Carry it home. Nairobi, East African Literature Bureau [1974] 89 p. DLC

Poems.

265
Muruah, George K. Never forgive father. Nairobi, East African Literature Bureau [1972] 318 p. (Student's book writing scheme) DLC

266
Mwaura, Joshua N. Sky is the limit. Nairobi, East African Literature Bureau [1974] 253 p. PZ4.M9928Sk

267
Mwaura, Mike. The renegade, Nairobi, East African Literature Bureau [1972] 166 p. PZ4.M993Re

268
Nazareth, Peter. In a brown mantle. Nairobi, East African Literature Bureau [1972] 157 p. PZ4.N335In

269
_______ Literature and society in modern Africa, essays on literature. Kampala, East African Literature Bureau [1972] 222 p. PR9340.5.N3 1972

Published in 1974 by Northwestern University Press, Evanston, Ill., under the title: An African view of literature.

A collection of essays by the author on the writings of Ngugi, Oculi, Kimenye, Carlin, Mangua, Rubadiri, and others.

270
Ngubiah, Stephen N. A curse from God. Nairobi, East African Literature Bureau [1970] 251 p. PR6064.G75C8

"East African Literature Bureau student's book-writing scheme."

271
Pulsations; an East African anthology of poetry. [Edited by Arthur Kemoli] Nairobi, East African Literature Bureau [1969?] xvi, 166 p. PR9898.E26P8

272
Tejani, Bahadur. Day after tomorrow. Nairobi, East African Literature Bureau [1971] 145 p. PZ4.T264Day

Novel on the South Asian situation in East Africa.

273
Thiong'o, Ngugi Wa. This time tomorrow. Nairobi, East African Literature Bureau [1970?] 50 p. PR6070.H52T5

Contents: The rebels.—The wound in the heart.—This time tomorrow.

Three plays.

274
Wandera, Billy O. Hand of chance. Kampala,

East African Literature Bureau [1970] 216 p. (Students' book-writing scheme)
PZ4.W246Han

275
Wanjala, Chris, *comp*. Faces at crossroads; a 'Currents' anthology. With an introd. by Angus Calder. Nairobi, East African Literature Bureau [1971] xv, 215 p. (EALB students' book writing scheme) PR9381.5.W3F3

276
——— *ed*. Singing with the night: a collection of East African verse. Nairobi, East African Literature Bureau [1974] 86 p. DLC

277
——— *ed*. Standpoints on African literature: a critical anthology. Nairobi, East African Literature Bureau [1973] xviii, 389 p. DLC

Contents: pt. 1. General.—pt. 2. East Africa.—pt. 3. West Africa.—pt. 4. South Africa.—pt. 5. Afro-Americans.

278
Writers in East Africa. Edited by Andrew Gurr and Angus Calder. Nairobi, East African Literature Bureau [1974] 150 p. DLC

On cover: Papers from a colloquium held at the University of Nairobi, June 1971.

Commerce and Trade

279
Agreement establishing an association between the European Economic Community and the United Republic of Tanzania, the Republic of Uganda, and the Republic of Kenya, and annexed documents. Signed on 24 September 1969. [Nairobi, Printed by All Africa Trading Co. Box 47450, Nairobi, under E.A. Community Authority Ref. CME/13/5/1, 1971?] [168] p. DCL–LL

On cover: Decision of the Association Council on the definition of the concept of "originating" products for the purpose of implementing Title I of the Agreement and on the methods of administrative co-operation.

280
Agreement establishing an association between the European Economic Community and the United Republic of Tanzania, the Republic of Uganda and the Republic of Kenya and annexed documents, signed on 24 September 1969. [Yaundé, 1969] 70 columns. 21 x 31 cm. DLC

281
Anglo-Belgian East African traffic convention. [London] Printed for the use of the Colonial Office, 1921. ([Gt. Brit.] Colonial Office. African no. 1084) DLC-Micro 03759

Collation of the original: 6 p.

[Gt. Brit.] Public Record Office. C.O. 879/120.

Text in English and French.

"The convention was signed on 15th March 1921 in identic terms with this draft."

282
Conference of Governors of British East African Territories. *Committee Appointed to Consider a Revision of the Customs Tariff of Kenya, Uganda and Tanganyika Territory*. Report. Nairobi, Printed by the Govt. Press, 1930.
DLC-Micro 23940 reel 10 folio 192

Collation of the original: 53 p.

G. Walsh, chairman.

At head of title: Conference of East African Governors.

Colonial Office Library East Africa pamphlet folio 192.

The Committee recommended against establishing a joint tariff advisory board.

283
Conference on Public Policy, *2d, University College, Nairobi, 1963*. Conferences on public policy, 1963/4: East African federation; [papers] [Nairobi? 1964?] HC517.E2C6 1963

The following papers concern commerce and trade:

[no. 7] Ghai, Dharam. Terrttorial distribution of benefits and costs of the East African Customs Union. 17 leaves.

Later revised as Territorial distribution of the benefits and costs of the East African Common Market, published in Colin Leys' Federation in East Africa; opportunities and problems (Nairobi, London, Oxford University Press, 1965 [i.e. 1966] HC517.E2L4) p. 72–82.

[no. 10] Newman, Peter. Customs union and co-ordinated planning in East Africa. 16 leaves.

Later revised as The economics of integration in East Africa, published in Colin Leys' Federation in East Africa; opportunities and problems (Nairobi, London, Oxford Press, 1965 [i.e. 1966] HC517.E2L4) p. [56]–71.

284
East Africa High Commission. The East African customs regulations, 1954. Nairobi, Printed by the High Commission Printer, 1954. 119 p. forms. DLC–LL

285
_______ The East African excise regulations, 1954. Nairobi, Printed by the High Commission Printer, 1954. 43 p. forms. DLC

286
_______ A schedule of international restrictions on the movement of goods as at 1st July, 1960. Nairobi, Govt. Printer, 1960. 6 p.

Source: Col. Off. Lib. Cat.

287
East Africa High Commission. *East African Customs and Excise Dept.* Abridged annual trade statistics of Kenya, Uganda, and Tanganyika. 1948?–1960. Mombasa, Commissioner of Customs and Excise. HF266.E3E28a

Superseded by a publication with the same title (item 301) issued by East African Customs and Excise of the East African Common Services Organization.

L.C. has 1958–60; DS has 1951, 1953–54, 1956–57, 1959–60.

288
_______ Annual trade report of Kenya, Uganda, and Tanganyika. 1949–60. [Mombasa, etc., Commissioner of Customs and Excise, etc.] HF266.E3A23

Supersedes the Annual trade report of Kenya and Uganda (item 328) issued by the Commissioner of Customs, Kenya and Uganda, of Kenya Colony and Protectorate, and the Trade report issued by the Customs Dept. of Tanganyika.

Superseded by a publication with the same title (item 302) issued by East African Customs and Excise of the East African Common Services Organization.

L.C. has 1949–60; DNAL has 1949–58.

289
_______ Invoicing procedure. Nairobi, Govt. Printer. 1956. 6 p. DS

290
_______ Official import and export list. Nairobi, Printed by the Govt. Printer, 1953. 129 p. IEN

"Based on the Standard international trade classification compiled by the Statistical Commission of the United Nations and . . . suitably modified to meet the requirements of East Africa."

291
_______ Trade and revenue report for Kenya, Uganda, and Tanganyika. 1949–61. Mombasa, Commissioner of Customs and Excise. monthly. HF266.E3A23

Vols. for 1949-Feb. 1954 printed in Dar es Salaam, Tanganyika.

Superseded by a publication with the same title (item 303) issued by East African Customs and Excise of the East African Common Services Organization.

Vols. for Jan. 1951, Jan. 1952, Jan. 1953, and Jan. 1954 include tables for the preceding year.

Cumulative trade statistics are included in the agency's Annual trade report of Kenya, Uganda, and Tanganyika (item 288).

L.C. has 1949–61 (scattered issues wanting).

East Africa High Commission. *East African Office, London.*

Note: After World War I the Association of East African Chambers of Commerce and the Convention of Associations of Kenya Colony urged "the immediate establishment of an office in London whose functions shall embrace those of a trade commissioner and those of an information bureau." The Eastern African Dependencies Trade and Information Office was established in London in 1925 by the governments of the East African territories and the Kenya-Uganda Transport Administration "to deal with enquiries as to, and foster, white settlement in available areas of Kenya, Uganda, Tanganyika, Zanzibar, Nyasaland, and Northern Rhodesia; also tourist traffic; commercial enquiries, particularly the development of markets for East African produce." The name of the office was shortened to East Africa Office in 1945. Thereafter, the office concerned itself primarily with trade matters, and economic information on and for Kenya, Tanganyika, Uganda, and Zanzibar. On January 1, 1948, the office came under the East Africa High Commission, and on December 9, 1961, it was reconstitued within the East African Common Services Organization. With the independence of the East African states in 1961–63, high commissions of each state took over the office's functions. Subsequently, the office was closed on June 30, 1966.

292

Report of the East African Commissioner. 1926–57. [London] annual. HC517.E2E3

Title varies: 1926–1937? Report on the work. Other slight variations in title.

Vols. for 1926–1944? issued by the agency under its earlier name: Eastern African Dependencies Trade and Information Office.

Superseded by the East Africa information digest (item 2), and the East Africa statistical digest (item 304).

Information on the Office's activities for 1948–65 is summarized in the Annual report of the East Africa High Commission (item 1569) issued by the Colonial Office of Gt. Brit., and in the Annual report (item 1581) issued by the East African Common Services Organization.

L.C. catalogs under: Eastern African Dependencies Trade and Information Office. Report.

L.C. has 1928–30, 1933–35, 1938, 1948–50; CtY has 1955–57; source for 1926–57: Col. Off. Lib. Cat.

293

East Africa High Commission. *East African Statistical Dept.* The balance of payments of East Africa. 1956–59/61? [Nairobi] annual. HG3883.A35A26

Period covered by report varies.

Title varies: 1956, An estimate of the balance of payments of East Africa.

No more published?

Each issue for 1956/58–1959/61 included revised statistics for the first two years of coverage, and estimates for the third year. Later statistics are included in the Economic and statistical review (item 761) issued by the East African Statistical Dept. of the East African Common Services Organization, and subsequently in the Economic and statistical review (item 763) issued by the East African Statistical Dept. of the East African Community.

L.C. has 1956–1959/61.

294

East Africa High Commission. *East African Statistical Dept. East African Unit.* External trade of East Africa; indices 1954–1958 & commentary. Nairobi, 1960. 9 p. HF266.E3A25

Later statistics are included in East African trade indices; revised external trade indices 1954–1961 with commentary (item 306) issued by the East African Statistical Dept. of the East African Common Services Organization.

295

East Africa High Commission. *Laws, statutes, etc.* Customs and excise tariff handbook. Nairobi, printed by the Govt. Printer, 1954. 40 p. IEN

296
_______ _______ Nairobi, Printed by the Govt. Printer, 1958. 29 p. DS

297
_______ _______ Mombasa [East African Customs and Excise Dept.] 1960. 35 p. DS

298
_______ _______ [Mombasa? East African Customs and Excise Dept.?] 1961. NNC
NNC catalogs under: East Africa High Commission. *Customs and Excise Dept.*

299
_______ The East African transfer traffic regulations, 1954. Nairobi, the High Commission Printer, 1954. 17 p. DS

East African Cargo Handling Services Ltd.
Note: The East African Cargo Handling Services Ltd. is a subsidiary corporation of the East African Harbours Corporation and the East African Railways Corporation. The accounts of the company are audited by the auditor-general of the East African Community. The company maintains its headquarters in Mombasa, Kenya, with branches in Dar es Salaam, Mtwara, and Tanga, Tanzania.
300
General Manager's annual report. 1950+ [Mombasa, Kenya] illus. HE559.A362E18a
L.C. has 1966–68, 1970+

301
East African Common Services Organization. *East African Customs and Excise.* Abridged annual trade statistics of Tanganyika, Uganda, and Kenya. 1961–66. Mombasa. DLC
Supersedes Abridged annual trade statistics of Kenya, Uganda, and Tanganyika (item 287) issued by the East African Customs and Excise Dept. of the East Africa High Commission.
Title varies: 1961–62? Abridged annual trade statistics of Kenya, Uganda, and Tanganyika.
Superseded by a publication with the same title (item 310) issued by the East African Customs and Excise Dept. of the East African Community.
L.C. has 1962; DS has 1961, 1964, and 1966.

302
_______ Annual trade report of Tanganyika, Uganda, and Kenya. 1961–66. [Mombasa, Commissioner of Customs and Excise]
HF266.E3A23
Supersedes the Annual trade report of Kenya, Uganda, and Tanganyika (item 288) issued by the East African Customs and Excise Dept. of the East Africa High Commission.
Order of countries listed in the title vaires.
Superseded by a publication with the same title (item 311) issued by the East African Customs and Excise Dept. of the East African Community.
L.C. has 1961–66 (1963 wanting) ; DNAL has 1961, 1964, and 1966.

303
_______ Trade and revenue report for Tanganyika, Uganda, and Kenya. 1962–67. Mombasa, Commissioner of Customs and Excise, East Africa. monthly. CtY-E
Supersedes a publication with the same title (item 291) issued by the East African Customs and Excise Dept. of the East Africa High Commission.
Title varies: 1962–63, Trade and revenue report for Kenya, Uganda, and Tanganyika. –1964, Trade and revenue report for Kenya, Tanganyika, and Uganda.
Superseded by the Trade and revenue report for Tanzania, Uganda, and Kenya (item 312) issued by the East African Customs and Excise Dept. of the East African Community.
Cumulative trade statistics are in the agency's Annual trade report of Tanganyika, Uganda, and Kenya.
CtY-E has 1962–67 (scattered issues wanting).

304
East African Comon Services Organization. *East African Office, London.* Statistical digest. 1958–1962? London. CSt-H
Supersedes in part the Report of the East African Commissioner (item 292) issued by the

East African Office, London, of the East Africa High Commission.
Title varies: 1958–196-? East Africa statistical digest.
No more published?
"A summary of trade statistics . . . including statistics of other selected economies and financial activities in the East African territories."
CSt-H has 1961–62; source for 1958+: Col. Off. Lib. Cat.

305
East African Common Services Organization. *East African Statistical Dept.* East African retained imports; stage of production and end use analysis. 1960/61. [Nairobi, 1962] DLC
No more published.
Later statistics are included in the agency's Economic and statistical review (item 761).
L.C. has 1960/61.

306
______ East African trade indices; revised external trade indices 1954–1961, with commentary. [Nairobi] 1963. 7p. DLC
Later statistics are included in the agency's Economic and statistical review (item 761).

307
East African Common Services Organization. *Laws, statutes, etc.* Customs and excise tariff handbook. [Mombasa?] 1963. 46 p. HJ6369.A25a
L.C. catalogs under: East African High Commission. *East African Customs and Excise Dept.*

308
East African Community. Agreement establishing an association between the European Economic Community and the United Republic of Tanzania, the Republic of Uganda, and the Republic of Kenya. [Nairobi] 1969. 31 p. MiEM
"Special issue: East African Community Gazette, Supplement no. 18."

309
______ East African customs and excise tariffs. [Nairobi] 1970+ 162p. DNAL
Loose-leaf for updating.

310
East African Community. *East African Customs and Excise Dept.* Abridged annual trade statistics of Tanzania, Uganda, and Kenya. 1967+ Mombasa. HF266.E3E3a
Supersedes Abridged annual trade statistics of Tanganyika, Uganda, and Kenya (item 301) issued by East African Customs and Excise of the East African Common Services Organization.
Title varies: 1967, Abridged annual trade statistics of Tanganyika, Uganda, and Kenya.
L.C. has 1967+

311
______ Annual trade report of Tanzania, Uganda, and Kenya. 1967+ [Mombasa, Statistical Branch, etc.] HF266.E3A23
Supersedes the Annual trade report of Tanganyika, Uganda, and Kenya (item 302) issued by East African Customs and Excise of the East African Common Services Organization.
Title varies: 1967, Annual trade report of Tanganyika, Uganda, and Kenya.
Each issue includes trade legislation enacted during the year by Kenya, Tanzania, and Uganda, with a detailed index of commodities.
L.C. has 1967+

312
______ Monthly trade statistics for Tanzania, Uganda, and Kenya. 1968+ [Mombasa] DLC
Supersedes Trade and revenue report for Tanganyika, Uganda, and Kenya (item 303) issued by East African Customs and Excise of the East African Common Services Organization.
Title varies: 1968–72, Trade and revenue report for Tanzania, Uganda, and Kenya.
Vol. for 1968 issued by the Commissioner of Customs and Excise; vols. for 1969+ issued by the agency's Statistical Branch.
December issue includes provisional statistics for past calendar year. Final cumulative statistics are in the agency's Annual trade report of Tanzania, Uganda, and Kenya.

L.C. has current issues only; CtY-E has 1968 + (scattered issues wanting).

312a

_______ Official import and export list (revised). [Mombasa? 1974] 79 p. DLC

313

Eastern African Dependencies Trade and Information Office. East African statistics, raw coffee. [London] monthly. DNAL

Comulative for calendar year.

Includes imports into Gt. Brit. from Kenya, Tanganyika, and Uganda, and re-exports from Gt. Brit. of coffee originally consigned from Kenya, Tanganyika, and Uganda.

DNAL has Dec. 1931-June 1939 (scattered issues wanting).

314

_______ Memorandum on the character and functions of His Majesty's Eastern African Dependencies Trade and Information Office, and also of its Advisory Committee appointed in London by the Secretary of State for the Colonies. [London? 193-?]

DLC-Micro 23940 reel 3 octavo 147

Collation of the original: 9 p.

Colonial Office Library East Africa pamphlet octavo 147.

315

_______ Notes on clove produce inspection. no. 1+ [London? 1934?+]

Two issues numbered 1.

DNAL received issues for 1930's; apparently not retained.

316

_______ Report on the East African pavilion at the Empire Exhibition, Glasgow, 1938. [London? 1938?]

DLC-Micro 23940 reel 5 octavo 255

Collation of the original: 24 p. illus.

Colonial Office Library East Africa pamphlet octavo 255.

317

_______ Tanganyika Territory; a brief commentary on its history, etc. London, n.d. 64 p. map. NNA

318

European Economic Community. Agreement establishing an association between the European Economic Community and the United Republic of Tanzania, the Republic of Uganda and the Republic of Kenya. [Arusha? 1968?] 38 leaves. DLC-LL

319

Gt. Brit. *Committee on Industry and Trade.* Memorandum on transport development and cotton growing in East Africa, submitted by the Committee on Industry and Trade to the Prime Minister on 2nd of July 1925. London, H.M. Stationery Off., 1925. 9 p. ([Gt. Brit. Parliament. Papers by command] Cmd. 2463)

HD9087.B6A5 1925

At head of title: Board of Trade.

Sir Arthur Balfour, chairman.

320

Gt. Brit. *Empire Marketing Board.* Production and trade of Kenya and Uganda. London, Printed and published by H.M. Stationery Off., 1930. 23 p. (*Its* [Production and trade reports] E.M.B./T.P.7) HC245.A45 no. 7

321

Gt. Brit. *Foreign Office.* Africa. Report for the half-year ending December 31, 1903, on the country produce traffic of the Uganda Railway. London, Printed for H.M. Stationery Off. by Harrison, 1904. 16 p. (*Its* Diplomatic and consular reports. Miscellaneous series, 1904, no. 607)

HC4.R6 1904 no. 607

[Gt. Brit. Parliament. Papers by command] Cd. 1767–11.

322

Gt. Brit. *Treaties, etc., 1910–1936 (George V).* Convention between Great Britain and Belgium with a view to facilitating Belgian traffic through the territories of East Africa. Signed at London, March 15, 1921. London, H.M.

Stationery Off., 1921. p. 187–196. ([Gt. Brit. Brit. Foreign Office] Treaty series, 1921, no. 11) JX636 1892 1921 no. 11
[Gt. Brit. Parliament. Papers by command] Cmd. 1327.
Text in English and French in parallel columns.

323
Gt. Brit. *Treaties, etc., 1936–1952 (George VI)*. Exchange of notes between His Majesty's Government in the United Kingdom and the French Government regarding the importation of raffia of French origin and of British East African coffee and New Zealand kauri gum. Paris, July 16/23, 1937. London, H.M. Stationery Off., 1937. 4 p. ([Gt. Brit. Foreign Office] Treaty series, 1937, no. 34) JX636 1892 1937 no. 34
[Gt. Brit. Parliament. Papers by command] Cmd. 5558.
Text in English and French.

324
Johnston, W. Proposed East African customs and excise department, memorandum by Commissioner of Customs, Kenya and Uganda. Entebbe, Printed by the Govt. Printer, 1948. 8 p. (Uganda. Legislative Council. Sessional paper no. 2 of 1948) J732.H6 no. 2 of 1948

325
Kampala agreement; the documents covering the decisions arrived at by the Kenya, Uganda, and Tanganyika Governments in redressing the imbalance of trade between them. [Dar es Salaam, Information Service of the United Republic of Tanganyika and Zanzibar] 1964. 12 p. HF3896.5.K35

326
Kenya and Uganda Railways and Harbours. Proposed abolition of country produce preferential tariffs; memorandum for the Uganda Tariff Committee submitted by the Acting General Manager, Kenya and Uganda Railways and Harbours. Nairobi, General Manager's Office, Kenya and Uganda Railways and Harbours, 1929. 12 p. DLC

327
Kenya Colony and Protectorate. Papers relating to the creation of an East African customs and excise department. [Nairobi? 1948?] (Kenya colony and Protectorate. [Legislative Council] Sessional paper no. 3 of 1948)
Source: Kenya debates, July 13, 1948.

328
Kenya Colony and Protectorate. *Commissioner of Customs.* Annual trade report of Kenya and Uganda. 1921–48. Nairobi, Printed and published by the Govt. Printer. HF266.K3A3
Report for 1921 covers period Apr.-Dec.
At head of title: Colony and Protectorate of Kenya and Uganda Protectorate.
Supersedes the Annual report issued by the Customs Dept. of the East Africa Protectorate, and the Trade report issued by the Customs Dept. of Uganda.
Title varies: 1921, Customs report.
Superseded by the Annual trade report of Kenya, Uganda, and Tanganyika (item 288) issued by the East African Customs and Excise Dept. of the East Africa High Commission.
L.C. has 1921–48 (1925 and 1942 wanting); DNAL has 1930–48 (1943 wanting).

329
Kenya Colony and Protectorate. *Customs Dept.* Customs and excise tariff. –1947. Nairobi, Printed and published by the Govt. Printer. DS
At head of title: Colony and Protectorate of Kenya and the Protectorate of Uganda.
Title varies.
Later information is included in the Customs and excise tariff handbook (items 295–98) issued by the East African Customs and Exice Dept. of the East Africa High Commission.
DS catalogs under: East Africa High Commission. *Laws, statutes, etc.* Customs and excise tariff, Colony and Protectorate of Kenya and the Protectorate of Uganda.
DS has 1945; source for 1933: Royal Comm. Soc. Cat.; source for 1934: Kenya Govt. Press rept., 1934; source for 1946–47: Kenya Govt. Print. rept., 1946–47.

330
——— Customs invoicing procedure. [Nairobi, Govt. Printer] 1945. 8 p.
Source: Kenya Govt. Print. rept., 1945.

331
——— Official import and export list, applicable to Colony and Protectorate of Kenya, Uganda Protectorate, Tanganyika Territory, Zanzibar Protectorate. Nairobi, Printed by the Govt. Printer, 1947. 78 p. IEN
At head of title: H.M. Customs Dept.
Issued from Mombasa by the Commissioner of Customs, Kenya and Uganda.
Amendment slip enclosed.
IEN catalogs under: Uganda. *Customs Dept.*

332
——— ——— Entebbe, Govt. Printer, 1947. 74 p. IEN
"Issued as a supplement to Uganda Gazette, dated 15th December, 1947."
IEN catalogs under: Uganda. *Customs Dept.*

333
Kenya Colony and Protectorate. *Tariff Committee.* Report. Nairobi, Printed by the Govt. Printer, 1929.
DLC-Micro 23940 reel 10 folio 183
Collation of the original: 61 p.
J. E. S. Merrick, chairman.
Colonial Office Library East Africa pamphlet folio 183.
Includes consideration of a customs union with Tanganyika and Uganda.

334
Martin, C. J. The growth of East Africa as shown by its external trade, by C. J. Martin, Director, East African Statistical Department. [Nairobi? 1956?] 16 p.
Source: Col. Off. Lib. Cat.

335
Snapnews. 195-?-1962. London, East Africa High Commission, East African Office. monthly.
"Items culled from all sections of the East African press."
Cited in the Annual report, 1962, issued by the East African Common Services Organization.

336
Tanganyika. Amalgamation of the Tanganyika Customs Dept. and the Kenya and Uganda Customs Depts. [Dar es Salaam? 1948?] 7 p. (Tanganyika. Legislative Council. Sessional paper, 1948, no. 3) MBU

337
Uganda. *Cutsoms Dept.* Official import and export list applicable to Colony and Protectorate of Kenya, Uganda Protectorate, Tanganyika Territory, Zanzibar Protectorate. Entebbe, Govt. Printer, 1947. 74 p. IEN
"Issued as a supplement to Uganda Gazette, dated 15th December, 1947."

Tourist Trade

East Africa Tourist Travel Association.

Note: Early in 1948, an interim body known as the East Africa Tourist Travel Office was established by the East Africa High Commission to study travel promotion in East Africa. In May 1948, the East Africa Tourist Travel Association was created as a nonprofit organization by the East Africa High Commission, the East African Railways and Harbours Administration, the East African Airways Corporation, and the governments of Kenya, Tanganyika, Uganda, and Zanzibar, along with a number of commercial firms. "The task of the Association has been declared to promote, foster and maintain tourist traffic to and within East Africa, and to safeguard the interests of tourists when in East Africa and to encourage the improvement and development of travel and allied services." The association was directed by an executive committee with headquarters in Nairobi and visitors' information bureaus in Kampala, Mombasa, and Dar es Salaam. Staff were maintained in the East African Office, London, and in New York. On June 30, 1963, Uganda withdrew from the association. In Tanganyika, the Dar es Salaam

Information and Tourist Association took over the functions of the Visitors' Information Bureau of the East Africa Tourist Travel Association. On November 30, 1965, the association was formally dissolved.

338

Annual report. 1948–1965? Nairobi. illus. DS
Period covered by report is irregular.
Vols. for 1948–1960/61 called also 1st-13th.
Vols. for 1958–59 and 1962–63 include the agency's Balance sheet, statements and accounts
Information on the activities of the East Africa Tourist Travel Association for the period 1948–61 is included in the Annual report of the East Africa High Commission (item 1569) issued by the Colonial Office of Gt. Brit; for the period 1961–63 in the Annual report (item 1581) issued by the East African Common Services Organization.
DS has 1951–63 (1952 and 1955 wanting); source for 1963–1965? Col. Off. Lib. Cat.

339

——— Balance sheet, statements and accounts. [Nairobi] annual. DS
Vols. for 1958–59 and 1962–63 are included in the agency's Annual report.
DS catalogs under: East Africa Tourist Travel Association. Statement of accounts.
DS has 1957.

340

——— List of officers, members and associates. Nairobi. DS
DS has 1957–58.

341

——— Monthly newsletter to all full members. [Nairobi?]
Cited in the agency's Annual report, 1963.

342

East Africa Tourist Travel Association. *Formation Committee.* Minutes, 1948. [Nairobi?]
Source: Col. Off. Lib. Cat.

343

Ouma, Josep P. Evolution of tourism in East Africa (1900-2000). Nairobi, East African Literature Bureau [1970] 117 p. illus., maps. G155.A26O9

344

Wright, Fergus C. Tourism in East Africa; a report of an economic enquiry carried out in Kenya, Tanganyika, Uganda and Zanzibar. London, Dept. of Technical Co-operation, 1962. 82 p.
Held by University of Cambridge African Studies Centre, England.

345

——— Tourism in East Africa; report of an economic enquiry carried out in Kenya, Tanganyika, Uganda and Zanzibar. London, Dept. of Technical Co-operation, 1962. [147] p.
Source: Royal Comm. Soc. Cat.

346

——— ——— [Rev.] London, Dept. of Technical Cooperation, 1962. 152 p.
Source: SOAS Cat. (suppl.)

Communications and Transportation

347
Bunning, A. J. F. Report on visit to Kenya, Uganda, Tanganyika, Northern and Southern Rhodesia, the port of Beira, Nyasaland and the Union of South Africa, 27th September to 18th December, 1948, by A. J. F. Bunning, Adviser on Inland Transport to the Secretary of State for the Colonies. London, Colonial Office, 1949. DLC-Micro 23940 reel 14 folio 419

Collation of the original: 12 leaves.

Colonial Office Library East Africa pamphlet folio 419.

348
Conference on Public Policy, *2d, University College, Nairobi, 1963.* Conferences on public policy, 1963/4: East African federation; [paper no. 5] (1) Some inter-territorial aspects of road and rail transport in East Africa. (2) The economics of inter-territorial relations [by] Arthur Hazlewood. [Nairobi? 1946?] 11, 7 leaves. HC517.E2C6 1963 no. 5

Later revised as The co-ordination of transport policy, published in Colin Leys' Federation in East Africa; opportunities and problems (Nairobi, London, Oxford University Press, 1965 [i.e. 1966] HC517.E2L4) p. [111]-123.

349
East African Transport Policy Board. Report on co-ordination of transport in Kenya, Uganda and the Tanganyika Territory, by Sir H. Osborne Mance. Nairobi, Printed by the Govt. Printer, 1937. 64 p. HE284.E3

L.C. also has on microfilm (23940, reel 4, octavo 217).

350
Gt. Brit. *Colonial Office. Committee on Private Enterprise in British Tropical Africa.* Private enterprise in British tropical Africa. Report of the committee appointed by the Secretary of State for the Colonies to consider and report whether, and if so what, measures could be taken to encourage private enterprise in the development of the British dependencies in East and West tropical Africa, with special reference to existing and projected schemes of transportation. London, H.M. Stationery Off. [1924] 26 p. ([Gt. Brit. Parliament. Papers by command] Cmd. 2016) HE284.A5 1924

Ronaldshay, chairman.

Includes information on transportation in East Africa, the proposed customs union of Kenya, Tanganyika, and Uganda, and the growing of cotton in Tanganyika

351
Van Rees, C. J. The development of motor vehicle ownership in East Africa. Nairobi, East African Statistical Dept., 1967. 27 leaves. HE5704.E2V35

"This review presents an analysis of the relative growths of different classes of motor vehicles."

Includes statistics for East Africa, Kenya, Tanzania, and Uganda for 1956–65.

Air Travel

352
Conference of Governors of British East African Territories. *Committee Appointed to Prepare a Scheme for Post-War Local Air Services in East Africa.* Report. Nairobi, Printed by the Govt. Printer, 1943.
DLC-Micro 23940 reel 7 octavo 339

Collation of the original: 22p.

H. L. G. Gurney, chairman.

At head of title: East African Governors' Conference.

Colonial Office Library East Africa pamphlet octavo 339.

Includes "Draft of the East African Territories (Air Transport) Order in Council" establishing East African Airways.

353
______ ______ Nairobi, 1945. 8 p. NNC

At head of title: East African Governors' Conference.

354
East Africa High Commission. *Administrator.* Report on civil aviation; annual report. 1958/59. Nairobi, Printed by the Govt. Printer. TL528.E2A3

Report year ends June 30.

Supersedes a publication with the same title issued by the Commissioner for Transport of the East Africa High Commission.

Superseded by the Annual report (item 357) issued by the Directorate of Civil Aviation, East Africa, of the East African Common Services Organization.

"Incorporating a report on the East African Directorate of Civil Aviation."

L.C. has 1958/59.

355
East Africa High Commission. *Commissioner for Transport.* Report on civil aviation; annual report. 1950–1957/58. Nairobi, Printed by the Govt. Printer. TL528.E2A3

Report year for 1950–1953? ends Dec. 31; for 1954/55–1957/58 ends June 30.

Report for 1954/55 covers period Jan. 1954-June 1955.

Superseded by a publication with the same title issued by the Administrator of the East Africa High Commission.

"Incorporating a report of the East African Directorate of Civil Aviation."

L.C. has 1950–52, 1954/55–1957/58.

Note: For information on the office of Commissioner for Transport, *see* note to item 436.

356
East Africa High Commission. *Court of Inquiry into the Accident to Dakota VP-KKH on 18th May, 1955.* Civil aircraft accident; report. Nairobi, Govt. Printer, 1955. 23 p. IEN

357
East Africa High Commission. *Directorate of Civil Aviation, East Africa.* Annual report. 1948–1959/60. [Nairobi] TL528.E2A3

Report year for 1948–53 ends Dec. 31; for 1954/55–1959/60 ends June 30.

Report for 1954/55 covers period Jan. 1954-June 1955.

Title varies: 1948–49, 1951–52, 1954/55–1958/59, Report.

Vols. for 1948–1958/59 issued by the agency under a variant name: East African Directorate of Civil Aviation.

Reports for 1950–52, and 1954/55–1957/58 are included in the Report on civil aviation; annual report (item 355) issued by the Commissioner for Transport of the East Africa High Commission; for 1958/59 is included in the Report on civil aviation; annual report (item 354) issued by the Administrator of the East Africa High Commission.

Superseded by a publication with the same title (item 366) issued by the Directorate of Civil Aviation, East Africa of the East African Common Services Organization.

L.C. has 1948–1959/60.

358
——— Aerodromes, Kenya, Tanganyika, Uganda, Zanzibar. [Nairobi?] 1951. 92 p.

Source: Col. Off. Lib. Cat.

359
——— Aeronautical information publication. [Nairobi, 1958] 1 v. (various pagings) DS

360
——— ——— Amendment list. [Nairobi?] irregular.

Source for no. 81, Mar. 1, 1967: Makerere Lib. Bull. no. 66.

361
East Africa High Commission. *Inter-territorial Committee on Ground Services for Civil Aviation in East Africa.* Report. Nairobi, 1948. DLC-Micro 23940 reel 14 folio 420

Collation of the original: 30 p.

G. R. Sandford, chairman.

Colonial Office Library East Africa pamphlet folio 420.

Paper laid on the table of the East Africa Central Legislative Assembly of the East Africa High Commission on April 26, 1949.

East African Airways Corporation.

Note: The East African Airways Corporation was established by the East African Territories (Air Transport) Order, 1945. On January 1, 1948, the corporation came under the jurisdiction of the East Africa High Commission, which approved the corporation's budget estimates. Under the terms of the East African Airways Corporation Act, 1967, the agency provides air transportation on a commercial basis for East Africa, and links the three partner states with each other by operating regional routes. The corporation is controlled by a board of directors, composed of a chairman appointed by the East African Authority, a director-general who is a director *ex-officio,* and eight others, two or whom are appointed by the East African Authority and the partner states. Under the Treaty for East African Co-operation, the corporation continues to maintain headquarters in Nairobi, Kenya.

362
Annual report. 1946+ [Nairobi] illus.
TL720.9.E27A3
Each issue includes an audited statement of the agency's accounts.
L.C. has 1948–53, 1957, 1959+

363
——— Timetable. [Embakasi, Nairobi Airport] 2 no. a year. illus. maps
L.C. received Nov. 1968; not retained.

364
East African Common Services Organization. *Accident Investigation Branch.* Civil aircraft accident: report of the East African Common Services Organization in the accident to DH 106 Comet 4 G-APDL, during its approach to Nairobi airport on 2nd February, 1964. [London?] H.M. Stationery Off., 1965. 9 p.
At head of title: Ministry of Aviation.
Source: Col. Off. Lib. Cat.

365
East African Common Services Organization. *Commission on the Constitutional Position of East African Airways.* Report of the Commission under the chairmanship of Stephen Wheatcroft. [Nairobi, 1965]
Source: Dar es Salaam Lib. Bull. no. 53.

366
East African Common Services Organization. *Directorate of Civil Aviation.* Annual report. 1960/61–1966/67. [Nairobi?] 7 v. in 2.
HE9884.A7E33a
Report year ends June 30.
Supersedes a publication with the same title (item 357) issued by the Directorate of Civil Aviation, East Africa of the East Africa High Commission.
Vols. for 1960/61–1961/62 issued by the agency under a variant name: Directorate of Civil Aviation, East Africa.
Superseded by a publication with the same title (item 368) issued by the Directorate of Civil Aviation of the East African Community.
L.C. has 1960/61–1966/67.

367
East African Community. Licensed operators providing [air] services in East Africa in 1972. *In* East African Community. Annual report. 1972. [Arusha, Tanzania?] p. 25–34.
JQ2945.A58E25 1972

East African Community *Directorate of Civil Aviation.*
Note: On January 1, 1948, the directorate took over the functions of the former East African Air Transport Authority, established in 1945 to oversee the East African Airways Corporation. The directorate is a non-self-contained service providing air-traffic, communications, and radio-navigation services in Kenya, Tanzania, and Uganda. The directorate is administered by a director-general from headquarters in Nairobi. Decentralization of the directorate was begun in 1969, in accordance with the Treaty of East African Co-operation, with the establishment of state directors' offices in each of the partner states.

368
Annual report. 1967/68+ [Nairobi]
TL528.E2E27a
Report year ends June 30.
Supersedes a publication with the same title (item 366) issued by the Directorate of Civil Aviation of the East African Common Services Organization.
L.C. has 1967/68+

369
——— Careers in civil aviation. [Nairobi, 1970?] 24 p. DLC

370
East African Community. *East African Legislative Assembly. Select Committee to Examine the Difficulties Faced by the East African Airways Corporation.* Report. [Arusha? 1972?]
The Committee was appointed June 17, 1972.
Cited in British Broadcasting Corporation, Monitoring Service, Summary of world broadcasts, pt. 4, The Middle East and Africa, 2d ser., ME/4019, June 20, 1972, p. B/5.

371
East African Community. *East African Statistical Dept.* Civil airports and airstrips in East Africa. Nairobi, 1967.
Source: Hofmeier.

372
Gt. Brit. *Air Ministry.* Civil air transport services. Note by the Secretary of State for Air on the proposed arrangements with Imperial Airways, Ltd., for the continued operation of (1) an air service between Khartoum and West Africa and (2) an air service between Kisumu and Lusaka. London, H.M. Stationery Off., 1938. 4 p. ([Gt. Brit. Parliament. Papers by command) Cmd. 5770) TL720.9.I5A6 1938b
"The route to be followed will be Kisumu, Nairobi, Moshi, Dodoma, Mbeye, Mpika (or Kasama, Ndola), Broken Hill and Lusaka."

373
Jambo news. [Nairobi, East African Airways Office of Public Relations] illus. MBU
Staff magazine.

374
Kenya. Sessional paper on a Government guarantee for a loan to the East African Airways Corporation to acquire a 4th super VC 10 aircraft. [Nairobi, 1967] 2 p. (Kenya. [National Assembly] Sessional paper no. 2 of 1967)
Information received from L.C. Office, Nairobi, Kenya; (publication not held by DLC).

375
Kenya. *Ministry of Power and Communications.* Government guarantee of bank overdraft facilities to be extended to East African Airways Corporation by the National Bank of Kenya Ltd. Nairobi, Printed by the Govt. Printer, 1970. 2 p. (Kenya. [National Assembly] Sessional paper no. 4 of 1970) DLC

376
——— Government guarantee of purchase moneys payable by East African Airways Corporation to B.A. (Holdings) Ltd. [Nairobi, 1969] 2 p. (Kenya. [National Assembly] Sessional paper no. 5 of 1969)
Information received from L.C. Office, Nairobi, Kenya; (publication not held by DLC).

377
——— Kenya Government guarantee of credits to the East African Airways Corporation by the Export Import Bank of the United States and the McDonnell Douglas Corp. in respect of the purchase of three DC-9 aircraft. [Nairobi, 1970] 3 p. (Kenya. [National Assembly] Sessional paper no. 10 of 1970)
Information received from L.C. Office, Nairobi, Kenya; (publication not held by DLC).

378
Kenya Colony and Protectorate. Agreement as to air survey between Khartoum and Kisumu. [London, Burchells, 1926]
DLC-Micro 23940 reel 9 folio 14
Collation of the original: [4] p.
At head of title: Kenya, Uganda and the Sudan. North Sea Aerial & General Transport ltd.
Colonial Office Library East Africa pamphlet folio 142.

379
Tanganyika. East African air transport policy.

Dar es Salaam, Govt. Printer, 1945. 8 p.
Source: Dar es Salaam Lib. Bull. no. 85.

380
World chart: all the important facts for the countries of the world. Nairobi, University Press of Africa [for] East African, International Airline of Africa, 1970. chart 90 x 120 cm. DLC

381
Zanzibar. *Legislative Council.* [Agreement between British Overseas Airways Corporation and East African Airways Corporation] (*Its* Sessional paper no. 3 of 1947) *In* Zanzibar. *Legislative Council.* Papers laid before the Legislative Council, 1947. Zanzibar, Printed by the Govt. Printer, 1948. p. 3–7. J733.J52 1947

Posts and Telecommunications

382
East Africa High Commission. *Posts and Telegraphs Dept.* Telephone directory, Mombasa, Nairobi. [Nairobi?] DS
DS has Feb. 1951.

383
East Africa High Commission. *Posts and Telegraphs Dept. Advisory Board.* Inter-territorial organisation. Scheme for the conversion of the East African Posts and Telegraphs Department into a self-contained department with its own capital account. Nairobi, 1947. 21 p. (Colonial paper no. 210) MBU
J. R. Leslie, chairman of the ad hoc committee.

East African External Telecommunications Company.
Note: Following a decision of the East African Communications Council of the East African Common Services Organization in the latter part of 1963, the company was created to take over the assets of Cable and Wireless Limited, a British firm based in London, which had operated telecommunications services in East Africa since 1910. Under the agreement, the then postmaster general acquired 60 percent of the share capital. With the creation of the East African Community, the share capital was transferred to the East African Posts and Telecommunications Corporation to be held on behalf of the East African Community. The corporation purchased the remaining 40 percent of the share capital held by Cable and Wireless in 1974.

384
Reports and accounts. [Nairobi] illus. annual. HE8490.E22E27a
Report year ends Mar. 31.
L.C. has 1965/66+ (1968/69 wanting)

East African Posts and Telecommunications Administration
Note: On January 1, 1948, the East African Posts and Telegraphs Department was made a non-self-contained service of the East Africa High Commission with headquarters in Nairobi, Kenya. On January 1, 1949, the status of the department was altered by the East African Posts and Telegraphs Department (Conversion) Order, 1949, to a self-contained service, i.e. a self-financed corporation. On October 1, 1951, the above developments were consolidated in the East African Posts and Telecommunications Act, in which the department was renamed the East African Posts and Telecommunications Administration. On January 1, 1964, the responsibility for the operation of the external telecommunications of East Africa was vested in the East African External Telecommunications Company Ltd. Under the Treaty for East African Co-operation, the administration was converted to a self-contained corporation within the East African Community and its name changed to East African Posts and Telecommunications Corporation. Headquarters were moved from Nairobi, Kenya, to Kampala, Uganda.

385
Annual report and accounts. 1948–67. [Nairobi, Govt. Printer] illus. HE7346.E3E2
Supersedes the Annual report (item 419) issued by the Posts and Telegraphs Dept. of Kenya Colony and Protectorate, and the agency's Operating accounts, 1949 (item 391).

Title varies: 1948–66, Annual report.

Vols, for 1948–50 issued by the agency under its earlier name: East African Posts and Telegraphs Dept.

Vol. for 1950 includes the Report of the Director of Audit, Kenya, on the appropriation and operating accounts; for 1951–67 includes the Report of the Auditor-General (1951–53 called Director of Audit) of the East African Common Services Organization (1951–60 called East Africa High Commission) on the accounts.

Superseded by a publication with the same title (item 404) issued by the East African Posts and Telecommunications Corporation.

L.C. has 1949–67.

386

——— Brief description for the use of members of the African Telecommunication Union of an experimental V.H.F. radio beam relay route operated between Nairobi and Nakuru in Kenya, by the East African Posts and Telegraphs Department. [Nairobi?] 1949. 3 p.

Issued by the agency under its earlier name: East African Posts and Telegraphs Dept.

Source: Col. Off. Lib. Cat.

387

——— Draft estimates of expenditure and revenue. 1949?–1967? [Nairobi] annual. MBU

Issued in 2 parts: pt. 1. Draft on estimates.—pt. 2. Memoranda.

388

——— Estimates of expenditure and revenue. 1949?–1967? [Nairobi] annual. DLC

Vols. for 1949?–1961 issued in 2 parts: pt. 1. Estimates.—pt. 2. Memoranda.

Superseded by Estimates of revenue and expenditure (item 405) issued by the East African Posts and Telecommunications Corporation.

"Approved by the East Africa Central Legislative Assembly."

L.C. has 1952–62 (scattered issues) ; MBU has 1949–67 (scattered issues wanting) .

389

——— List of post offices in East Africa. [Nairobi?] 1968.

Source: Makerere Lib. Bull. no. 72.

390

——— Kenya, Tanganyika, and Uganda post office telephone directory. [Nairobi] 2 no. a year. DLC

Superseded by the Kenya telephone directory (item 401) the Tanganyika telephone directory (item 402) and the Uganda telephone directory (item 403) ?

L.C. has Sept. 1949.

391

——— Operating accounts. 1948–51. Nairobi, Printed by the Govt. Printer. annual. DLC

Issued by the agency under its earlier name: East African Posts and Telegraphs Dept.

Superseded by a section entitled Report of the Director of Audit, Kenya, on the appropriation and operating accounts, in the agency's Annual report (item 385) .

L.C. has 1949; source for 1948–51: Royal Comm. Soc. Cat.

392

——— Post office directory of private box and private bag renters, Kenya. [Nairobi]
HE7350.K4A45

Superseded by a publication with the same title (item 407) issued by the Regional Director, Kenya of the East African Posts and Telecommunications Corporation.

L.C. catalogs under title: Post office directory of private box & private bag renters, Kenya.

L.C. has June 1966; source for June 1963: Col. Off. Lib. Cat.

393

——— Post office directory of private box and private bag renters, Tanzania (excluding Zanzibar and Pemba) . [Dar es Salaam]

Superseded by Post office directory of private box and private bag renters, Tanzania (item 409) issued by the Regional Director, Tanzania of the East African Posts and Telecommunications Corporation.

Source for 1967: Dar es Salaam Lib. Bull. no. 86.

394

_______ Post office directory, Tanganyika: list of box numbers of private bag renters, 1962–1963. Dar es Salaam [1962] xvii, 187 p.

Source: Col. Off. Lib. Cat.

395

_______ Post office directory, Uganda. [Entebbe?]

Source for Oct. 1966: Makerere Lib. Bull no. 65.

396

_______ Post office guide. 1948–1966? [Nairobi, Printed by the Govt. Printer] irregular.
HE7350.E3A28

Vols. for 1948–51 issued by the agency under its earlier name: East African Posts and Telegraphs Dept.

Vol. for 1966 issued in 3 parts: v. 1. Inland postal and remittance services and general information.—v. 2. International postal and remittance services.—v. 3. Guide to telecommunications services.

Superseded by a publication with the same title (item 406) issued by the East African Posts and Telecommunications Corporation.

L.C. has 1948, 1951, 1953, 1956, 1960–1961/62, and 1966; DS has 1959.

397

_______ _______ Supplement. Nairobi, Printed by the Govt. Printer. irregular.
HE7350.E3A282

L.C. has no. 2–3, Jan.–Oct. 1954 for 1953 ed.; no. 1–2, Feb.–Mar. 1956 for 1956 ed.; and no. 1, Oct. 1961 for 1961/62 ed.

398

_______ Press notice. [Kampala?]

L.C. received no. 39/67, Oct. 23, 1967; not retained.

399

_______ Revised international parcel postage rates effective 1st July, 1969. Nairobi, Govt. Printer, 1969. 9 p. DLC

400

_______ Staff list; European officers. 1949?–1961? Nairobi, Govt. Printer. annual.

"For official use only."

No more published?

Source for 1949–61: Col. Off. Lib. Cat.

401

_______ Telephone directory, Kenya. 1950?–1967. [Nairobi] 2 no. a year. DLC

Title varies: 1950?–1959, Kenya telephone directory.

Superseded by a publication with the same title (item 408) issued by the Regional Director, Kenya, of the East African Posts and Telecommunications Corporation.

L.C. has July 1956–67 (scattered issues wanting).

402

_______ Telephone directory, Tanzania. 1950?–1967? [Dar es Salaam] 2 no. a year. DLC

Title varies: 1950?–1959, Tanganyika telephone directory.—1960–1965? Telephone directory, Tanganyika.

Superseded by a publication with the same title (item 410) issued by the Regional Director, Tanzania, of the East African Posts and Telecommunications Corporation.

L.C. has May 1952, Oct. 1956, Mar. 1958–1960.

403

_______ Telephone directory, Uganda. 1950?–1967? [Kampala] 2 no. a year. DLC

Superseded by a publication with the same title (item 412) issued by the Regional Director, Uganda, of the East African Posts and Telecommunications Corporation.

L.C. has 1965; Cst-H has 1961.

East African Posts and Telecommunications Corporation.

Note: Under the Treaty for East African Co-operation, the corporation succeeded the East African Posts and Telecommunications Administration on January 1, 1968. The director general of the agency is responsible to the Board of Directors, of which he is an *ex of-*

ficio member. The directors, appointed by the East African governments, formulate and control the policy of the corporation. The Board of Directors may be advised on matters of policy by the Communications Council of the East African Community. On January 10, 1968, the postal and telecommunications services of Zanzibar were integrated with those of the mainland. The headquarters of the corporation are located in Kampala, Uganda, with regional direrectors in Dar es Salaam, Tanzania, Kampala, Uganda, and Nairobi, Kenya.

404
Annual report and accounts. 1968+ [Kampala] illus. DLC
Supersedes a publication with the same title (item 385) issued by the East African Posts and Telecommunications Administration.
Each issue includes the Accounts of the Corporation audited by the auditor-general of the East African Community.
L.C. has 1968+

405
——— Estimates of revenue and expenditure. 1968?+ Kampala. annual. NNUN
Supersedes Estimates of expenditure and revenue (item 388) issued by the East African Posts and Telecommunications Administration.
NNUN has 1969+

406
——— Post office guide. 1970/71+ [Nairobi] irregular. DLC
Supersedes a publication with the same title (item 396) issued by the East African Posts and Telecommunications Administration.
Issued in three parts: v.1. Inland postal and remittance services and general information.—v. 2. International postal and remittance services.—v. 3. Telecommunications services.
L.C. has 1970/71+

406a
——— Posts and telecommunications: East Africa telex directory, March 1974. [Kampala, Uganda, 1974?] 99 p. DLC

407
East African Posts and Telecommunications Corporation. *Regional Director, Kenya.* Post office directory of private box & private bag renters, Kenya. [Nairobi] CSt-H
Supersedes a publication with the same title (item 392) issued by the East African Posts and Telecommunications Administration.

408
——— Telephone directory, Kenya. 1968+ Nairobi. illus. DLC
Supersedes a publication with the same title (item 401) issued by the East African Posts and Telecommunications Administration.
Each issue includes separate sections for the departments of the East African Community in Kenya, and for the ministries of the Kenya Government.
L.C. has 1968+

409
East African Posts and Telecommunications Corporation. *Regional Director, Tanzania.* Post office directory of private box and private bag renters, Tanzania. [Dar es Salaam] annual. DLC
Supersedes Post office directory of private box and private bag renters, Tanzania (excluding Zanzibar and Pemba) (item 393) issued by the East African Posts and Telecommunications Administration.
L.C. has 1969, 1972–73.

410
——— Telephone directory, Tanzania. Kitabu cha orodha ya simu, Tanzania. 1968+ Dar es Salaam. illus. DLC
Supersedes a publication with the same title (item 402) issued by the East African Posts and Telecommunications Administration.
Text in English and Swahili.
Each issue includes separate sections for the departments of the East African Community in Tanzania, and for the ministries of the Tanzania Government.
L.C. has 1968+

411
East African Posts and Telecommunications Cor-

poration. *Regional Director, Uganda.* Post office directory of private box and private bag renters, Uganda. [Kampala] CSt-H

412
——— Telephone directory, Uganda. 1968+ Kampala. illus. DLC

Supersedes a publication with the same title (item 403) issued by the East Africa Posts and Tele-communications Administration.

Each issue includes separate sections for the departments of the East African Community in Uganda, and for the ministries of the Uganda Government.

L.C. has 1968+

413
East African Posts and Telecommunications Corporation. *Salaries Review Commission.* Report. [Kampala] 1971. 292 p. in various pagings. DLC

G. L. Binaisa, chairman.

414
East African Posts and Telecommunications Corporation. *Stamp Bureau.* Philatelic bulletin. v. 1+ Kampala, May 1965+ illus. quarterly. DLC

Vols. for 1965–1967? issued by the agency under its earlier name: East African Posts and Telecommunications Administration. Stamp Bureau.

L.C. has May 1965, and June 1969+

415
Gt. Brit. *Air Ministry.* Empire air mail scheme (Kisumu-Luska auxiliary service). Note by the Secretary of State for Air on the principal provisions proposed to be embodied in an agreement with Imperial Airways, Limited, for the operation by an associated company, Wilson Airways, Limited, of a light trunk landplane service between Kisumu and Lusaka (referred to in Cmd. 5414). London, H.M. Stationery Off., 1937. 3 p. ([Gt. Brit. Parliament. Papers by command] Cmd. 5523) HE6939.A4A5 1937d

"The route to be followed will be Kisumu, Nairobi, Moshi, Dodoma, Mboya, Mpika (or Kasama, Ndola) and Lusaka."

416
Gt. Brit. *Colonial Office.* East Africa Protectorate, correspondence, October, 1905, to March, 1909, relating to the mail service and the improvement of steamship communication. [London] Printed for the use of the Colonial Office, 1910. (*Its* African no. 877, confidential) DLC-Micro 03759

Collation of the original: 66 p.

[Gt. Brit.] Public Record Office. C.O. 879/96.

Includes information on Zanzibar, the East Africa Protectorate, Uganda, and German East Africa.

417
Kenya. Government guarantee for a loan by the IBRD (World Bank) to the East African Posts and Telecommunications Corporation. The Guarantee (Loans) Act Cap. 461. [Nairobi, 1973?] 3 p. (Kenya. [National Assembly] Sessional paper no. 2 of 1973)

Information received from L.C. Office, Nairobi, Kenya; (publication not held by DLC).

418
Kenya. *Ministry of Power and Communications.* Kenya Government guarantee for a loan to the East African Posts and Telecommunications Corporation by the International Bank for Reconstruction and Development. Nairobi, Printed by the Govt. Printer, 1970. 4 p. (Kenya. [National Assembly] Sessional paper no. 3 of 1970) DLC

419
Kenya Colony and Protectorate. *Posts and Telegraphs Dept.* Annual report. 1926–47. Nairobi. HE7350.K4A3

At head of title, 1926: Kenya Colony and Protectorate and Uganda Protectorate; 1927–32: Colony and Protectorate of Kenya and Uganda Protectorate; 1933–47?: Colony and Protectorate of Kenya, Uganda Protectorate, and Mandated Territory of Tanganyika.

Supersedes the Annual report issued by the Posts and Telepgraphs Dept. of Tanganyika.

Title varies: 1926–28, Abridged report.—

1929–35, Abridged annual report.

Issued by the agency under variant names: 1926–28, Post and Telepgraph Dept.; 1933–35, Post and Telegraphs Dept.

Superseded by the Annual report (item 385) issued by the East African Posts and Telegraphs Dept.

L.C. has 1926–38; source for 1926–47: Royal Comm. Soc. Cat.

420

——— Kenya and Uganda post office guide. Nairobi. irregular.

Source for 1917: Royal Empire Soc. Cat.; source for 1929–30: Makerere Lib. Bull. no. 39; source for 1932: Royal Comm. Soc. Cat.; source for 1934: Kenya Govt. Press rept., 1934.

421

——— Post office circulars. [Nairobi, Govt. Printer] biweekly.

Source for 1946–47: Kenya Govt. Print. rept., 1946–47.

422

——— Telephone directory. [Nairobi, Govt. Printer]

Source for 1934: Kenys Govt. Press rept., 1934.

423

Mackay, James A. East Africa; the story of East Africa and its stamps. [London] Philatelic Publishers ltd. [in association with East African Posts and Telecommunications Corporation, c1970] 192 p. illus. HE6185.A6M3

424

Postgen. v. 1+ 1956+ [Kampala, East African Posts and Telecommunications Corporation] illus. quarterly. HE7350.E3P6

Vols. for 1956–67 issued by the agency under its earlier name: East African Posts and Telecommunications Administration.

"The staff magazine of the East African Posts and Telecommunications Corporation."

L.C. has Mar. 1963+ (scattered issues wanting); source for 1956+: Makerere Lib. Union list.

425

Whitson, H. A. Report on the East African Posts and Tele-Communications Administration industrial relations. [Nairobi?] 1960. 11 p. (East African Posts and Tele-Communications Administration. Press notice 38/60) MBU

426

——— Report on the industrial relations machinery within the E.A.P.&T. Administration. Nairobi, East Africa High Commission, 1961?] 11 p.

At head of title: East Africa High Commission. East African Posts and Telecommunications Administration.

Source: Col. Off. Lib. Cat.

Railroads and Harbors

427

Bandari zetu. no. 1+ 1969+ Dar es Salaam, East African Harbours Corporation. biweekly. DLC

Title translated: Our harbors.

Text in English and Swahili.

L.C. has no. 20, Aug. 1970+

428

Carson, John B. The preliminary survey for the Kenya and the Uganda railway, 1891–1892. Nairobi, Eagle Press, 1950. 16 p. map. (Treasury of East African history) IEN

429

Churchill, W. S. Uganda Railway. [London, Printed at the Foreign Office by J. W. Harrison] for the use of the Colonial Office [1906] ([Gt. Brit. Colonial Office] African no. 862, confidential) DLC-Micro 03759

Collation of the original: 12 p. fold. map. [Gt. Brit.] Public Record Office. C.O. 879/93.

Includes a proposal to expand the Uganda Railway to the Congo, with a "Sketch to show existing and projected railways."

430

Commonwealth Shipping Committee. Interim

report on East African shipping services. London, H.M. Stationery Off., 1924. 10 p. HE905.E3C6

At head of title: Imperial Shipping Committee.

H. J. Mackinder, chairman.

431
East Africa High Commission. The East African Railways and Harbours Administration Act, 1950. Nairobi, Printed by the Govt. Printer, 1950. 70, xviii p. DLC-LL

At head of title: East African Railways and Harbours.

432
——— The East African Railways and Harbours Administration Pensions Regulations, 1950. Nairobi, Printed by the Govt. Printer [1950] 33 p. DLC-LL

433
——— Note by the East Africa High Commission on the traffic problems arising from the congestion at the port of Dar es Salaam. Nairobi, Govt. Printer [1948] 4 p. map.

Sir P. E. Mitchell, chairman.

Source: Col. Off. Lib. Cat.

434
——— Port of Dar es Salaam; report upon possibilities of development into a major port, by a committee consisting of A. F. Kirby, W. Urquhart [and] A. M. Smith. Nairobi, 1949. 47 p. illus., charts (part col.), col. maps, col. plan. HE560.D3E3

435
East Africa High Commission. *Audit Dept.* Report by the Auditor-General, East Africa High Commission services on the accounts of the East African Railways and Harbours Administration. 1951–1961? [Nairobi, Printed by the Govt. Printer] annual. DLC

Supersedes the Report by the Director of Audit, Kenya, on the accounts of the East African Railways and Harbours (item 598) issued by the Audit Dept. of Kenya Colony and Protectorate.

Title varies slightly.

Superseded by the Report by the Auditor-General, East African Common Services Organization, on the accounts of the East African Railways and Harbours Administration (item 447) issued by the Audit Dept. of the East African Common Services Organization.

Financial accounts are included also in the Annual report (item 459) issued by the East African Railways and Harbours Administration.

L.C. has 1951, 1956–59; IEN has 1951, and 1954.

East Africa High Commission. *Commissioner for Transport.*

Note: The position of member for transport was created by the East Africa High Commission Order in Council, 1947, beginning on January 1, 1948. With the assent of the East Africa Central Legislative Assembly, the member was renamed commissioner for transport. The commissioner was responsible for the East African Railways and Harbours Administration and the Directorate of Civil Aviation, East Africa. He regularly submitted the annual reports of the administration and the directorate to the chairman of the East Africa High Commission. The commissioner's office was located at the headquarters of the East African Railways and Harbours Administration in Nairobi, Kenya. When a vacancy occurred in 1959, the general manager of the East African Railways and Harbours Administration was appointed also acting commissioner for transport. The commissioner of transport made no separate annual report to the East Africa High Commission. However, he was responsible for the summary report and letter of transmittal prefacing the annual reports of the East African Railways and Harbours Administration, and the Directorate of Civil Aviation, East Africa. No further prefatory statements of the commissioner appear after 1960. With the reorganization of the East Africa High Commission into the East African Common Services Organization in 1961, the functions of the commissioner were taken over by the Ministerial Communications Committee.

436
Financial arrangements for the construction and operation of Mtwara Port and the Southern Province Railway in Tanganyika. [Nairobi? 1955?]

Source: E.A.H.C. proceedings, Sept. 6. 1955.

437
_______ The future of the Southern Province Railway in Tanganyika. [Nairobi? 1951?] (Transport Advisory Council Memorandum, no. 84)

Source: E.A.H.C. proceedings, Apr. 3, 1951.

438
_______ Report on a proposed extension of the railway from Kampala westwards [to Mityana] [Nairobi? 1950?] (Transport Advisory Memorandum, no. 72)

Source: E.A.H.C. proceedings, Jan. 16, 1951.

439
_______ Report on the proposed construction of a branch line to Mikumi. [Nairobi? 1958?]

Source: E.A.H.C. proceedings, Oct. 7, 1958.

440
_______ Reports of the Commissioner for Transport, East Africa High Commission, and of the General Manager on the administration of the East African Railways and Harbours. 1948–54. [Nairobi, Printed by the Govt. Printer] illus., col. maps. annual. **HE99.E3A3**

At head of title: East African Railways and Harbours.

Supersedes the Report of the General Manager on the administration of the railways and harbours (item 585) issued by Kenya and Uganda Railways and Harbours, and the Report of the General Manager issued by the Tanganyika Railways and Ports Services.

Superseded by the Annual report (item 459) issued by the East African Railways and Harbours Administration.

L.C. has 1948–51, 1953–54.

441
East Africa High Commission. *Mombasa Committee of Enquiry.* Report of the Committee of Inquiry Appointed Consequent Upon a Resolution Dated 25th April, 1952, of the East Africa Central Legislative Assembly. [Nairobi, Printed by the High Commission Printer, 1953] 35 p. NNC

R. E. Norton, chairman.

The inquiry concerned tranpsort in East Africa, with special reference to correcting the delay in the clearance of goods received at the port of Mombasa, Kenya.

The following entries (items 442–44) are arranged alphabetically and concern the implementation of the recommendations in the committee's report.

442
East Africa High Commission. Decisions on the recommendations contained in the Report of the Committee of Inquiry into the Working of the Port of Mombasa. Nairobi, Govt. Printer, 1953. 10 p. ([East Africa High Commission. East Africa Central Legislative Assembly] Sessional paper) NNC

443
East African Railways and Harbours Administration. General Manager's comments [on the] Mombasa Committee of Enquiry, being memoranda on the Committee's Report prepared for the consideration of Transport Advisory Council and its sub-committees. Nairobi, 1953. 36 p. NNC

444
_______ General Manager's preliminary comments on the Report of the Norton Committee of Enquiry into Mombasa port working, February 1953. Nairobi, 1953. 12, 32, 2 leaves. DS

Includes also Transport Advisory Council Memorandum no. 253 [on the] Report of the Committee of Enquiry Appointed to Consider and Advise upon Certain Matters Connected with the Port of Mombasa [and] Council Memorandum no. 262 [General-Manager's additional comments on the] Mombasa Port Inquiry Committee's report.

445
East African Common Services Organization. Port working party. [Mombasa, Port Manager's Office, 1962] 9 p. CaQML

At head of title: East African Railways and Harbours.

T.p. wanting in CaQML photocopy.

446
——— Request to the United Nations Development Programme for assistance from the U.N. Special Fund, with a training and development project for the East African Railways and Harbours. Nairobi, 1966. 63 p.

Cited in Bibliography on Kenya issued by the Documentation Centre of the African Training and Research Centre in Administration for Development of Tangier (Tánger, 1970) p. 2.

447
East African Common Services Organization. *Audit Dept.* Report by the Auditor-General, East African Common Services Organization, on the accounts of the East African Railways and Harbours Administration. 1962?–1968? [Nairobi, printed by the Govt. Printer] annual. DLC

Supersedes the Report by the Auditor-General, East Africa High Commission services on the accounts of the East African Railways and Harbours Administration (item 435) issued by the Audit Dept. of the East Africa High Commission.

L.C. has 1963.

448
East African Community. *East African Legislative Assembly. Select Committee on the Reorganization of the East African Railways Board of Directors.* Report, June 26, 1974. [Arusha. Tanzania? 1974] 185 p.

E. K. Ntende, chairman.

Recommended the merging of the positions of director general and chairman of the East African Railways Corporation and a staff reduction of 10 per cent.

Cited in British Broadcasting Corporation, Monitoring Service, Summary of world broadcasts, pt. 4, The Middle East and Africa, 2d ser., ME/4638, June 29, 1974, p. B/7–8.

449
East African Community. *East African Legislative Assembly. Select Committee to Inquire into the Harbours Operations.* Report. [Arusha? 1974]

Cited in Africa research bulletin, economic, financial and technical series, v. 11, no. 9, Oct. 31, 1974, p. 3252.

450
East African Community. *Treaties, etc. International Bank for Reconstruction and Development, May 25, 1970.* Letter agreement (third East African railways project) between International Bank for Reconstruction and Development and East African Community. Dated May 25, 1970. [Washington] 1970. 8 p. (Loan no. 674EA) CLL

Conformed copy.

East African Harbours Corporation.

Note: The corporation was established on June 1, 1969, as one of the two successors to the defunct East African Railways and Harbours Administration. The headquarters for the corporation are located in Dar es Salaam, Tanzania. The board of directors consists of a chairman, a director-general, three directors appointed by the East African Authority, and three directors appointed by the partner states.

451
Annual report and accounts. 1969+ [Dar es Salaam] illus. HE559.E28E2a

First report covers period June-Dec. 1969.

Supersedes in part the Annual report (item 459) issued by the East African Railways and Harbours Administration.

Includes a summary in Swahili.

L.C. has 1969+

451a

_______ Approved estimates of expenditure and revenue and capital works program. 1970. Dar es Salaam. annual. HE559.A362E183c

Supersedes the agency's Programme of capital expenditure (item 455).

Superseded by the agency's Approved expenditure and revenue budgets and capital works programme.

L.C. has 1970.

452

_______ Approved expenditure and revenue budgets and capital works programme. 1971?+ Dar es Salaam, Office of the Director General. annual. HE559.A362E183b

Supersedes the agency's Approved estimates of expenditure and revenue and capital works program.

Cover title: Approved revenue and expenditure budgets and capital works programme, original varies.

L.C. has 1971+

453

_______ The East African Harbours regulations, 1970. [Nairobi?] 1970. 72 p. DLC

454

_______ Information on East African maritime ports. Dar es Salaam [1970?] 28 p. illus. HE559.A362E183 1970

455

_______ Programme of capital expenditure. 1969. Nairobi, Govt. Printer. annual. HE559.A362E183a

Supersedes in part a publication with the same title (item 481) issued by the East African Railways and Harbours Administration.

Superseded by the agency's Approved estimates of expenditure and revenue and capital works program (item 451a).

L.C. has 1969.

456

_______ Tariff book of harbour dues charges (all ports) in force from 1st May 1974. [Dar es Salaam] 1974. 90 leaves. HE559.E27E37 1974

457

_______ Tariff book of harbour dues & charges (applicable to all ports) in force from 1st May 1974. [Dar es Salaam] 1974. 90 leaves. DLC

East African Railways and Harbours Administration.

Note: On August 31, 1948, the East Africa Central Legislative Assembly passed the East African Railways and Harbours (Transitional Provisions) Act creating the East African Railways and Harbours Administration as a self-contained (i.e., self-financing) service of the East Africa High Commission by merging the Kenya and Uganda Railways and Harbours with the Tanganyika Railways and Ports Services. A comprehensive East African Railways and Harbours Act (item 431) replaced the Transitional Provisions Act on May 17, 1950. Article 71 of the Treaty for East African Co-operation, establishing the East African Community on December 1, 1967, provided for the creation of two new corporations from the defunct administration. On June 1, 1969, Article 71 came into force. As a result, the East African Railways Corporation has maintained the offices of the former administration in Nairobi, Kenya, while the East African Harbours Corporation has moved to new headquarters in Dar es Salaam, Tanzania. During its existence, the administration is often referred to simply as East African Railways and Harbours in many official publications.

458

An agreement made this fifth day of November, 1948, between the Chief Port Authority for and on behalf of the East African Railways and Harbours (Hereinafter referred to as "The Authority") of the one part and the Tanganyika Landing and Shipping Company, Limited . . . [Dar es Salaam, Govt. Printer] 1947. 9 p. CaQML

On cover: EACSO.

Title page missing in CaQML copy.

CaQML catalogs under: East African Common Services Organization.

459

_______ Annual report. 1955–68. [Nairobi,

Printed by the Govt. Printer] illus., col. maps. HE3420.E3A35

Supersedes the Reports of the Commissioner for Transport, East Africa High Commission, and of the General Manager on the administration of the East African Railways and Harbours (item 440).

Vols. for 1955–60 include the report of the Commissioner for Transport.

Superseded by the Annual report and accounts (item 451) issued by the East African Harbours Corporation, and the Annual report (item 518) issued by the East African Railways Corporation.

L.C. has 1955–68.

460
_______ The case for a rail link between East and Central Africa. Nairobi, 1963.

Source: Hofmeier.

461
_______ Dar es Salaam becomes a modern port. [n.p., 1957] [28] p. illus. DBRE

462
_______ Dar es Salaam, gateway to Tanganyika and the Belgian Congo; the story of the building of three deep-water berths completed in 1956. [London, 195–?] [30] p. illus.

Source: Col. Off. Lib. Cat.

463
_______ Draft estimates of revenue and expenditure. 1949–68. [Nairobi?] annual. HE3420.E3A34

Supersedes the Draft estimates and memoranda (item 566) issued by the Kenya and Uganda Railways and Harbours.

Superseded in part by a publication with the same title (item 519) issued by the East African Railways Corporation.

L.C. has 1949 bound with the agency's Estimates of revenue and expenditure; source for 1955–56: Makerere Lib. Bull. no. 68.

464
_______ East African locomotives. [Nairobi? Govt. Printer, between 1948 and 1966] 1 v. (unpaged) DLC

465
_______ East African railways and harbours; expenditure instructions. Nairobi, Govt. Printer, 1958. [2] 21 leaves.

Source: Col. Off. Lib. Cat.

466
_______ The East African Railways and Harbours transport services in Tanganyika since amalgamation on the 1st May, 1948; being a note published at the request of Transport Advisory Council. Nairobi, Govt. Printer, 1952. 69 p. NNC

467
_______ East African Railways and Harbours; western Uganda extension, Kampala-Kasese. [n.p., 195–?] map. DLC-G&M

Scale 1:250,000.

Blue line print.

468
_______ Estimates of expenditure on capital, betterment and renewal works. 1948?–1966. Nairobi. annual. HE3420.E3A33

Title varies slightly.

Vols. for 1958–66 issued in 2 parts: Harbours.—Railways.

Superseded by the agency's Programme of capital expenditure (item 481).

L.C. has 1950–65.

469
_______ Estimates of revenue and expenditure. 1949–67. Nairobi, Printed by the Govt. Printer. annual. HE3520.E3A34

Supersedes the Estimates of the revenue and expenditure (item 567) issued by the Kenya and Uganda Railways and Harbours, and the Estimates of the revenue and expenditure issued by the Tanganyika Railways and Ports Services.

Superseded in part by a publication with the same title (item 520) issued by the East African Railways Corporation.

"Passed by the East Africa Central Legislative Assembly."

Each issue includes revised estimates for the preceding year.

L.C. has 1950–63.

470
——— General Manager's report to the Ministerial Communications Committee on the Kilombero railway extension to Kidatu. [Nairobi? 1962?] (Memorandum no. 17)
Source: E.A.C.S.O. debates, May 22, 1962.

471
——— General rules, 1953. Made under Section 99 of the East African Railways and Harbours Administration Act, 1950. For observance of employees. Nairobi, 1953. 189 p.
Source: BM Cat., 1968.

472
——— Harbours Advisory Council minutes and memoranda. 1948+ [Nairobi, Govt. Printer] irregular.
Supersedes the Advisory Council minutes and memoranda, harbours (item 564) issued by the Kenya and Uganda Railways and Harbours.
Title varies: 1948–49, Advisory Council minutes, harbours.
Source for 1948–55: Kenya Govt. Print. rept., 1948–55.

473
——— Look ahead with E.A.R.&H. [Nairobi, 196–?] [9] p. illus., map. DLC
Recruitment brochure.

474
——— Map of northern section of link line. [Nairobi? 1964?] DLC-G&M
Scale not given.
Photograph positive in color.
Shows southwestern Tanganyika.
"Physiographical details from Tanganyika Geological Survey map no. G.S. 1463. Z.2098.825.9/60. Rainfall from Meteorological Dept. of E.A.C.S.O. map of 10% probability of annual rainfall of East Africa 1961."

475
——— Memorandum to the International Bank for Reconstruction and Development. Nairobi, 1963. 2 v. maps. MCM
Contents: [v. 1] Rolling stock requirements, phase I.—[v. 2] Rolling stock requirements, phases II & III.

476
——— Motive power report 1957; being an investigation into the possible use of diesel or electric traction as a means of increasing line capacity on the Mombasa-Nairobi-Nakuru sections, and allied matters. [Nairobi, 1957?] 2 v. in 1.
Source: Col. Off. Lib. Cat.

477
——— Nairobi-Nakuru realignments. [Nairobi? 1950?] map. DLC-G&M
Scale 1:253,440.

478
——— Port of Dar es Salaam, Tanganyika. Dar es Salaam, 1956. 67 p. illus., maps. DLC

479
——— The Port of Mombasa. [Nairobi? 1966] map. DLC-G&M
Scale not given.
On verso: Shipping companies serving the port and their agents, and charges.

480
——— Port of Mombasa (Kilindini harbour-Mombasa old port): port booklet. Nairobi, 1950. 56 p. DS
1947 ed.: Port of Mombasa (Kilindini harbour-Mombasa old port) (item 581) issued by Kenya and Uganda Railways and Harbours.

481
——— Programme of capital expenditure. 1967–68. Nairobi. annual. DLC
Supersedes the agency's Estimates of expenditure on capital, betterment and renewal works (item 468).
Superseded by publications with the same

titles (items 455 and 520a) issued by the East African Harbours Corporation, and the East African Railways Corporation.

L.C. has 1967–68.

482

_______ R.M.S. 'Victoria'. [Nairobi, 1961?] [24] p. illus.

Source: Dar es Salaam Lib. Bull. no. 88.

483

_______ Rail, road and inland marine services. [London, Cook, Hammond & Kell, 1957] map. DLC–G&M

Scale 1:3,600,000.

Shows Kenya, Tanganyika, and Uganda.

484

_______ _______ Nairobi, Govt. Printer [1960?] map. DLC-G&M

Scale not given.

"Supplement to Saben's Uganda directory, 1960/61."

Shows Kenya, Tanganyika, and Uganda.

485

_______ _______ Nairobi, Govt. Printer, 1961. map. DLC-G&M

Scale not given.

Shows Kenya, Tanganyika and Uganda.

486

_______ _______ [Nairobi? 1963?] map. DLC-G&M

Scale 1:5,000,000.

Shows Kenya, Tanganyika, and Uganda.

487

_______ Rail-served industrial areas of East Africa. Nairobi, 1959. 37 p. maps. DLC

488

_______ _______ [2d ed.] Nairobi, 1961. 99 leaves. maps. DLC

489

_______ Railway Advisory Council minutes and memoranda. 1948+ [Nairobi, Govt. Printer] irregular.

Supersedes the Advisory Council minutes and memoranda, railways (items 565) issued by the Kenya and Uganda Railways and Harbours.

Title varies: 1948–49, Advisory Council minutes, railways.

Source for 1948–55: Kenya Govt. Print. rept., 1948–55.

490

_______ Railway, marine and road motor services tariff book. no. 1–5. Nairobi, Printed by the Govt. Printer, 1951–68. irregular. HE284.E2E32

Issued in 2 parts: pt. 1. General conditions. —pt. 2. Rates, fares and charges.

Continued in part by the Tariff book (item 521) issued by the East Africa Railways Corporation.

Updated by amendments contained in Correction slip.

L.C. has no. 1 (1951), and no. 5 (1968); DS has no. 4 (1965).

491

_______ Railway, steamer and road time table. General information and fares. Nairobi, Printed by the Govt. Printer. DBRE

DBRE has no. 7 (1948).

492

_______ Railway tariff policy. [Nairobi? Govt. Printer, 1964] 7 p. ([East African Common Services Organization. Central Legislative Assembly] Sessional paper no. 1 of 1964) HE2204.E37

At head of cover title: East African Railways and Harbours.

493

_______ Report on an engineering survey of a rail link between the East African and Rhodesian railway systems. Nairobi, 1952. 91 p. fold. col. maps. TF119.T3E2.

494

_______ Report on the Kilombero railway proj-

ect. Nairobi, 1961.
Source: Hofmeier.

495

——— Report on the proposed extension of the Kilosa-Mikuma branch line to Kidatu. Nairobi, 1961.
Source: E.A.C.S.O. debates, May 22, 1962. and Hofmeier.

496

——— A review of localisation and training. Nairobi, General Manager's Office, 1961. 21, 22 leaves. HE3419.E3Z6 1961

497

——— Special notice. [Nairobi] irregular.
"Special notices are sent out as occasion demands, in addition to the Weekly notices, and are numbered consecutively with the weekly notices."
Note: Individual special notices are entered in this guide by subject. They can be identified by consulting the index to this guide under East African Railways and Harbours Administration, *Special notice*.

498

——— Staff list, senior officers and supervisory staff. 1949?–1968? Nairobi, Govt. Printer. annual.
Title varies: 1949?–54, Staff list, European staff.
Source for 1949–62: Col. Off. Lib. Cat.

499

——— Staff regulations. 1951+ Nairobi, Printed by the Govt. Printer. HE284.Z7E23a
L.C. has 1951; source for 1951–62: Col. Off. Lib. Cat.

500

——— Station and port distance tables. 1st Oct. 1951, in force until further notice. Nairobi, Printed by the Govt. Printer, 1951. 70 p. HE3414.E3
"For use in conjunction with East African Railways and Harbours tariff book no. 1" (item 490).

501

——— Station and port distance tables. 1st January 1956, in force until further notice. Nairobi, Printed by the Govt. Printer, 1955. 76 p. DLC
"For use in conjunction with East African Railways and Harbours tariff book no. 2" (item 490).

502

——— Statistics of rail operation. Nairobi. 2 no. a year.
Source: Hofmeier.

503

——— Superannuation fund regulations, revised June 1950. [Nairobi, Printed by English Press, 1950] 57 p. DLC

504

——— Tariff of harbour dues and charges no. 2, applicable to Tanzania ports only. [Dar es Salaam?] 1968. 62 leaves. DLC
Issued 1st January 1968; in force until further notice.
"This tariff is prepared and published by authority of the General Manager in exercise of the powers conferred upon him under the provisions contained in the E.A.R.&H. Act."

505

——— Temporary distance tables. [Nairobi?]
Source for 1965: Makerere Lib. Bull. no. 68.

506

——— Tide tables for East African ports. Mombasa.
L.C. received 1960; not retained.

507

——— Time table. 1948?–1969? Nairobi, map. 2 no. a year. DLC
Title varies slightly.
"This time table and all information printed

herein is subject to the conditions and regulations published in the Tariff book of the East African Railways and Harbours" (item 490).

Includes information on rail, road, and marine services.

L.C. has current issues only; DBRE has 1952–60 (scattered issues).

508
______ The way to the west . . . the story of the extension of the railway through Uganda from Kampala to Kasese by the East African Railways and Harbours, 1950–1956. [Kampala? 1957?] [30] p. illus., map.
Source: Col. Off. Lib. Cat.

509
______ Weekly notice. Nairobi. irregular.
Cited in the agency's Special notice (item 496).

510
East African Railways and Harbours Administration. *Kenya and Uganda Section.* First supplementary estimates, 1948. Nairobi [1948] 9 p.
Source: BM Cat., 1965.

511
______ Renewals, betterment and capital works progress. Railways: list of works in progress and proposed new works. Nairobi. DLC
L.C. has 1949.

512
East African Railways and Harbours Administration. *Railway Administration. Dar es Salaam District.* Annual report. [Dar es Salaam?]
Source: Hofmeier.

513
East African Railways and Harbours Administration. *Railway Administration. Mwanza District.* Annual report. [Dar es Salaam?]
Source: Hofmeier.

514
East African Railways and Harbours Administration. *Railway Administration. Tabora District.* Annual report. [Dar es Salaam?]
Source: Hofmeier.

515
East African Railways and Harbours Administration. *Railway Administration. Tanga District.* Annual report. [Dar es Salaam?]
Source: Hofmeier.

516
East African Railways and Harbours Administration. *Tanganyika Section.* Estimate of expenditure on works in progress and proposed. 1949+ Dar es Salaam. IEN

517
East African Railways and Harbours Commission. Report of the East African Railways and Harbours Commission, 1962. Nairobi, 1963. 68 p. MiEM
Hans Harres, chairman.
"Reported to the East African Common Services Authority on 26th February, 1963."
Provided salary increases and changes in the conditions of service for staff, effective July 1, 1963.

The following entry includes the views of the staff and management and concerns the implementation of the recommendations in the commission's report.

517a
East African Railways and Harbours Administration. Proposals for the implementation of the recommendations of the Report of the East African Railways and Harbours Commission, 1962 [Nairobi, Printed by the Govt. Printer, 1963] 42 p. ([East African Common Services Organization. Central Legislative Assembly] Sessional paper no. 2 of 1963)
HE3419.E3E37
At head of title: East African Railways and Harbours.

East African Railways Corporation.
Note: The corporation was created from the

former East African Railways and Harbours Administration on June 1, 1969. Headquarters are maintained in Nairobi, Kenya. The board of directors consists of a chairman, a director general, and three members appointed by the East African Authority, and three resident directors, one appointed by each of the partner states. In mid–1974, the corporation was decentralized, with regional offices having responsibility for their finances.

518

Annual report. 1969+ [Arusha] illus. HE3419.E3E38

First report covers period June-Dec. 1969. Supersedes in part a publication with the same title (item 459) issued by the East African Railways and Harbours Administration.

L.C. has 1969+

519

______ Draft estimates of revenue and expenditure. 1969+ [Nairobi?] annual. DLC

Supersedes in part a publication with the same title (item 463) issued by the East African Railways and Harbours Administration.

L.C. has 1969.

520

______ Estimates of revenue and expenditure. 1968+ Nairobi, Printed by the Govt. Printer. annual. DLC

Supersedes in part a publication with the same title (item 469) issued by the East African Railways and Harbours Administration.

"Approved by the Board of Directors . . ."

L.C. has 1968+

520a

______ Programme of capital expenditure. Nairobi. annual. HE3419.E3E382a

Supersedes in part a publication with the same title (item 481) issued by the East African Railways and Harbours Administration.

Suspended 1973–74.

L.C. has 1970+

521

______ Tariff book. no. 5+ Nairobi. irregular. Supersedes in part and continues the numbering of Railway, marine and road motor services tariff book (item 490) issued by the East African Railways and Harbours Administration.

Cited in the following item.

522

______ ______ Amendment pages, correction slip. Nairobi, Chief Traffic Manager's Office. DLC

L.C. has no. 27, 1973.

523

East African Railways Corporation. *Salaries and Terms of Service Review Commission.* Report. [Nairobi] East African Railways Corp., 1972. 186 p. HD4966.R12E354 1972

Dunstan A. Omari, chairman.

524

Gateways of Eastern Africa. no. 1–4; June-Nov./Dec. 1971. [Mombasa, East Africa Harbours Corporation] illus. bimonthly. HE550.G37

"Staff magazine of the East African Harbours Corporation."

No more published.

L.C. has June-Nov./Dec. 1971.

525

Gibb, Roger. Report by Mr. Roger Gibb on railway rates and finance in Kenya, Uganda, and Tanganyika Territory, September 1932. London, H.M. Stationery Off., 1933. 56 p. ([Gt. Brit. Parliament. Papers by command] Cmd. 4235) HE3419.E3G5

Map on verso of last diagram.

Issued also without the parliamentary series numbering:

526

______ ______ [London, 1933] 56 p. fold. map. HE3419.E3G5 1933a

The following entry concerns the implementation of the recommendations in Gibb's Report.

527

Tanganyika. Memorandum setting out the views

and conclusions arrived at by the Railway Advisory Council of the Tanganyika Territory on certain questions raised by Mr. Roger Gibb's Report. [Dar es Salaam? 1933?] (Tanganyika. Legislative Council. Sessional paper, 1933, no. 4)

Source: Tanganyika debates, Oct. 31, 1933.

528

Gt. Brit. *Colonial Office.* Report on the railway systems of Kenya, Uganda, and Tanganyika, by Lieutenant-Colonel F. D. Hammond, Special Commissioner for Railways, Eastern Africa. London, Crown Agents for the Colonies, 1921. 2 v. HE3412 1921

Contents: pt. 1. Kenya and Uganda.—pt. 2. Tanganyika.—pt. 3. Future development.

The following entry concerns the implementation of the recommendations in Hammond's Report.

529

Kenya Colony and Protectorate. *Governor, 1925–1930 (Sir E. W. M. Grigg).* Memorandum on railway development. Nairobi, Printed at the Govt. Printer, 1926.
DLC-Micro 23940 reel 9 folio 106

Collation of the original: 16 p.

Colonial Office Library East Africa pamphlet folio 106.

Includes extensive comment on Hammond's Report and recommends the linking up of East Africa's railroads.

530

Gt. Brit. *Colonial Office.* Steamer services on lakes Victoria and Kioga; information for second officers. [London] Printed for the use of the Colonial Office [1914] (*Its* African no. 1030)
DLC-Micro 03759

Collation of the original: 3 p.

[Gt. Brit.] Public Record Office. C.O. 879/116.

531

Gt. Brit. *Crown Agents' Office.* East Africa. Agreement for the establishment of a service of steamers, viâ the Suez canal, between the United Kingdom and East Africa. London, H.M. Stationery Off., printed by Darling, 1910. 3 p. ([Gt. Brit. Parliament. Papers by command] Cd. 5428) HE905.E3A5 1910

By R. L. Antrobus and M. A. Cameron, crown agents acting for the East Africa, Uganda, and Nyasaland protectorates and Zanzibar, of the one part, and the Union Castle Mail Steamship Company, ltd., of the other part.

532

Gt. Brit. *Foreign Office.* Account showing the money issued from the consolidated fund under the provisions of the Uganda railway acts, 1896 (59 & 60 Vict. c. 38) and 1902 (2 Edw. VII. c. 40), and of the money expended and borrowed, and securities created under the said acts; together with the Report of the Comptroller and Auditor General thereon. 1896/97–1906/7. London, Printed for H.M. Stationery Off. by Eyre and Spottiswoode. annual. J301.K6

Report year ends Mar. 31.

Title varies: 1896/97–1899/1900, Account showing the money issued from the consolidated fund under the Uganda Railway Act, 1896 (59 & 60 Vict. c. 38), and of the money expended and borrowed, and securities created under the said act; together with the Report of the Comptroller and Auditor General thereon.—1900/1–1901/2, Account showing the money issued from the consolidated fund under the provisions of the Uganda railway acts, 1896 (59 & 60 Vict. c. 38) and 1900 (63 & 64 Vict. c. 11), and of the money expended and borrowed, and securities created under the said acts; together with the Report of the Comptroller and Auditor General thereon.

The accounts are issued as individually numbered reports and papers in the following volumes of the British House of Commons Sessional papers: v. 52 (1898), no. 188; v. 51 (1899), no. 108; v. 47 (1900), no. 109; v. 37 (1901), no. 153; v. 55 1902), no. 193; v. 36 (1903), no. 196; v. 49 (1904), no. 184; v. 49 (1905), no. 166; v. 65 (1906), no. 113; v. 47 (1907), no. 74; v. 62 (1908), no. 80.

L.C. has 1896/97–1906/7.

533

______ Correspondence respecting the Uganda

Railway. London, Printed for H.M. Stationary Off. by Harrison [1901?] 65 p. (*Its* Africa no. 6 (1901)) J301.K6 1901 v. 48

[Gt. Brit. Parliament. Papers by command] Cd. 670.

Includes Colonel T. Gracey's report on the Uganda Railway prior to its opening for public traffic.

534

_______ Final report of the Uganda Railway Committee. London, Printed for H.M. Stationery Off. by Harrison [1904?] 32 p. (*Its* Africa no. 11 (1904)) J301.K6 1904 v. 62

[Gt. Brit. Parliament. Papers by command] Cd. 2164.

535

_______ Memoranda relating to the Uganda Railway, 1902. London, Printed for H.M. Stationery Off. by Harrison [1902?] 11 p. (*Its* Africa no. 5 (1902)) J301.K6 1902 v. 69

[Gt. Brit. Parliament. Papers by command] Cd. 1082.

536

_______ Memoranda relating to Uganda Railway. London, Printed for H.M. Stationery Off. by Harrison [1900?] 9 p. (*Its* Africa no. 4 (1900)) J301.K6 1900 v. 56

[Gt. Brit. Parliament. Papers by command] Cd. 97.

Presents a higher estimate for railway construction.

537

_______ Memorandum relating to the Uganda Railway Bill. London, Printed for H.M. Stationery Off. by Eyre and Spottiswoode, 1896. 4 p. ([Gt. Brit. Parliament. Papers by command] C. 8049) J301.K6 1896 v. 59

At head of title: Uganda Railway.

538

_______ Papers relating to the Mombasa railway survey and Uganda. London, Printed for H.M. Stationery Off. by Harrison [1892?] 147 p. map. (*Its* Africa no. 4 (1892)) J301.K6 1892 v. 56

[Gt. Brit. Parliament. Papers by command] C. 6555.

Includes the charter granted to the Imperial British East Africa Company, Sept. 3, 1888, the Africa Order in Council, 1889, and reports by Capt. F. D. Lugard.

539

_______ Papers respecting proposed railway from Mombasa to Lake Victoria Nyanza. London, Printed for H.M. Stationery Off. by Harrison [1892?] 11 p. (*Its* Africa no. 2 (1892)) J301.K6 1892 v. 56

[Gt. Brit. Parliament. Papers by command] C. 6560.

540

_______ Report by the Mombasa-Victoria (Uganda) Railway Committee on the progress of the works, 1898–1899; with a map. London, Printed for H.M. Stationery Off. by Harrison [1899?] 18 p. fold. map. (*Its* Africa no. 6 (1899)) J301.K6 1899 v. 63

[Gt. Brit. Parliament. Papers by command] C. 9333.

541

_______ Report by the Mombasa-Victoria (Uganda) Railway Committee on the progress of the works, 1899–1900 (with a map and section). London, Printed for H.M. Stationery Off. by Harrison [1900?] 13 p. fold. map. (*Its* Africa no. 7 (1900)) J301.K6 1900 v. 56

[Gt. Brit. Parliament. Papers by command] Cd. 355.

542

_______ Report by the Mombasa-Victoria (Uganda) Railway Committee on the progress of the works, 1900–1901 (with a map). London, Printed for H.M. Stationery Off. by Harrison [1901?] 12 p. (*Its* Africa no. 8 (1901)) J301.K6 1901 v. 48

[Gt. Brit. Parliament. Papers by command] Cd. 674.

543

_______ Report by the Mombasa-Victoria

(Uganda) Railway Committee on the progress of the works, 1901–1902 (with two maps and a section). London, Printed for H.M. Stationery Off. by Harrison [1902?] 15 p. 2 fold. maps. (*Its* Africa no. 4 (1902)) J301.K6 1902 v. 69
[Gt. Brit. Parliament. Papers by command] Cd. 1080.

544
_______ Report by the Mombasa-Victoria (Uganda) Railway Committee on the progress of the works and revenue working, 1902–1903, (with two maps). London, Printed for H.M. Stationery Off. by Harrison [1903?] 22 p. 2 maps. (*Its* Africa no. 12 (1903))
J301.K6 1904 v. 62
[Gt. Brit. Parliament. Papers by command] Cd. 1770.

545
_______ Report on Mombasa-Victoria Lake railway survey. London, Printed for H.M. Stationery Off. by Eyre and Spottiswoode, 1893. 125 p. 7 fold. maps. ([Gt. Brit. Parliament. Papers by command] C. 7025)
J301.K6 1893/94 v. 62
At head of title: Mombasa, Victoria Lake Railway Survey.

546
_______ Report on the construction and working of the Mombasa to Victoria (Uganda) railway and steamboat service on Lake Victoria, 1903–1904. London, Printed for H.M. Stationery Off. by Harrison [1905?] 40 p. (*Its* Africa no. 16 (1904)) J301.K6 1905 v. 56
[Gt. Brit. Parliament. Papers by command] Cd. 2332.

547
_______ Report on the progress of the Mombasa-Victoria (Uganda) Railway, 1896–97. London, Printed for H.M. Stationery Off. by Harrison [1897?] 7 p. (*Its* Africa no. 4 (1897))
J301.K6 1897 v. 62
[Gt. Brit. Parliament. Papers by command] C. 8435.

548
_______ Report on the progress of the Mombasa-Victoria (Uganda) railway, 1897–98. London, Printed for H.M. Stationery Off. by Harrison [1898?] 5 p. fold. map. (*Its* Africa no. 8 (1898)) J301.K6 1898 v. 60
[Gt. Brit. Parliament. Papers by command] C. 8942.

549
_______ Report on the Uganda Railway by Sir Guilford Molesworth, K.C.I.E., dated March 28, 1899. London, Printed for H.M. Stationery Off. by Harrison [1899?] 36 p. maps. (*Its* Africa no. 5 (1899)) J301.K6 1899 v. 63
[Gt. Brit. Parliament. Papers by command] C.9331.

550
_______ Report on the working of the Uganda Railway and the steamboat service on Lake Victoria, 1904–1905. London, Printed for H.M. Stationery Off. by Darling, 1905. 40 p. ([Gt. Brit. Parliament. Papers by command] Cd. 2716) J301.K6 1906 v. 80
At head of title: British East Africa Protectorate.

551
_______ Return giving dates of purchase and prices paid for rails, sleepers, girders, locomotives, carriages, and bridge work obtained for the construction of the Uganda Railway. London, Printed for H.M. Stationery Off. by Harrison [1903?] 2 p. (*Its* Africa no. 5 (1903))
J301.K6 1903 v. 45
[Gt. Brit. Parliament. Papers by command] Cd. 1625.

552
_______ Return of the names of the British and American firms who tendered for the supply of certain bridges for the Uganda Railway, and the amounts of the various tenders. London, Printed for H.M. Stationery Off. by Harrison [1901?] 3 p. (*Its* Africa no. 1 (1901))
J301.K6 1901 v. 48
[Gt. Brit. Parliament. Papers by command] Cd. 434.

553
_______ Return showing (1) The capital ex-

penditure of the Uganda Railway, (2) The charge involved upon the exchequer by the capital expenditure, (3) The gross and net earnings of the line for each year since it was opened. London, Printed for H.M. Stationery Off. by Darling, 1908. 3 p. ([Gt. Brit. Parliament. Papers by command] Cd. 4354)
J301.K6 1908 v. 73

At head of title: Uganda Railway.

554
Gt. Brit. *Treaties, etc., 1952– (Elizabeth II).* Exchange of letters constituting an agreement between the Government of the United Kingdom of Great Britain and Northern Ireland and the Government of the United States of America on the subject of a loan for the development of certain port facilities in Kenya and Tanganyika. London, June 26, 1953. London, H.M. Stationery Off., 1953. 9 p. ([Gt. Brit. Foreign Office] Treaty series, 1953, no. 70) JX636 1892 1953 no. 70

[Gt. Brit. Parliament. Papers by command] Cmd. 8965.

The loan was for new port construction at Mombasa, Kenya, and at Tanga, Tanganyika.

555
Gt. Brit. *War Office. General Staff. Geographical Section.* Mombasa-Victoria (Uganda) Railway and Busoga Railway. Southampton, Printed at the Ordnance Survey Office, 1913. (*Its* G.S.G.S. no. 2687) map. DLC-G&M

Scale 1:1,500,000.

"Compiled ... from Provisional map of East Africa Protectorate, 1:1,500,000, G.S.G.S. no. 2542, and various maps of Uganda."

556
Gt. Brit. *War Office. Intelligence Division.* Map shewing the Mombasa-Victoria (Uganda) Railway. Revised. London, Stanford, 1903. (*Its* I.D.W.O. no. 1413) DLC-G&M

Scale 1:1,584,000.

557
Hill, Mervyn F. Permanent way. Nairobi, East African Railways and Harbours [1949–60?] 2 v. illus., fold. col. maps, plates, ports.
HE3420.K45H5

Contents: [v. 1] The story of the Kenya and Uganda Railway, being the official history of the development of the transport system in Kenya and Uganda.—v. 2. The story of the Tanganyika Railways.

558
——— ——— [2d ed.] Nairobi, East African Railways and Harbours [1961+] illus., fold. col. maps, plates, ports. HE3420.K45H52

Contents: [v. 1] The story of the Kenya and Uganda Railway, being the official history of development of the transport system in Kenya and Uganda.

559
Industrial relations machinery, *1962*. [Nairobi, Printed by the Govt. Printer, 1962] 25 p.
DLC-LL

At the head of title: East African Railways and Harbours.

Includes the Constitution of the Central Joint Council, composed of representatives of management and trade unions, with a "Memorandum of agreement made between the General Manager of the East African Railways and Harbours [and others]" and model constitutions.

560
Kenya. Government guarantee for a loan by the IBRD (World Bank) to the East African Harbours Corporation. [Nairobi, 1972?] 2p. (Kenya. [National Assembly] Sessional paper no. 5 of 1972)

Information received from L.C. Office, Nairobi, Kenya; (publication not held by DLC).

561
Kenya. *Ministry of Power and Communications.* Government guarantee for a loan to the East African Harbours Corporation by the International Bank for Reconstruction and Development. The Loans (Guarantee) Act 1966. [Nairobi, 1969] 3 p. (Kenya. [National Assembly] Sessional paper no. 2 of 1969)

Information received from L.C. Office, Nairobi, Kenya; (publication not held by DLC).

562
_______ Government guarantee in respect of an I.B.R.D. loan to the East African Railways Corporation. Nairobi, Printed by the Govt. Printer, 1970. 5 p. (Kenya. [National Assembly] Sessional paper no. 1 of 1970) DLC

563
_______ Kenya Government guarantee for loan to the East African Community for the purpose of the East African Railways Corporation by the Government of the United Kingdom and Northern Ireland and for a loan by the Government of the Federal Republic of West Germany to the East African Railways Corporation and of commercial credits by Associated Electrical Industries Ltd. and Andrew Barclays Ltd. to the East African Railways Corporation. [Nairobi, 1970] 3 p. (Kenya. [National Assembly] Sessional paper no. 9 of 1970)

Information received from L.C. Office, Nairobi, Kenya; (publication not held by DLC).

564
Kenya and Uganda Railways and Harbours. Advisory Council minutes and memoranda, harbours. -1947. [Nairobi Govt. Press]

Superseded by Advisory Council minutes, harbours (item 472) issued by the East African Railways and Harbours Administration.

Source for 1934: Kenya Govt. Press rept., 1934; source for 1945–47: Kenya Govt. Print. rept., 1945–47.

565
_______ Advisory Council minutes and memoranda, railways. -1947. [Nairobi, Govt. Printer]

Superseded by Advisory Council minutes, railways (item 489) issued by the East African Railways and Harbours Administration.

Source for 1934: Kenya Govt. Press rept., 1934; source for 1945–47: Kenya Govt. Print. rept., 1945–47.

566
_______ Draft estimates and memoranda. 1926?–1948? [Nairobi, Govt. Printer] annual.

Supersedes the Draft estimates (item 615) issued by the Uganda Railway.

Superseded by the Draft estimates of revenue and expenditure (item 463) issued by the East African Railways and Harbours Administration.

Source for 1948: Kenya Govt. Print. rept., 1947.

567
_______ Estimates of the revenue and expenditure. 1926?–1948. Nairobi, Printed by the Govt. Printer. annual. HE3420.E3A34

Supersedes the Estimates of revenue and expenditure (item 616) issued by the Uganda Railway.

Superseded by the Estimates of revenue and expenditure (item 469) issued by the East African Railways and Harbours Administration.

Supplements accompany some issues.

Bound with the Estimates of revenue and expenditure (item 469) issued by the East African Railways and Harbours Administration.

L.C. has 1945–48.

568
_______ General Manager's bulletin. no. 1–25; Feb. 1931–Dec. 1939. Nairobi, Printed by the Govt. Printer. quarterly. HE3419.K4A35

Includes information on finances, traffic, tonnage, rates, and responses to government reports on transportation.

L.C. catalogs under: Kenya Colony and Protectorate. Kenya and Uganda railways and harbours. General manager's bulletin.

L.C. has Feb. 1931–Dec. 1939.

569
_______ General rule book. [Nairobi, Govt. Printer, 1946?] 112 p.

Source: Kenya Govt. Print. rept., 1946.

570
_______ Goods' agent instructions. [Nairobi, Govt. Printer, 194–?]

Cited in following item.

571
_______ _______ Amendments. [Nairobi, Govt.

Printer, 1947] 12 p.
Source: Kenya Govt. Print. rept., 1947.

572
——— Gratuity regulations, 1945. [Nairobi, Govt. Printer, 1945? 12 p.
Source: Kenya Govt. Print. rept., 1945.

573
——— Harbours dues tariff list, 1934. [Nairobi, Govt. Printer, 1934] 54 p.
Source: Kenya Govt. Press rept., 1934.

574
——— The harbours regulations, 1945. Nairobi [Govt. Printer] 1945. 57 p. DS

575
——— List of works in progress and proposed new works. [Estimates of expenditure for 1948] [Nairobi, 1947] 22 p.
Source: BM Cat., 1965.

576
——— Memoranda submitted to the Railway Advisory Council, 30th October, 1945. Nairobi, Printed by the Govt. Printer, 1945.
DLC-Micro 23940 reel 13 folio 374
Collation of the original 51 p.
Colonial Office Library East Africa pamphlet folio 347.
Includes 152–211, which deal with all facets of the railway.

577
——— Memoranda submitted to the Railway Advisory Council, 27th June, 1946. Nairobi, Printed by the Govt. Printer, 1946.
DLC-Micro 23940 reel 7 octavo 351
Collation of the original: 54 p.
Colonial Office Library East Africa pamphlet octavo 351.
The Memoranda concern the construction of railway road services to the Lumbwa-Kericho-Sotik area of Kenya.

578
——— Memorandum on the proposal to realign and regrade the main line between Gilgil and Nakuru. Nairobi, Printed by the Govt. Printer [1940?]
DLC-Micro 23940 reel 6 octavo 286
Collation of the original: 29 p. fold. map.
Colonial Office Library East Africa pamphlet octavo 286.

579
——— Military traffic instructions. [Nairobi, Govt. Printer, 194–?]
Cited in the following item.

580
——— ——— Amendments. [Nairobi, Govt. Printer, 194–?+] irregular.
Source for 1947: Kenya Govt. Print. rept., 1947.

581
——— Port of Mombasa (Kilindini harbour-Mombasa old port). Nairobi, 1947. 47 p. map. DS
A later edition entitled Port of Mombasa (Kilindini harbour-Mombasa old port): port booklet (item 480) was issued in 1950 by the East African Railways and Harbours Administration.

582
——— Provident fund regulations, 1945. [Nairobi, Govt. Printer, 1945?] 12 p.
Source: Kenya Govt. Print. rept., 1945

583
——— Railway Council minutes, 1931–33. [Nairobi, Govt. Printer] 1934.
Source: Kenya Govt. Press rept., 1934.

584
——— Railway tariff book. [Nairobi, Govt. Printer]
Source for 1934: Kenya Govt. Press rept., 1934.

585
——— Report of the General Manager on the administration of the railways and harbours.

1925–47. Nairobi, Printed by the Govt. Printer. annual. HE3419.K4A3

Supersedes Report of the General Manager on the administration of the railway and marine services (item 620) issued by the Uganda Railway.

Title varies: 1925–26, Report of the acting General Manager on the administration of the railway and marine services.

Vols. for 1925-26 issued by the agency under a variant name: Kenya and Uganda Railway.

Vols. for 1930–38 issued in two parts.

Superseded by Reports of the Commissioner for Transport, East Africa High Commission, and of the General Manager on the administration of the East African Railways and Harbours (item 440) issued by the Commissioner for Transport of the East Africa High Commission.

L.C. has 1925–47 (1930, pt. 2, and 1934, pt. 2 wanting).

586

_______ Revised dress regulations for officers of the marine services of the Kenya and Uganda Railways and Harbours. [Nairobi?] 1935. (General Manager's circular no. 1 of 1935)

DLC-Micro 23940 reel 3 octavo 199

Collation of the original: 3 p.

Colonial Office Library East Africa pamphlet octavo 199.

587

_______ A short account of the early history, development and plans for the future of the Kenya and Uganda Railways and Harbours. Nairobi, Printed by the Govt. Printer, 1948.

DLC-Micro 23940 reel 8 octavo 397

Collation of the original: 11 p. illus., map.

Colonial Office Library East Africa pamphlet octavo 297.

588

_______ Staff regulations. Nairobi, Govt. Printer.

Source for 1934–45: Col. Off. Lib. Cat.

589

_______ Summary of the main provisions of the Kenya and Uganda Railways and Harbours superannuation fund rules, 1939. Nairobi, 1939.

DLC-Micro 23940 reel 12 folio 333

Collation of the original: 14 p.

Colonial Office Library East Africa pamphlet folio 333.

590

_______ Superannuation fund rules. Nairobi, Printed by the Govt. Printer, 1939.

DLC-Micro 23940 reel 7 octavo 343

Collation of the original: 52 p.

Includes Amendments.

Colonial Office Library East Africa pamphlet octavo 343.

591

_______ Tariff of harbour dues and charges. Nairobi. irregular. DS

DS has no. 5, Aug. 1, 1945.

592

_______ Time table. [Nairobi, Govt. Printer]

Source for no. 5, 1946: Kenya Govt. Print. rept., 1946.

593

_______ Weekly notices to staff. [Nairobi, Govt. Printer]

Source for 1947: Kenya Govt. Print. rept., 1947.

594

_______ Working time table. [Nairobi, Govt. Printer]

Source for no. 12, 1945: Kenya Govt. Print. rept., 1945.

595

Kenya and Uganda Railways and Harbours. [*First*] *Departmental Committee on the Amount of Contributions to Renewals Funds Necessary to Allow for Depreciation of Wasting Assets.* Report. Nairobi, Printed by the Govt. Printer, 1930.

DLC-Micro 23940 reel 10 folio 203

Collation of the original: 59 p.

H. E. Goodship, chairman.
Colonial Office Library East Africa pamphlet folio 203.

596
Kenya and Uganda Railways and Harbours. *Second Departmental Committee on the Amount of Contribution to Renewals Funds Necessary to Allow for Renewing Wasting Assets.* Report. Nairobi, Printed by the Govt. Printer, 1935.
DLC-Micro 23940 reel 10 folio 204
Collation of the original: 62 p.
A. E. Hamp, chairman.
Colonial Office Library East Africa pamphlet folio 204.

597
Kenya Colony and Protectorate. *Audit Dept.* Kenya and Uganda Railways and Harbours. Report on the audit of accounts. 1926?–1947? Nairobi, Printed by the Govt. Printer. annual.
HE3420.K46A32
Superseded by the agency's Report by the Director of Audit, Kenya, on the acounts of the East African Railways and Harbours.
L.C. has 1929, and 1932; NN has 1931–32; source for 1931+: Royal Comm. Soc. Cat.

598
——— Report by the Director of Audit, Kenya, on the accounts of the East African Railways and Harbours. 1948?–1950. Nairobi, Printed by the Govt. Printer. annual.
HE3420.K46A32
Supersedes the agency's Kenya and Uganda Railways and Harbours. Report on the audit of accounts.
Superseded by the Report by the Auditor-General, East Africa High Commission services on the accounts of the East African Railways and Harbours Administration (item 435) issued by the Audit Dept. of the East Africa High Commission.
L.C. has 1950.

599
Kenya Colony and Protectorate. *Legislative Council.* Amalgamation of the Kenya and Uganda Railways and Harbours and Tanganyika Railways and Ports Services. Nairobi, Printed by the Govt. Printer, 1948. 10 p. (Kenya [Colony and Protectorate] Legislative Council. Sessional paper no. 1 [of] 1948)
J731.H62 1948 no. 1

600
O'Callaghan, F. L. Uganda Railway. Chatham [Eng.] Royal Engineers Institute, 1900. 20 p. fold. map, 9 fold. plates. ([Gt. Brit. Army] Corps of Royal Engineers. Professional papers, v. 26, paper 8) TA7.G72 1900 v. 26
L.C. also has on microfilm (23940, reel 1, octavo 7).

601
Ongalo, M. E. East African Railways Corporation. [Nairobi?] 1967. map 93 x 72 cm.
G8401.P3E2 1967.06
Scale 1:2,000,000.
Blue line print.

602
Overseas Consultants, *inc., New York.* Report on central African rail link development survey, by Overseas Consultants, inc. [and] Sir Alexander Gibb & Partners. [New York] 1952. 2 v. illus., 14 maps (3 fold. in pocket)
HE3417.09 1952
At head of title: United Kingdom Government, Colonial Office.
Survey of proposed railway routes through central and southwestern Tanganyika, and Northern Rhodesia. Includes information on the economies and transportation systems of Northern Rhodesia, Nyasaland, and Tanganyika.

603
——— Report on preliminary reconnaissance for a survey of a link betwen the East African and Rhodesian railway systems, November 1949, by Overseas Consultants, inc. [and] Sir Alexander Gibb & Partners. [New York, 1949] 22 leaves. 4HE 1253

604
Permanent way *(Motion picture).* California

Texas Oil Corp., 1963. Made by East African Railways and Harbours Administration.

29 min. sd. color. 16 mm. (Caltex international public relations series)

Credits: Director, Hal Morey; photographers, Roger Eastell, Hal Morey, Robin Ridgway.

Summary: Describes the building of a railroad which initiated growth and development in East Africa.

Also issued in 35 mm.

Available for loan from Association-Sterling Film, Inc., 600 Grand Ave., Ridgefield, N.J., 07657.

605

Pringle, Patrick. The story of a railway. Adapted from Permanent way: the story of the Kenya and Uganda railway, by M. F. Hill. London, Evans [1960] 69 p. illus., maps. MiEM

"The East African Literature Bureau originally planned this book."

606

SPEAR. v. 1+ June 1952+ [Nairobi] East African Railways Corporation and East African Harbours Corporation. illus. HE3411.S15

Quarterly, 1952–54; bimonthly, 1955–Apr. 1966; irregular, v. 7, no. 9+

Vols. for June 1952–1969 issued by the East African Railways and Harbours Administration; for 1969–70 (v. 8, no. 9–10) issued by the East African Railways Corporation.

Title varies: June 1952–Mar. 1953, Staff magazine.—June 1953–Mar. 1954, EAR&H magazine.—June 1954–Dec. 1964, Magazine.

"Journal of the East African Railways and Harbours corporations."

L.C. has June 1952+

607

Sikio. no. 1+ Feb. 1960+ [Nairobi, East African Railways Corporation] illus. biweekly. DLC

Title translated: Listen.

Vols. for Feb. 1960–June 1969 issued by the East African Railways and Harbours Administration.

The staff newspaper of the East African Railways Corporation.

Text in English or Swahili.

L.C. has December 10, 1963+ (scattered issues wanting).

608

Tanganyika. Amalgamation of the Tanyanyika Railways and Ports Services and the Kenya and Uganda Railways and Harbours. [Dar es Salaam? 1948?] 11 p. (Tanganyika. Legislative Council. Sessional paper, 1948, no. 1) MBU

609

______ Financial guarantees in respect of the operations of the port of Mtwara and the railway system Mtwara-Lumesule Juu as they affect the Overseas Food Corporation, the Tanganyika Government and the East African Railways and Harbours Administration. [Dar es Salaam? 1951?] (Tanganyika. Legislative Council. Sessional paper, 1951, no. 1)

Source: Tanganyika debates, Feb. 7, 1951.

610

Uganda. Amalgamation of the Kenya and Uganda Railways and Harbours and the Tanganyika Railways and Ports Services. Entebbe, Printed by the Govt. Printer, 1948. 11 p. (Uganda. Legislative Council. Sessional paper no. 1 of 1948) J732.H6 no. 1 of 1948

611

______ East African Railways and Harbours' case for the shortening of the main line between Tororo and Kampala. Entebbe, Printed by the Govt. Printer [1960] 2 p. (Uganda. [Legislative Council] Sessional paper no. 8 of 1958/59) MBU

612

______ Report on the working of the Western Uganda Extension. [Entebbe] annual?

Source for 1959: Uganda debates, Sept. 22, 1960.

613

Uganda. *Economic Committee Appointed to Consider and Report upon the Most Productive Route to be Followed by the Proposed*

Extension of the Uganda Railway into the Protectorate. Report. Entebbe, Printed by the Govt. Printer, 1923.

DLC-Micro 23940 reel 9 folio 95

Collation of the original: 10 p. fold. map.

G. N. Loggin, chairman.

Map of "Proposed railway extensions: Eastern Province" scale 1:500,000.

Colonial Office Library East Africa pamphlet folio 95.

Uganda Railway

Note: In 1896 the Parliament of Great Britain approved the construction of a railroad from the port of Mombassa across the East Africa Protectorate to Lake Victoria. The construction of the railroad reached Lake Victoria at Kisumu, then called Port Florence, in January 1902. A fleet of steamers connected ports in Uganda, notably Entebbe, Kampala, and Jinja, with Kisumu. Before World War I, railroad lines were constructed in both the East Africa Protectorate and Uganda. In 1924 a railroad was built from Nakuru, Kenya Colony and Protectorate (formerly the East Africa Protectorate), on the main line from Mombasa to Kisumu, across Kenya and into Uganda.

On February 3, 1926, the Kenya and Uganda (Transport) Order in council was issued, and the name of the railroad was changed to the Kenya and Uganda Railways and Harbours. From that date, the control of the railroad, harbor, and steamship services was vested in the high commissioner for transport, who was the governor of Kenya Colony and Protectorate.

614

[Correspondence recommending Jeeranjee and Co., Karachi, Coolie Contractors] Mombasa, 1892–1903.

DLC-Micro 23940 reel 10 folio 214

Collation of the original: [3] leaves.

Colonial Office Library East Africa pamphlet folio 214.

615

_______ Draft estimates. [Nairobi?] annual.

Source for 1926: Uganda debates, Oct. 22, 1925.

616

_______ Estimates of revenue and expenditure. [Nairobi?] annual?

Source for 1924: Uganda debates, Nov. 16, 1923.

617

_______ From Mombasa to Lake Victoria Nyanza by steamer round the great lake. Nairobi, 1916. 36 p.

1911 ed.: The Uganda Railway, British East Africa, from Mombasa to Lake Victoria Nyanza, and by steamer round the great lake (item 623).

Source: Royal Empire Soc. Cat.

618

_______ Official tariff book, no. 11, 1st January, 1924. Nairobi, 1925. 202 p. MH-BA

619

_______ Rail and steamer time tables, in force on and from 1st July 1924. Nairobi, 1924. 54 p.

Source: Royal Empire Soc. Cat.

620

_______ Report of the General Manager on the administration of the railway and marine services. 1905/6?–1924. Nairobi. annual.

HE3420.U6A3

Report year for 1905/6?–1920/21 ends Mar. 31; for 1921–24 ends Dec. 31.

Report for 1921 covers period Apr.-Dec.

At head of title: –1919/20, East Africa Protectorate; 1920/21–1921, The Colony and Protectorate of Kenya.

Suspended 1907–1909?

Title varies: –1914/15, Administration report, railway. Report of the General Manager—1915/16, Administration report, railways. Report of the . . . General Manager.—1916/17–1919/20, Administration report, railways, East Africa and Uganda. Report of the General Manager, Uganda Railway (varies slightly).

Superseded by Report of the acting General Manager on the administration of the railway and marine services (item 585) issued by the Kenya and Uganda Railways and Harbours.

L.C. catalogs 1912/13–1919/20 under: East Africa Protectorate. Administration report, railways. East Africa and Uganda . . . with the call no.: HE3419.E3A3; L.C. catalogs 1920/21–1921 under: Kenya Colony and Protectorate. Kenya and Uganda railways and harbours. Report . . . on the administration of the railways and harbours, with the call no.: HE3419.K4A3.

L.C. has 1912/13–1924; source for 1905/6, 1912/13–1916/17: BM Cat. 1965; source for 1910/11–1924: Royal Comm. Soc. Cat.

621

——— Station and port distance table. Nairobi, 1924. 138 p.

Source: Royal Empire Soc. Cat.

622

——— Uganda Railway and East Africa lakes. Nairobi, 1916. 23 p.

Source: Royal Empire Soc. Cat.

623

——— The Uganda Railway, British Africa, from Mombasa to Lake Victoria Nyanza, and by steamer round the great lake. [London, Waterlow, 1911?] 30 p. illus., map.

HE3420.U6 1911

1916 ed.: From Mombasa to Lake Victoria Nyanza by steamer round the great lake (item 617).

624

United Nations. *Development Programme.* East African Railways and Harbours training and development project: plan of operation. [Arusha? East African Community] 1969. 39 leaves. DLC

625

Whitson, H. A. A report on industrial relations in the East African Railways and Harbours. Nairobi, 1960. [12] p. MBU

A supplement to Sikio (item 607).

626

——— Report on the state of industrial relations in the East African Railways and Harbours Administration. [Nairobi? 1960] 42 p.

HD6869.R1W45

Submitted to the Governor of Kenya as chairman of the East African High Commission.

The following entry concerns the implementation of the recommendations in Whitson's Report.

627

East African Railways and Harbours Administration. Proposals for the implementation of the recommendations of the Report on the state of industrial relations in the East African Railways and Harbours Administration. [Nairobi] Govt. Printer, 1961. 11 p. ([East Africa High Commission. East Africa Central Legislative Assembly] Sessional paper no. 6 of 1961)

Source: Col. Off. Lib. Cat.

Roads

628

Bonney, R. S. P., *and* N. F. Stevens. Vehicle operating costs on bituminous, gravel and earth roads in East and Central Africa; research into the ratio of vehicle operating costs on different types of road surfacing. London, H.M. Stationery Off., 1967. 42 p. illus., map. (Road research technical paper no. 76)

TE7.H33 no. 76

Includes information for Kenya and Uganda.

629

East African Community. Report on exploratory mission in the field of motor vehicle assembly for East Africa, by J. H. Stephens. [Nairobi] 1969. 39 p.

Source: UNECA, New acq. May/June 1970.

630

East African Railways and Harbours Adminis-

tration. Tanganyika and Uganda coach services. [Nairobi? 1956?] 2 maps. DLC-G&M
Scale 1:3,131,893.
Pictorial maps.
General information and time table on verso.
Shows places of interest and road service stations.

631
East African Railways and Harbours Administration. *Tanzania Road Services.* Annual report. [Dar es Salaam?]
Source: Hofmeier.

632
——— Monthly report. [Dar es Salaam?]
Source: Hofmeier.

633
O'Reilly, M. P., K. Russam, *and* F. H. P. Williams. Pavement design in the tropics: investigation of subgrade conditions under roads in East Africa. London, H.M. Stationery Off., 1968. 123 [1] p. illus. (Road research technical paper no. 80) TE7.H33 no. 80

634
Pollitt, H. W. W. Colonial road problems; impressions from visits to East Africa and Northern Rhodesia, and Nyasaland. London, H.M. Stationery Off., 1954. 77 p. illus., maps. (Colonial research publications, no. 17)
JV33.G7A52 no. 17
Includes information on road construction for Kenya, Tanganyika, Uganda, and Zanzibar.

635
Tanganyika. *Committee of Inquiry into the East African Railways Road Services in Tanganyika.* Report. Dar es Salaam, Govt. Printer, 1954. 74 p. illus. IEN
M. A. Carson, chairman.

Description and Travel

636
Brown, Alice. East Africa in pictures. [Nairobi?] Printed and published by the English Press in collaboration with the East Africa Tourist Travel Association [1964?] [56] p. (chiefly illus.) WvU

637
East Africa: gateway to safari. Edited by Mervyn Cowie. [Nairobi, Ministry of Tourism and Wildlife, 1970] [32] p. (chiefly col. illus.)
QH46.E28
Forward [sic] by Jan Mohamed, Assistant Minister for Tourism & Wildlife, Republic of Kenya.

638
East Africa Tourist Travel Association. Dar es Salaam guide. [Nairobi? 1953?] 76 p. illus.
Cited in the agency's Annual report, 1953.

639
——— East Africa in a nutshell; a travel digest of Kenya, Tanganyika, Uganda, and Zanzibar. [Nairobi, 1960] 24 p. illus. DLC

640
——— East Africa, land of sunshine. Compiled and drawn by D. O. Mathews for the East Africa Tourist Travel Association. Glasgow, 1949. map. DLC-G&M
Scale 1:3,300,000.
Pictorial map.

641
——— ——— Compiled and drawn by D. O. Mathews for the East Africa Tourist Travel Association. [Glasgow?] 1954. map. DLC-G&M
Scale 1:5,700,000.
Pictorial map.

642
_______ _______ Glasgow, 1962. map. DLC-G&M

Scale 1:2,925,000.
Pictorial map.
Text and illus. on verso.

643
_______ East Africa travel agents' counter book: Kenya, Tanganyika, Uganda, Zanzibar. [2d ed.] [Nairobi, 195–?] 1 v. (loose-leaf) DLC
See also item 663.

644
_______ Exploring East Africa. [Nairobi, 1954] 32 p. illus. NN
Caption title: East Africa, Kenya-Uganda-Tanganyika-Zanzibar.

645
_______ _______ [Nairobi] 1958. 24 p. illus., map.
Source: Col. Off. Lib. Cat.

646
_______ _______ [Nairobi, 1959] 24 p. illus., map. DLC

647
_______ A guide to Dar es Salaam. [Dar es Salaam, 1958?] 55 p. illus. CSt-H

648
_______ _______ [Dar es Salaam, Tanganyika Standard, 1962?] 64 p. illus. WvU

649
_______ Guide to hotels, safari lodges and restaurants of East Africa. 6th ed. Nairobi [1959 or 1960]
Cited in the agency's Annual report, 1959/60.

650
_______ _______ 8th ed. [Nairobi? 1963]
Cited in the agency's Annual report, 1963.

651
_______ A guide to Mombasa and the coast. [Nairobi, 1953] 64 p. illus., maps. InU

652
_______ The hotels, safari lodges, and restaurants of East Africa. Nairobi [1953?] 1 v. (unpaged) illus. TX910.E2E23 1953

653
_______ _______ Nairobi, 1959.
Source: Mascarenhas.

654
_______ _______ [Nairobi, 1964?] 699 p. illus., map.
Source: Col. Off. Lib. Cat.

655
_______ Information bulletin. Overseas edition. Nairobi, Kenya Colony.
L.C. received no. 3, 6, and 10; July 1950, Aug. 1951, and June 1952; apparently not retained.

656
_______ Kenya. Photos by K.I.O. [and others] 3 ed. rev. Nairobi, 1952. 1 v. (unpaged) DLC

657
_______ Mombasa. [Nairobi, 1957?] 68 p. illus., maps. DT434.M7E2 1957
Cover title: A guide to Mombasa and the coast.

658
_______ Mombasa [a guide to Mombasa and the coast] Rev. ed. [Nairobi?] 1960.
Source: Col. Off. Lib. Cat.

659
_______ Nairobi; a visitor's guide. [Nairobi, 1953] 63 p. illus., maps (part fold.) NN

660
_______ National parks, Uganda, Belgian Congo. Nairobi [195–?] 9 p. illus.

Source: Col. Off. Lib. Cat.

661
——— Stronghold of the wild. Nairobi [1959?] [32] p. illus., col. map. DLC
A German ed. was issued in 1963.
National parks and game reserves in Kenya, Tanganyika, and Uganda.

662
——— ——— [Nairobi, 1965] 31 p. illus. QL337.E25E27 1960z

663
——— Travel agents counter book: East Africa . . . [Nairobi]
Source for 1951–55: Col. Off. Lib. Cat.
See also item 643.

664
——— Uganda/Belgian Congo booklet. [Nairobi? 1957?]
Text in English and French.
Cited in the agency's Annual report, 1957.

665
——— Visit East Africa. [Nairobi, 1955?]
Cited in the Annual report of the East Africa High Commission, 1955, issued by the Colonial Office of Gt. Brit.

666
East African Airways Corporation. Guide to the East African territories of Kenya, Tanganyika, Uganda, & Zanzibar. Edited by L. S. Levin. Salisbury, A. J. Levin [1959?] 356 p. illus. ICU

667
Eastern African Dependencies Trade and Information Office. Kenya. Rev. ed. London, 1929. 116 p. DS

668
——— ——— London, 1931. 119 p. illus., map.
Source: Royal Comm. Soc. Cat.

669
——— ——— Rev. ed. London, H.M. Eastern African Dependencies Trade and Information Office [1935] 120 p. illus., fold. col. map. DT434.E2E25 1935
Cover title: Kenya; Britain's most attractive colony.

670
——— ——— Rev. ed. London, H.M. Eastern African Trade and Information Office [1938] 120 p. illus., fold. col. map. DT434.E2E25 1938
Cover title: Kenya; Britain's most attractive colony.
Map wanting in L.C. copy.

671
——— Uganda. London [1935] 106 p. illus., fold. col. map. NN

672
——— ——— London, H.M. Eastern African Trade and Information Office [1938] 112 p. illus., fold. col. map. DT434.U2E3
Cover, and running title: Uganda, the pearl of Africa.
Map wanting in L.C. copy.

673
East African Railways and Harbours Administration. Inland marine services. [Nairobi, Govt. Printer, 195–?] folder [2] p. col. maps. DLC
Tourist broshure on East Africa's inland lakes.

674
Gt. Brit. *Foreign Office*. Despatches addressed by Dr. Livingstone, Her Majesty's consul, inner Africa, to Her Majesty's Secretary for Foreign Affairs, in 1870, 1871, and 1872. London, Printed by Harrison, 1872. 24 p. ([Gt. Brit. Parliament. Papers by command] C. 598) J301.K6 1872 v. 70
Includes information on Ujiji and Zanzibar.

675
Hawkins (D.A.) ltd., *Nairobi*. 16 safari maps of

East Africa's national parks & game reserves. Compiled with the assistance of the Kenya National Parks, Uganda National Parks, and Tanganyika National Parks, and the Kenya Game Dept., and with the co-operation of the Automobile Association of East Africa and the E.A. Tourist Travel Association. Nairobi [1964?] 15, [1] p. (chiefly col. maps) 31 x 49 cm. fold. to 31 x 12 cm. G2501.D5H3 1964

Title from p. [16] (outside when folded).

676
Information for sportsmen and travellers in East Africa. London, Crown Agents for the Colonies [1922?]
DLC-Micro 23940 reel 3 octavo 171

Collation of the original: 48 p.

Colonial Office Library East Africa pamphlet octavo 171.

677
Kampala. [Nairobi?] East Africa Tourist Travel Association in collaboration with Uganda Dept. of Information for Kampala Municipal Council [1953?] 6 p.

Cited in the Annual report, 1953, issued by the East Africa Tourist Travel Association.

678
Kenya, your queries answered. 4th ed. rev. [Nairobi?] East Africa Tourist Travel Association for the Kenya Government [1953?] 52 p. illus., map.

Cited in the Annual report, 1953, issued by the East Africa Tourist Travel Association.

679
Kenya and Uganda Railways and Harbours. Kenya Colony and Uganda Protectorate, via the Kenya and Uganda Railway. [London, H.M. Eastern African Dependencies' Trade and Information Office, 1935?] 20 p. illus., fold. map. DBRE

680
_______ Travel guide to Kenya and Uganda. [London, 1929?] 182 p. illus., fold. map. DS

Cover title: Travel in Kenya and Uganda.

681
_______ _______ Nairobi, 1930. 182 p. illus.

Source: Royal Comm. Soc. Cat.

682
_______ _______ [Nairobi, East African Standard, 1930] 264 p. illus., maps. NNC

683
_______ _______ Nairobi, 1931. 196 p. illus., fold. col. map. IU

Cover title: Travel in Kenya and Uganda.

At head of title: No. 3–1931.

684
_______ _______ Nairobi [1932] 203 p. illus., maps (part fold.) IU

At head of title: No. 4, 1932.

685
_______ _______ [Nairobi? 1934] 218 p. illus., fold map. HE3411.K42A22

At head of title: No. 5–1934.

Cover title: The traveller's guide.

686
_______ _______ [Nairobi, 1950] 264 p. illus., fold. map. CSt-H

687
_______ Travel information for ocean steamship passengers landing at Mombasa. [Nairobi, Printed by the Govt. Printer] 1931. 32 p. NBuG

At head of title: Kenya and Uganda.

688
_______ The travellers' guide to Kenya and Uganda. Nairobi, 1936. 231 p. illus., fold. col. map. DT434.E2K38

689
_______ _______ Nairobi, Kenya Colony [1937] 231 p. illus., maps (1 fold.) CSt-H

At head of title: No. 7–1937.

690
——— ——— [Nairobi? 1939] 246 p. illus., fold. map. OOxM

691
Ngorongoro and the Serengeti plains. [Nairobi?] East Africa Tourist Travel Association for National Parks of Tanganyika, 1954. 8 p. illus., map.
Cited in the Annual report, 1954, issued by the East Africa Tourist Travel Association.

692
Queen Elizabeth National Park. [Nairobi?] East Africa Tourist Travel Association for Uganda National Parks [1953?] 4 p. illus.
Cited in the Annual report, 1953, issued by the East Africa Tourist Travel Association.

693
Safari. no. 1–25? Nairobi, East Africa Tourist Travel Association, 1952–64? irregular
Source: SCOLMA, Mar 1969.

694
Uganda Railway. Information re. British East Africa and Uganda. Nairobi, 1916. 38 p. illus., maps.
Source: Royal Empire Soc. Cat.

695
——— On "Safari" in the British East African highlands. Nairobi, 1916. 16 p.
Source: Royal Empire Soc. Cat.

Economics

696
Conference of Directors of Social and Economic Research Institutes in Africa, *Nairobi, 1971.* Economic independence in Africa, edited by Dharam Ghai. Nairobi, East African Literature Bureau [1973] xxii, 235 p. DLC

697
Conference of East African Directors of Public Works, *10th, Entebbe, 1957.* Minutes of the tenth conference of the East African Directors of Public Works, held at Entebbe, Uganda, on 28th October to 2nd November, 1957. [n.p., 1957?] 31 leaves.
Source: Col. Off. Lib. Cat.

698
Conference of East African Directors of Public Works, *12th, Nairobi, 1959.* Minutes of the twelvth conference of the East African Directors of Public Works, held at Nairobi, Kenya. [Nairobi? 1959?]
Source: Col. Off. Lib. Cat.

699
Commonwealth Economic Committee. Commonwealth development and its financing. London, H.M. Stationery Off., 1961+ maps (part fold.), plates. HC259.C67
Name of agents in America stamped on t.p., v. 1–3: British Information Services, New York.
The following individual titles concern East Africa:
9. Uganda. 1966. [66] p.
Includes a survey of the economy of Uganda for 1957–64, with information on investment funds, transport, fuel and power, and production.
11. Kenya. 1967. 98 p.

East Africa High Commission. *East African Production and Supply Council.*
Note: In 1942 the Conference of Governors of British East African Territories created the East African Production and Supply Council to coordinate the imports policy and the distribution of locally produced food, and to control prices in East Africa during World War II. The council continued after 1945, and was

reconstituted under the East Africa High Commission in 1948. Its primary function was to regulate imports of food and material. From 1948 to 1954 the executive of the council acted as executive of the East African Industrial Council and the East African Timber Advisory Board and also performed the function of secretariat to the East Africa Hides, Tanning and Allied Industries Bureau. On December 16, 1954, the East Africa Central Legislative Assembly approved the redesignation of the council's executive as the Department of Economic Co-ordination. The council's advisory function was transferred to the newly created Committee for Economic Co-ordination. In December 1956 all references to the council in the East Africa (High Commission) Order in Council, 1947, were changed to read Department of Economic Co-ordination.

700
Report of the Executive to Council. 1948?–1953/54. [Nairobi, Govt. Printer] DLC

Vol. for 1953/54 covers period Jan. 1953-June 1954.

Superseded by the Report (item 742) issued by the Dept. of Economic Co-ordination of the East Africa High Commission.

Includes reports on the activities of the East African Industrial Council, the East African Timber Advisory Board, and the East African Hides, Tanning and Allied Industries Bureau.

The Council's activities for 1948–54 are summarized in the Annual report of the East Africa High Commission (item 1569) issued by the Colonial Office of Gt. Brit.

L.C. has 1953/54.

701
East Africa High Commission. *East African Statistical Dept.* Bibliography of economics in East Africa (Kenya, Tanganyika, Uganda and Zanzibar). [Nairobi] 1958. [30] leaves. Z7165.A42E3

702
_______ Estimates of geographical income and net product. [1st-5th] 1947–1947/51. Nairobi, Printed by the Govt. Printer. annual (cumulative) HC517.K4A32

At head of title: Colony and Protectorate of Kenya.

Title varies: 1947, National income and output.

Other slight variations in title.

Statistics for gross domestic product for 1954–58 are included in Domestic income and product in Kenya (item 706) issued by the agency's Kenya Unit. Later statistics are included in the Statistical abstract issued by the Central Bureau of Statistics of Kenya.

L.C. has 1947/51; IEN has 1947/49; NN-Sc has 1947/50; source for 1947, 1947/48: Col. Off. Lib. Cat.

703
_______ Estimates of the geopraphical income [of the] Uganda Protectorate for the years 1950–52. [Entebbe, Printed by the Govt. Printer, 1953] 23 p. HC517.U2E3

Later cumulative estimates are contained in The geographical income of Uganda, 1950–56 (item 709) issued by the agency's Uganda Unit.

704
_______ Preliminary estimates of the geographical income and net product for the years 1950 and 1951. Entebbe, Printed by the Govt. Printer, 1952. 5 p. DLC

At head of title: Uganda Protectorate.

Later cumulative statistics are contained in the agency's Estimates of the geographical income for the years 1950–52, and in The geographical income of Uganda, 1950–1956 (item 709) issued by the agency's Uganda Unit.

705
East Africa High Commission. *East African Statistical Dept. Kenya Unit.* Capital formation in Kenya, 1954–1960. [Nairobi] East African Statistical Dept., 1961. 14 p. HC517.K43C32

"The purpose of this publication is to present the revised figures from 1954 to 1959 and certain preliminary figures for 1960 with a general review of the changes in capital formation during the past decade."

706

——— Domestic income and product in Kenya; a description of sources and methods with revised calculations from 1954 to 1958. [Nairobi, Printed by the Govt. Printer, 1959] 97 p. HC517.K4E22

Later statistics of domestic income and product are included in the Statistical abstract issued by the Statistics Division of the Ministry of Economic Planning and Development of Kenya.

707

——— A survey of capital assets held in Kenya, 1958. [Nairobi] 1960. 8 p. HC517.K43C33

A survey of physical assets covering both fixed capital and working capital.

708

East Africa High Commission. *East African Statistical Dept. Tanganyika Office.* The gross domestic product of Tanganyika, 1954–1957. [Dar es Salaam, Printed by the Govt. Printer, 1959] 35 p. HC557.T3A56

Later information on the gross domestic product is included in the Statistical abstract issued by the Central Statistical Bureau of Tanzania.

See also item 951.

709

East Africa High Commission. *East African Statistical Dept. Uganda Unit.* The geographical income of Uganda, 1950–1956. [Entebbe, Govt. Printer] 1957. 23 p. HC517.U2E35

At head of title: Uganda Protectorate.

710

——— The geographical income of Uganda, 1957. [Entebbe, Govt. Printer] 1958. 9 p. NNC

At head of title: Uganda Protectorate.

711

——— The gross domestic product of Uganda, 1954–1959. [Entebbe, Govt. Printer] 1961. 47 p. HC517.U2E36

At head of title: Uganda Protectorate.

712

East African Common Services Organization. *East African Metric Commission.* Report. [Nairobi] 1967. 36 p. QE88.E26

P. N. Nayer, chairman.

713

East African Common Services Organization. *East African Statistical Dept.* The gross domestic product of the Protectorate of Zanzibar, 1957–1961. [Nairobi, 1963] 17 p. HC517.Z33I54

714

East African Standing Committee on the Metric System. Metric handbook for the consumer. Arusha, East African Community, Common Market and Economic Affairs Secretariat [1973?] 27 p. DLC

715

Economist Intelligence Unit, ltd., *London.* The economy of East Africa; a study of trends, prepared for the East African Railways and Harbours Administration. [Nairobi] East African Railways and Harbours Administration, 1955. 237 p. 3 fold. maps. HC17.E2E34

716

Gt. Brit. *Colonial Office.* An economic survey of the colonial territories, 1951. v. 2. The East African territories: Kenya, Tanganyika, Uganda, Zanzibar, and the Somaliland Protectorate. London, H.M. Stationery Off., 1952. 203 p. (*Its* Colonial no. 281–2) HC259.A19 v. 2

717

Gt. Brit. *Commercial Relations and Exports Dept.* British East Africa; economic and commercial conditions in British East Africa (Kenya, Uganda, Tanganyika and Zanzibar). 1921–52. London, H.M. Stationery Off. irregular. HC517.E2A3

Vol. for 1948 covers period 1938–47; for 1952 covers period 1948–51.

Vols. for 1948–52 issued as Overseas economic surveys.

Title varies: 1921–28, 1934/36–1937/38, Report on economic and commercial conditions in British East Africa (varies).—1929–1932/34, Economic conditions in Africa.

Subtitle varies slightly.

Vols. for 1921–45 issued by the Dept. of Overseas Trade; for 1948 by the Export Promotion Dept.

L.C. has 1921–52.

718
Gt. Brit. *Ministry of Overseas Development. Statistics Division.* The developing countries: charts of economic indicators. [1st]-2d issue; 1969–70. [London] 2 v. HC59.7.G74

Merged in 1971 with the agency's. The developing countries: tables of economic indicators, to form The developing countries, economic indicators: charts and tables, issued by the Division when the Ministry's name became Overseas Development Adminitration.

Includes charts for Kenya, Tanzania, and Uganda.

L.C. has 1969–70.

719
——— The developing countries: tables of economic indicators. [London, H.M. Stationery Off., 1969] 48 p. HC59.7.G743

Merged in 1971 with the agency's The developing countries: charts of economic indicators, to form The developing countries: charts and tables, issued by the Division when the Ministry's name became Overseas Development Administration.

Includes tables for Kenya, Tanzania, and Uganda.

720
Jerome, Abraham. National agrarianism. Nairobi, East African Literature Bureau [1973] 2 v. DLC

Contents: v. 1. Africa in search of an ideology.—v. 2. Racism and economics.

721
Newman, Peter. Foreign investment and economic growth: the case of East Africa, 1963–1970. Nairobi, East African Common Services Organization, 1964. 25, 11 leaves. CtY-E

Later published with the same title in Conference on Public Policy, *3d, Dar es Salaam, 1964,* Problems of foreign aid; proceedings (Dar es Salaam, Institute of Public Administration, University College [1965] HC60.C627 1964) p. [138]–161.

722
Oloya, J. J. Coffee, cotton, sisal, and tea in the East African economies, 1945–1962. Nairobi, East African Literature Bureau [1969] 87 p. maps. HF3899.E32O4

723
——— Some aspects of economic development, with special reference to East Africa. Nairobi, East African Literature Bureau [1968] 151 p. illus. HC517.E2O35

724
Robinson, Edward A. G. Report on the needs for economic research and investigation in East Africa. [Entebbe, Uganda, Printed by the Govt. Printer. 1955] 26 p. HC515.R6

At head of title: Uganda Protectorate.

For the governments of Kenya and Uganda with some reference to Tanganyika.

Cost of Living

725
Conference of Governors of British East African Territories. *Statistical Dept.* Index numbers of retail prices of commodities in Nairobi, 1924 to June 1930. Prepared under the direction of A. Walter, Statistician to the Conference of East African Governors, and Director of the Meteorological Service. [Nairobi? 1930] 7 p. (*Its* Memoir no. 1) MiEM

At head of title: Bulletins of statistical research.

726
——— Price of commodities in Kenya Colony, 1924 to 1930. Prepared under the direction of A. Walter, Statistician to the Conference of East African Governors, and Director of the Meteorological Service. [Nairobi? 1932] 29, 52 p. (*Its* Memoir no. 6) MiEM

727
East Africa High Commission. *East African Statistical Dept.* Kenya interim report on the European family budget survey carried out during the month of March, 1952. [Nairobi] 1952. 12 p. NNC

728
______ Methods of compiling indices, affecting cost of living allowances of Europeans and Asians in Kenya Colony and Protectorate. Nairobi, Govt. Printer, 1948. 13 p. NNC

At head of title: Colony and Protectorate of Kenya.

729
______ The pattern of income, expenditure and consumption of African labourers in Dar es Salaam, August 1950. [Nairobi] 1951. 27 p. NIC

At head of title: Tanganyika.

Reprinted July 1954.

730
______ The pattern of income, expenditure and consumption of African unskilled labourers in Jinja. 1951–52. [Nairobi?] annual. HD7064.U42J54

At head of title: Uganda Protectorate.

Later information is included in The patterns of income, expenditure and consumption of African unskilled workers in Jinja, June 1965, issued by the Statistics Branch of the Ministry of Planning and Community Development of Uganda.

L.C. has 1951–52.

731
______ The patterns of income, expenditure and consumption of African unskilled workers in Kampala. 1949–57. [Entebbe] irregular. HD7064.U42K32

Suspended 1954–56.

Title varies: 1949, Report on a cost of living survey carried out among African labourers in Kampala and district.— 1950, The pattern of income expenditure and consumption of African labourers in Kampala.—1951–52, The pattern of income, expenditure and consumption of African unskilled labourers in Kampala.

Later information is included in a publication with the same title issued by the Statistics Division of the Ministry of Planning and Community Development of Uganda.

L.C. has 1949–57 (1953 wanting); 1953 cited in vol. for 1957.

732
______ Report on the European family budget survey carried out during March and June 1952 [in Nairobi] Nairobi, 1953. 17 p. DLC

At head of title: Kenya.

733
East Africa High Commission. *East African Statistical Dept. Kenya Unit.* The pattern of income, expenditure and consumption of Africans in Nairobi. 1950–1957/58. [Nairobi] irregular. HD7064.N34E37a

At head of title, 1950: Kenya Colony and Protectorate; 1957/58: Kenya.

Suspended 1951–56.

Title varies: 1950, The pattern of income, expenditure and consumption of African labourers in Nairobi.

Vol. for 1950 issued by the agency under a variant name: East African Statistical Dept.

Later information is included in The pattern of income, expenditure and consumption of African middle income workers in Nairobi, July, 1963, issued by the Ministry of Finance and Economic Planning of Kenya.

L.C. has 1950–1957/58.

734
______ Wage earners' index of consumer prices in Nairobi; a description of the method of compilation. [Nairobi] 1960. [10] p. DLC

735
East Africa High Commission. *East African Statistical Dept. Tanganyika Office.* Household budget survey of Africans living in Dar es Salaam, 1956/1957. [Dar es Salaam] 1958. 35 p.

Source: UNECA. New acq., Jan./Feb. 1965.

736
______ The pattern of income, expenditure and consumption of African workers in Tanga, February 1958. [Dar es Salaam?] 1958. 22 leaves. HD7064.T32T35

At head of title: Tanganyika.

Family budget survey of 60 African families.

737
East Africa High Commission. *East African Statistical Dept. Uganda Unit.* Index of retail prices in African markets: Kampala. [Nairobi] 1957. 10 leaves. HB235.E2A53

At head of title: Uganda Protectorate.

738
______ The patterns of income, expenditure and consumption of African unskilled workers in Fort Portal, February, 1960. [Entebbe?] 1960. 41 p. DLC

At head of title: Uganda Protectorate.

739
______ The patterns of income, expenditure and consumption of African unskilled workers in Mbale. 1950–58. [Entebbe] irregular. DLC

Suspended 1951–57.

Title varies: 1950, The patterns of income, expenditure and consumption of African labourers in Mbale.

Vol. for 1950 issued by the agency under a variant name: East African Statistical Dept.

Later information is included in a publication with the same title issued by the Statistics Division of the Ministry of Planning and Economic Development of Uganda.

L.C. has 1958; vol. for 1950 cited in the Annual report, 1958/59, issued by the East African Statistical Dept. of the East Africa High Commission.

740
East African Common Services Organization. *East African Statistical Dept.* The pattern of income, expenditure and consumption of unskilled workers in Zanzibar; report on a survey carried out in April 1962. [Nairobi, 1963] 25 p. HD7064.Z35E27 1963

At head of title: Zanzibar Protectorate.

Results of a family budget survey of 48 workers from government departments and commercial enterprises.

Economic Cooperation

741
Conference on Public Policy, *2d, University College, Nairobi, 1963.* Conference on public policy, 1963/4: East African federation; [paper no. 11] Economic union and industrial development in East Africa [by] Benton F. Massell. [Nairobi? 1964?] [47] leaves. HC517.E2C6 1963 no. 11

Later revised as Economic union in East Africa: an evaluation of the gains ([Santa Monica, Calif., Rand Corp.] 1964. 29 p. illus. [Rand Corporation. Paper] P2971. AS36.R28 no. 2971).

East Africa High Commission. *Dept. of Economic Co-ordination.*

Note: On December 16, 1954, the executive of the defunct East African Production and Supply Council of the East Africa High Commission became the Department of Economic Co-ordination. The department acted as the secretariat to the Committee for Economic Coordination, created in September 1955. The committee considered questions of common East African interest, such as the marketing of agricultural produce, the protection of secondary industries, and the revision of customs tariff and railway freight rates. The department also acted as agent for the buying and selling of agricultural produce and dealt with matters of industrial and trade development in East Africa. When the East African Common Services Organization replaced the East Africa High Commission on December 9, 1961, the duties and responsibilities of the department were divided between the Trade and Marketing Division and the Economic Division of the Treasury of the East African Common Services Organization.

742
Report. 1954/55–1955/57? Nairobi, Printed by the Govt. Printer. annual. HC517.E2A32

Report year ends June 30.

Supersedes the Report of the Executive to Council (item 700) issued by the East African Production and Supply Council of the East Africa High Commission.

No more published?

Each issue includes reports of the East African Industrial Council, and the East African Timber Advisory Board. Summary reports of the department's activities for the period 1955–60 are included in the Annual report of the East Africa High Commission (item 1569) issued by the Colonial Office of Gt. Brit.

L.C. has 1954/55–1955/57.

743
East African Community. *Common Market and Economic Affairs Secretariat.* Review of economic integration activities within the East African Community, 1973. [Arusha?] 1973. 156 p. DLC

744
Gt. Brit. *Foreign Office.* Exchange of letters recording the views of the Government of the United Kingdom of Great Britain and Northern Ireland and the Government of the United States of America concerning arrangements for the establishment of revolving loan funds in the Uganda Protectorate and Tanganyika with counterpart funds derived from United States economic aid under Section 9 (c) of the Mutual Security Act of 1952. London, June 24, 1953. London, H.M. Stationery Off. [1953] 5 p. (*Its* United States, 1953, no. 3) HG188.U45G72

[Gt. Brit. Parliament. Papers by command] Cmd. 8994.

745
Gt. Brit. *Parliament. House of Commons. Select Committee on Overseas Aid. Subcommittee E.* Minutes of evidence; East Africa session 1969–70. London, H.M. Stationery Off., 1970. 73 p. MiEM

746
Gt. Brit. *Treasury.* Colonial Loans Act. 1949. Statement of guarantee given by the Treasury on 15th March, 1955, in pursuance of Section 1 of the Colonial Loans Act, 1949, as amended by Section 1 of the Colonial Loans Act, 1952, on a loan proposed to be made to the East Africa High Commission by the International Bank for Reconstruction and Development. Treasury chambers, 28th March 1955, Henry Brooke. Presented pursuant to Act 12 and 13 Geo. 6, Ch. 50, Section 1 (5). Ordered by the House of Commons to be printed, 28th March 1955. London, H.M. Stationery Off., 1955. [2] p. ([Gt. Brit. Parliament. 1954/55. House of Commons. Reports and papers] 98) J301.K6 1954/55 v. 8

747
Kenya. Government guarantee for a loan by the Government of Sweden to the E.A. Development Bank. [Nairobi, 1972?] 2 p. (Kenya. [National Assembly] Sessional paper no. 4 of 1972)

Information received from L.C. Office, Nairobi, Kenya; (publication not held by DLC).

748
______ Government guarantee for a loan by the IBRD (World Bank) to the E.A. Development Bank. [Nairobi, 1972] 2 p. (Kenya. [National Assembly] Sessional paper no. 3 of 1972)

Information received from L.C. Office, Nairobi, Kenya; (publication not held by DLC).

Statistics

749
Conference of Governors of British East African Territories. *Statistical Dept.* Memoir. no. 1–7? [Nairobi? 1930–1932?] irregular. MiEM

At head of title: no. 1–2? Bulletins of statistical research; no. 3–7?: Dept. of Statistical Research. British East Africa.

No more published?

MiEM has no. 1, 3–7; NN has mo. 1–5.

Individual titles in this series are listed in this guide under subject, e.g. Finance—Banks and banking, Finance—Taxation, etc. They can be identified by consulting the index to this guide under Conference of Governors of British East African Territories, Statistical Dept, *Memoir.*

750
_______ Report on the Statistical Department of the Conference of East African Governors. 1926/29–1931? [Nairobi?] annual. HA37.A4C6

Reports for 1926/29 issued in combined form.

No more published?

L.C. has 1930–31; source for 1926/29–1931: Col. Off. Lib. Cat.

East Africa High Commission. *East African Statistical Dept.*

Note: In 1925, Albert Walter was appointed statistician to the Kenya government. In 1926, he was detailed to the Conference of Governors of British East African Territories as its first statistician. The Kenya government provided staff for the statistician in Nairobi. In 1948, upon the creation of the East Africa High Commission, the statistician and his staff became the East African Statistical Department, still headquartered in Nairobi. On July 1, 1956, the following units were created within the department: the East African Unit and the Kenya Unit, at Nairobi, Kenya; the Tanganyikan Unit (called Tanganyika Office, a variant name, by the Library of Congress), at Dar es Salaam, Tanganyika; and the Uganda Unit, at Entebbe, Uganda. On the eve of the creation of the East African Common Services Organization in 1961, the units were reconstituted as government statistical departments within Kenya, Tanganyika, and Uganda. In Kenya, the Kenya Unit became the Economics and Statistics Division of the Treasury. In Tanganyika, the Tanganyika Office became the Economics and Statistics Division of the Treasury. In Uganda, the Uganda Unit became the Statistics Branch of the Ministry of Economic Development. The East African Unit was apparently renamed the East African Statistical Department of the East African Common Services Organization.

751
Annual report. 1948–1961/62. [Nairobi] HA37.A4A3

Report year for 1948–53 ends Dec. 31; for 1954/55–1961/62 ends June 30.

"Discontinued for distribution purposes."

Each report includes a list of the agency's publications issued during the year.

Information on the activities of the agency for 1948–61 is included in the Annual report of the East Africa High Commission (item 1569) issued by the Colonial Office of Gt. Brit.; information for 1962–67 is included in the Annual report (item 1581) issued by the East African Common Services Organization; and for 1968 and subsequent years in the Annual report (item 1596) issued by the East African Community.

L.C. has 1952, 1956/57, 1958/59–1961/62.

752
_______ Quarterly economic and statistical bulletin. no. 1–52; Sept. 1948-June 1961. Nairobi. HC517.E2A33

Title varies: 1948-June 1952, East African economic and statistical bulletin.

Superseded by the Economic and statistical review (item 761) issued by the East African Statistical Dept. of the East African Common Services Organization.

Each issue contains data on population, migration and tourism, external and interterritorial trade, transport and communications, employment and earnings, retail prices and cost of living, banking and currency, public finance, domestic income and product, agriculture and forestry, building and construction, mining, commerce, and fuel and power, for East Africa, Kenya, Tanganyika, and Uganda. Appended to each issue are a list of the agency's publications, and a list of introductory articles on the above topics.

L.C. has Sept. 1948-June 1961.

753
_______ Statistical abstract [of the Colony and Protectorate of Kenya] 1955–60. Nairobi, Printed by the Govt. Printer. annual. HA1977.K4A3

Superseded by the Statistical abstract issued by the Economics and Statistics Division of Kenya.

Statistical data for Kenya for the period 1948–60 is included also in the agency's Quarterly economic and statistical bulletin.

Contents: Land and climate.—Constitution.—Population and vital statistics.—Migration.—

External and interterritorial trade.—Transport and communications.—Agriculture.—Forestry.—Mining.—Fuel and power.—Commerce and industry.—Building.—Currency and banking.—Public finance.—Domestic income and product.—Retail price and cost of living.—Employment and earnings.—Public health.—Education.—Justice.—Balance of payments.

L.C. has 1955–60.

754

East Africa High Commission. *East African Statistical Dept. Tanganyika Office.* Monthly statistical bulletin. 1949–June 1961. Dar es Salaam, Printed by the Govt. Printer. DLC

Vols. for 1951–52 called also New series.

Supersedes the Trade and information report issued by the Customs Dept. of Tanganyika.

Title varies: 1949-Apr. 1951, Monthly statistical supplement.

Continued by a publication with the same title issued by the Economics and Statistics Division of Tanganyika.

L.C. has 1951–61; IEN has 1949–61.

755

______ Statistical abstract. 1938/51–1960. Dar es Salaam, Printed by the Govt. Printer. annual. HA2131.A3

At head of title: Tanganyika.

Suspended 1953.

Superseded by a publication with the same title issued by the Economics and Statistics Division of Tanganyika.

Contents: Land and climate.—Constitution.—Population.—Migration.—External and inter-territorial trade.—Transport and communications.—Agriculture and animal husbandry.—Forestry.—Mining.—Water supply.—Fuel and power.—Commerce and industry.—Co-operative societies. — Building. — Currency and banking.—Public finance.—National accounts of Tanganyika.—Retail prices and cost of living.—Employment and earning.—Public health.—Education.—Justice.

L.C. has 1938/51–1960.

756

East Africa High Commission. *East African Statistical Dept. Uganda Unit.* Statistical abstract. 1957–60. Entebbe, Printed by the Govt. Printer. annual. HA1977.U35A26

At head of title: Uganda Protectorate.

Superseded by a publication with the same title issued by the Statistics Branch of the Ministry of Economic Development of Uganda.

Contents: Land and climate.—Population.—Migration.—External and interterritorial trade.—Transport and communications.—agriculture.—Fishing.—Forestry.—Mining. — Fuel and power.—Industry and commerce.—Banking and currency.—Public finance.—Gross domestic product and capital formation.—Retail prices and cost of living.—Employment and earnings.—Public health.—Education.—Justice.

L.C. catalogs under: Uganda. *Ministry of Economic Development. Statistics Branch.* Statistical abstract.

L.C. has 1957–60.

757

East African Common Services Organization. *East African Statistical Dept.* Credit market statistics manual for Kenya. Compiled by M. Selsjord. Nairobi, 1966. 36, [55] leaves. forms. DJBF

758

______ Credit market statistics manual for Tanzania. Compiled by Mikael Selsjord. Nairobi, 1967. 32, [13] leaves. DJBF

759

______ Credit market statistics manual for the East African common institutions. Compiled by Mikael Selsjord. Nairobi, 1967. 8, [22] leaves. forms. DJBF

760

______ Credit market statistics manual for Uganda. Compiled by Mikael Selsjord. Nairobi, 1967. 20, [13] leaves. DJBF

761

______ Economic and statistical review. no. 1–24; Dec. 1961-Sept. 1967. [Nairobi] quarterly. HC517.E2A34

Supersedes the Quarterly economic and statistical bulletin (item 752) issued by the East African Statistical Dept. of the East Africa High Commission.

Continued by a publication with the same title (item 763) issued by the East African Statistical Dept. of the East African Community.

L.C. has Dec. 1961-Sept. 1967.

762
_______ Supplement to the credit market statistics manuals for Kenya, Tanzania, Uganda, and the East African common institutions. compiled by Mikel [i.e. Mikael] Selsjord. Nairobi, 1967. 19 leaves. DJBF

Appendices wanting in DJBF copy.

763
East African Community. *East African Statistical Dept.* Economic and statistical review. no. 25+ Dec. 1967+ [Nairobi] quarterly (irregular) HC517.E2A34

Supersedes and continues the numbering of a publication with the same title (item 761) issued by the East African Statistical Dept. of the East African Common Services Organization.

Each issue includes statistics for population, migration and tourism, external and interstate trade, transportation and communications, employment, retail price index numbers, production, banking, currency, insurance, public finance, domestic income and product, and balance of payments.

Some issues include articles with cumulative statistics on economics, trade, etc., e.g. Statistics of Kenya and Uganda imports, 1923–1948, by Arthur Hazlewood, in no. 46; Mar. 1973, p. viii-xxv.

L.C. has Dec. 1967+

764
_______ Statistical survey of the East African Community institutions. 1972+ [Nairobi] annual. HD4350.E25E28a

Includes statistics for the East African Railways Corporation, the East African Harbours Corporation, the East African Posts and Telecommunications Corporation, the East African Airways Corporation, the general fund services, and the East African Development Bank.

L.C. has 1972+

Natural Resources

East African Natural Resources Research Council.

Note: The East African Central Legislative Assembly created the council in Act no. 15 of 1962. The council succeeds to the functions of the former East African Agricultural and Fisheries Research Council, dissolved in 1962. The research organizations under the council's advisory control are the East African Agriculture and Forestry Research Organization, East African Freshwater Fisheries Research Organization, East African Marine Fisheries Research Organization, East African Veterinary Research Organization, Tropical Pesticides Research Institute, and by voluntary association, the East African Trypanosomiasis Research Organization. Research recommendations of the organizations are sent to "research co-ordinating committees" for consideration. Approved programs are published in *Research programmes* (item 69) issued by the East African Common Services Organization. Financial approval must be realized by the East African Legislative Assembly and confirmed by the East African Authority.

765
Annual report. 1962/63+ [Nairobi] S535.A23E27

Report year ends June 30.

Vol. for 1962/63 covers period Jan. 1962–June 1963; for 1964/65 covers period July 1963–June 1965.

Supersedes a publication with the same title (item 52) issued by the East African Agricultural and Fisheries Research Council of the East Africa High Commission.

Each issue includes summary reports, and lists of publications for East African Agriculture and Forestry Research Organization, East African Freshwater Fisheries Research Organization, East African Marine Fisheries Research Organization, East African Veterinary Research Organization, and the Tropical Pesti-

cides Research Institute.
L.C. and MiEM have 1962/63+

766
Gt. Brit. *Directorate of Overseas Surveys.* East Africa. [Tolworth, Surrey?] 1961. (*Its* D.O.S. (Misc.) 299A-H) 8 maps. DLC-G&M
Scale 1:4,000,000.

Contents: General.—Physical features.—Mineral resources, forests and game reserves.—Rainfall probability, population and main drainage basins.—Vegetation.—Geology.—Soils.—Roads and railways.

Accompanies Edward W. Russell's The natural resources of East Africa.

767
Russell, Edward W., *ed.* The natural resources of East Africa. Nairobi, D. A. Hawkins in association with East African Literature Bureau [1962] 144 p. illus., maps (6 col.)
HC517.E2R8

Later editions were published in 1969, and in 1972, by Oxford University Press with the title: East Africa; its peoples and resources.

Each chapter listed below was issued also separately.

Contents: 1. The history of East Africa, by A. T. Mason.—2. The archaeology of East Africa, by L. S. B. Leakey.—3. The demography of East Africa, by J. G. C. Blacker.—4. Commerce and industry in East Africa, by L. W. Aldous.—5. The physiography and geology of East Africa, by E. P. Saggerson.—6. The soils of East Africa, by R. M. Scott.—7. The climate of East Africa, by J. F. Griffiths.—8. Water requirements of East African crops, by H. C. Pereira and J. S. G. McCulloch.—9. The natural vegetation of East Africa, by C. G. Trapnell and I. Langdale-Brown.—10. Agriculture and land tenure in East Africa: Kenya, by L. H. Brown; Uganda, by G. W. Anderson; Tanganyika, by M. Lunan and D. P. Allan.—11. Forestry in East Africa: Forestry in Kenya, by E. J. Honoré; Forestry in Tanganyika, by R. G. Sangster; Forestry in Uganda, by W. E. M. Logan.—12. East African wild life as a natural resource, by H. F. Lamprey.

Colonial Concessions

The following entries (items 768–82) are arranged chronologically, and cover the period 1903–1917, and 1928.

768
Gt. Brit. *Foreign Office.* Return of concessions in the East Africa and Uganda protectorates. London, Printed for H. M. Stationery Off. by Harrison, 1903. 3 p. (*Its* Africa no. 7 (1903))
J301.K6 1903 v. 45
[Gt. Brit. Parliament. Papers by comand] Cd. 1628.

769
______ ______ London, Printed for H.M. Stationery Off. by Harrison, 1904. 30 p. (*Its* Africa no. 9 (1904))
J301.K6 1904 v. 62
[Gt. Brit. Parliament. Papers by command] Cd. 2100.

770
Gt. Brit. *Colonial Office.* Correspondence, 1905: March 3 to December 29, relating to concesions in Uganda, the East Africa Protectorate, and Somaliland. [London] Printed for the use of the Colonial Office, 1906. (*Its* African no. 772, confidential)
DLC-Micro 03759
Collation of the original: xxxvi, 271 p.
[Gt. Brit.] Public Record Office. C.O. 879/87.
"Continued by African no. 844."
Includes information on the Jewish settlement scheme in the East Africa Protectorate, and the concessions for Lake Magadi, the Tana river, the Mabira forest, the Kilindini harbor, and for rubber, coal, electricty, papyrus, the railway, and other land grants.

771
______ Further correspondence, 1906, relating to concessions in Uganda, the East Africa Protectorate, and Somaliland. [London] Printed for the use of the Colonial Office, 1907. (*Its* African no. 844, confidential)
DLC-Micro 03759

Collation of the original: lxvi, 396 p.
[Gt. Brit.] Public Record Office. C.O. 879/92.
"In continuation of African no. 772; continued by African no. 869."
Includes information on the Uganda Railway, the Lake Magadi scheme, Mabira forest reserve, Kilindini harbor, settler schemes, and other land grants totaling 516 for the year.

772
_______ Further correspondence, 1907, relating to concessions in Uganda, the East Africa Protectorate, and Somaliland. [London] Printed for the use of the Colonial Office, 1908. (*Its* African no. 869, confidential)
DLC-Micro 03759
Collation of the original: lxvii, 425 p. fold. map.
[Gt. Brit.] Public Record Office. C.O. 879/95.
"In continuation of African no. 844; continued by African no. 914."
Includes information on fiber and silk concessions, the Tana river concession to Mongolia, ltd., Lake Magadi Railway, the Mombasa water supply, the British East Africa Corporation, and the land rights of the Masai, and other African peoples in the East Africa Protectorate and in Uganda.

773
_______ Further correspondence, 1908, relating to concessions in Uganda and the East Africa Protectorate. [London] Printed for the use of the Colonial Office, 1909. (*Its* African no. 914, confidential) DLC-Micro 03759
Collation of the original: lii, 383 p. 6 maps.
[Gt. Brit.] Public Record Office. C.O. 879/99.
"In continuation of African no. 869; continued by African no. 929."
Includes informatioin on the Juba and Tana river concessions, the Mabira and Budongo forest leases, the Southern Abyssinian Expedition, the Lake Magadi soda scheme, the Mombasa water supply, Boer immigration, African land rights, and cotton and railway concessions.

774
_______ Further correspondence, 1909, relating to concessions in the East Africa Protectorate, Uganda, and Nyasaland. [London] Printed for the use of the Colonial Office, 1910. (*Its* African no. 929, confidential) DLC-Micro 03759
Collation of the original: xxxix, 308 p. 6 maps.
[Gt. Brit.] Public Record Office. C.O. 879/101.
"In continuation of African no. 914; continued by African no. 951."
Includes information on the Mombasa water supply, the Lake Magadi soda scheme, leases for the Arabuko, Budongo, Mwele, and Sekoki forests, the Mackenzie concessions at Malindi, the Uganda Railway, and other cotton and rubber leases.

775
_______ Further correspondence, 1910, relating to concessions in Nyasaland, Uganda, and the East Africa Protectorate. [London] Printed for the use of the Colonial Office, 1911. (*Its* African no. 951, confidential) DLC-Micro 03759
Collation of the original: lxvii, 503 p. 2 maps.
[Gt. Brit.] Public Record Office. C.O. 879/104.
"In continuation of African no. 929; continued by African no. 965."
Includes information on the development of Jubaland, land grants to missionary societies in the East Africa Protectorate, Malindi concessions, Budongo and Mwele forest leases, and the Jinja-Kakindu Railway.

776
_______ Further correspondence, 1911, relating to concessions in Nyasaland, Uganda, and the East Africa Protectorate. [London] Printed for the use of the Colonial Office, 1912. (*Its* African no. 965, confidential) DLC-Micro 03759
Collation of the original: lxii, 422 p.
[Gt. Brit.] Public Record Office. C.O. 879/107.
"In continuation of African no. 951; continued by African no. 985."
Includes information on the Kenia, Bugoma, Budongo, and Mabira forest leases, the Lake

Magadi scheme, the Jinja-Kakindu Railway, the Nairobi Electric Light and Power Company, loans for construction of piers at Kilindini, and Native land settlement in Buganda (p. 269–292 and 314–315).

777

_______ Further correspondence, 1912, relating to concessions in Nyasaland, Uganda, and the East Africa Protectorate. [London] Printed for the use of the Colonial Office, 1913. (*Its* African no. 985, confidential)

DLC-Micro 03759

Collation of the original: xl, 274 p.

[Gt. Brit.] Public Record Office. C.O. 879/110.

"In continuation of African no. 965; continued by African no. 998."

Includes information on forest policy in Uganda, and concessions in the Bugoma, Budongo, Mwele, Mabira, and Kenia forests; pier construction at Kilindini, the Kampala Electric Lighting concession, and other timber, rubber, and land leases.

778

_______ Further correspondence, 1913, relating to concessions in Nyasaland, Uganda, and the East Africa Protectorate. [London] Printed for the use of the Colonial Office, 1914. (*Its* African no. 998, confidential)

DLC-Micro 03759

Collation of the original: lxi, 404 p.

[Gt. Brit.] Public Record Office. C.O. 879/111.

"In continuation of African no. 985; continued by African no. 1016."

Includes information on the alienation of crown and agricultural lands in the East Africa Protectorate, the recruitment of Arab, Indian, and Somali labor for the East Africa Protectorate, railway extension in the East Africa Protectorate, and the Mabira forest lease, and the Nairobi Electric Power and Lighting Company concession.

Includes also Proposed harbor improvements at Kilindini (p. 221–234) by Coode, Matthews, Fitzmaurice and Wilson.

779

_______ Further correspondence, 1914, relating to concessions in Nyasaland, Uganda, and the East Africa Protectorate. [London] Printed for the use of the Colonial Office, 1915. (*Its* African no. 1016, confidential) DLC-Micro 03759

Collation of the original: xxxix, 318 p.

[Gt. Brit.] Public Record Office. C.O. 879/115.

"In continuation of African no. 998; continued by African no. 1032."

Includes information on the alienation of land in the East Africa Protectorate and Uganda, the land settlement policy in Zanzibar; the recruitment of Indian and Somali labor for the East Africa Protectorate; the Uganda Railway extension to Uasin Gishu plateau and the North Kavirondo area; the recruitment of Kikuyu labor for use in the coastal areas of the East Africa Protectorate; forced labor in Uganda; water rights on the Thika river; and the Mabira and Mwele forest leases.

Includes also the Report (p. 279–284) of the Committee on the Amalgamation of East African Railways (T. R. Wynne, chairman); the Land Settlement Decree, 1914, of Zanzibar, and Memorandum concerning the proposed steps which government intend to take to settle the question of the ownership of the land in the Zanzibar Protectorate (p. 247–253); and Observations on the Recommendations, 1912, of the Commission to Inquire into the Question of Native Labour in British East Africa (p. 114–117) by Governor Belfield of the East Africa Protectorate.

780

_______ Further correspondence, 1915, relating to concessions in Nyasaland, Uganda, and the East Africa Protectorate. [London] Printed for the use of the Colonial Office, 1916. (*Its* African no. 1032, confidential)

DLC-Micro 03759

Collation of the original: xv, 111 p.

[Gt. Brit.] Public Record Office. C.O. 879/116.

"In continuation of African no. 1016; continued by African no. 1042."

Includes information on the revision of the lease of East African Estates, ltd.; land tenure in Uganda; Kenya and Mwele forest concessions; and other mica and rubber concessions.

Includes also Recommendations (p. 60–69) on the Reports of the Committee Appointed to Consider the Question of Native Land Settlement in Ankole, Bunyore, Busoga and Toro, of Uganda, by F. J. Jackson, Governor of Uganda; and the Agreement (p. 97–105) on the Nairobi Electric Power and Lighting concession.

781

——— Further correspondence, 13th January 1916 to 22nd January 1917, relating to concessions in Nyasaland, Uganda, and the East Africa Protectorate. [London] Printed for the use of the Colonial Office, 1918. (*Its* African no 1042. confidential) DLC-Micro 03759

Collation of the original: 56 p.

[Gt. Brit.] Public Record Office. C.O. 879/117.

"In continuation of African no. 1032."

Includes Note on land in East Africa Protectorate for intending settlers (p. 1–4) by H. Conway Belfield, Governor; amendments to Nairobi Electric Power and Lighting Company's draft concession; lumber leases in Uganda, and other land leases.

782

Uganda. Grant of timber concessions in the Minziro forest in Tanganyika Territory and Uganda. Entebbe, Govt. Printer, 1928. 10 p.

Cited in An East African forest bibliography, compiled by A. L. Griffith and B. E. St. L. Stuart, and issued by the East African Agriculture and Forestry Research Organization of the East Africa High Commission ([Nairobi, 1955]) p. 68.

Education

783

Arrow. [no.] 1+ 1957+ [Nairobi, D. A. Hawkins] illus. 9 no. a year.

Early numbers issued by the East African Literature Bureau "on behalf of the departments of education, of Kenya, Tanganyika Uganda and Zanzibar . . . to provide reading material in graded English for school children . . ."

L.C. received June 1965; not retained.

784

Clarke, Edith R. Activities and games for tropical schools. London, Macmillan, in association with the East African Literature Bureau, 1957. 119 p. illus. CLU

785

Conference of Directors of Education of Kenya, Tanganyika, Uganda and Zanzibar, held at Makerere, January 18th–19th, 1937. Proceedings. [Kampala? 1937?]

E. R. J. Hussey, chairman.

Source: Col. Off. Lib. Cat.

786

Conference on Muslim Education, *Dar es Salaam, 1958.* Proceedings of the Conference on Muslim Education held in Dar es Salaam on 20th–22nd November, 1958. [Nairobi, Printed by authority and printed by the Govt. Printer, 1959] 40 p. LC904.C66 1958

At head of title: East Africa High Commission.

"In preparing the account which forms Part One of the Proceedings of the Conference the aim has been to summarize the discussions of the Conference relating to the principal suggestions and proposals made by Professor Serjeant and Mr. Griffiths in their original Report and to present as clearly as possible the Conference's own recommendations on them."

See also item 800.

787

East Africa High Commission. *East African Literature Bureau.* Annual report. 1949–1960/61. [Nairobi] illus. Z965.B7

Report year for 1949–53 ends Dec. 31; for

1954/55–1960/61 ends June 30.

Report for 1954/55 covers period Jan. 1954–June 1955.

Superseded by a publication with the same title (item 793) issued by the East African Literature Bureau.

L.C. has 1950–1960/61; IEN has 1949–1960/61.

788
_______ Books on East African history, customs, languages, published by the East African Literature Bureau. Nairobi, 1961. 14 p. illus. DLC

789
_______ Catalogue of books, 1955. Nairobi [1955?] 22 p. DLC

790
_______ Catalogue of books published by or in association with the East African Literature Bureau and available throughout East Africa. Kampala, Eagle Press, 1960. 59 p. illus. Z3585.E25 1960

Photo reproduction.

791
East Africa High Commission. *East African Literature Bureau. Advisory Council.* Minutes of the third meeting . . . held on the 23rd August, 1950 at 9:30 a.m. in the rooms of the Uganda Society, Kampala, 1950. [37] p.

Source: Col. Off. Lib Cat.

792
East Africa High Commission. *East African Office, London.* European education in East Africa. [London?] 1958. 18 p.

Fees, etc. as at January 1958.

Source: Col. Off. Lib. Cat.

East African Literature Bureau.

Note: The East African Literature Bureau was established in 1948 as an agency of the East Africa High Commission (later the East African Common Services Organization, at present the East African Community). The purpose of the E.A.L.B. is the publication and distribution of low-priced literature on a variety of topics in English, Swahili, and other African languages. Special encouragement is given to African authors through its students' book-writing scheme (see the section on The Arts—East African Literature (English)). Attention is also paid to the production of adult literacy readers, textbooks, and practical guides for the African home. The bureau publishes under its own name and under the imprint "The Eagle Press." In the 1950's certain manuscripts received by the bureau were transmitted to commercial publishers for publication. A description of the bureau's activities is included in the agency's *Annual report* and also in C. S. Sabiti's "The Work of the East African Literature Bureau," published in the East African Library Association's *Papers Presented at the Fourth East African Library Association Conference, Makerere University, Kampala, 16–19 September, 1970* [n.p.] 1972 *(EALA Bulletin no. 12)* p. 144–152. Z857.E3E2 1972.

This bibliography contains a selection of East African Literature Bureau publications in English and Swahili held by American libraries. Individual titles are listed by author under their respective subject, e.g., The Arts—East African Literature (English); Education—Textbooks; Swahili, etc. Books on topics of interest to individual partner states, namely, Kenya, Tanzania, and Uganda, or in local languages, e.g., Gikuyu, Ganda, etc., will be found in subsequent guides to official publications. All nonbook material has been omitted. For a comprehensive listing of titles currently available from the bureau, see its *Complete catalogue* (item 795).

793
Annual report. 1961/62+ Nairobi. illus. DLC

Report year ends June 30.

At head of title, 1961/62–1966/67: East African Common Services Organization; 1967/68+: East African Community.

Supersedes a publication with the same title (item 787) issued by the East African Literature Bureau of the East Africa High Commission.

L.C. has 1961/62–1967/68 (1962/63 wanting).

794
_______ Catalogue of books and visual aids published by or in association with East African Literature Bureau and available from bookshops throughout East Africa. 1961–1968/69. Nairobi. illus. Z5819.E15
Frequency varies.
Title varies.
Superseded by the agency's Complete catalogue.
L.C. has 1961–1968/69.

795
_______ Complete catalogue. 1971+ Nairobi. irregular. Z3585.E26a
Supersedes the agency's Catalogue of books and visual aids published by or in association with East African Literature Bureau and available from bookshops throughout East Africa.
L.C. has 1971, and 1973+

796
Gt. Brit. *Board of Education.* Educational systems of the chief Crown Colonies and possessions of the British Empire, including reports on the training of native races. pt. 2. West Africa, Basutoland, Southern Rhodesia, East Africa Protectorate, Uganda, Mauritius, Seychelles. London, H.M. Stationery Off., 1905. xvi, 345 p. (*Its* Special reports of educational subjects, v. 13) L341.A7 v. 13
[Gt. Brit. Parliament. Papers by command] Cd. 2378.
L.C. has also a second copy in the Reports and Papers issued by the House of Commons of the Parliament of Gt. Brit. with the call no.: J301.K6 1905 v. 26.

797
Gt. Brit. *Colonial Office.* Report by Professor C. H. Phillips to the Secretary of State for the Colonies on mass education in East Africa. [London? 1947?]
Source: Dar es Salaam Lib. Bull. no. 58.

798
Gt. Brit. *Colonial Office. Advisory Committee on Education in the Colonies.* Report of the Biology Sub-committee on the replies from the British East African territories to the Secretary of State's despatch on the place of biology in education. [London? 1933]
Source: SOAS Cat.

799
_______ Report of the sub-committee appointed to consider the educational policy underlying paragraph 19 of the Report of the Conference of Directors of Education of Kenya, Tanganyika, Uganda and Zanzibar, held in June 1932. [n.p., 1933] (A.C.E.C. 44/33)
Source: SOAS Cat.

800
Gt. Brit. *Fact-Finding Mission to Study Muslim Education in East Africa.* Report by the fact-finding mission to study Muslim education in East Africa. Nairobi, Govt. Printer, 1958. 23 p. MBU
At head of title: East Africa High Commission.
Signed by: V. L. Griffiths and R. B. Serjeant.
See also item 786.

801
Hawkridge, D. G. A proposal for an integrated plan for programmed learning research and applications in East Africa, prepared by D. G. Hawkridge at the request of the directors of the departments and institutes of education, the University College of Makerere [and other universities] [n.p.] 1968. 26 leaves.
Source: London. Univ. Inst. of Educ. Cat.

802
Huxley, Julian S. Biology and its place in native education in East Africa. [London, Colonial Office, Advisory Committee on Education in the Colonies, 1931] 44 p. ([Gt. Brit.] Colonial Office. Advisory Committee on Education in the Colonies. African (East) no. 1134, Apr. 1930)
Source: Royal Comm. Soc. Cat.

803
Kazimi, Ali A. An inquiry into Indian education in East Africa. Nairobi, Printed by the

Govt. Printer, 1948. 111 p. LA1561.K3
At head of cover title: Colony and Protectorate of Kenya.
Includes the history of Indian education and statistical data for Kenya, Uganda, Tanganyika and Zanzibar.
L.C. also has on microfilm (23940, reel 7, octavo 381).

804
Richards, C. G. A proposed literature organization for East Africa; the preliminary scheme for carrying out the proposals accepted in principle by the East African governments prepared by the Adviser on Literature for Africans in conjunction with representatative bodies in Kenya, Uganda, Tanganyika and Zanzibar. [Nairobi? 1947?]
DLC-Micro 23940 reel 13 folio 395
Collation of the original: 29 leaves.
Colonial Office Library East Africa pamphlet folio 395.

805
Technical education and vocational training in East Africa. Report of a mission on behalf of the East African Governments, October, 1947 [by H. C. Weston and A. J. Ellis] London, Crown Agents for the Colonies on behalf of the governments of Kenya, Tanganyika, Uganda, and Zanzibar, 1948. 27 p.
Source: Col. Off. Lib. Cat.

806
Turner, G. C. A review of African secondary education in East Africa, Dec. 1946. [n.p., 1946?] 36 p. (loose-leaf)
Source: Tang. Lib. Ser. East Africana.

Adult Education

807
Teaching adults: a handbook for developing countries. Edited by Roy Prosser and Ron Clarke. Nairobi, East African Literature Bureau [1972] 175 p. CtY

808
Young, T. R. Teaching adults; advice to teachers. Nairobi, Eagle Press, 1958. 35 p. WvU

Health Education

809
Chilton, N. Magonjwa yaletwayo na vimelea na matibio yake. A description of the common parasitic diseases of East Africa, with notes on their diagnosis and treatment for Swahili-speaking rural dressers. 2d ed. rev. Dar es Salaam, Printed by the Govt. Printer, 1942. 45 p.
Text in English and Swahili.
Source: Dar es Salaam Lib. Bull. no. 90.

810
______ ______ 3d ed. rev. [Dar es Salaam? 1946] 47 p. (Course of lectures for East Africa rural dressers) 4RC 257
Text in English and Swahili.

811
Ebrahim, C. J. Child care in the tropics. Nairobi, East African Literature Bureau [1971] 112 p. illus. RJ61.E17

812
______ The newborn in tropical Africa. Nairobi, East African Literature Bureau [1969] 111 p. illus. DLC

813
______, *ed.* Practical maternal and child health problems in tropical Africa. Nairobi, East African Literature Bureau [1968] 63 p. illus.
RG518.A3E2

814
______ Practical mother and child health in developing countries. Nairobi, East African Literature Bureau [1974?] 108 p. DLC

815
Koeune, Esther. How to teach hygiene, home nursing and first aid: a book for primary

schools and welfare centres in East Africa. With a foreword by R. Y. Dunlop. Nairobi, Eagle Press, 1950. 64 p. illus. DHU
2d rev. ed. was issued in Nairobi by Longmans of Kenya in 1966 [c1963].
Issued also in Swahili.

816
_______ Jinsi ya kufundisha afya, uuguzi wa nyumbani na msaada wa kwanza; kitabu kwa skuli za primary na majengo ya maendeleo katika Afrika Mashariki. Dar es Salaam, East African Literature Bureau, 1962. 77 p. illus. DLC
Title translated: How to teach hygiene, home nursing and first aid.
Text in Swahili.
Issued also in English.

817
_______ Mafundisho ya afya katika skuli za chini. Nairobi, East African Literature Bureau, 1971+ illus. LB3409.A42K63
First published 1962.
Title translated: The teaching of health in junior schools.
Text in Swahili.
L.C. has kitabu cha kwanza.

818
_______ The teaching of health-training in the junior school. Book one, class I to III. Nairobi, Eagle Press, 1953. 106 p. illus. DHU

819
_______ _______ Book two, class IV. Nairobi, Eagle Press, 1953. 75 p. illus. DHU

820
Mamuya, S. J. Maarifa mapya ya kuwaelimisha watu afya na mambo mengine. [Das es Salaam, East African Literature Bureau] 1970 [i.e. 1971] 222 p. illus. DLC
Title translated: New information on teaching health, and other topics.
Text in Swahili.

821
Mandao, Martha. Tupigane na safura. Nairobi, East African Literature Bureau [1967] 17 p. illus. DLC
Title translated: Let's fight hookworms.
Text in Swahili.

822
Twining, Helen Mary Twining, *Baroness.* The home care of the mental patient in the village. Nairobi, East African Literature Bureau [1966] 22 p. illus. RC480.5.T85

Higher Education

823
Conference on the University of East Africa, *Nairobi, 1967.* Background information. [Nairobi? 1967] 72 leaves. illus. LG418.N3C6 1967

824
_______ _______ Supplement. Nairobi, 1967. 19 leaves. DLC

825
_______ Report. [Kampala, Printed by Uganda Press, 1967] 141 p. LG418.N3C6 1967b

826
Dar-es-Salaam. University College. Plans and perspectives [submissions to the] University of East Africa Kenya Conference, October 1967. Dar-es-Salaam [1967] 77 p. DLC

East African Examination Council.
Note: The council was created in 1967 to administer the examinations for the high school certificates in East Africa in cooperation with the University of East Africa. After the University of East Africa was dissolved in 1970, the University of Dar es Salaam, the University of Nairobi, and Makerere University continued to cooperate with the council in a joint program. Funds are provided to the council by the three East African governments independently, and through the East African Community.

827
Annual report. 1967/68+ [Kampala, Uganda] LB3058.E2E23a

Report year ends June 30.
Includes results of examinations in subjects, and award of certificates for Kenya, Tanzania, and Uganda.
L.C. has 1967/68+

828
_______ East African advanced certificate of education: regulations and syllabuses. Kampala. annual. DLC
L.C. has 1974+

829
_______ East African certificate of education: regulations and syllabuses. Kampala. annual. LB3058.T3E37a
L.C. has 1974+

830
Giffen, Edmund, *and* D. H. Alexander. Report by E. Giffen and D. H. Alexander to the chairman of the East Africa High Commission on a visit to the Royal Technical College of East Africa in November and December, 1956. [n.p., 1957?] 47 [i.e. 46] leaves. CLU
Also issued as Appendix II to Higher education in East Africa (item 834).

831
Gt. Brit. *Commission on Higher Education in East Africa.* Higher education in East Africa. Report of the Commission appointed by the Secretary of State for the Colonies. London, H.M. Stationery Off., 1937. 136 p. fold. map. ([Gt. Brit. Colonial Office] Colonial no. 142) LA1563.A5 1937
De La Warr, chairman.
Minority report (p. 123–130) signed: John Murray.
A report upon the higher education in East Africa, with particular reference to Uganda, and the working of Markerere College, Kampala, Uganda.

832
Gt. Brit. *Working Party on Higher Education in East Africa.* Report. [Nairobi, Printed for the East African Governments by the Govt. Printer, 1959] 48 p. map. LA1563.A53
J. F. Lockwood, chairman.

833
The Higher College of East Africa; proceedings of the inter-territorial conference held at Makerere, Uganda, on the 21st, 23rd and 24th May, 1938 to examine the practical steps necessary to implement the recommendations of the Commission on Higher Education in East Africa for the establishment of a higher college. Entebbe, Printed by the Govt. Printer, 1938. DLC-Micro 23940 reel 5 octavo 244
Collation of the original: 34 p. fold. map.
W. H. Kauntze, chairman.
Colonial Office Library East Africa pamphlet octavo 244.
Representatives from Kenya, Tanganyika, Uganda, and Zanzibar recommended the creation of Makerere College to be located in Kampala, Uganda.

834
Higher education in East Africa. Entebbe, Govt. Printer [1958] 123 p. MdU
J. F. Lockwood, chairman.
"This White paper is issued jointly by the governments of Kenya, Tanganyika, and Uganda, and His Highness's Government of Zanzibar."
Appendix I: Report of the Working Party on Higher Education in East Africa, July-August, 1955 (Sir Alexander M. Carr-Saunders, chairman).—Appendix II: Report by E. Giffen and D. H. Alexander ... on a visit to the Royal Technical College of East Africa in November and December, 1956.

835
Nairobi. Royal Technical College of East Africa. Memorandum by governing council on the Report of the Working Party on Higher Education, 1955. [Nairobi, 1957?] 14, [2] p. (Council paper 134)
Source: Col. Off. Lib. Cat.

836
Quinquennial Advisory Committee. Report,

1960. [Nairobi, Printed for the East African Governments by the Govt. Printer, Kenya, 1960] 15 p. LA1563.Q5

E. B. David, chairman.

The Committee was appointed "to consider the proposals for, and the estimated cost of, higher education in East Africa in the five years from 1961 to 1966."

837

Tanganyika. Higher education in East Africa. [Dar es Salaam? 1958?] (Tanganyika. Legislative Council. Government paper, 1958, no. 1)

Source: Tanganyika debates, May 6, 1958.

838

Uganda. Minutes by the Government on Makerere College in relation to higher education for Africans in East Africa. [Entebbe? Govt. Press, 1936?]

DLC-Micro 23940 reel 11 folio 279

Collation of the original: 9 p.

Colonial Office Library East Africa pamphlet folio 279.

Appendixes include: Summary of report of the Sub-committee of the Advisory Committee on Education in the Colonies on the subject of university education in Africa together with the Minute theron of the East African Directors of Education.—Speech by His Excellency the Governor at Makerere on the 21st December, 1935.

839

University of East Africa. Draft university development plan for the triennium 1964/67. [Entebbe] 1963. 106 p.

Source: Dar es Salaam Lib. Bull. no. 79.

840

_______ First degree courses. Kampala [196-?]

Source: Dar es Salaam Lib. Bull. no. 85.

841

_______ The University of East Africa development plan, second triennium, 1967–70. [Kampala, Uganda, 1967] 101 p.

LG421.K37A53

On cover: The University of East Africa triennial development plan, 1967–70.

842

University of East Africa. *Committee on Needs and Priorities.* Report, 1962. Entebbe, Printed by the Govt. Printer [1963] 122 p.

LG421.E57U54 1963

843

University of East Africa. *Grants Committee.* Report. Kampala.

Source for 1964, and 1967: Makerere Lib. Union list.

844

Working Party on Entrance Levels and Degree Structure of the University of East Africa. Report. [n.p.] 1964. 71 p. WvU

845

Working Party on Higher Education in East Africa. Report. Submitted to East African Authority at Arusha, January 31, 1969. [Arusha, 1969] 69, [43] leaves. LA1558.W67

George D. Stoddard, chairman.

Recommended the creation of national universities in Kenya, Tanzania, and Uganda, and the dissolving of the University of East Africa.

Teacher Education

846

Callander, J. F. Suggestions for head teachers. Nairobi, East African Literature Bureau, 1961. 65 p. illus. WvU

847

Conference on Institutes of Education, *Mombasa, Kenya, 1964.* A report. Edited and reported by: Arthur J. Lewis [and] L. V. Lieb. [Mombasa? 1964?] 99 p. LB2130.C66 1964

848

Conference on Teacher Education for East Africa, *5th, Makerere University College, 1967.* A report. Edited by Carl J. Manone. [Kampala, Uganda, 1967?] 141 p. L106 1967.C6

849
Lieb, L. V. A report of the University of East Africa Conference on Permanent Staffing of Teacher Education Institutions, April 4–6, 1966, Dar es Salaam, Tanzania, East Africa. Edited and reported by L. V. Lieb. [n.p., 1966?] xxii, 111 p. LB2175.A42L53
Includes information on teacher education for Kenya, Tanzania, and Uganda.

850
University of East Africa Conference on New Directions in East African Teacher Education: Innovation, Implementation, and Evaluation, *7th, Mombasa, 1968.* A report. Edited by Carl J. Manone. [Mombasa? Kenya, 1968] 152 p. LB1727.A355U5 1968

851
University of East Africa Conference on Teacher Education, *8th, Dar es Salaam, 1969.* Staffing teacher education institutions in East Africa: supply and demand, training, and utilization; a report. Edited by Carl J. Manone. [Dar es Salaam, 1969] 1. v. (various pagings) LB1727.A355U53 1969
Includes Progress reports, 1968/69, of the Kenya Institute of Education, of the Institute of Education, University College, Dar es Salaam, of the National Institute of Education, Makerere University College, and of the Institute of Education of the University of Zambia.

852
Universities of Eastern Africa Conference on Teacher Education, *9th, National Institute of Education (Uganda), 1970.* Critical issues in teacher education; proceedings. Edited by Carl J. Manone. [Kampala, Uganda, 1971?] 177 p. LB1727.A355U49 1970
Includes Progress reports, 1969/70, of the Kenya Institute of Education, of the Institute of Education, University of Dar es Salaam, of the National Institute of Education, Makerere University, and of the Institute of Education, University of Zambia.

853
Universities of Eastern Africa Conference on Teacher Education, *10th, University of Nairobi, 1971.* The role of teacher education in promoting rural transformation; proceedings. Carl J. Manone, editor. [Kampala, National Institute of Education, 1972] 169 p. LB1727.K4U54 1971
Includes Progress reports, 1970/71, of the Kenya Institute of Education, of the Institute of Education, University of Dar es Salaam, of the National Institute of Education, Makerere University, and of the Institute of Education, University of Zambia.

854
Universities of Eastern Africa Conference on Teacher Education, *11th, Dar es Salaam, 1972.* Strategies for educational change. Dar es Salaam, University of Dar es Salaam, Institute of Education, 1972. 78 p. DLC

Technical and Vocational Education

Home Economics

855
Hume, Violet R. Watoto wetu: ulinzi na malezi yao, kimeandikwa kwa Kiingereza na V. R. Hume pamoja na J. M. Wigram. Kimefasiriwa kwa Kiswahili na Hyder M. Matano. Nairobi, East African Literature Bureau [1973] 175 p. illus. DLC
Title translated: Our children: their supervision and upbringing.
Text in Swahili.

856
Koeune, Esther. The African housewife and her home. With a foreword by H. Neatby. Nairobi, Eagle Press, East African Literature Bureau, 1952. 186 p. illus. DHU

857
——— ——— Dar es Salaam, East African Literature Bureau [1971] 193 p. illus. TX115.K63

858
_______ Cooking for the family in East Africa. Kampala, Eagle Press, 1953. 91 p. illus. DHU

859
_______ _______ Kampala, East African Literature Bureau [1970] 95 p. illus.
TX661.K64 1970

"First published 1953. New edition containing Tanganyika recipes 1955 ... Reprinted 1970."

860
Lyth, Nora. Kufuma kumefanywa rahisi. Nairobi, East African Literature Bureau, 1972. 31 p. illus. DLC

First published 1964.

Title translated: Knitting made easy.

Text in Swahili.

861
Maletnlema, T. N. Utunzaji wa mama na watoto vijijini. (Rural mother and child care). Nairobi, East African Literature Bureau [1971] 256 p. illus. DLC

Text in Swahili.

862
Pelham-Johnson, M. Binti Leo kwake. Tabora, T.M.P. Book Dept., 1967. 35 p. illus.
TX162.P45 1967

"First published 1950 E[ast] A[frican] L[iterature] B[ureau]."

Title translated: Today's woman at home.

Text in Swahili.

Textbooks

863
Desai, N. C., *and* K. S. Forland. Elementary chemical calculations. Nairobi, East African Literature Bureau [1968] 59 p. (Let's find out about...) DLC

864
Entwistle, A. R. Handbook of physical education for schools. Book I, boys and girls, standards I-IV. Kampala, Eagle Press, 1957. 168 p. DHU

865
Gregory, R. M. The teaching of homecraft; a handbook for African teachers. Nairobi, Eagle Press, 1958. 95 p. illus. WvU

866
Hastie, Catherine. How to organize handcraft competitions in women's groups. Kampala, East African Literature Bureau, 1962. 55 p. illus. DLC

867
Jury, S. J. Cash accounting for the African trader. Nairobi, Pitman, Eagle Press [1951] 31 p. DHU

868
King, M. C. Notes for teachers on the school compound and garden. Nairobi, Eagle Press, 1957. 25 p. illus. DHU

869
Kingsbury, O. A. Economics for East Africa. Nairobi, East African Literature Bureau. Eagle Press, 1959. 146 p. CSt-H

Textbook of the elements of economic theory.

870
_______ _______ [2d ed.] Nairobi, Highway Press, 1965 [sic, i.e. 1968] 146 p. illus.
HB171.5.K517

871
Kurtz, Margaret A. Secretarial dictation. Nairobi, East African Literature Bureau [1971] 175 p. DLC

872
McKenzie, John C. Creative activities, art and craftwork for primary I and II. Nairobi, East African Literature Bureau, 1962. 19 p. illus. DLC

873
——— ——— Nairobi, East African Literature Bureau [1971] 19 p. illus. DLC

874
McKilliam, K. R. A handbook for literacy teachers. Nairobi, East African Literature Bureau [1964] 62 p. illus. LB1573.M176

875
McNeil, R. T. Handbook of physical education for schools. Book III, boys, standard V-VII. Kampala, Eagle Press, 1957. 135 p. illus. DHU

876
Millar, Douglas J. A four-year course of lessons in physical education for African primary schools. Nairobi, East African Literature Bureau, Eagle Press, 1960. 117 p. WvU

877
——— A four-year course of lessons in physical education for primary schools. Nairobi, East African Literature Bureau [1971] 117 p. DLC

878
Ng'weno, Hilary. Let's find out about atoms. Edited by Dr. P. Gacii. Nairobi, East African Literature Bureau [1970] 45 p. illus. (Popular science readers series) DLC

879
——— Let's find out about energy and machines. Edited by P. Gacii. Nairobi, East African Literature Bureau [1969] 47 p. illus. (Popular science readers series) DLC

880
——— Let's find out about heat. Edited by P. Gacii. Nairobi, East African Literature Bureau [1968] 37 p. illus. (Popular science readers series) DLC

881
——— Let's find out about light. Edited by P. Gacii. Nairobi, East African Literature Bureau [1968] 34 p. illus. (Popular science readers series) DLC

882
——— Let's find out about sound. Edited by P. Gacii. Nairobi, East African Literature [1968] 27 p. illus. (Popular science readers series) DLC

883
——— Let's find out about the universe. Edited by P. Gacii. Nairobi, East African Literature Bureau [1968] 44 p. illus. (Poplar science readers series) DLC

884
Pelham-Johnson, M. F. Muhtasari ya kazi ya kushona, sehemu ya kwanza, madarasa ya II-V. Nairobi, Eagle Press, 1951. 8 p. illus. DHU

Title translated: Scheme of work for sewing classes, part one, standards II-V.

Text in Swahili.

885
——— Scheme of work for sewing classes, part two, standards VI-VIII and school certificate work. Nairobi, Eagle Press, 1951. 8 p. illus. DHU

886
Perren, G. Guide to teaching English in African primary and intermediate schools together with schemes of work. Kampala, Eagle Press, 1954. 49 p. DHU

887
Phiri, Desmond D. Hints to private students. Dar es Salaam, East African Literature Bureau [1966] 69 p. DLC

First published 1961.

"This book is written, therefore, in response to a widely felt need among young men and women who have the ambition to study and would like to be suitably advised on how to do so successfully."

888
Place, James. A school history of Britain and

western Europe for East Africa, book two. Nairobi, Eagle Press, 1954. 91 p. DHU

889
Popkin, J. M. Geography, history, civics; lessons for standard three in African primary schools. Kampala, Eagle Press, 1954. 56 p. illus. DHU

890
Roberts, Helen M. In the beginning, retold from the Bible. Published for Adult Literacy Organizing Centre, Nairobi. Nairobi, East African Literature Bureau, 1962. 42 p. illus. DLC

891
Ross, F. E. How to mark out fields, grounds, courts and tracks. Foreword by A. Evans. Nairobi, Eagle Press, 1954. 28 p. illus. DHU

892
Smith, J. Stephen. Aids to scoutmasters in East Africa. Nairobi, Eagle Press, 1951. 49 p. illus. DHU

893
Thorkil, Søe. Technical drawing for civil engineers. [Nairobi] East African Literature Bureau [1973] 69 p. illus. DLC

Finance

Banks and Banking

894
Conference of Governors of British East African Territories. *Statistical Dept.* Analysis of bank statistics for British East Africa, 1927 to 1931. Part I: Kenya Colony and Protectorate. Prepared under the direction of A. Walter, Statistician to the Conference of East African Governors, and Director of the Meteorological Service. [Nairobi? 1931] 35, 33 p. *(Its* Memoir no. 4) MiEM

895
Conference on Public Policy, *2d, University College, Nairobi, 1963.* Conferences on public policy, 1963/4: East African federation; [paper no. 9] Central banking in an East African federation [by] Brian Van Arkadie. [Nairobi? 1964?] 7 leaves. HC517.E2C6 1963 no. 9

Later revised as Central banking in an East African federation, published in Colin Leys' Federation in East Africa; opportunities and problems (Nairobi, London, Oxford University Press, 1965 [i.e. 1966] HC517.E2L4) p. [145]-157.

896
East African Common Services Organization. *East African Statistical Dept.* Statistics of commercial banks; assets [and] liabilities. Nairobi. annual. MBU

No more published.

Later information on the assets and liabilities of commercial banks is included in the agency's Economic and statistical review (item 761).

MBU received 1967; apparently not retained.

897
_______ Statistics of the commercial banks: Kenya. –1967? Nairobi. monthly. MBU

Superseded by Statistics of the commercial banks, assets and liabilities: Kenya (item 901) issued by the East African Statistical Dept. of the East African Community.

Statistical data on the Kenya commercial banks is included also in the agency's Economic and statistical review (item 761).

MBU has 1965–67 (scattered issues wanting).

898
_______ Statistics of the commercial banks:

Tanzania. –1967? Nairobi. monthly. MBU
Superseded by Statistics of the commercial banks, assets and liabilities: Tanzania (item 902) issued by the East African Statistical Dept. of the East African Community.
Statistical data on the Tanzania commercial banks is included also in the agency's Economic and statistical review (item 761).
MBU has 1965–67 (scattered issues wanting).

899
——— Statistics of the commercial banks: Uganda. –1968? Nairobi. monthly. MBU
Superseded by Statistics of the commercial banks, assets and liabilities: Uganda (item 903) issued by the East African Statistical Dept. of the East African Community.
Statistical data on the Uganda commercial banks is included also in the agency's Economic and statistical review (item 761).
MBU has 1965–68 (scattered issues wanting).

900
——— Statistics of the commercial banks: Zanzibar. –1967? Nairobi. monthly. MBU
MBU has 1965–67 (scattered issues wanting).

901
East African Community. *East African Statistical Dept.* Statistics of the commercial banks, assets and liabilities: Kenya. [Nairobi?] monthly.
Supersedes Statistics of the commercial banks: Kenya (item 897) issued by the East African Statistical Dept. of the East African Common Services Organization.
Statistical data on the Kenya commercial banks is included also in the agency's Economic and statistical review (item 763), and also in the Statistical abstract issued by the Central Bureau of Statistics of Kenya.
Source for July-Dec. 1969: Makerere Lib. Bull. no. 77.

902
——— Statistics of the comercial banks, assets and liabilities: Tanzania. [Nairobi?] monthly.
Supersedes Statistics of the commercial banks: Tanzania (item 898) issued by the East African Statistical Dept. of the East African Common Services Organization.
Statistical data on the Tanzania commercial banks is included also in the agency's Economic and statistical review (item 763).
Source for July-Dec. 1969: Makerere Lib. Bull. no. 77.

903
——— Statistics of the commercial banks, assets and liabilities: Uganda. [Nairobi?] monthly.
Supersedes Statistics of the comercial banks: Uganda (item 899) issued by the East African Statistical Dept. of the East African Common Services Organization.
Statistical data on the Uganda commercial banks is included also in the agency's Economic and statistical review (item 763).
Source for July-Dec. 1969: Makerere Lib. Bull. no. 77.

East African Development Bank.
Note: The East African Development Bank was created on December 1, 1967, by the Treaty for East African Co-operation, Articles 21–22, and annex VI, the Charter of the East African Development Bank. The bank invests in industrial projects in the manufacturing and processing areas of the economies of the three partner states. One of the objectives of the bank is to provide additional industrial development incentive for the two less developed partner states, Tanzania and Uganda, by using a formula for investment of 38.75 percent for Tanzania and Uganda, and 22.5 percent for Kenya. The bank is located in new headquarters in Kampala, Uganda, with regional offices in Dar es Salaam, Tanzania, and Nairobi, Kenya.

904
Annual report. 1968+ [Kampala, Uganda]
HG3729.A37E24
First report covers period Dec. 1, 1967–Dec. 31, 1968.
L.C. has 1968+

905

_______ Guide to investors. Kampala [1968] 7 p. DLC

906

East African Posts and Telecommunications Administration. Report on the Kenya Post Office Savings Bank. 1961–67. [Nairobi] annual. HG1956.K4E2a

Supersedes in part the agency's Report on the Kenya, Uganda and Tanganyika post office savings banks.

Superseded by a publication with the same title (item 910) issued by the East African Posts and Telecommunications Corporation.

Statistical data on the Kenya Post Office Savings Bank is included also in the Economic and statistical review (item 761) issued by the East African Statistical Dept. of the East African Common Services Organization, and also in the Statistical abstract issued by the Statistics Division of the Ministry of Economic Planning and Development of Kenya.

L.C. and DJBF have 1961–67.

907

_______ Report on the Kenya, Uganda and Tanganyika post office savings banks. 1948–60. [Nairobi, Govt. Printer] annual. HG1946.A4E4

Supersedes the Annual report on the Kenya, Uganda and Tanganyika savings banks (item 915) issued by the Audit Dept. of Kenya Colony and Protectorate.

Title varies: 1948–58, Report on the Kenya, Uganda and Tanganyika savings banks.

Vols. for 1948–1950? issued by the agency under its earlier name: East African Posts and Telegraphs Dept.

Superseded by the agency's Report on the Kenya Post Office Savings Bank, the agency's Report on the Tanganyika Post Office Savings Bank, and the agency's Report on the Uganda Post Office Savings Bank (item 909).

Statistical data for the post office savings banks is included also in the Quarterly economic and statistical bulletin (item 752) issued by the East African Statistical Dept. of the East Africa High Commission, and also in the statistical abstracts of Kenya, Tanganyika, and Uganda.

L.C. catalogs 1952 under: Kenya Colony and Protectorate. *Audit Dept.* (HG1946.K4A3).

L.C. has 1952–60; source for 1948–60: SCOLMA, May 1969.

908

_______ Report on the Tanzania Post Office Savings Bank. 1961–67. [Nairobi] annual. HG1956.T35E2a

Supersedes in part the agency's Report on the Kenya, Uganda and Tanganyika post office savings banks.

Title varies: 1961–63, Report on the Tanganyika Post Office Savings Bank.

Superseded by a publication with the same title (item 911) issued by the East African Posts and Telecommunications Corporation.

Statistical data on the Tanzania Post Office Savings Bank is included also in the Economic and statistical review (item 761) issued by the East African Statistical Dept. of the East African Common Services Organization, and also in the Statistical abstract issued by the Central Statistical Bureau of Tanzania.

L.C. and DJBF have 1961–67.

909

_______ Report on the Uganda Post Office Savings Bank. 1961–67. [Nairobi?] annual. DLC

Supersedes in part the agency's Report on the Kenya, Uganda and Tanganyika post office savings banks (item 907).

Superseded by a publication with the same title (item 912) issued by the East African Posts and Telecommunications Corporation.

Statistical data on the Uganda Post Office Savings Bank is included also in the Economic and statistical review (item 761) issued by the East African Statistical Dept. of the East African Common Services Organization, and also in the Statistical abstract issued by the Statistics Division of the Ministry of Planning and Economic Development of Uganda.

L.C. and DJBF have 1961–67.

910

East African Posts and Telecommunications Corporation. Report on the Kenya Post Office Savings Bank. 1968+ [Nairobi] annual. HG1956.K4E2a

Supersedes a publication with the same title (item 906) issued by the East African Posts and Telecommunications Administration.

Statistical data on post office savings banks in Kenya is included also in the Economic and statistical review (item 763) issued by the East African Statistical Dept. of the East African Community, and also in the Statistical abstract issued by the Central Bureau of Statistics of Kenya.

L.C. has 1968+

911

——— Report on the Tanganyika Post Office Savings Bank. 1968+ [Nairobi] annual.
HG1956.T35E2a

Supersedes Report of the Tanzania Post Office Savings Bank (item 908) issued by the East African Posts and Telecommunications Administration.

Title varies: 1968– , Report on the Tanzania Post Office Savings Bank.

Statistical data on post office savings banks in Tanzania is included also in the Economic and statistical review (item 763) issued by the East African Statistical Dept. of the East African Community, and also in the Statistical abstract issued by the Bureau of Statistics of Tanzania.

L.C. and DJBF have 1968+ (1969 wanting).

912

——— Report on the Uganda Post Office Savings Bank. 1968+ [Nairobi?] annual.
HG1956.U4E2a

Supersedes a publication with the same title (item 909) issued by the East African Posts and Telecommunications Administration.

Statistical data on post office savings banks in Uganda is included also in the Economic and statistical review (item 763) issued by the East African Statistical Dept. of the East African Community, and also in the Statistical abstract issued by the Statistics Division of the Ministry of Planning and Economic Development of Uganda.

L.C. has 1968+

913

International Conference on Special Problems of Development Banks in Eastern Africa, *Kampala, Uganda, 1969*. Summary report. [Berlin] German Foundation for Developing Countries, Conferences and Documentation Division [1969] 45 p. (German Foundation for Developing Countries. Dok 489 B/a, It 31/69)
HC59.7.D385 no. 489 B/a

"In cooperation with East African Development Bank and Kreditanstalt für Wiederaufbau, October 20 to 25, 1969."

914

Kenya. *Treaties, etc. June 6, 1967*. Charter of the East African Development Bank; constituting annex VI to the Treaty for East African co-operation, signed at Kampala, Uganda, on 6th June, 1967, on behalf of the governments of the United Republic Tanzania, the sovereign State of Uganda and the Republic of Kenya. [Entebbe, Govt. Printer, 1971] 27 p. DLC–LL

915

Kenya Colony aind Protectorate. *Audit Dept.* Annual report on the Kenya, Uganda and Tanganyika savings banks. 1937–47. Nairobi, Printed by the Govt. Printer. HG1946.K4A3

Superseded by the Report on the Kenya, Uganda and Tanganyika savings banks (item 907) issued by the East African Posts and Telegraphs Dept.

Each issue includes statistical data for a ten year period.

L.C. has 1937–38.

916

Kenya Colony and Protectorate. *Posts and Telegraphs Dept.* Post office savings bank instructions. [Nairobi, Govt. Printer, 1946?] 32 p.

Source: Kenya Govt. Print. rept., 1946.

Currency

East African Currency Board.

Note: The East African Currency Board was created in December 1919 and charged with responsibility for issuing the lawful money of Kenya, Tanganyika, and Uganda. The board's offices were located in the office of the Crown Agents for the Colonies in London. On January 1, 1936, Zanzibar joined the currency area. During and after World War II the East African shilling was also the currency of Aden, certain areas of occupied Italian East Africa, and British Somaliland (until 1961). In 1960, the board was reconstituted within the framework of the East African Common Services Organization and moved from London to Nairobi, Kenya. In June 1965, the finance ministers of Kenya, Tanzania, and Uganda announced that national banks would be established in each country and that separate currencies would be issued. Tanzania began to issue its own currency notes on June 14, 1966, with Uganda following on August 15, 1966, and Kenya changing on September 14, 1966. During 1967, the board's currency functions were terminated in all three countries. On January 1, 1972, the central banks of Kenya, Tanzania, and Uganda assumed responsibility for any further redemption of the board's outstanding East African shillings. "A brief outline history of the Board" is included in the agency's final report [1971/72] (item 918).

917
Regulations defining the constitution, duties and powers of the East African Currency Board, as revised and approved on 11th January 1949 [by A. Creech-Jones, Secretary of State for the Colonies] [London? 1949?]
DLC-Micro 23940 reel 14 folio 416

Collation of the original: [3] leaves.

Colonial Office Library East Africa pamphlet folio 416.

Revokes "the regulations defining the constitution, duties and powers of the Board dated 11th July, 1932, and the regulations dated the 29th October, 1935."

918
______ Report. 1920/21-[1971/72] [Nairobi] annual. HG1350.E3A3

Report year ends June 30.

Vols. for 1920/21-1958/59 published in London by Waterlow.

Vol. for 1920/21 includes "Regulations defining the constitution, duties and powers of the East African Currency Board."

L.C. catalogs 1971/72 under: East African Currency Board. The final report of the East African Currency Board, with the call no.: HG1350.E2E37 1972.

L.C. has 1920/21-1971/72 (1940/41 and 1943/44 wanting).

919
Gt. Brit. *Colonial Office*. East Africa, correspondence, 2nd February, 1911, to 19th December, 1913, relating to currency questions in East Africa. [London] Printed for the use of the Colonial Office, 1915. (*Its* African no. 976, confidential) DLC-Micro 03759

Collation of the original: 58 p.

[Gt. Brit.] Public Record Office. C.O. 879/109.

Includes the Report (p. 16-18) of the East Africa Protectorate Currency Committee, and a memorandum on proposed currency changes in the East Africa Protectorate and Uganda (p. 30-37) by C. C. Bowring, Acting Governor of the East Africa Protectorate.

Insurance

920
East Africa High Commission. *East African Statistical Dept*. East Africa insurance statistics. 1950/58-1959. Nairobi, annual (irregular). HG8725.E3A2

Vol. for 1950/58 issued by the agency's East African Unit.

Superseded by a publication with the same title issued by the East African Statistical Dept. of the East African Common Services Organization.

"Statistics of insurance in East Africa, covering the years 1947 to 1951 were first published in 1953 in the East African Statistical Bulletin no. 21. Another set of figures for the years 1947 to 1957 was published in Bulletin no. 42, 1958. For this issue [i.e. 1950/58] the figures published in 1953 were revised and superseded."

Includes statistics for East Africa, Kenya, Tanganyika, and Uganda.

L.C. has 1950/58-1959.

921
East African Common Services Organization. *East African Statistical Dept*. East Africa insurance statistics. 1960-65. [Nairobi] annual (irregular). HG8725.E3A2

Supersedes a publication with the same title issued by the East African Statistical Dept. of the East Africa High Commission.

Superseded by a publication with the same title issued by the East African Statistical Dept. of the East African Community.

Includes statistics for East Africa, Kenya, Tanzania, and Uganda.

L.C. has 1960–65.

922
East African Community. *East African Statistical Dept.* East Africa insurance statistics. 1966–67. [Nairobi] annual (irregular) HG8725.E3A2

Supersedes a publication with the same title issued by the East African Statistical Dept. of the East African Common Services Organization.

No more published.

Includes statistics for East Africa, Kenya, Tanzania, and Uganda.

L.C. has 1966–67.

Public Finance (including Budget)

The following entries (items 923–59) are arranged chronologically.

1890–1947

923
Great Britain. Regulations for the guidance of the accounting officers of the protectorates of Uganda, British Central Africa, and British East Africa, in rendering accounts of the receipts and expenditure for imperial audit. [London? 189–?] DLC-Micro 23940 reel 8 folio 2

Collation of the original: 34 p. (chiefly forms).

Colonial Office Library East Africa pamphlet folio 2.

924
Gt. Brit. *Colonial Office.* East Africa; papers relating to the estimates of the East African protectorates for 1907 and 1907–8. [London] Printed for the use of the Colonial Office, 1907. (*Its* African no. 865, confidential) DLC-Micro 03759

Collation of the original: 58 p.

[Gt. Brit.] Public Record Office. C.O. 879/94.

Includes budget estimates for the East Africa Protectorate, Uganda, Somaliland, and the Uganda Railway.

925
——— East Africa, papers relating to the estimates of the East African protectorates for 1908 and 1908–9. [London] Printed for the use of the Colonial Office, 1908. (*Its* African no. 895, confidential) DLC-Micro 03759

Collation of the original: 93 p.

[Gt. Brit.] Public Record Office. C.O. 879/97.

Includes budget estimates for Uganda, the East Africa Protectorate, and the Uganda Railway.

926
——— East Africa, papers relating to the estimates of the East African protectorates for 1909 and 1909–10. [London] Printed for the use of the Colonial Office, 1910. (*Its* African no. 921, confidential) DLC-Micro 03759

Collation of the original: 114 p. fold. map.

[Gt. Brit.] Public Record Office. C.O. 879/100.

Includes budget information for the East Africa Protectorate and Uganda.

927
——— East Africa, papers relating to the estimates of the East African protectorates for 1910 and 1910–11. [London] Printed for the use of the Colonial Office, 1911. (*Its* African no. 944, confidential) DLC-Micro 03759

Collation of the oriignal: 161 p.

[Gt. Brit.] Public Record Office. C.O. 879/103.

Includes budget information for the East Africa Protectorate and Uganda.

928
——— East Africa, papers relating to estimates of the East African protectorates for 1911 and 1911–12. [London] Printed for the use of the Colonial Office, 1913. (*Its* African no. 964, confidential) DLC-Micro 03759

Collation of the original: 191 p.

[Gt. Brit.] Public Record Office. C.O. 879/105.

Includes budget information for the East Africa Protectorate and Uganda.

929

——— East Africa, correspondence, 19th October 1911–31st August 1913, relating to the estimates of the East African protectorates. [London] Printed for the use of the Colonial Office, 1914. (*Its* Arfican no. 983, confidential)
DLC-Micro 03759

Collation of the original: xxi, 338 p.

[Gt. Brit.] Public Record Office. C.O. 879/109.

Includes budget information for the East Africa Protectorate, Uganda, and the Uganda Railway.

930

——— East Africa, correspondence, September, 1913–September, 1914, relating to the estimates of the East African protectorates. [London] Printed for the use of the Colonial Office, 1915. (*Its* African no. 996, confidential)
DLC-Micro 03759

Collation of the original: xxi, 298 p.

[Gt. Brit.] Public Record Office. C.O. 879/111.

Includes information on estimates for the East Africa Protectorate, Uganda, and Zanzibar.

931

——— East Africa, further correspondence, 16th September 1914–23rd September 1915, relating to the estimates of the East African protectorates. [London] Printed for the use of the Colonial Office, 1916. (*Its* African no. 1027, confidential) DLC-Micro 03759

Collation of the original: 163 p.

[Gt. Brit.] Public Record Office. C.O. 879/116.

Includes budget information for the East Africa Protectorate, Uganda, and Zanzibar.

932

——— Operations in East Africa; correspondence, 6th February 1915 to 13th March 1917, relating to war expenditure. [London] Printed for the use of the Colonial Office, 1918. (*Its* African no. 1040, confidential)
DLC-Micro 03759

Collation of the original: xxxvi, 218 p.

[Gt. Brit.] Public Record Office. C.O. 879/117.

Includes information on the East Africa Protectorate, Uganda, Zanzibar, the Uganda Railway, and German East Africa.

933

——— East Africa, further correspondence, 27th October 1915 to 15th August 1917, relating to the estimates of the East African protectorates. [London] Printed for the use of the Colonial Office, 1918. (*Its* African no. 1041, confidential) DLC-Micro 03759

Collation of the original: 176 p.

[Gt. Brit.] Public Record Office. C.O. 879/117.

Includes budget information for the East Africa Protectorate, Uganda, and Zanzibar.

934

——— East Africa, further correspondence, 1918–1920, relating to the estimates of the East African colonies and protectorates. [London] Printed for the use of the Colonial Office, 1923. (*Its* African no. 1063, confidential)
DLC-Micro 03759

Collation of the original: 378 p.

[Gt. Brit.] Public Record Office. C.O. 879/119.

Includes budget information for the East Africa Protectorate, Uganda, Tanganyika (1920 only), and Zanzibar (1918–19 only).

935

——— East Africa, further correspondence, 1921–1922, relating to the estimates of the East African colonies and protectorates. [London] Printed for the use of the Colonial Office, 1923. (*Its* African no. 1089, confidential)
DLC-Micro 03759

Collation of the original: 354 p.

[Gt. Brit.] Public Record Office. C.O. 879/120.

Includes budget information for Kenya, Uganda, and Zanzibar.

936

Gt. Brit. *Inter-departmental Committee on the Apportionment of the East African War Expenditure.* Report London, Printed by H.M. Stationery Off. Press [1925]

DLC-Micro 23940 reel 2 octavo 75

Collation of the original: 23 p

Walter Guinness, chairman.

Colonial Office Library East Africa pamphlet octavo 75.

"Terms of reference: 'To report as to the precise liabilities of Kenya Colony, the Uganda Protectorate and the Nyasaland Protectorate in respect of the East African war expenditure under the arrangements made during the war; what rate of interest, if any, should be charged thereon, and from what date.' "

937

Great Britain. Palestine and East Africa loans. Memorandum explaining financial resolution. London, H.M. Stationery Off., 1926. 3 p. ([Gt. Brit. Parliament. Papers by command] Cmd. 2696) J301.K6 1926 v. 23

938

Gt. Brit. *Colonial Office. East African Guaranteed Loan Committee.* East Africa. Report of the East African Guaranteed Loan Committee appointed by the Secretary of State for the Colonies. London, H.M. Stationery Off., 1926. 47 p. ([Gt. Brit. Parliament. Papers by command] Cmd. 2701) HJ1594.A5 1926

Sir George Schuster, chairman.

"First interim report of the East African Guaranteed Loan Committee:" p. 44–47.

939

——— East Africa. Report of the East African Guaranteed Loan Committee appointed by the Secretary of State for the Colonies, 1926–1929. London, H.M. Stationery Off., 1930. 20 p. ([Gt. Brit. Parliament. Papers by command] Cmd. 3494) HJ1594.A5 1929

Sir George Schuster, chairman, 1926–1928; Richard H. Jackson, chairman, 1928–1929.

"The present report covers the work of the East African Guaranteed Loan Committee between the date of the passing of the Palestine and East Africa Loans Act (December 1926) and the transfer of their functions to the Colonial Development Advisory Committee (September 1929)."—p. [2]

The following entry concerns the implementation of the recommendations in the committee's report.

940

Tanganyika. *Governor, 1924–1931 (Cameron).* Despatch from the Governor to the Secretary of State on the subject of loan funds to be raised under the Palestine and East African Loan (Guarantee) Act, 1926. [Dar es Salaam? 1928?] (Tanganyika. Legislative Council. Sessional paper, session 1927/28, part 2)

Source: Tanganyika debates, May 18, 1928, and Tanganyika Blue book, 1934.

941

Gt. Brit. *Colonial Office.* Palestine and East Africa loans (guarantee). Memorandum on proposed financial resolution. London, H.M. Stationery Off., 1931. 4 p. ([Gt. Brit. Parliament. Papers by command] Cmd. 3848) J301.K6 1930/31 v. 23

1948-61

942

East Africa High Commission. Draft estimates of revenue and expenditure of the non-self-contained services. 1948–1961/62? [Nairobi, Printed by the Govt. Printer] annual. HJ81.A2

Report year for 1948–53 ends Dec. 31; for 1954/55–1961/62 ends June 30.

Subsequent Draft estimates issued by the East African Common Services Organization, and the East African Community are "not for distribution outside the East African Community."

L.C. has 1948–50, 1955/56–1957/58.

943

East Africa High Commission. *Auditor-General.* Auditor-General's report; Accountant General's report; financial statements. 1948–1960/61. Nairobi. annual. HJ81.A14

Report year for 1948–53 ends Dec. 31; for 1954–1960/61 ends June 30.

Report for 1954 covers period Jan.-June 1954.

Cover title: Financial statements and reports thereon by the Auditor-General and Accountant General (varies slightly).

At the head of title: East Africa High Commission (non-self-contained services).

Title varies: 1948, Financial report and statement.—1949, Annual report of the chief accounting officer.—1950, Financial statements and report thereon by the Director of Audit, Kenya.—1951, Financial statements and report thereon by the Acting Director of Audit, East Africa High Commission services.—1952–53, Director of Audit's report; Accountant General's report; financial statements.

Superseded by a publication with the same title (item 954) issued by the Auditor-General of the East African Common Services Organization.

L.C. has 1956/57–1960/61; MBU has 1948–1960/61.

944

East Africa High Commission. *Laws, statutes, etc.* Estimates of revenue and expenditure of the non-self-contained services. 1948–1961/62. [Nairobi, Printed by the Govt. Printer] annual. DLC-LL

Report year for 1948–53 ends Dec. 31; for 1954/55–1961/62 ends June 30.

"Passed by the East Africa Central Legislative Assembly.'

Superseded by the Estimates of expenditure (general fund services) (item 955) issued by the East African Common Services Organization.

L.C. has 1948–1961/62 (1960/61 wanting).

945

East Africa High Commission. Memorandum on the estimates of revenue and expenditure of the non-self-contained services. Nairobi, Printed by the Govt. Printer, annual. DLC

Memorandum for 1954 covers period Jan.-June 1954.

Cover title: Memorandum on the estimates of revenue and expenditure of the East Africa High Commission non-self-contained services.

Each issue includes revised estimates approved by the Standing Committee on Finance of the East Africa Central Legislative Assembly of the East Africa High Commission.

L.C. has 1954/55; NNC has 1952–54.

946

——— Financial orders, 1952. [Nairobi? 1952?] 1 v. (unpaged) HJ1596.E2 1952

947

East Africa High Commission. *East African Statistical Dept. Uganda Unit.* Background to the budget, five years of progress. [Entebbe, Govt. Printer, 1955] 21 p. DLC

Issued by the agency under its earlier name: East Africa High Commission, East African Statistical Dept., Entebbe Branch.

Includes information on revenue and expenditure, geographical income, population, employment, standard of living, and external trade for 1950–54. The budget survey for 1957/58 and subsequent years is contained in the Background to the budget issued by the Ministry of Finance of Uganda.

948

——— Good housekeeping; the story of Uganda's budget. Entebbe, East African Statistical Dept., and Dept. of Information. col. illus. annual. CSt–H

CSt-H has 1955/56–1957/58.

949

East Africa High Commission. *East African Statistical Dept. Tanganyika Office.* Budget survey. 1956/57–1961/62. [Dar es Salaam?] annual. HJ86E.E3

Report year ends June 30.

Superseded by a publication with the same title issued by the Economics and Statistics Division of Tanganyika.

Each issue includes estimates for the fiscal year and statistical data for the preceding 4-year period.

L.C. has 1956/57–1961/62.

950
East Africa High Commission. East Africa High Commission 1948 to 1957; a decade of service to East Africa: designed to illustrate the budget statement of the Financial Secretary on the 1958–59 estimates of the non-self-contained services. [Nairobi, High Commission Printer, 1958] [20] p. illus.

Source: Col. Off. Lib. Cat.

951
East Africa High Commission. *East African Statistical Dept. Tanganyika Office.* Public finance in Tanganyika, an analysis. [Dar es Salaam, Govt. Printer, 1959] 46 p.
HJ1654.T3A55

"Economic and functional analyses of the central and local governments' accounts in Tanganyika."

A complementary study to the agency's The gross domestic product of Tanganyika, 1954–1957 (item 708).

952
Gt. Brit. *East African Economic and Fiscal Commission.* East Africa, report. London, H.M. Stationery Off. [1961] 83 p. ([Gt. Brit. Parliament. Papers by comand] Cmnd. 1279)
HC517.E2A57

At head of title: Colonial Office.

Jeremy Raisman, chairman.

Includes information on the East African Common Market, taxation, and the financing of services and research of the East Africa High Commission.

The following entry concerns the implementation of the recommendations in the commission's report.

953
Kenya Colony and Protectorate. Sessional paper on the report of the East African Economic and Fiscal Commission. [Nairobi, Printed by the Govt. Printer] 1961. 4 p. (Kenya Colony and Protectorate. [Legislative Council] Sessional paper no. 3 of 1961) J731.H62 no. 3 of 1961

Cover title: Report of the Economic and Fiscal Commission.

1962-67

954
East African Common Services Organization. *Auditor-General.* Auditor-General's report; Accountant General's report: financial statements. 1961/62–1967/68. [Nairobi] annual.
DLC

Report year ends June 30.

Cover title: Financial statements and reports thereon by the Auditor-General and Accountant General (varies slightly).

At head of title 1961/62: East Africa High Commission (non-self-contained services) East African Common Services Organization (general fund services); 1962/63–1966/67: East African Common Services Organization (general fund services); 1967/68: East African Common Services Organization/East African Community (general fund services).

Supersedes a publication with the same title (item 943) issued by the Auditor-General of the East Africa High Commission.

Superseded by a publication with the same title (item 958) issued by the Auditor-General of the East African Community.

L.C. catalogs 1961/62–1963/64 under: East Africa High Commission. *Auditor-General.* Auditor-General's report; Accountant-General's report; financial statements (HJ81.A14).

L.C. has 1961/62–1967/68.

955
East African Common Services Organization. *Laws, statutes, etc.* Estimates of expenditure (general fund services). 1962/63–1967/68? Nairobi, Govt. Printer] annual. DLC-LL

Report year ends June 30.

Supersedes the Estimates of revenue and expenditure of the non-self-contained services (item 944) issued by the East Africa High Commission.

"Not for distribution outside the East African Community."

L.C. has 1962/63–1967/68 (1964/65 wanting); source for 1964/65: Col. Off. Lib. Cat.

956
Conference on Public Policy, *2d, University College, Nairobi, 1963.* Conferences on public policy, 1963/4: East African federation; [paper no. 4] Joint fiscal instructions and policy in East Africa [by] Urusula Hicks. [Nairobi? 1964?] 17 leaves. HC517.E2C6 1963 no. 4

1968-74

957
East African Community. Estimates of expenditure. 1967/68+ [Arusha?] annual. NNUN

Report year ends June 30.

Vol. for 1967/68 [suppl.] covers period Dec. 1967–June 30, 1968.

Supersedes the Estimates of expenditure (general fund services) (item 955) issued by the East African Common Services Organization.

"Not for distribution outside the East African Community."

DJBF has 1967/68–1969/70; NNUN has 1968/69+

958
East African Community. *Auditor General.* Auditor-General's report; Accountant General's report; financial statements. 1968/69+ [Arusha] annual. DLC

Report year ends June 30.

Cover title: Financial statements and reports thereon by the Auditor-General and Accountant General.

At head of title: East African Community (general fund services).

Supersedes a publication with the same title (item 954) issued by the Auditor-General of the East African Common Services Organization.

L.C. has 1968/69+

959
East African Community. Financial regulations, 1970. Arusha, 1972. 128 leaves. DLC

Taxation

960
Conference of Governors of British East African Territories. *Statistical Dept.* Proportionate taxation in Kenya, 1925 to 1927. [Nairobi, 1931] (*Its* Memoir no. 2) NN

961
East Africa High Commission. *East Africa Central Legislative Assembly. Select Committee on the East African Income Tax (Management) Bill.* Report, 1958. Nairobi, 1958. 265 p. MBU

J. Hinchey, chairman.

962
East Africa High Commission. *East African Income Tax Dept.* Proposals for (a) amendments to the income tax laws to provide for allowances in respect of capital expenditure. (b) amendments to the excess profits tax laws in connexion with the winding up of the tax. Nairobi, Printed by the Govt. Printer, 1946.
DLC-Micro 23940 reel 7 octavo 352

Collation of the original: 53 p.

At head of title: Colony and Protectorate of Kenya, Protectorate of Uganda, Tanganyika Territory, Protectorate of Zanzibar.

Issued by the agency under an earlier name: Joint Income Tax Dept. of East Africa.

Colonial Office Library East Africa pamphlet octavo 352.

963
______ Proposals for an East African Income Tax Act. Nairobi, Govt. Printer [1951] 97 p. IEN

964
______ Report. 1950–1960/61. Nairobi, Printed, and schedules prepared by East African Statistical Dept. annual. HJ4791.A22

Report year for 1950–53 ends Dec. 31; for 1954/55–1960/61 ends June 30.

Report for 1954/55 covers period Jan. 1954–June 1955.

Title varies: 1950–1954/55, Annual report.

Superseded by a publication with the same

title (item 971) issued by the East African Income Tax Dept.

Each issue includes statistics on assessments made, and income tax collection paid to Kenya, Tanganyika, Uganda, and Zanzibar.

L.C. has 1951–1960/61 (1953 wanting).

965
East Africa High Commission. *East African Revenue Advisory Board.* Report on the East African Income Tax (Management) Act, 1952. Nairobi, 1953. 73 p. NNC

966
East African Commission of Inquiry on Income Tax. Report. [Nairobi, East Africa High Commission, 1957] 212 p. HJ4791.E2

E. Coates, chairman.

The following entries (items 967–69) are arranged alphabetically, and concern the implementation of the recommendations in the commission's report.

967
Kenya Colony and Protectorate. Income tax proposals. Nairobi. Printed by the Govt. Printer, 1958. 24 p. (Kenya Colony and Protectorate. [Legislative Council] Sessional paper no. 5 of 1957/58)
J731.H62 no. 5 of 1957/58

"The Government intentions in regard to the Coates Commission recommendations referred to in the Budget proposals for 1957/58 are here set out in the order of those recommendations as they appear in the summary of Chapter XX of the Coates Report. References to the "Management Act" relate to the East African Income Tax (Management) Act, 1952, which is at present in course of being revised."

968
Tanganyika. *Legislative Council.* Government proposals on the recommendations of the East African Commission of Inquiry on Income Tax, 1956–57. Dar es Salaam, Printed by the Govt. Printer, 1958. 16 p. (*Its* Government paper, 1958, no. 3) J801.H62 1958 no. 3

969
Uganda. A statement of intentions in respect of recommendations made in the Report of the East African Commission of Inquiry on Income Tax, 1956–57. Entebbe, Printed by the Govt. Printer [1958] 25 p. (Uganda. Legislative Council. Sessional paper no. 11 of 1957/58) CSt-H

970
East African Community. *Laws, statutes, etc.* East African laws of income tax. [Nairobi, Printed by East African Community Printer, 1971+] 1 v. (loose-leaf) DLC

Title from spine.

East African Income Tax Dept.

Note: The East African Income Tax Department was the sole agency responsible for the collection of income tax in East Africa for the period 1940–1973. At the outbreak of World War II, Tanganyika, Uganda, and Zanzibar made a request to the Kenya government for it to authorize its commissioner of income tax to set up a joint department to operate throughout East Africa. Legislation establishing the department came into effect on January 1, 1940. On January 1, 1948, the department came under the jurisdiction of the newly created East Africa High Commission. Under the Treaty for East African Co-operation of 1967, the department was the agency responsible for the assessment and collection of income tax in Kenya, Tanzania, and Uganda, with headquarters remaining in Nairobi, Kenya. A commissioner-general headed the department with a commissioner for income tax for Kenya, Tanzania, and Uganda. Effective January 1, 1974, the department was dissolved. Its functions were taken over by the treasuries of the three partner states, with subsequent amendment of the Treaty for East African Co-operation.

During the period January 1, 1952–March 31, 1960, the department also assessed and collected income tax for Aden.

971
Report. 1961/62–1971/72? [Nairobi, E.A. Community (CPS) Printer] annual. DLC

Report year ends June 30.

At head of title, 1961/62–1965/66: East African Common Services Organization; 1966/67–1971/72? East African Community.

Supersedes a publication with the same title (item 964) issued by the East African Income Tax Dept. of the East Africa High Commission.

No more published?

Each issue includes tax assessments, analyzed by status, residence, main trade group, and changeable income, with averages for Kenya, Tanzania, and Uganda.

L.C. has 1961/62–1971/72.

972
______ The East African Income Tax Management Act. Rev. ed. Nairobi, East African Community Printer, 1970. 1 v. (loose-leaf) DLC

973
______ A guide to income tax in East Africa. Nairobi [1969] 62 p. DLC-LL

L.C. catalogs under: East African Community. *East African Income Tax Dept.*

974
East African tax cases. v. 1–3; 1943/54–1958/63. Nairobi, East African Common Services Organization Printer. MiU-L

At head of title of v. 1: East Africa High Commission.

"Being reports of cases relating to income tax decided in the Court of Appeal for Eastern Africa, the Supreme Court of Kenya and the High Courts of Tanganyika, Uganda and Zanzibar."

975
Gt. Brit. *Board of Inland Revenue.* Income taxes outside the United Kingdom. 1966+ London, H.M. Stationery Off. annual. HJ4629.G59

Vol. 2 of each year includes summaries of income tax which were in force in the East African Community.

L.C. has 1966–71.

976
Gt. Brit. *Treaties, etc., 1952– (Elizabeth II).* Exchange of notes between the Government of the United Kingdom of Great Britain and Northern Ireland and the Government of Denmark extending to the Federation of Rhodesia and Nyasaland, and to Kenya, Uganda, Tanganyika, and Zanzibar the Convention of March 27, 1950 for the avoidance of double taxation and the prevention of fiscal evasion with respect to taxes on income. Copenhagen, January 17, 1959. London, H.M. Stationery Off., 1959. [6] p. ([Gt. Brit. Foreign Office] Treaty series, 1959, no. 81) JX636 1892 1959 no. 81

[Gt. Brit. Parliament. Papers by command] Cmnd. 903.

977
______ Exchange of notes between the Government of the United Kingdom of Great Britain and Northern Ireland and the Government of Sweden extending to the Federation of Rhodesia and Nyasaland, and to Kenya, Uganda, Tanganyika and Zanzibar the Convention of March 30, 1949, for avoidance of double taxation and the prevention of fiscal evasion with respect to taxes on income. Stockholm, May 28, 1958. London, H.M. Stationery Off., 1959. 5 p. ([Gt. Brit. Foreign Office] Treaty series, 1959, no. 75) JX636 1892 1959 no. 75

[Gt. Brit. Parliament. Papers by command] Cmnd. 891.

978
Kenya. *Laws, statutes, etc.* East African Income Tax (Management) Act, 1958 (as amended for 1965) and amended acts together with subsidiary legislation, rules, territorial rates and allowances acts, double taxation agreements, etc., prepared by the taxation service of the East African Income Tax Department. [1965 ed.] Nairobi, Printed by Print. and Packaging Corp. [1966?+] 1 v. (loose-leaf) DLC-LL

At head of title: East African Income Tax Department.

On spine: East Africa laws of income tax.

"This print of the legislation is not published by authority and accordingly cannot be quoted as authoritative in any legal proceedings."

979
United States. *Internal Revenue Service.* Report on tax administration in the East African Common Services Organization; a tax assistance survey. [Nairobi?] USAID, Kenya, 1964. 14 leaves. DLC-LL

980
Woods, *Sir* Wilfrid W. A report on a fiscal survey of Kenya, Uganda and Tanganyika. [Nairobi, Printed by the Govt. Printer, 1946] 178 p. HJ1594.W6

At head of title: Conference of East African Governors.

The report is a review of the system, distribution, and incidence of existing taxation, both direct and indirect, and an examination of existing methods of assessment and collection of taxes, with recommendations.

Geography and Maps

981
East Africa. London, Printed for H.M. Stationery Off. by Fosh & Cross [1947?] map. DLC-G&M

Scale not given.

S.O. code no. 70–538–5–5.

982
East African Railways and Harbours Administration. East Africa. [Nairobi?] 1963. map. DLC-G&M

Scale 1:3,750,000.

Photograph positive in color.

"Drawn by E.A.R.&H. Jan. 1961. Rainfall & population data obtained from map 3 of the Report of the East Africa Royal Commission, 1953–55, corrected to October 1963."

983
Gt. Brit. *Army. East Africa Command.* Map catalogue, East Africa Command. [Nairobi?] Survey Directorate, H.Q. East Africa Command, 1945. 49 p. maps. DLC-G&M

Includes index maps.

984
Gt. Brit. *Army. East African Force.* Chart of approximate magnetic declination epoch May 1942: Central & East Africa. 2d ed. Nairobi, 1942. (*Its* E.A.F. no. 817) DLC-G&M

Scale 1:12,000,000.

"Drawn and printed by E.A. Survey Group, July 1942. Magnetic data compiled by B.E.A. Meteorological Service, Nairobi, May 1942."

985
______ Chart of approximate magnetic declination epoch May 1944: Central & East Africa. 3d ed. [Nairobi?] 1944. (*Its* E.A.F. no. 1590) DLC-G&M

Scale 1:12,000,000.

"The magnetic information has been compiled from the most recent data available. This chart supersedes all previous publications."

"Restricted."

986
______ [East Africa] [Nairobi, n.d.] maps 51 x 66 cm. or smaller. G8320 50.G71

Scale 1:50,000.

Sheets compiled from aerial photographs.

Military Grid.

Transportation classified.

Hydrography shown.

Cultural features shown by symbols.

Vegetation shown by symbols.

Index to adjoining sheets in margin.

987
______ East Africa. [Nairobi] 1943+ maps 80 x 61 cm. or smaller. G8320 100.G7

Scale 1:100,000.

Reproduced from French originals.

Military Grid system (Metre Grid).

Transportation classified.

Hydrography shown.

Elevation shown by form lines, hachures, spot heights.

Cultural features shown by symbols.
Set complete in 7 sheets.
Index to adjoining sheets in margin.

988
_______ East Africa 1:25,000. [Nairobi] 1940+ col. maps 68 x 77 cm. or smaller. G8320 25.G7
Scale 1:25,000.
Composite set of various E.A.F. maps at 1:25,000.
Zone H Grid system.
Topography shown by contours and spot heights.
Transportation classified.
Hydrography shown.
Index to adjoining sheets in margin.

989
_______ East Africa 1:50,000. [Nairobi] 1940+ col. maps 80 x 63 cm. G8320 50.G7
Scale 1:50,000.
Composite set of various E.A.F. maps at 1:50,000.
Topography shown by contour lines and spot heights.
Transportation classified.
Hydrography shown.
Index to adjoining sheets in margin.

990
_______ East Africa 1:125,000. [Nairobi] 1906+ col. maps 73 x 54 cm. or smaller. G8320 125.G7
Scale 1:125,000.
Topography shown by contour lines and spot heights.
Transportation classified.
Cultural features shown by symbols.
Vegetation shown by symbols.
Index to adjoining sheets in margin.

991
_______ East Africa 1:250,000. [Nairobi] 1940+ col. maps 82 x 61 cm. or smaller. G8320 250.G7
Scale 1:250,000.
Composite set of various E.A.F. maps at 1:250,000.
Military Grid system.
Topography shown by contours and spot heights.
Transportation classified.
Hydrography shown.
Reliability diagram, boundary diagram, and index to adjoining sheets in margins.

992
_______ East Africa 1:250,000. Compiled at the Survey Office, Khartoum ... , grid added by AMS, 1951. 2d ed. AMS. [Washington, Printed by Army Map Service, Corps of Engineers, 1951+] col. maps 47 x 66 cm. (A.M.S. Y501) G8320 s250.G71
Scale 1:250,000.
Coverage complete in 188 sheets.
Most sheets have added series designation: G.S.G.S. 8003.
Includes "Index to adjoining sheets."

993
_______ East Africa 1:500,000. Compiled, drawn and printed by E.A. Survey Group. [Nairobi, 194-?+] col. maps 47 x 47 cm. (*Its* E.A.F. series) G8320 s500.G7
Scale 1:500,000.
Various issues of some sheets, with various E.A.F. series numbers for individual sheets, and grids. Some have air information.
Relief shown by contours and spot heights.
Terrain shown by symbols.
Cultural features shown by symbols.
Index to adjoining sheets, boundary, reliability and grid reference diagram.

994
_______ Eastern Africa. Compiled, drawn and printed by E.A. Survey Group. [Nairobi?] 1942. (*Its* E.A.F. no. 1129) DLC-G&M
Scale: 1:12,000,000.
At head of title: "Security."

995
_______ Tribal map of eastern Africa. [Nairobi? 194–?] map on 2 sheets. (*Its* E.A.F. no. 1549) DLC-G&M
Shows Kenya, Uganda, and northern Tanganyika.
L.C. has sheet 1 only.

996
Gt. Brit. *Army. East African Survey Group.* [East]

Africa 1:1,000,000. [Nairobi] 1939+ col. maps 47 x 69 cm. or smaller. G8320 s1000.G7

Scale 1:1,000,000.

Coverage of Africa east of 24° E in 33 sheets. Various issues of some sheets, with various E.A.F. series numbers, some with grids.

Relief shown by contours, spot heights and altitude tints. Terrain shown by symbols.

Cultural features shown by symbols.

Index to adjoining sheets in margins.

997

Gt. Brit. *Army. Middle East Forces.* East Africa; index gazetteer showing place-name on [E.A.-F.] 1:500,000 map series, compiled by Survey Directorate, General Headquarters, Middle East. Cairo, 1946–47. 2 v. in 3.
G8420 s500.G7 Suppl.

Vol. 2 published by Directorate of Military Survey, War Office.

Maps to which this index gazetteer applies were issued by the East African Force of the Army of Gt. Brit.

Contents: v. 1. Kenya, Uganda & Tanganyika.—v. 2–2a. Abyssinia, Eritrea, British, French & Italian Somaliland & part of the Sudan.

998

Gt. Brit. *Colonial Office.* Correspondence, 8 July, 1905, to 31st December, 1906, relating to the survey of British colonies and protectorates in Africa. [London] Printed for the use of the Colonial Office, 1907. (*Its* African no. 777, confidential) DLC-Micro 03759

Collation of the original: xvii, 210 p. illus., fold maps.

[Gt. Brit.] Public Record Office. C.O. 879/87.

"Continued by African no. 885."

Includes information on the mapping and surveying of the East Africa Protectorate and Uganda.

Includes also the Annual reports, 1904/5–1905/6, of the Land and Survey Office of Uganda, the Annual report, 1905, of the Land Office of the East Africa Protectorate, and Report on survey, East Africa Protectorate, by G. E. Smith, commissioner on the Anglo–German Boundary Commission.

999

Gt. Brit. *Colonial Survey Committee.* Special report on the triangulations of Eastern and Central Africa including Kenya, Northern Rhodesia, Nyasaland, Tanganyika Territory, and Uganda. London, H.M. Stationery Off., 1928. 58 p. 2 maps. ([Gt. Brit.] Colonial Office. Colonial no. 33) QB296.A17G7 1928

At head of title: Issued by the Colonial Office.

Includes corrections to reports of boundary commissions for the period 1893 to 1914.

L.C. also has parts of a preliminary version of this report on microfilm under the title: Notes on East African triangulation (Colonial Office Library East Africa pamphlet folio 137) (DLC-Micro 23940 reel 9 folio 137).

1000

Gt. Brit. *Crown Agents for Oversea Governments and Administrations.* Contract for air photography of certain areas in the Arusha District of Tanganyika ... 6th February 1958, [with Fairey Air Surveys] [London? Crown Agents on behalf of the East Africa High Commission, 1958] 50 p. fold. map.

Source: Col. Off. Lib. Cat.

1001

——— Contract for air photography of certain areas of Tanganyika [with Fairey Air Surveys Limited] Agreement, specification, schedule to specification, letters (including the tender), map. [London?] Office of the Crown Agents for Oversea Governments and Administrations, E. F. Turner, 1960. 51 p. map.

At head of title: The East Africa High Commission.

Source: Col. Off. Lib. Cat.

1002

Gt. Brit. *Directorate of Military Survey.* East Africa 1:250,000. [London, etc.] 1958+ col. maps 47 x 69 cm. (*Its* Series Y503)
G8400 s250.G7

Scale 1:250,000.

A series coordinated by, and in part issued by, Directorate of Military Survey, chiefly in quadrangles 1° of latitude by 1.5° of longitude, numbered according to the scheme of the

International map of the world. Index map indicates completion in 116 sheets.

Includes various issues of sheets, some issued by Uganda Lands and Surveys Dept., some by Survey of Kenya, some by Tanganyika Survey Division, and some reprinted by Royal Corps of Engineers or by U.S. Army Map Service. Some sheets by Survey of Kenya have added series designation: SK34.

Relief variously shown by contours, gradient tints, spot heights, etc.

Each sheet includes reliability and boundaries diagrams, and index to adjoining sheets.

Accompanied by index map, by U.S. Army Map Service, on sheet 27 x 38 cm.

1003

_______ East Africa 1:500,000. [London] D. Survey, War Office and Air Ministry, 1958+ col. maps 47 x 47 cm. (*Its* Series Y401)
G8320 s500.G72

Scale 1:500,000; 1 inch 7,891 miles.

Issued in 2° quadrangles; some oversize.

Based on series of same title issued by the East African Forces, and its revision issued by British General Staff Geographical Section as series GSGS 4355. Some sheets bear this additional designation. Sheets reprinted by U.S. Army Map Service are issued as its Series Y401.

Relief shown by contours, form-lines, hachures, etc.

Marginal maps on each sheet: Index to adjoining sheets.—Boundary diagrams.—Reliability diagram.

1004

Gt. Brit. *Directorate of Overseas Surveys.* Central & East Africa: air photo cover up to 31st March 1967. [Tolworth, Surrey?] 1967. map. (*Its* D.O.S. (Misc.) 73/A) DLC-G&M

Scale not given.

Map 2A–1967.

1005

_______ Central & East Africa field survey. [Tolworth, Surrey?] 1967. map. (*Its D.O.S.* (Misc.) 73/C) DLC-G&M

Scale not given.

Map 2F-1967.

Includes field survey up to Mar. 31, 1967, with preliminary triangulation (D.O.S.) and and first order tellurometer traverse (D.O.S.) for Kenya, Tanzania, and Uganda.

1006

_______ Central & East Africa: mapping. [Tolworth, Surrey?] 1967. map (*Its* D.O.S. (Misc.) 73/B) DLC-G&M

Scale not given.

Map 2M-1967.

1007

_______ Central & East Africa [mapping: field survey and air photo cover, mainly of 1:50,000) up to 31st March 1959. [Tolworth, Surrey?] 1959. map on 4 sheets. (*Its* D.O.S. (Misc.) 73/A-D) DLC-G&M

Scale not given.

From the Annual report, 1958/59, issued by the Directorate of Overseas Surveys of Gt. Brit.

The following entries (items 1008–11) are maps to the report (item 11) issued by the East Africa Royal Commission of Great Britain.

1008

_______ East Africa, general. [London?] 1954. map. (D.C.S. (Misc.) 203a) DLC-G&M

Scale 1:3,000,000.

"Drawn by Directorate of Colonial Surveys from information supplied by the Royal Commission to East Africa."

Map 1.

Shows "alienated lands" in Kenya, Tanganyika, and Uganda.

Issued by the agency under a variant name: Directorate of Colonial Surveys.

1009

_______ East Africa: population, tsetse fly and rainfall. [London?] 1954. map. (D.C.S. (Misc.) 203b) DLC-G&M

Scale 1:3,000,000.

"Drawn by Directorate of Colonial Surveys from information supplied by the Royal Commission to East Africa."

Map 2.

Issued by the agency under a variant name: Directorate of Colonial Surveys.

1010
_______ East Africa: population, tsetse fly and rainfall. [London?] 1954. map. (D.C.S. (Misc.) 203c) DLC-G&M
Scale 1:3,000,000.
"Drawn by Directorate of Colonial Surveys from information supplied by the Royal Commission to East Africa."
Map 3.
Issued by the agency under a variant name: Directorate of Colonial Surveys.

1011
_______ Kenya: boundaries, land units, population, tsetse fly and rainfall. map. [London?] 1954. (D.C.S. (Misc.) 203d) DLC-G&M
Scale 1:2,000,000.
"Drawn by Directorate of Colonial Surveys from information supplied by the Royal Commission to East Africa."
Map 4.
Issued by the agency under a variant name: Directorate of Colonial Surveys.

1012
Gt. Brit. *War Office. General Staff.* Co-ordination of surveys in East Africa. [London?] 1926. DLC-Micro 23940 reel 9 folio 138
Collation of the original: [4] leaves.
On leaf 4: G.S.G.S.
Colonial Office Library East Africa pamphlet folio 138.

1013
_______ Positions, azimuths and lengths of sides of Capt. Whitehouse's triangulation round the southern shores of Lake Victoria. Computed by the Topographical Section of the General Staff. London, 1907. 4 p.
Source: War Off. Cat.

1014
_______ Positions, azimuths and length of sides of the Anglo-German Boundary Commission triangulation, 1902–1906, from Zanzibar to Mount Ruwenzori. Recomputed under the direction of the Topographical Section of the General Staff. London, 1907. 12 p.
Source: War Off. Cat.

1015
Gt. Brit. *War Office. General Staff. Geographical Section.* East Africa. [Nairobi] 1942+ col. maps 90 x 60 cm. (*Its* GSGS 8041) G8320 125.G71
Scale 1:125,000.
E.A.F. 1173.
Military Grid (Metre Grid).
Transportation classified.
Cultural features shown by symbols.
Vegetation shown by symbols.
Hydrography shown.
Index to adjoining sheets in margin.
DLC-G&M catalogs under: Gt. Brit. *Army. General Staff Geographical Section.*

1016
_______ East Africa 1:500,000. [London] 1946+ col. maps 47 x 47 cm. (*Its* G.S.G.S. 4355) (Series Y401). G8320 s500.G71
Scale 1:500,000.
Reprinted from East African Force series (G8320 s500.G7). Various issues of some sheets. Some sheets reprinted by Army Map Service or Directorate of Military Surveys with UTM grid.
Relief shown by contours and spot heights.
Cultural features shown by symbols.
Index to adjoining sheets in margins.

1017
Hoy, Harry E. East Central Africa, base map prepared by Harry E. Hoy for OQMG. [London?] 1950. DLC-G&M
On face of map: Environmental Protection Section. Research & Development Branch.
Scale not given.
Shows Kenya and Uganda.

History

Prehistory

1018
British Museum (*Natural History*). Fossil mammals of Africa. no. 1–22. London, 1951–67. illus. irregular. QE881.B76

Suspended 1960–64.

No. 18–22 included also in the agency's Bulletin, Geology series.

Superseded by Fossil vertebrates of Africa.

The following numbers relating to East Africa are held by L.C.:

no. 1. Clark, *Sir* Wilfrid E. L. G., *and* L. S. B. Leakey. The Miocene Hominoidea of East Africa. 1951. 117 p.

no. 3. Clark, Sir Wilfrid E.L.G., *and* D. P. Thomas. Associated jaws and limb bones of *Limnopithecus macinnesi*. 1951. 27 p.

no. 4. MacInnes, Donald G. Miocene Anthracotheriidae from East Africa. 1951. 24 p.

no. 5. Clark, *Sir* Wilfrid E. L. G., *and* D. P. Thomas. The Miocene Lemuroids of East Africa. 1952. 20 p.

no. 6. MacInnes, Donald G. The Miocene and Pleistocene Lagomorpha of East Africa. 1953. 30 p.

no. 7. Whitworth, T. The Miocene Hyracoids of East Africa. 1954. 58 p.

no. 9. Clark, *Sir* Wilfrid E. L. G. A Miocene lemuroid skull from East Africa. 1956. 6 p.

no. 10. MacInnes, Donald G. Fossil Tubulidentata from East Africa. 1956. 38 p.

no. 11. Butler, Percy M. Erinaceidae from the Miocene of East Africa. 1956. 75 p.

no. 12. MacInnes, Donald G. A new Miocene rodent from East Africa. 1957. 35 p.

no. 13. Butler, Percy M. Insectivora and Chiroptera from the Miocene rocks of Kenya Colony. 1957. 35 p.

no. 14. Leakey, L. S. B. Some East African Pleistocene Suidae. 1958. 132 p.

no. 15. Whitworth, T. Miocene ruminants of East Africa. 1958. 50 p.

no. 16. Napier, John R., *and* P. R. Davis. The fore-limb skeleton and associated remains of *Proconsul africanus*. 1959. 69 p.

L.C. binds no. 18–22 in the Bulletin of the British Museum (Natural History) Geology, with the call no.: QE1.B65

no. 18. Butler, Percy M. East African Miocene and Pleistocene chalicotheres. *In* Bulletin of the British Museum (Natural History) Geology, v. 10, no. 7. London, 1965. p. [163]–237. QE1.B65 v. 10 no. 7

no. 19. Savage, Robert J. G. The Miocene Carnivora of East Africa. *In* Bulletin of the British Museum (Natural History) Geology, v. 10, no. 8. London, 1965. p. [239]–316. QE1.B65 v. 10 no. 8

no. 20. Gentry, Alan W. Fossil Antilopini of East Africa. *In* Bulletin of the British Museum (Natural History) Geology, v. 12, no. 2. London, 1966. p. [43]–106. QE1.B65 v. 12 no. 2

no. 21. Hooijer, Dirk A. Miocene rhinoceroses of East Africa. *In* Bulletin of the British Museum (Natural History) Geology, v. 13, no. 2. London, 1966. p. [117]–190. QE1.B65 v. 13 no. 2

no. 22. Gentry, Alan W. *Pelorovis oldowayensis* Reck, an extinct bovid from East Africa. *In* Bulletin of the British Museum (Natural History) Geology, v. 14 no. 7. London, 1967. p. [243]–299. QE1.B65 v. 14 no. 7

1019
Cole, Sonia M. Early man in East Africa. London, Macmillan, 1958. 104 p. illus. (Treasury of East African history) GN865.E2C6

"The MS. for this book was received through the East African Literature Bureau."

1020
Leakey, L. S. B. A contribution to the study of the Tumbian culture in East Africa. Nairobi, Coryndon Memorial Museum, 1945. 59 p. illus., map. (Coryndon Memorial Museum, *Nairobi*. Occasional papers, no. 1) DT421.C622 no. 1

1021
——— Notes on the genus *Simopithecus,* with a description of a new species from Olduvai. Nairobi, Coryndon Memorial Museum, 1958. 14 p. 10 plates. (Coryndon Memorial Museum, *Nairobi.* Occasional papers, no. 6)
DT421.C622 no. 6

1022
Leakey, Margaret. Introduction to the study of the early prehistory of East Africa. [Nairobi?] National Museums of Kenya, The Education Section, 1973. 22 p. DLC
On cover: Early prehistory of East Africa.

Slave Trade

1023
Collister, Peter. The last days of slavery; England and the East African slave trade, 1870–1900. Dar es Salaam, East African Literature Bureau, 1961. 150 p. illus., 4 maps. (Treasury of East African history) HT1327.C59

The following entries (items 1024–76) are arranged chronologically.

1024
Great Britain. Slave trade (Zanzibar). Return to an address of the honourable the House of Commons dated 22 February 1859 for copies or extracts of the letters of the Government of Bombay to Her Majesty's Secretary of State for India, or the Court of Directors, forwarding letters written in August and September 1858, by Captain Rigby, the Company's agent at Zanibar, on the subject of the slave trade at Zanibar and along the Mozambique coast. India Office, 3 March 1859, J. W. Kaye, Secretary in Political and Secret Department (Mr. Kinnaird). [London] Ordered by the House of Commons to be printed, 1859. 14 p. ([Gt. Brit. Parliament, 1859. House of Commons, session 1. Reports and papers] 111)
J301.K6 1859 session 1 v. 27

1025
——— Class B. East coast of Africa. Correspondence respecting the slave trade and other matters, from January 1 to December 31, 1869. London, Printed by Harrison, 1870. 103 p. ([Gt. Brit. Parliament. Papers by command] C. 141) J301.K6 1870 v. 61

1026
——— Class B. East coast of Africa. Correspondence respecting the slave trade and other matters, from January 1 to December 31, 1870. London, Printed by Harrison, 1871. 70 p. ([Gt. Brit. Parliament. Papers by command] C. 340) J301.K6 1871 v. 62

1027
Gt. Brit. *Committee on the East African Slave Trade.* Report, addressed to the Earl of Clarendon. London, Printed by Harrison, 1870. 13 p. map. ([Gt. Brit. Parliament. Papers by command] C. 209) J301.K6 1870 v. 61

1028
Great Britain. East Coast of Africa; recent correspondence respecting the slave trade. London, Printed by Harrison, 1871. 24 p. ([Gt. Brit. Parliament. Papers by command] C. 385)
J301.K6 1871 v. 62

1029
Gt. Brit. *Parliament. House of Commons. Select Committee on Slave Trade (East Coast of Africa).* Report . . . together with the proceedings of the committee, minutes of evidence, appendix and index. [London] Ordered by the House of Commons to be printed, 1871. xxiv, 242 p. ([Gt. Brit. Parliament, 1871. House of Commons. Reports and papers] 420)
J301.K6 1871 v. 12
Russell Gurney, chairman.

1030
Great Britain. Class B. East coast of Africa. Correspondence respecting the slave trade and other matters, from January 1 to December 31, 1871. London, Printed by Harrison, 1872. 86 p. ([Gt. Brit. Parliament. Papers by command] C.657) J301.K6 1872 v. 54

1031
_______ Class B. East coast of Africa. Correspondence respecting the slave trade and other matters, from January 1 to December 31, 1872. London, Printed by Harrison, 1873. 69 p. ([Gt. Brit. Parliament. Papers by command. C. 867–1]) J301.K6 1873 v. 61

1032
_______ Correspondence respecting Sir Bartle Frere's mission to the East coast of Africa, 1872–73. London, Printed by Harrison, 1873. 156 p. fold. map. ([Gt. Brit. Parliament. Papers by command. C. 820]) J301.K6 1873 v. 61

Frere's mission was concerned primarily with the slave trade, but the correspondence includes considerable information on Zanzibar and the Sultan, the East African coast and its peoples, resident Asians, and European missions.

1033
Gt. Brit. *Treaties, etc., 1837–1901 (Victoria).* Treaty between Her Majesty and the Sultan of Zanzibar for the suppression of the slave trade. Signed at Zanzibar, June 5, 1873. London, Printed by Harrison, 1874. 2 p. ([Gt. Brit. Foreign Office] Slave trade, no. 2 (1874)) J301.K6 1874 v. 62

[Gt. Brit. Parliament. Papers by command] C. 889.

1034
Gt. Brit. *Foreign Office.* Correspondence with British representatives and agents, and reports from naval officers relative to the East African slave trade, from January 1 to December 31, 1873. London, Printed by Harrison, 1873. 160 p. (*Its* Slave trade no. 8 (1874)) J301.K6 1874 v. 62

[Gt. Brit. Parliament. Papers by command] C. 1064.

1035
_______ Reports on the present state of the East African slave trade. London, Printed by Harrison, 1874. 19 p. (*Its* Slave trade no. 5 (1874)) J301.K6 1874 v. 62

[Gt. Brit. Parliament. Papers by command] C. 946.

1036
_______ Further reports on East African slave trade [by F. Elton] London, Printed by Harrison, 1874. 25 p. 2 col. maps (1 fold.) (*Its* Slave trade no. 7 (1874)) J301.K6 1874 v. 62

[Gt. Brit. Parliament. Papers by command] C. 1062.

1037
_______ Correspondence with British representatives and agents abroad and reports from naval officers, relative to the East African slave trade. London, Printed by Harrison, 1875. 139 p. (*Its* Slave trade no. 1 (1875)) J301.K6 1875 v. 71

[Gt. Brit. Parliament. Papers by command] C. 1168.

Covers 1874.

1038
Gt. Brit. *Treaties, etc., 1837–1901 (Victoria).* Treaty between Her Majesty and the Sultan of Zanzibar, supplementary to the Treaty for the suppression of the slave trade of June 5, 1873. Signed at London, July 14, 1875. London, Printed by Harrison, 1876. 2 p. ([Gt. Brit. Foreign Office] Zanzibar no. 1 (1876)) J301.K6 1876 v. 84

[Gt. Brit. Parliament. Papers by command] C. 1387.

1039
Gt. Brit. *Foreign Office.* Communications from Dr. Kirk, respecting the suppression of the land slave traffic in the dominions of the Sultan of Zanzibar. London, Printed by Harrison, 1876. 6 p. (*Its* Slave trade no. 3 (1876)) J301.K6 1876 v. 70

[Gt. Brit. Parliament. Papers by command] C. 1521.

1040
_______ Correspondence with British representatives and agents abroad, and reports from naval officers, relating to the slave trade. London, Printed by Harrison, 1876. 360 p. (*Its* Slave trade no. 4 (1876)) J 301.K6 1876 v. 70

[Gt. Brit. Parliament. Papers by command] C. 1588.

Zanzibar and East Africa: p. 1–181.

1041

_______ Slave trade. Despatches with respect to the practice of the slave trade by the subjects of the native princes of India. London, Printed by Eyre and Spottiswoode for H.M. Stationery Off., 1876. 15 p. ([Gt. Brit. Parliament. Papers by command] C. 1546) J301.K6 1876 v. 70

Includes correspondence on Indian involvement in the East African slave trade, with particular reference to Zanzibar.

1042

_______ Correspondence with British representatives and agents abroad, and reports from naval officers, relating to the slave trade. London, Printed by Harrison, 1877. 382 p. 3 fold. maps. (*Its* Slave trade no. 2 (1877)) J301.K6 1877 v. 78

[Gt. Brit. Parliament. Papers by command] C. 1829.

Zanzibar: p. 172–323.

1043

_______ Annual report of the Commander-in-Chief in the East Indies on the slave trade. London, Printed by Harrison, 1878. 5 p. (*Its* Slave trade no. 4 (1878)) J301.K6 1878 v. 67

[Gt. Brit. Parliament. Papers by command] C. 2140.

Includes information on the slave trade for Zanzibar and the East African coast.

1044

_______ Correspondence with British representatives and agents abroad, and reports from naval officers, relating to the slave trade. London, Printed by Harrison, 1878. 447 p. (*Its* Slave trade no. 3 (1878)) J301.K6 1878 v. 67

[Gt. Brit. Parliament. Papers by command] C. 2139.

Zanzibar: p. 247–388.

1045

_______ _______ London, Printed by Harrison, 1879. xvii, 322 p. (*Its* Slave trade no. 1 (1879)) J301.K6 1878/79 v. 66

[Gt. Brit. Parliament. Papers by command] C. 2422.

Zanzibar: p. 157–253.

1046

_______ _______ London, Printed by Harrison, 1880. xviii, 336 p. (*Its* Slave trade no. 5 (1880)) J301.K6 1880 v. 69

[Gt. Brit. Parliament. Papers by command] C. 2720.

Zanzibar: p. 188–270.

1047

_______ _______ London, Printed by Harrison, 1881. 438 p. 4 fold. maps. (*Its* Slave trade no. 1 (1881)) J301.K6 1881 v. 85

[Gt. Brit. Parliament. Papers by command] C. 3052.

Zanzibar: p. 278–378.

1048

_______ _______ London, Printed by Harrison, 1882. 355 p. (*Its* Slave trade no. 1 (1882)) J301.K6 1882 v. 65

[Gt. Brit. Parliament. Papers by command] C. 3160.

Zanzibar: p. 139–322.

1049

_______ Correspondence with British representatives and agents abroad, and reports from naval officers and the Treasury, relative to the slave trade, 1882–83. London, Printed for H.M. Stationery Off. by Harrison, 1883. 218 p. (*Its* Slave trade no. 1 (1883)) J301.K6 1883 v. 66

[Gt. Brit. Parliament. Papers by command] C. 3547.

Zanzibar: p. 85–197.

1050

_______ Correspondence with British representatives and agents abroad, and reports from naval officers and the Treasury, relative to the slave trade, 1883–84. London, Printed by Harrison, 1884. 144 p. (*Its* Slave trade no. 1 (1884)) J301.K6 1884 v. 75

[Gt. Brit. Parliament. Papers by command] C. 3849.

Zanzibar: p. 66–139.

1051
______ Correspondence with British representatives and agents abroad, and reports from naval officers and the Treasury, relative to the slave trade, 1884–85. London, Printed by Harrison, 1885. 83 p. (*Its* Slave trade no. 1 (1885))
J301.K6 1884/85 v. 73

[Gt. Brit. Parliament. Papers by command] C. 4523.

Zanzibar: p. 39–83.

1052
______ Correspondence with British representatives abroad, and reports from naval officers and the Treasury, relative to the slave trade, 1885. London, Printed by Harrison, 1886. 185 p. (*Its* Slave trade no. 1 (1886))
J301.K6 1886 v. 62

[Gt. Brit. Parliament. Papers by command] C. 4776.

Zanzibar: p. 89–181.

1053
______ Correspondence relative to the slave trade, 1886. London, Printed for H.M. Stationery Off. by Harrison, 1887. 193 p. (*Its* Slave trade no. 1 (1887)) J301.K6 1887 v. 78

[Gt. Brit. Parliament. Papers by command] C. 5111.

Includes information on the East coast of Africa and Zanzibar.

1054
______ Correspondence relative to the slave trade, 1887. London, Printed for H.M. Stationery Off. by Harrison, 1888. 233 p. (*Its* Slave trade no. 1 (1888)) J301.K6 1888 v. 93

[Gt. Brit. Parliament. Papers by command] C. 5428.

Includes information on the East coast of Africa and Zanzibar.

1055
______ Reports on slave trade on the East coast of Africa, 1887–88. London, Printed for H.M. Stationery Off. by Harrison, 1888. 87 p. (*Its* Africa no. 7 (1888)) J301.K6 1888 v. 74

[Gt. Brit. Parliament. Papers by command] C. 5578.

1056
______ Correspondence respecting suppression of slave trade in East African waters. London, Printed for H.M. Stationery Off. by Harrison, 1888. 4 p. (*Its* Africa no. 6 (1888))
J301.K6 1888 v. 74

[Gt. Brit. Parliament. Papers by command] C. 5559.

1057
______ Correspondence relative to the slave trade, 1888–89. London, Printed for H.M. Stationery Off. by Harrison, 1889. 103 p. (*Its* Slave trade no. 1 (1889)) J301.K6 1889 v. 72

[Gt. Brit. Parliament. Papers by command] C. 5821.

Includes information on the East African coast and Zanzibar.

1058
Gt. Brit. *Treaties, etc., 1837–1901 (Victoria).* Agreement betwen Great Britain and Zanzibar respecting the right of search in Zanzibar waters, slavery, etc. Signed at Zanzibar, September 13, 1889. *In* Gt. Brit. *Foreign Office.* British and foreign state papers. 1888/89; v. 81. London [189–?] p. 1291–92.
JX103.A3 1888/89 v. 81

"Laid before Parliament in Africa no. 6 (1895)."

1059
______ General Act of the Brussels Conference relative to the African slave trade. Signed at Brussels, July 2, 1890. London, Printed for H.M. Statioinery Off. by Harrison, 1892. 109 p. ([Gt. Brit. Foreign Office] Treaty series, 1892, no. 7) JX636 1892 1892 no. 7

[Gt. Brit. Parliament. Papers by command] C. 6557.

Text in English and French.

Signed by Great Britain, Germany, Zanzibar, and other powers.

1060
Zanzibar. *Laws, statutes, etc.* Anti-slavery decree issued by the Sultan of Zanzibar, dated August 1, 1890. London, Printed for H.M. Stationery Off. by Harrison, 1890. 3 p. ([Gt. Brit. Foreign Office] Africa no. 1 (1890-91))
J301.K6 1890/91 v. 57
[Gt. Brit. Parliament. Papers by command] C. 6211.

1061
Gt. Brit. *Foreign Office.* Papers relating to the trade in slaves from East Africa. London, Printed for H.M. Stationery Off. by Harrison, 1891. 11 p. (*Its* Africa no. 6 (1891))
J301.K6 1890/91 v. 57
[Gt. Brit. Parliament. Papers by command] C. 6373.

1062
_______ Papers relative to slave trade and slavery in Zanzibar. London, Printed for H.M. Stationery Off. by Harrison, 1892. 8 p. (*Its* Africa no. 6 (1892)) J301.K6 1892 v. 74
[Gt. Brit. Parliament. Papers by command] C. 6702.

1063
_______ Returns of slaves freed in Zanzibar waters through Her Majesty's ships, 1892–93. London, Printed for H.M. Stationery Off. by Harrison, 1893. 4 p. (*Its* Africa no. 12 (1893))
J301.K6 1893/94 v. 85
[Gt. Brit. Parliament. Papers by command] C. 7247.

1064
_______ Paper respecting the traffic in slaves in Zanzibar. London, Printed for H.M. Stationery Off. by Harrison, 1893. 5 p. (*Its* Africa no. 6 (1893)) J301.K6 1893/94 v. 85
[Gt. Brit. Parliament. Papers by command] C. 7035.

1065
_______ Correspondence respecting slavery in Zanzibar. London, Printed for H.M. Stationery Off. by Harrison, 1895. 43 p. (*Its* Africa no. 6 (1895)) J301.K6 1895 v. 71
[Gt. Brit. Parliament. Papers by command] C. 7707.

1066
_______ Correspondence respecting slavery in the Zanizbar dominions. London, Printed for H.M. Stationery Off. by Harrison, 1896. 47 p. (*Its* Africa no. 7 (1896)) J301.K6 1896 v. 59
[Gt. Brit. Parliament. Papers by command] C. 8275.

1067
_______ Abolition of the legal status of slavery in Zanzibar and Pemba. London, Printed for H.M. Stationery Off. by Harrison, 1897. 6 p. (*Its* Africa no. 2 (1897)) 301.K6 1897 v. 62
[Gt. Brit. Parliament. Papers by command] C. 8433.

1068
_______ Instructions to Mr. Hardinge respecting the abolition of legal status of slavery in the islands of Zanzibar and Pemba. London, Printed for H.M. Stationery Off. by Harrison, 1897. 7 p. (*Its* Africa no. 1 (1897))
J301.K6 1897 v. 62
[Gt. Brit. Parliament. Papers by command] C. 8394.

1069
_______ Correspondence respecting the abolition of the legal status of slavery in Zanzibar and Pemba. London, Printed for H.M. Stationery Off. by Harrison, 1898. 86 p. (*Its* Africa no. 6 (1898)) J301.K6 1898 v. 60
[Gt. Brit. Parliament. Papers by command] C. 8858.

1070
_______ Correspondence respecting the status of slavery in East Africa and the islands of Zanzibar and Pemba. London, Printed for H.M. Stationery Off. by Harrison, 1899. 59 p. (*Its* Africa no. 8 (1899)) J301.K6 1889 v. 63
[Gt. Brit. Parliament. Papers by command] C. 9502.

1071
_______ Correspondence respecting slavery and the slave trade in East Africa and the islands of Zanzibar and Pemba. London, Printed for H.M. Stationery Off. by Harrison, 1900. 22 p. (*Its* Africa no. 3 (1900)) J301.K6 1900 v. 56
[Gt. Brit. Parliament. Papers by command] Cd. 96.

1072
_______ _______ London, Printed for H.M. Stationery Off. by Harrison, 1902. 28 p. (*Its* Africa no. 4 (1901)) J301.K6 1901 v. 48
[Gt. Brit. Parliament. Papers by command] Cd. 593.

1073
_______ _______ London, Printed for H.M. Stationery Off. by Harrison, 1902. 28p. (*Its* Africa no. 6 (1902)) J301.K6 1903 v. 45
[Gt. Brit. Parliament. Papers by command] Cd. 1389.
Covers the year 1901.

1074
_______ Correspondence respecting slavery in the islands of Zanzibar and Pemba. London, Printed for H.M. Stationery Off. by Harrison, 1904. 6 p. (*Its* Africa no. 14 (1904))
J301.K6 1905 v. 56
[Gt. Brit. Parliament. Papers by command] Cd. 2330.

1075
_______ Despatch from His Majesty's agent and consul-general at Zanzibar transmitting a new slavery decree, signed at Zanzibar, June 9, 1909. London, Printed for H.M. Stationery Off. by Harrison, 1909. 3 p. (*Its* Africa no. 3 (1909)) J301.K6 1909 v. 59
[Gt. Brit. Parliament. Papers by command] Cd. 4732.

1076
Gt. Brit. *Colonial Office*. Memorandum on anti-slavery legislation in tropical Africa, with special reference to the Tanganyika Territory [by C. Strachey. London] Printed for the use of the Colonial Office, 1921. (*Its* African (East) no. 1090, confidential) DLC-Micro 03759
Collation of the original: 10 p.
[Gt. Brit.] Public Record Office. C.O. 879/120.
Includes brief surveys of anti-slavery legislation for the East Africa Protectorate and Zanzibar.
"The question of the present position in Tanganyika is dealt with in a separate memorandum [i.e. C.O./9846/21, not printed]"

Colonial Partition

The following entries (items 1077–91) are arranged chronologically.

1077
Gt. Brit. *Treaties, etc., 1837–1901 (Victoria)*. Agreement between the British and German governments, respecting the Sultanate of Zanzibar and the opposite East African mainland, and their spheres of influence, 29th October/1st November, 1886. *In* Hertslet, *Sir* Edward. The map of Africa by treaty, 3d ed. London, H.M. Stationery Off., 1909. v. 3, p. 882–86. ([Document] no. 264) JX1026 1909.H45 v. 3

1078
_______ _______ Adhesion of Sultan of Zanzibar to Agreement between Great Britain and Germany of 29th October/1st November, 1886. 4 December 1886. *In* Hertslet, *Sir* Edward. The map of Africa by treaty, 3rd ed. London, H.M. Stationery Off., 1909. v. 3, p. 887. ([Document] no. 265) JX1026 1909.H45 v. 3

1079
Gt. Brit. *Foreign Office*. Further correspondence relating to Zanzibar. [London] Printed for H.M. Stationery Off. by Harrison, 1887. 60 p. (*Its* Africa no. 3 (1887)) J301.K6 1887 v. 59
[Gt. Brit. Parliament. Papers by command] C. 4609.
Includes information on the European partition of East Africa, and the creation of the boundary commission.

1080

_______ _______ London, Printed for H.M. Stationery Off. by Harrison, 1888. 135 p. (*Its* Africa no. 1 (1888)) J301.K6 1888 v. 74

[Gt. Brit. Parliament. Papers by command] C. 5315.

Includes British, German, and Portuguese correspondence on the European partition of East Africa, with special reference to Kilwa, and other southern dominions of the Sultan of Zanzibar.

1081

_______ Correspondence respecting the Anglo-German agreement relative to Africa and Heligoland. London, Printed for H.M. Stationery Off. by Harrison, 1890. 11 p. (*Its* Africa no. 6 (1890)) J301.K6 1890 v. 51

[Gt. Brit. Parliament. Papers by command] C. 6046.

Text in English and German.

In return for Heligoland, Germany relinquished her claims to British East Africa.

1082

_______ Despatch to Sir E. Malet respecting the affairs of East Africa. London, Printed for H.M. Stationery Off. by Harrison, 1890. 3 p. (*Its* Africa no. 5 (1890)) J301.K6 1890 v. 51

[Gt. Brit. Parliament. Papers by command] C. 6043.

Includes Anglo-German negotiations to limit German claims in British East Africa.

1083

Gt. Brit. *Treaties, etc., 1837–1901 (Victoria).* Agreement between Great Britain and Germany respecting Zanzibar, Heligoland, and the spheres of influence of the two countries in Africa. Signed at Berlin, 1 July 1890. *In* Gt. Brit. *Foreign Office.* British and foreign state papers. 1889/90; v. 82. London [189–?] p. 35–47. JX103.A3 1889/90 v. 82

Supplemented by the Agreement of July 25, 1893.

Text in English and German in parallel columns.

1084

_______ Protocols between the governments of Her Britannic Majesty and of His Majesty the King of Italy for the demarcation of their respective spheres of influence in eastern Africa. Signed at Rome, March 24 and April 15, 1891. London, Printed for H.M. Stationery Off. by Harrison, 1891. 3 p. ([Gt. Brit. Foreign Office] Italy no. 1 (1891)) J301.K6 1890/91 v. 96

Text in English and Italian.

The northern boundary of British East Africa is defined as the Juba river from Kismayu to the Blue Nile.

1085

Gt. Brit. *War Office. Intelligence Division.* General map of eastern equatorial Africa. London, Published on behalf of the War Office by Edward Stanford, 1889. Revised 1st Jan. 1892. (*Its* no. 748) DLC-G&M

Scale 1:3,801,600 or 60 miles to 1 inch.

Shows "spheres of influence, protectorates, or dominions."

1086

Gt. Brit. *Treaties, etc., 1837–1901 (Victoria).* Agreement between Great Britain and Germany respecting boundaries in East Africa. Signed at Berlin, July 25, 1893. London, Printed for H.M. Stationery Off. by Harrison, 1893. 4 p. 2 maps. ([Gt. Brit. Foreign Office] Treaty series, 1893, no. 14) JX636 1892 1893 no. 14

[Gt. Brit. Parliament. Papers by command] C. 7203.

Text in English and German in parallel columns.

Demarcation of the boundary between British and German East Africa.

1087

_______ Agreement between Great Britain and Zanzibar respecting the possessions of the Sultan of Zanzibar on the mainland and adjacent islands, exclusive of Zanzibar and Pemba. Signed at Zanzibar, December 14, 1895. *In* Gt. Brit. *Foreign Office.* British and foreign state papers. 1894/95; v. 87. London, 1900. p. 968. JX103.A3 1894/95 v. 87

1088
_______ Notes exchanged between Great Britain and Zanzibar, relative to the boundary between the Sultan's mainland territories and the of the British East Africa Protectorate. Zanzibar, July 13, 1899. *In* Gt. Brit. *Foreign Office.* British and foreign state papers. 1899/1900; v. 92. London, 1903. p. 115–6.
JX103.A3 1899/1900 v. 92

1089
Gt. Brit. *Treaties, etc., 1901–1910 (Edward VII).* Agreement between the United Kingdom and Germany relative to the boundary of the British and German spheres of interest between lakes Nyasa and Tanganyika. Signed at Berlin, February 23, 1901. London, Printed for H.M. Stationery Off., by Harrison, 1902. 6 p. fold. map. ([Gt. Brit. Foreign Office] Treaty series, 1902, no. 8) JX636 1892 1902 no. 8

[Gt. Brit. Parliament. Papers by command] Cd. 1009.

Text in English and German in parallel columns

1090
Gt. Brit. *Ordnance Survey Office.* Anglo-German boundary: East Africa 1904–1905. Southampton, 1906. map on 5 sheets. (*Its* GSGS no. 2224) DLC-G&M

Scale 1:100,000 or 1.5783 miles to 1.

1091
Gt. Brit. *Treaties, etc., 1901–1910 (Edward VII).* Agreement between the United Kingdom and Ethiopia relative to the frontiers between British East Africa, Uganda, and Ethiopia. Signed at Addis Ababa, December 6, 1907. London, Printed for H.M. Stationery Off. by Harrison, 1908. 4 p. 2 fold. maps. ([Gt. Brit. Foreign Office] Treaty series, 1908, no. 27)
JX636 1892 1908 no. 27

[Gt. Brit. Parliament. Papers by command] Cd. 4318.

Imperial British East Africa Company

1092
Gt. Brit. *Foreign Office.* Correspondence respecting the retirement of the Imperial British East Africa Company. London, Printed for H.M. Stationery Off. by Harrison, 1895. 25 p. (*Its* Africa no. 4 (1895)) J301.K6 1895 v. 71

[Gt. Brit. Parliament. Papers by command] C. 7646.

Includes a list of the Companys assets as at June 30, 1894.

1093
Gt. Brit. *Treaties, etc., 1837–1901 (Victoria).* Agreement between the Sultan of Zanzibar and British Acting Agent and Consul-General, respecting the administration of the British East Africa Company of certain of His Highness' possessions on the mainland and islands lying off the coast. Zanzibar, 21 August 1889. *In* Hertslet, *Sir* Edward. The map of Africa by treaty, 3d ed. London, H.M. Stationery Off., 1909. v. 1, p. 359–61. ([Document] no. 66)
JX1026 1909.H45 v. 1

Imperial British East Africa Company.

Note: In April 1888, William Mackinnon and a group of British philanthropists and businessmen created the Imperial British East Africa Company from the British East African Association. By its charter, based on the concession of May 1887 from the sultan of Zanzibar, the company administered a narrow strip of the East African mainland which served as a base for further penetration of the upper Nile basin and, in particular, of Uganda. The company was poorly managed and underfinanced for its commercial and administrative activities. Uganda was evacuated by the company in April 1893, with a protectorate being proclaimed by the British Foreign Office in June 1894. In 1895, the East Africa Protectorate took over the remaining territory lying between Uganda and the East Africa coast. Both protectorates remained under the Foreign Office until 1905, when they were transferred to the Colonial Office. After the company's withdrawal, a protracted controversy ensued with the British government over compensation to the company. The company was terminated in 1897.

Additional information on the company's publications and remaining archives is included in A. T. Matson's *The records of the Imperial British East Africa Company, 1888–1897* (Library materials on Africa, v. 10, no. 2, Oct. 1972: 83–88).

1094

Agreement between the Imperial British East Africa Company and Witu. March 18, 1891. *In* Gt. Brit. *Foreign Office.* British and foreign state papers. 1890/91; v. 83. London, 1897. p. 921–23. JX103.A3 1890/91 v. 83

1095

______ Charter granted to the Imperial British East Africa Company. Westminster, September 3, 1888. *In* Gt. Brit. *Foreign Office.* British and foreign state papers. 1887/88; v. 79. London [1895] p. 641–50.
JX103.A3 1887/88 v. 79

1096

______ ______ London, Harrison, 1888.
DLC-Micro 23940 reel 8 folio 1

Collation of the original: 4 p.

Signed: Muir Mackenzie.

Colonial Office Library East Africa pamphlet folio 1.

"Extract from the London Gazette of Friday, September 7, 1888."

1097

______ Imperial British East Africa Company to G. S. Mackenzie Esq.—power of attorney [1888], [*and* Transfer of power of attorney to John William Buchanan, 1889] 7 leaves. photostat.

Source: Col. Off. Lib. Cat.

1098

______ Treaty between the British East Africa Company and King Mwanga of Uganda. Kampala, March 30, 1892. *In* Gt. Brit. *Foreign Office.* British and foreign state papers, 1891/92; v. 84. London, 1898. p. 59–61.
JX103.A3 1891/ v. 84

Terminated by Agreement of May 29, 1893.

1099

McDermott, P. L., *comp.* British East Africa; or IBEA; a history of the formation and work of the Imperial British East Africa Company. London, Chapman and Hall, 1893. 16, 382 p. illus., port., col. map. DT431.M11

"Compiled with the authority of the Directors from official documents and the records of the company."

Includes "A sketch map of IBEA showing stations of the Imp.B.R.E. Africa Co., proposed railway and routes of Capt. Lugard 1891–92 by E. G. Ravenstein."

Appendixes include the following documents: Concession given by the Sultan of Zanzibar to the British East African Association.—[Imperial British East Africa Company] founders' agreement, 1888.—Royal charter, dated 3rd September 1888.—Baron Lambermont's award.—Agreement between His Highness the Sultan of Zanzibar and Gerald Herbert Portal, Acting English Consul-General.—Manda and Patta concession, correspondence.—Italian agreement of 3rd August 1889.—Agreement of July 1, 1890.—Settlement of Witu.—Treaty with Mwanga, dated March 30th, 1892.—Correspondence relating to company's withdrawal from Uganda.—Article IX. of the German company's concession.—Decrees, etc., relating to slavery and the slave trade.—Correspondence relating to the placing of the company's concession teritory within the free zone under the Berlin Act.

1100

______ ______ New ed. London, Chapman and Hall, 1895. 20, 632 p. illus., port., col. map.
NRU

The following documents are added to the new ed.: Neutralisation of ports under the Berlin Act.—Extract from report on meteorological observations in British East Africa for 1893.—Decrees, etc., relating to slavery and the slave trade.

Includes a list of the Company's directors and staff.

1101

Ravenstein, E. G. A sketch map of IBEA showing stations of the Imp.Br.E. Africa Co., proposed railway and routes of Capt. Lugard

1891–92. London & Liverpool, Philip [189–?] DLC-G&M

Scale 1:5,000,000.

1102
Vere-Hodge, Edward R. Imperial British East Africa Company. London, Macmillan, Published in association with the East African Literature Bureau, 1960. 95 p. illus. HF3508.A3V4

1103
Zanzibar. *Treaties, etc., 1870–1888 (Bargash bin Said).* [Concession given by the Sultan of Zanzibar to the Imperial British East Africa Company of powers over his Mrima (i.e. coastal) dominions and its dependencies, from Vanga to Kipini. Zanzibar, 24th May 1887] [Zanzibar? 1887?] 16 leaves.

Text in English (8 leaves), and Arabic (6 leaves), with H.M. Consul's registration notes (2 leaves).

Photocopy.

Source: Col. Off. Lib. Cat.

1104
Zanzibar. *Treaties, etc., 1888–1890 (Khalifa bin Said).* Concession given by His Highness the Sayyid Khalifa, Sultan of Zanzibar, to the Imperial British East Africa Company. Zanzibar-October 9, 1888. *In* Gt. Brit. *Foreign Office.* British and foreign state papers. 1887/88; v. 79. London [1895] p. 373–79. JX103.A3 1887/88 v.79

1105
Zanzibar. *Treaties, etc., 1890–1893 (Ali bin Said).* Concession by the Sultan of Zanzibar to the Imperial British East Africa Company of certain islands and of certain places on the Benadir coast. March 4, 1890. *In* Gt. Brit. *Foreign Office.* British and foreign state papers. 1890/91; v. 83. London, 1897. p. 918–9. JX103.A3 1890/91 v. 83

1106
——— ——— Supplementary agreement concluded between His Highness Seyyid Ali, G.C.S.I., Sultan of Zanzibar, and Mr. George Mackenzie, Director and Acting Administrator-in-chief of the Imperial British East Africa Company. March 5, 1891. (*In* Gt. Brit. *Foreign Office.* British and foreign state papers. 1890/91; v. 83. London, 1897. p. 919–20. JX103.A3 1890/91 v. 83

Industry

1107
East Africa High Commission. *Dept. of Economic Co-ordination.* An examination of the trends and prospects of sugar production and consumption in East Afirca, 1950–1970. Nairobi, 1960. 16, [4] leaves. DJBF

East Africa High Commission. *East African Hides and Leather Bureau.*

Note: In mid-1949, the East African Hides and Allied Industries Bureau replaced the Hides, Skins, and Leather Control, established during World War II. Headquarters of the bureau were located at Nairobi, with an experimental research laboratory at Muguga, Kenya. The bureau was charged by the East Africa High Commission to improve the quality of East African skins for export. The executive of the East African Production and Supply Council acted as secretariat to the bureau. The bureau was advised by the Interterritorial Hides and Skins Advisory Committee, supported by the East African Hides, Skins and Exporters Association, the East African Hides and Skins Dealers Association, and the East African Tanner Association. On December 16, 1954, the bureau came under the control of the Department of Economic Co-ordination of the East Africa High Commission. In September 1958 the laboratory at Muguga was closed down. On December 31, 1960, the bureau's Inspection Service was terminated. After 1960, the bureau was to act as the secretariat to the Interterritorial Hides and Skins Advisory Committee and to continue to compile statistics on exports and tanning.

1108

Report. 1950–1956/57. Nairobi, Printed by the Govt. Printer. illus. annual. HD9778.A5A25

Reports for 1956/57 issued in combined form.

Vols. for 1950–55 issued by the agency under an earlier name: East African Hides, Tanning and Allied Industries Bureau.

Information on the Bureau's activities for the period 1949–60 is included in the Annual report of the East Africa High Commission (item 1569) issued by the Colonial Office of Gt. Brit. Statistics on skin exports for 1961–66 is contained in the Annual report (item 1581) issued by the East African Common Services Organization.

L.C. has 1953–1956/57.

East Africa High Commission. *East African Industrial Council.*

Note: In September 1943, the Conference of Governors of British East African Territories established the East African Industrial Council to coordinate the policy of the East African Industrial Research Board with the activities of the East African Management Board during the Second World War. The council was reconstituted by the East Africa High Commission on January 1, 1948, and delegated an advisory body to the commission on "questions of policy relating to industrial development in East Africa." The council also was the licensing authority under the Industrial Licensing Ordinances passed by Kenya, Tanganyika, and Uganda in 1952–53. The purpose of the ordinances was to protect industrial development by the avoidance of uneconomic competition in certain articles, notably cotton and woolen piece goods, glassware, metal frames, and glazed earthenware. These items were not to be manufactured for sale in any territory except under license approved by the council. On December 16, 1954, the council came under the Department of Economic Co-ordination of the East Africa High Commission. On Dec. 9, 1961, the council was transferred to the Economic Co-ordination Division of the East African Common Services Organization, and continued its licensing activities. The council apparently ceased to function after 1964. Reports on the council are included in the Annual report of the East Africa High Commission (item 1569) issued by the Colonial Office of Gt. Brit., and subsequently in the Annual report (item 1581) issued by the East African Common Services Organization.

1109

Some notes on industrial development in East Africa. [Nairobi, Printed by the Govt. Printer] 1956. 63 p. illus., fold. map. HC517.E2E2

L.C. catalogs under: East Africa High Commission.

1110

——— ——— 2d ed. [Nairobi, Printed by the Govt. Printer, 1959] 65 p. illus. HC517.E2A45

L.C. catalogs under: East Africa High Commission.

1111

East Africa High Commission. *East African Statistical Dept. Kenya Unit.* Kenya survey of industrial production. 1954–57. [Nairobi, Govt. Printer] annual. HC517.K4E23

Suspended 1955.

Vol. for 1954 issued by the agency under a variant name: East African Statistical Dept.

Later information on industrial production in Kenya is included in Census of manufacturing 1961, issued by the Ministry of Finance and Economic Planning of Kenya Colony and Protectorate.

L.C. has 1954–57.

1112

East Africa High Commission. *East African Statistical Dept. Tanganyika Office.* Report on the survey of industrial production in Dar es Salaam for 1954. Dar es Salaam, 1956. 18 p.

Source: Dar es Salaam Lib. Bull. no. 79.

1113

——— Survey of industrial production, 1956. [Dar es Salaam? 1957?]

Includes statistics for Dar es Salaam, Arusha, Moshi, Mwanza, Tabora, and Tanga.
Cited in the following item.

1114
_______ Survey of industrial production, 1958. Dar es Salaam, 1960. 34, [15] p. DLC
At head of title: Tanganyika.
Includes statistics for industrial establishments in Tanganyika having more than five employees.

1115
East Africa High Commission. *Maize and Produce Control.* Balance sheets and accounts as at 31st July, 1950. [Nairobi, 1951] 9 p.
Source: Col. Off. Lib. Cat.

1116
East African Common Services Organization. Directory of business. 1964?+ Nairobi. quarterly.
Source: Col. Off. Lib. Cat.

1117
East African Development Bank. Industry in East Africa and role of the East African Development Bank: speech of the Director- General, East African Development Bank, to UNIDO Workshop on Financial Planning of Industrial Projects. Dar es Salaam [n.d.] 9 leaves.
Source: Tang. Lib. Ser. East Africana.

East African Industrial Research Organization.
Note: In April 1942, the East African Industries Technical Advisory Committee was replaced by the East African Industrial Research and Development Board, which was charged not only with continuing research begun by the defunct committee but also with translating industrial research into industrial production for the war effort. Further reorganization occured in September 1943, with the creation of the East African Industrial Council to coordinate the policies of two executive boards: the East African Industrial Management Board, responsible for the construction and staffing of factories, and the East African Industrial Research Board, responsible for all industrial research. There were two local branches of the East African Industrial Research Board, the Tanganyika Industrial Committee, 1943–47, and the Uganda Industrial Committee, 1943–45. The two committees dealt with local research and assisted their respective governments in setting up small-scale industries not falling within the scope of the East African Industrial Research Board. On January 1, 1948, the board became a non-self-contained service of the East Africa High Commission. On April 1, 1955, the East African Industrial Research Board was absorbed into the East African Industrial Research Organization, created by the East Africa High Commission with a grant received from the Colonial Development and Welfare Fund to stimulate new industry in East Africa and to provide technical advisory service to existing industries too small to afford their own research. The board continued to function as a scientific advisory body to the organization. However, the board has not met since August 24, 1966. It is anticipated that a new East African Industrial Research Council will absorb the East African Industrial Research Board and will coordinate the activities of the East African Industrial Research Organization with those of two new research institutes to be established in Tanzania and Uganda under the policy control and direction of the Common Market Council. The headquarters of the organization is located in Nairobi, Kenya. Topics of research undertaken by the organization include ceramics, coffee and other food processing, and chemical engineering.

1118
Annual report. 1943+ Nairobi. T177.A5E34
Report year for 1943–53 ends Dec. 31; for 1954/55+ ends June 30.
At head of title, 1948–1960/61: East Africa High Commission; 1961/62–1966/67: East African Common Services Organization; 1967/68+ East African Community.
Vols. for 1943–53 called also 1st-11th.
Vols. for 1943–53 issued by the agency under its earlier name: East African Industrial Research Board.
Vols. for 1944–47 include the Report of the

Tanganyika Industrial Committee; for 1944–45 include the Report of the Uganda Industrial Committee.

L.C. has 1943+

1119

——— Report C.R. 1+ [Nairobi? 1956+] irregular.

The following numbers have been identified in the agency's Research catalogue: 1942–1969; a brochure giving an account of the work and type of research undertaken by EAIRO since its inception:

1. Report of tests on a stationary bed coffee dryer. 1956.

2. Report on investigations into the performance of the Wilken coffee dryer. 1956.

3. Report on further investigations into the Wilken bed-type coffee dryer. 1957.

4. The performance of radial-flow and floor ventilated silos when finishing partially dried parchment coffee. 1957.

5. Research into the mechanical drying of East African Arabica parchment coffee. 1957.

6. Report on the performance of a bed-dryer using a 48-hour drying cycle. 1957.

7. The effect of moisture content, sunlight and drying temperature on the quality of Arabica coffee. 1957.

8. Some further effect of chemical and photochemical treatment on the quality of Arabica coffee beans. 1957.

9. The effect of light frequency on the quality of Arabica coffee beans. 1958.

10. Some characteristics of parchment coffee in storage and other properties. 1959.

11. Investigation into the nature and cause of "onion-flavour" taint in Kenya coffee. 1960.

12. Fermentation of coffee. 1963.

13. The quality of Kenya coffee as refined by the Out-Turn report (1953–63). 1967. 2 v.

Contents: v. 1. Text.—v. 2. Figures.

1120

——— Research catalogue: 1942–1969; a brochure giving an account of the work and type of research undertaken by EAIRO since its inception. [Nairobi, Printed by EAC Printer, 1969?] 81 p. illus. T177.K4E17

On cover: East African Community.

Includes an alphabetical list of research topics, e.g. building materials, coffee, lemongrass, phosphatic fertilizers, etc. with bibliographic references to the agency's Annual report, Technical pamphlet, and other technical research reports.

1121

——— Technical pamphlet. no. 1–17? [Nairobi] 1942?–1955? illus. irregular. DLC

No. 1–9 issued by the East African Industries Technical Advisory Committee; no. 10–16 by the East African Industrial Research Board.

No more published?

L.C. has no. 5 on microfilm (23940, reel 6, octavo 324), 10, 11 on microfilm (23940, reel 6, octavo 325), 12–17; DNAL has no. 2, 4–16.

The following numbers have been identified:

no. 1. On the manufacture of glass bottles. 1942?

Cited in the agency's Annual report, 1943.

no. 2. A new pattern of hoe. 1942. [5] p.

Reprinted in 1946.

no. 3. Castor oil and its conversion into a drying oil. [1942?]

Source: Col. Off. Lib. Cat.

no. 4. A simple filter for reconditioning the used lubricating oil of petrol engines. 1942. 11 p.

no. 5. Weller, H. O. Brick-making in East Africa. 1943. 12 p.

See also no. 14.

no. 6. Colet Birch, W. Paints and substitute distempers from East African materials; a summary of results of investigations by the Research Branch of the Board. 1943. 9 p.

no. 7. French, M. H. Notes on methods of small-scale tanning. 1943. 12 p.

no. 8. Weller, H. O. Improved lime mortars as substitutes for portland cement mortars; a short account of an investigation by the Board into the value of Kenya pozzuolanas. 2d ed. 1944. 8 p.

First published in 1943.

no. 9. Paper making as a home industry. 1943. 8 p.

no. 10. Glover, J., *and* L. Goldstucker. Small

scale pottery manufacture; an account of the development of a small pottery factory using only African workmen. 1944. 15 p.

no. 11. The design of furnaces for burning sawdust and other comminuted fuels. 1945. 10 p.

no. 12. Weller, H. O. The manufacture of roofing titles in East Africa. 1945. 15 p.

no. 13. _____ Building limes. 1946. 8 p.

no. 14. _____ Brick-making in East Africa. 2d ed. 1945. 15 p.

Revised edition of no. 5.

no. 15. Campbell, A. J. Design for a small wood-fired up-draught kiln. 1947. 10 p.

no. 16. Colet Birch, W. Clays, red and black, and Nairobi building stone; an attempt to use them for the manufacture of bricks and tiles, with a note on the application of the laboratory results on a manufacturing scale, by A. J. Campbell. Nairobi, Printed by the Govt. Printer, 1953. 22 p.

no. 17. Cole, A. F. C., R. A. F. Brenan, *and* T. A. Koenig. The pelletizing of cetyl alcohol. 1955. 5 p.

East African Industries Technical Advisory Committee.

Note: In July 1941 the East African Industries Technical Advisory Committee was established by the Conference of Governors of British East African Territories to provide liaison between research and supply organizations in East Africa during World War II. The committee absorbed the functions of the former *ad hoc* Committee on Munitions and Equipment, and the defunct *ad hoc* Comittee on Petroleum Fuel Substitutes. During the committee's existence, it studied industrial possibilities for East Africa and coordinated research on industrial problems. In April 1942 the committee was succeeded by the East African Industrial Research and Development Board.

1122

Bulletin. no. 1–3; Sept. 1941–Apr. 1942. Nairobi. irregular. DNAL

No. 2, Nov. 1941, issued by the East African Substitutes Committee.

DNAL has Sept. 1941–Apr. 1942.

East African Substitutes Committee.

Note: In June 1941, the East African Substitutes Committee was created in liaison with the East African Industries Technical Advisory Committee. The task of the committee was to investigate local products that could replace imported materials cut off with the initiation of World War II. In November 1943, the East African Substitutes Committee was absorbed into the Tanganyika Industrial Committee, a local branch of the East African Industrial Research Board.

1123

Technical pamphlet. no. 1–2. [Dar es Salaam, 1941?–1943?] irregular. DNAL

No more published?

The following numbers are held by DNAL:

no. 1. On edible oils, salad oils, ghee and ghee subsitutes.

no. 2. Manufacture of hand-made paper.

1124

Grant, Julius. Report on pulp and paper production in Uganda Protectorate and Kenya Colony. [London? Pulp and Paper Research Co., ltd., 1956] 185 leaves. illus. HD9837.U32G7

The survey was authorized by the Uganda Development Corporation and the Minister of Forest Development, Game and Fisheries of Kenya Colony and Protectorate.

1125

Kenya Colony and Protectorate. *Forest Dept.* Memorandum on the East African bamboo (*Arundinaria alpina*) with special reference to its utilisation for the manufacture of paper-pulp. Nairobi [Printed by the Govt. Printer] 1922. 6, 2 p. DNAL

1126

Llewelyn, D. A. B. Coffee drying; preliminary report to the Coffee Board of Kenya. Nairobi, 1955. 88 leaves.

At head of cover title: East African Industrial Research Board.

Source: Col. Off. Lib. Cat.

Labor

1127
Conference of Governors of British East African Territories. *Statistical Section.* Analysis of wages paid to African employees in Kenya for the month of November, 1946. Nairobi, 1947. 47 leaves. NNUN

1128
Conference on Public Policy, *2d, University College, Nairobi, 1963.* Conferences on public policy, 1963/4: East African federation; [paper no. 14] The integration of labour policy [by] T. J. Mboya. [Nairobi? 1964?] 7, 6, 7 leaves. HC517.E2C6 1963 no. 14

Appendix A: Joint statement issued in Kampala on 20th August, 1962 by the three ministers then responsible for labour—Mr. Mboya (Kenya), Mr. Onama (Uganda), and Mr. Kamaliza (Tanganyika).—Appendix B: Minutes of a meeting of the Triapartite Labour Conference on East Africa, held in Dar es Salaam on 15th and 16th November, 1962.

Later revised without the appendixes as East African labour policy and federation, published in Colin Leys' Federation in East Africa; opportunities and problems (Nairobi, London, Oxford University Press, 1965 [i.e. 1966] HC517.E2L4) p. [102]-110.

1129
East Africa High Commission. *East African Statistical Dept.* Earnings of African labour. 1947–48. [Nairobi] annual. CSt-H

At head of title: Kenya Colony and Protectorate.

CSt-H catalogs under: East African Common Services Organization. *East African Statistical Dept.*

Cst-H has 1947–48.

1130
______ Enumeration of employees in building construction [in] Uganda, April 1955. [Nairobi] 1955. 8 p. HD8039.B892U3

Later statistics are included in the Statistical abstract issued by the Statistics Division of the Ministry of Planning and Community Development of Uganda.

1131
______ Report on African labour census 1947 [in Kenya] Prepared under the direction of C. J. Martin, Director [of the] East African Statistical Dept. [Nairobi?] 1948. 5 p. DLC

Later reports are issued by the Labour Dept. of Kenya Colony and Protectorate.

1132
______ Report on the enumeration of African employees [in Tanganyika] July 1952. [Nairobi, 1953] 32, [51] p. HD5841.T3A5

1133
______ Report on the enumeration of non native employees [in] Kenya. 1946–52. [Nairobi] annual. HD5841.K4A3

At head of title, 1946–49: Colony and Protectorate of Kenya; 1952: Kenya.

Suspended 1950–51.

Title varies: 1946–49, Report on census of non native employees.

Later information is included in the agency's Reported employment and wages in Kenya.

L.C. has 1947–52.

1134
______ Reported employment and wages in Kenya. 1954–1948/60. [Nairobi, Printed by the Govt. Printer] annual. HD5841.K4A32

At head of title: Kenya.

Reports for 1955/56 issued in combined form.

Title varies: 1959, Reported employment and earnings in Kenya.

Superseded by Reported employment and earnings in Kenya issued by the Economics and Statistics Division of Kenya Colony and Protectorate.

Vol. for 1948/60 includes a summary, but not complete statistical data, from earlier reports. Information on non-African employees for 1946–52 is included in the agency's Report on the enumeration of non native employees [in] Kenya.

L.C. has 1954–1948/60.

1135
East Africa High Commission. *East African Statistical Dept. Uganda Unit.* Enumeration of employees. 1948–60. [Entebbe] annual. HD8791.E3A32

At head of title: Uganda Protectorate.

Suspended 1953–54.

Title varies: 1948–49, Report on the enumeration of African labour.—1950–52, Report on the enumeration of African employees in Uganda.

Superseded by a publication with the same title issued by the Statistics Branch of the Office of the Prime Minister of Uganda.

L.C. catalogs under: East Africa High Commission. *East African Statistical Dept.* Report on the enumeration of African employees in Uganda.

L.C. has 1949, and 1956–60; DJBF has 1950–60.

1136
_______ Enumeration of employees in cotton ginneries: Uganda. 1953–1957? [Entebbe] annual. HD8039.T42U43a

Suspended 1956.

No more published?

Later statistics are included in the Statistical abstract issued by the Statistics Division of the Ministry of Planning and Community Development of Uganda.

L.C. has 1953–57.

1137
Northcott, Clarence H. African labour efficiency survey. London, H.M. Stationery Off., 1949. 123 p. (Colonial research publications, no. 3) JV33.G7A52 no. 3

At head of title: Colonial Office.

A survey to investigate the economic and social conditions of 7,000 African employees of the Kenya and Uganda Railways and Harbours in Nairobi during the first half of 1947.

1138
Orde-Browne, *Sir* Granville St. John. Labour conditions in East Africa. London, H.M. Stationery Off., 1946. 94 p. fold. map. ([Gt. Brit.] Colonial Office. Colonial no. 193) HD8799.E407

Includes information on labor conditions in Kenya, Tanganyika, Uganda, and Zanzibar.

Language and Linguistics

1139
Whiteley, Wilfred H., *and* A. E. Gutkind. A linguistic bibliography of East Africa. Kampala, Uganda, East African Swahili Committee, and the East African Institute of Social Research, 1954. 62 leaves. Z7106.W5

"Addenda et corrigenda slip inserted."

Includes an unannotated list of books and periodical articles on the languages of Kenya, Tanganyika, and Uganda, with a separate section on Swahili.

1140
_______ _______ Supplement. no. 1–2; Nov. 1954–Nov. 1955. Kampala, Uganda, East African Swahili Committee, and the East African Institute of Social Research. Z7106.W52

1141
_______ _______ Rev. ed. Kampala, East African Swahili Committee, 1958. 1 v. (loose-leaf) Z7106.W523

1142
_______ _______ Supplement. no. 1+ Apr. 1960+ Kampala, East African Swahili Com-

mittee, and East African Institute of Social Research, Makerere College. Z7106.W52

Swahili Linguistics

Note: Swahili is the lingua franca of East Africa. This section includes Swahili literature; material on Swahili linguistics; and Swahili readers and textbooks issued by the East African Literature Bureau, the Institute of Swahili Research and its predecessors, and publications issued by partner states of the East African Community. Official publications in Swahili on other topics will be included in subsequent guides to official publications of Kenya, Tanzania, and Uganda. Additional titles may be found in Marcel van Spaandonck's *Practical and systematical Swahili bibliography; linguistics, 1850–1963* (Leiden, Brill, 1965. xxiii, 61 p. Z7108.S8S65), and Alberto Mioni's "La bibliographie de langue swahili; remarques et supplément à la Swahili Bibliography de M. Van Spaandonck" (*In Cahiers d'études africaines,* 27, v. 7, 3. cahier. Paris, 1967. p. [485]–532. DT1.C3 no. 27).

East African Swahili Committee.

Note: The Inter-territorial Language (Swahili) Committee was created to establish a standard form of Swahili for educational purposes in Kenya, Tanganyika, Uganda, and Zanzibar. The committee convened first in Nairobi, Kenya, in 1930, and thereafter met annually in one of the major cities of East Africa. Initially, each of the four governments appointed two officials, one of whom was the director of education, and two nonofficials. In 1948, when the committee came under the East Africa High Commission, membership was reduced to eight, two from each jurisdiction. During its first years, the committee made Kiunguja, the dialect of Swahili spoken in Zanzibar, the model for a "standard Swahili," with an orthography and rules for spelling, and it approved the use of specialized terms for various subjects, e.g., law, education, etc. Throughout the 1930's and 1940's, the committee gave its official imprimatur to books conforming to the standard language. This practice ceased sometime after the creation of the East African Literature Bureau in 1948. On September 1, 1952, the committee moved from Nairobi, Kenya, to become affiliated with Makerere College, Kampala, Uganda. In 1965, the committee was absorbed into the Institute of Swahili Research, University College, Dar es Salaam, Tanzania. The institute was financed by the governments of Kenya and Tanzania, the Calouste Gulbenkian Foundation, the British Ministry of Overseas Development, and the Rockefeller Foundation. In 1969, the institute was formally constituted within the Faculty of Arts and Social Science of the University College, Dar es Salaam (now the University of Dar es Salaam) to strengthen its financial support. On July 30, 1973, the Inter-university Committee for East Africa resolved that the institute should become an interstate establishment in order to serve all three universities of the East African Community as an East African research center of the Swahili language.

Activities of the institute and its predecessor, the East African Swahili Committee, have included substantial research in the fields of literature, linguistics, and language history, with special emphasis on the collection and preservation of Swahili manuscripts (see J. W. T. Allen's *The Swahili and Arabic manuscripts and tapes in the library of the University College Dar-es-Salaam; a catalogue* (Leiden, Brill, 1970. xvi, 116 p. Z6605.S85A4)). Current projects include the compilation of a definitive dictionary of Swahili, the preparation of material for the teaching of Swahili, and the publication of the institute's journal, Kiswahili (item 1149).

1143
[Annual report] –1963/64? [Dar es Salaam] ICRL

Report year ends June 30.

Period covered by report is irregular.

Title varies.

No more published?

Annual reports for 1958/59, 1960/61, 1961/62, and 1963/64 are included in no. 30, 32, v. 33 [pt.] 2, and 34 [pt.] 1 of Swahili (item 1158). Earlier reports, with informal minutes, or draft minutes, are in the agency's Journal, and Bulletin.

ICRL has 1953/54–1955 on microfilm; source for 1952–56: Makerere Lib. Union list.

1144
——— Quinquennial report 1952–57. Kampala, Makerere College [1958] 20 p.
Source: Col. Off. Lib. Cat.

1145
Education Conference, *Dar es Salaam, Tanganyika Territory, 1925.* Conference between government and missions, convened by His Excellency the Governor, Sir Donald Cameron. Report of proceedings, held at Dar es Salaam, 5th to 12th October, 1925. [Dar es Salaam, Govt. Printer] 1925. 177 p. map. NNMR
Cover title: Report of the Education Conference, 1925, together with the Report of the Committee for the Standardization of the Swahili Language.

1146
Inter-territorial Language (Swahili) Committee to the East African Dependencies. Amendments to Bishop Steere's "Swahili exercises." Dar es Salaam [n.d.] 2 v.
Source: Dar es Salaam Lib. Bull. no. 80.

1147
——— A standard English-Swahili dictionary (founded on Madan's English-Swahili dictionary) by the Inter-territorial Language Committee of the East African Dependencies under the direction of the late Frederick Johnson. London, Oxford University Press, 1939. 635, [1] p. PL8703.15

1148
——— A standard Swahili-English dictionary (founded on Madan's Swahili-English dictionary) by the Inter-territorial Language Committee for the East African Dependencies under the direction of the late Frederick Johnson. London, Oxford University Press, 1939. 548 p. PL8703.153

1149
Kiswahili. v. 40 [no.] 2+ Sept. 1970+ Dar es Salaam, Chuo Kikuu. semiannual. PL8701.K58
Supersedes and continues the numbering of Swahili (item 1158).
"Jarida la Chuo cha Uchunguzi wa Lugha ya Kiswahili."
Text in English and Swahili.
L.C. has Sept. 1970+

1150
Kiswahili fasihi na ufanisi. Kijarida. no. 1+ Okt. 1971+ Dar es Salaam, Chama cha Kiswahili, Chuo Kikuu. DLC
Title translated: Correct usage of Swahili. Explanation.
L.C. has Okt. 1971.

1151
Lambert, H. E. Chi-chifundi; a dialect of the southern Kenya coast. Kampala [Uganda] East African Swahili Committee, 1958. 111 p. (Studies in Swahili dialect, 5) PL8704.Z9G3
Text in English and Swahili.

1152
——— Chi-jomvu and Ki-ngare; sub-dialects of the Mombasa area. Kampala, East African Swahili Committee, 1958. 119 p. (Studies in Swahili dialect, 3) DLC
Text in English and Swahili.

1153
——— Ki-vumba; a dialect of the southern Kenya coast. Kampala, East African Swahili Committee, 1957. 101 p. (Studies in Swahili dialect, 2) DLC
Text in English and Swahili.

1154
Mulika. no. [1]+ [Dar es Salaam, Chuo cha Unchunguzi wa Lugha ya Kiswahili, 1971?+] 12 no. a year. PL8701.M8
First issue has no number or date; no. 2+ have no date.
Title translated: Ray [of light]
Papers on the study of Swahili.
L.C. has no. [1]+

1155
Newall, H. W., *comp.* Notes in Ki-Swahili as spoken in King's African Rifles. Kampala, Govt. Printer [c1928] 24 p.
Source: Royal Comm. Soc. Cat.

1156
Prins, Adriaan H. J. A Swahili nautical dictionary. Dar es Salaam, Chuo cha Uchunguzi wa Lugha ya Kiswahili, 1970. 95 p. (Preliminary studies in Swahili lexicon, 1) V24.P86

Contents: pt. 1. Swahili-English.—pt. 2. English-Swahili.

1157
Sarufi na ufasaha. no. 1–2? Kampala, East African Swahili Committee, 1955–56? IEN

No more published?

Title translated: Grammar and style.

The following numbers are held by IEN:
no. 1. Kopoka, O. B. Vihusiano. 1955. 18 p.
no. 2. ______ Miao. [1956?] 56 p.

1158
Swahili. 1930-Mar. 1970. Dar es Salaam, Institute of Swahili Research. PL8701.E2

Annual, 1930–57, 1960–61; 2 no. a year, 1958–59, 1962/63–1970.

Vols. for 1930–61 called also no. 1–32; no. 31–32 called also "New series" v. 1, pt. 2–3; vols. for 1962/63–1970 called also v. 33–40/1.

Title varies: 1930–53, Bulletin.—1954–58, Journal.

Issued by the agency under earlier names: 1930–53, East African Inter-territorial Language (Swahili) Committee (varies); 1954–64, East African Swahili Committee.

Continued by Kiswahili (item 1149).

Supplements accompany some numbers.

Text in English and Swahili.

L.C. catalogs under: East African Swahili Committee. Journal.

L.C. has 1952–70 (most supplements wanting); ICRL has 1952–68 (1955 wanting) on microfilm; the Library of the University of Dar es Salaam has earlier and more complete holdings.

1159
Uganda. *Governor, 1925–1932* (*Gowers*). Development of Kiswahili as an educational and administrative language in the Uganda Protectorate. Entebbe, Printed by the Govt. Printer, 1928. 7 p. 4PL 227

1160
Whiteley, Wilfred H. The dialects and verse of Pemba; an introduction. Kampala, East African Swahili Committee, Makerere College, 1958. 61 p. map. (Studies in Swahili dialect, 4) PL8704.Z9P4

"Corrigenda" slip inserted.

Text in English and Swahili.

1161
______ Ki-mtang'ata; a dialect of the Mrima coast, Tanganyika. Kampala, East African Swahili Committee, Makerere College, 1956. 64 p. (Studies in Swahili dialect, 1) DLC

Text in English and Swahili.

Swahili Literature

Unless otherwise noted, the text of the following entries (items 1162–1224) is in Swahili.

1162
Abdallah bin Hemedi 'lAjjemy. Habari za Wakilindi. Imehaririwa na J. W. T. Allen na William Kimweri bin Mbago bin Kibwana bin Maiwe wa Kwekalo (Mlungui) bin Kimweri Zanyumbai. Nairobi, East African Literature Bureau, 1962. 254 p. illus. DT443.A58

Title translated: A history of the Kilindi.

1163
______ The Kilindi. Edited by J. W. T. Allen and William Kimweri bin Mbago bin Kibwana bin Maiwe Kwekalo (Mlungui) bin Kimweri Zanyumbai. Nairobi, East African Literature Bureau, 1963. xxxvi, 238 p. illus. DT443.A5813

Translation of Habari za Wakilindi.

Text in English.

1164
Abdulla, Muhammed Said. Mzimu wa watu wa kale. Nairobi, East African Literature Bureau [1968] 85 p. illus. PL8704.A36 1968

First published 1960.

Title translated: A spirit of the past.

"A detective story from Zanzibar; first prize winner in the Swahili story-writing competition, 1957/58."

1165
Abedi, K. Amri. Sheria za kutunga mashâiri, na Diwani ya Amri. Kampala, Eagle Press, 1954. 148 p. DHU
Title translated: The poems of Amri with an essay on Swahili poetry and the rules of versification.

1166
_______ _______ Dar es Salaam, East African Literature Bureau, 1963. xvi, 130 p. PL8701.A3
"Introductory study, by H. E. Lambert."

1167
Abubakr, Abdulla M. The life of Khalifa Abubakr Siddik. Nairobi, Eagle Press, 1952. 31 p. DHU

1168
Akilimali Snow-White, K. H. A. Diwani ya Akilimali. Nairobi, East African Literature Bureau, 1963. 79 p. (Johari za Kiswahili, 4) PL8704.A5
Title translated: The poems of Akilimali.

1169
_______ _______ Dar es Salaam, East African Literature Bureau, 1966. 79 p. (Johari za Kiswahili, 4) PL8704.A5A6 1966

1169a
_______ Usanifu wa ushairi. Nairobi, East African Literature Bureau [1974] 163 p. (Johari za Kiswahili, 13) DLC
Title translated: The art of poetry.

1170
Baker, E. C. Mwarabu na binti wake; na hadithi nyingine. Nairobi, Oxford University Press, 1968. 82 p. DLC
"First published by the East African Literature Bureau, 1950."
Title translated: The Arab and his daughter, and other tales.

1171
el-Buhriy, Hemedi bin Abdallah. Utenzi wa Abdirrahmani na Sufiyani. The history of Abdurrahman and Sufian, by Hemed Abdallah Saidi Abdallah Masudi el Buhry el Hinawy. With translation by Roland Allen and notes by J. W. T. Allen. Dar es Salaam, East African Literature Bureau, 1961. 132 p. (Johari za Kiswahili, 2) PL8704.B82 1961
Swahili text and English prose translation on opposite pages.

1172
_______ Utenzi wa Kadhi Kasim bin Jaafar. Umehaririwa na Mohamed Burhan Mkelle. [Dar es Salaam] Chuo cha Uchunguzi wa Lugha ya Kiswahili [1972?] 56 p. PL8704.B82U8 1972
Title translated: The poems of Kadhi Kassim bin Jaafar.

1173
_______ Utenzi wa Kutawafu Nabii. The release of the Prophet, with translation by Roland Allen. Edited by J. W. T. Allen. Kampala [East African Swahili Committee] 1956. 72 p. PL8701.E2 no. 26 suppl.
"Supplement to the East African Swahili Committees [sic] Journal no. 26, June 1956."

1174
_______ Utenzi wa Seyyidna Huseni bin Ali. The history of Prince Hussein son of Ali, umetungwa na Hemed Abdallah. With translation and notes by J. W. T. Allen. Dar es Salaam, East African Literature Bureau, 1965. 130 p. (Johari za Kiswahili, 6) PL8704.B83 1965
Swahili text and English prose translation on opposite pages.

1175
_______ Utenzi wa vita vya Wadachi kutamalaki Mrima, 1307 A.H. The German conquest of the Swahili coast, 1891 A.D., by Hemedi bin Abdallah bin Said bin Abdallah bin Masudi el Buhriy. With translation and notes by J. W. T. Allen. [2d ed.] Dar es Salaam, East African Literature Bureau, 1960. 84 p.

(Johari za Kiswahili [no. 1]) PL8704.B84 1960
First published as a supplement to Journal no. 25, June 1955, of the East African Swahili Committee.
Swahili text and English prose translation on opposite pages.

1176
Cory Hans. Sikilizeni mashairi. Picha zimechorwa na binti wake. [4th ed.] Mwanza, Lake Print. Works [1966] 42 p. illus. PL8704.C67S5 1966
"1st edition published by the East African Literature Bureau, Nairobi."
Title translated: Listen to poetry.

1177
East African Swahili Committee. List of manuscripts in the East African Swahili Committee Collection, University College Library, Dar es Salaam, compiled and edited by Jan Knappert and H. Ball [of the] East African Swahili Committee. [Dar es Salaam] 1964. 25 p. (Dar es Salaam. University College. Library. Library bulletin and accessions list, no. 24) CSt-H

1178
Farsi, S. S. Swahili sayings from Zanzibar. Dar es Salaam, East African Literature Bureau, 1958. 2 v. in 1. PN6519.S9F3
Text in English and Swahili on opposite pages.
Contents: 1. Proverbs.—2. Riddles and superstitions.

1179
Farsy, Muhammad Saleh. Kurwa na Doto; maelezo ya makazi katika kijiji cha Unguja yaani Zanzibar. Dar es Salaam, East African Literature Bureau, 1960. 62 p. PL8704.F3
Added t.p.: Kurwa and Doto; a novel depicting life in a typical Zanzibar village.

1180
Ganzel, Eddie. Ndoto ya mwendawazimu. Dar es Salaam, East African Literature Bureau [1972] 93 p. illus. PL8704.G35
Title translated: The dream of a madman.

1181
Hamid ibn Muhammad, *called Tipoo Tib*. Maisha ya Hamed bin Muhammed el Murjebi, yaani Tippu Tip, kwa maneno yake mwenyewe. Kimefasiriwa na W. H. Whiteley. Nairobi, East African Literature Bureau [1966] 141 p. maps. (Johari za Kiswahili, 8) DT361.H33
"First published as a supplement to the East African Swahili Committee Journals no. 28/2, July 1958, and no. 29/1, January 1959 . . ."
Title translated: The life of Hamed bin Muhammed el Murjebi, also known as Tippu Tip, as told in his own words.
"The text . . . is that originally collected by Brode and published by him in the *Mitteilungen des Seminars für Orientalische Sprachen* 1902–3."

1182
Hinawy, Mbarak Ali. Al-Akida and Fort Jesus, Mombasa; the life-history of Muhammad bin Abdallah bin Mbarak Bakjashweini, with songs and poems of his time. London, Macmillan, 1950. 88 p. illus. IEN
Text in English and Swahili.

1183
__________ Al-Akida and Fort Jesus, Mombasa. [2d ed.] Nairobi, East African Literature Bureau [1970] 79 p. illus. DT432.H56 1970
"First edition by East African Literature Bureau and Macmillan and Co., Ltd . . . 1950."
"Utenzi wa Al-Akida (a Swahili poem)" by Abdallah bin Mas'ud bin Salim al-Mazrui: p. [67]–69.
Text in English and Swahili.

1184
Hisi zetu. Kimeandikwa na S. D. Kiango na T. S. Y. Sengo. Dar es Salaam, Chuo cha Uchunguzi wa Kiswahili, Chuo Kikuu, 1973+ DLC
Title translated: Our feelings.
Short stories.
L.C. has 1, 1973.

1185
Hyslop, Graham. Afadhali mchawi. Dar es Sa-

laam, Oxford University Press [1969, c1957] 26 p. PL8704.H9A7 1969
"First published by the East African Literature Bureau 1957."
Title translated: It's better to have a wizard.
A play in two acts.

1186
_______ Mgeni karibu. Nairobi, Oxford University Press [1966, c1957] 14 p. PL8704.H9M45 1966
"First published by East African Literature Bureau 1957."
Title translated: Welcome stranger.
A play.

1187
Jamaliddini, Abdul Karim bin. Utenzi wa Vita vya Maji-Maji; [with] historical introduction by Margaret Bates. Translated by W. H. Whiteley. [n.p.] 1957. 72 p. (East African Swahili Committee. Journal, no 27, June 1957. Supplement) MBU
Title translated: Poems of the Maji Maji rebellion.
Text in English and Swahili.

1188
Kabeya, John B. Mtemi Mirambo; mtawala shujaa wa Kinyamwezi. Nairobi, East African Literature Bureau [1966] 90 p. illus., geneal. tables, map. (Wananchi mashuhuri wa Tanzania) DT446.M54K3
"Watu mashuhuri wa Tanzania."
Title translated: Mtemi Mirambo; great ruler of the Nyamwezi people.

1189
Katalambula, Faraji H. Simu ya kifo. Dar es Salaam, East African Literature Bureau, 1965. 76 p. illus. PL8704.K3
Title translated: Trail of death.
"The manuscript of this book was one of those highly commended in the novel writing competition organised by the E.A. Literature Bureau, 1963."

1190
Kezilahabi, Euphrase. Rosa Mistika. Nairobi, East African Literature Bureau [1971] 119 p. PL8704.K4R6
A novel.

1191
Kiimbila, J. K. Ubeberu utashindwa. Dar es Salaam, Chuo cha Uchunguzi wa Kiswahili [c1971] 133 p. PL8704.K517U2
Title translated: Capitalism will fail.
A novel.

1192
Kijuma, Muhammad. Utenzi wa Fumo Liyongo. [Dar es Salaam] Chuo cha Uchunguzi wa Lugha ya Kiswahili, Chuo cha Dar es Salaam, 1973. 28 p. PL8704.K518U8
Title translated: The poem of King Liyongo.
See also item 1219.

1193
Kuboja, Nacksso J. Mbojo: simba-mtu. Nairobi, East African Literature Bureau [1971] 104 p. illus. PL8704.K84M3
Title translated: Mbojo: the lion-man.
The story is based on the myth of human lions in the Singida region of Tanzania.

1194
Kuria, Henry. Nakupenda, lakini . . . Nairobi, East African Literature Bureau, Eagle Press, 1961. 42 p. NN
Title translated :I love you, but . . .
A play.

1195
_______ _______ Nairobi, Oxford University Press [1968, c1957] 42 p. PL8704.K87N3 1968
"First published by East African Literature Bureau 1957."

1196
Lambert, H. E. Diwani ya Lambert. Imehaririwa na Mathias E. Mnyampala. Nairobi, East African Literature Bureau [1971] 50 p. (Johari za Kiswahili, 10) PL8704.L3D5
Title translated: Poems of Lambert.

1197
Lesso, Zuberi H. Utenzi wa zinduko la ujamaa. Nairobi, East African Literature Bureau [1972] 62 p. PL8704.L43U8
Title translated: A poem on the awakening of socialism [in Tanzania]

1198
Mashairi ya Mambo leo. Poems from the Swahili newspaper "Mambo leo" selected by the Inter-territorial Language Committee. London, Sheldon Press, 1966–67. 2 v. in 1. PL8704.A2M33
"First published in book form 1946."

1199
Matola, S., *comp.* Waimbaji wa juzi: Mw. Shabaan [sic, et al.] Walioharriri nyimbo ni S. Matola, Mw. Shabaan [sic], W. H. Whiteley. Habari nyingine zimekusanywa na A. A. Jahadhmy. [Dar es Salaam, Chuo cha Uchunguzi wa Lugha ya Kiswahili, 1966] 124 p. PL8704.A2M34
Title translated: Singers of the year before last.

1200
Mnyampala, Mathias E. Diwani ya Mnyampala. Dar es Salaam, East African Literature Bureau, 1963. 156 p. (Johari za Kiswahili, 5) PL8704.M58
Title translated: Poems of Mnyampala.

1201
——— Fasili johari ya mashairi. [Dar es Salaam] Halmashauri ya Kiswahili ya Afrika Mashariki, 1964. 83 p. DLC
"Supplement 1 to the Journal 33, 2 of the Swahili Committee, February, 1964."
Title translated: Cut jewels of poetry.
Text in Swahili, with an introd. in English by H. E. Lambert.

1202
——— Utenzi wa Enjili Takatifu. [Mombasa] Halmashauri ya Kiswahili ya Afrika Mashariki [1963] 87 p. (East African Swahili Committee. Journal. no 33/1. Supplement.) ICRL
Title translated: Poems of the Holy Gospel.

1203
——— ——— [Ndanda, Tanzania] Ndanda Mission Press [1967?] 119 p. illus. PL8704.M584

1204
——— Waadhi wa ushairi. Pamoja na utangulizi ulioandikwa na K. Amri Abedi. Dar es Salaam, East African Literature Bureau, 1965. 87 p. (Johari za Kiswahili, 7) PL8704.M585
Title translated: Speeches on the art of poetry.

1205
Muhammad, Saleh. Utenzi wa jengo lenye itifaki: baiti 334. The structure of harmony: [334 verses, by] Mtungaji Saleh Muhammad. Nairobi, East African Literature Bureau [1974] 68 p. (Johari za Kiswahili, 12) DLC
Text in Swahili and English.
Poetry.

1205a
Musiba, Aristablus E. Kufa na kupona. Nairobi, East African Literature Bureau [1974] 117 p. PL8704.M86K8
Title translated: Death and life.
A novel.

1206
Mwaruka, Ramadhani. Utenzi wa Jamhuri ya Tanzania. Nairobi, East African Literature Bureau [1968] 64 p. DT444.M9
Title translated: The epic of the Republic of Tanzania.
A poem on the history of Tanzania.

1207
Ngali, Mwanyengela. Mwana Taabu, na michezo mingine ya kuigiza. Kampala, East African Literature Bureau [1971] 77 p. PL8704.N35M9
Title translated: Daughter Taabu, and other plays.

Contents: Mwana-Taabu.—Kifo cha penzi. —"Mwerevu mjinga."

1208
Ngugi, Gerishon. Nimelogwa! Nisiwe na mpenzi. Dar es Salaam, East African Literature Bureau, 1961. 78 p. CtY
Title translated: I am under a spell! I cannot have a lover.
A play.

1209
_______ Nimelogwa nisiwe na mpenzi! mchezo wa kuigiza. Dar es Salaam, East African Literature Bureau [1971] 78 p. PL8704.N44N5
Title translated: I am under a spell; I cannot have a lover! a play.

1210
Nurru, Saidi M. Ndoa ya mzimuni. Nairobi, East African Literature Bureau [1974] 60 p. DLC
Title translated: Marriage of a ghost.

1211
Nyasulu, Godfrey. Laana ya Pandu. Nairobi, East African Literature Bureau [1974] 97 p. DLC
Title translated: The curse of Pandu.

1212
Nyasulu, Godfrey, *and* J. Mkabarah. Michezo ya kuigiza na hadithi. Nairobi, East African Literature Bureau [1970] 252 p. PL8704.N8A6 1970
Title translated: Plays and a story.
Contents: Wavivu [na] Godfrey Nyasulu.—Sikupendi tena [na] Jumaa Mkabarah.—Wikondeji [na] Godfrey Nyasulu.

1213
Omari, Cuthbert K. Mwenda kwao. [Dar es Salaam, Chuo cha Uchunguzi wa Lugha ya Kiswahili, 1971] 157 p. PL8704.042M9
Title translated: One who goes home.
A novel.

1214
Pavumapo palilie, na hadithi nyingine. [Nairobi] Longman; kwa maafikiano na British Broadcasting Corporation [1972, c1971] 40 p. (Hekaya za kuburudisha) PL8704.A2P3 1972
Contents: Suleiman, M. Wivu mwovu.—Mohamed, S. A. Mzee Khamis, leo wapi?—Said, M. M. Malipo duniani hesabu ahera.—Nassor, M. G. Ndoa ziko mbinguni.—Nassor, F. H. Pavumapo palilie.—Abeid, R. K. Ushirikina si mzuri.—Hilal, A. M. A. Maryam na siku ya mwanzo ya Dakhalia.—Suleiman, M. Pesa moto.

1215
Robert, Shaaban. Adili na nduguze. Picha zimechorwa na R. E. Bush. London, Macmillan, 1968. 65 p. illus. PL8704.R54A67 1968
First published in 1952.
Title translated: Adili and his brothers.
"The manuscript for this book was received through the East African Literature Bureau."

1216
_______ Kusadikika, nchi iliyo angani. [Dar es Salaam] Nelson [1967] 58 p. illus. (Diwani ya Shaaban, 2) PL8704.R54 1967 no. 2
First published 1951.
Title translated: Kusadikika, a country of promise.
"The publishers wish to acknowledge the assistance they have received from the East African Literature Bureau in the preparation of this volume . . . "

1217
_______ Wasifu wa Siti binti Saad; mwimbaji wa Unguja. [Dar es Salaam] Nelson [1967] 77 p. illus. (Diwani ya Shaaban, 3) PL8704.R54 1967 no. 3
"First published as supplement to no. 28/1 of East African Swahili Committee Journal 1958."
Title translated: Description of Siti, daughter of Saad; singer of Zanzibar.

1218
Semghanga, Francis H. J. Teuzi za nafsi. Dar es Salaam, Chuo cha Uchunguzi wa Lugha ya Kiswahili [1971] 68 p. PL8704.S4T4
Title translated: Self criticism.
A poem.

1219
Utenzi wa Fumo Liongo. Dar es Salaam, East African Swahili Committee [1964] ICRL
Collation of the original: 13 p.
Title translated: The poem of King Liongo.
ICRL has positive microfilm.
See also item 1192.

1220
Utenzi wa Mkunumbi, mhariri Lyndon Harries. Pamoja na tafsiri ya Kiingereza na maelezo. Pamoja na maandishi ya Kiarabu yaliyoandikwa na Yahya Ali Omar. Dar es Salaam, East African Literature Bureau [1967] 72 p. (Johari za Kiswahili, 9) PL8704.U77
"It is not clear whether Muhammad Kijuma ... was the copyist or the author."
Title translated: A poem about Mkunumbi.

1221
Utenzi wa Nushur. Umekusanywa na Haji Chum. Dar es Salaam, East African Literature Bureau [1974] 75 p. (Johari za Kiswahili, 11) DLC
Title translated: Poems of Nushur.
Poems about life on earth, and life after death.

1222
Utenzi wa Vita vya Uhud. The Epic of the Battle of Uhud. Collected and compiled by Haji Chum. Edited, with a translation and notes, by H. E. Lambert. Dar es Salaam, East African Literature Bureau, 1962. 97 p. (Johari za Kiswahili, 3) PL8704.U8
Text in Swahili and English in opposite columns.

1223
Zani, Zacharish M. S. Mashairi yangu. Kampala, Eagle Press, 1953. 279 p. DHU
Title translated: My poems.

1224
——— ——— Tabora, T.M.P. Book Dept., 1967. 33 p. DLC

Swahili Readers and Textbooks

Unless otherwise noted, the text of the following entries (items 1225–85) is in Swahili.

1225
Allen, Winifred E. Mwanzo wa masomo. Dar es Salaam, East African Literature Bureau [1966] 2 v. illus. CSt
First published 1958.
Title translated: Primary readers.
Contents: 1. Kitabu cha kwanza.—2. Kitabu cha pili.

1226
Barker, Ronald D. Visa vya mzee Rufiji. Dar es Salaam, East African Literature Bureau, 1962–65. 5 v. (Hadithi za Tanganyika) CSt
Title translated: Adventures of 'Rufiji'.
Contents: 1. Nilivyofika na kukaa Afrika. How I settled in Africa.—2. Mwanga wa shetani. The devil's light.—3. Uchawi na mazingaombwe. Witchcraft and conjuring tricks.—4. Safari yetu ya kwenda Rufiji. Our journey to Rufiji.—5. Kapteni Aliyeshambuliwa na simba. The captain who was attacked by a lion.

1227
Bryce, V. K. Kazi za wanadamu. Dar es Salaam, East African Literature Bureau [1960?] 8 v. illus. CSt
Title translated: The work of men.
Contents: 1. Mtu wa simu.—2. Askari wa polisi.—3. Dreva wa gari la Moshi.—4. Dreva wa lori.—5. Mkulima.—6. Mwuguzi.—7. Tarishi.—8. Mwalimu.

1228
Bull, A. F. Tusome Kiswahili; mafunzo ya Kiswahili kwa madarasa V-VIII, katika vitabu vinne. London, Nairobi, Oxford University Press, 1960–61. 4 v. PPiD
Title translated: Let's learn Swahili; a Swahili language course for Standards V-VIII in four volumes.
"The manuscript was received through the East African Literature Bureau."

1229
_______ Tusome Kiswahili; mafunzo ya Kiswahili kwa madarasa V-VIII. Nairobi, Oxford University Press [1968–69, c1961–65] 4 v. PL8701.B8
Title translated: Let's learn Swahili; a Swahili language course for Standards V-VIII.
"The manuscript was received through the East African Literature Bureau."

1230
Christian Council of Tanganyika. *Literacy Subcommittee.* Tuandike barua; kitabu cha watu wazima. Dar es Salaam, East African Literature Bureau, 1963. 22 p. PL8701.C5
Title translated: Let's write a letter; a book on letter writing for new literates.

1231
Defoe, Daniel. Robinson Kruso na kisiwa chake. [London] Nelson [c1962] [60] p. illus. (Hadithi za Tanganyika) PPiD
Translation of Robinson Crusoe.
"The text was translated into Swahili by members of the [East African] Literature Bureau staff."

1232
_______ _______ [Rev. ed.] [London] Nelson [1964] [60] p. illus. (Hadithi za Tanganyika) WU
"The text was translated into Swahili by members of the [East African] Literature Bureau staff."

1233
_______ _______ [Rev. ed.] [London] Nelson [1966] [60] p. illus. (Kitabu cha kupendeza) DLC
"The publishers wish to acknowledge the assistance they have received from the East African Literature Bureau in preparing this book for publication."

1234
Diva, David E. Binti wa mfanyi biashara na hadithi nyingine. London, University of London Press [1965, c1951] 31 p. CSt
Title translated: The merchant's daughter and other stories.
"The manuscript of this book was received from the East African Literature Bureau."

1235
_______ Hadithi na vitendo. London, University of London Press [1965–66, c1951] 4 v. CSt
Title translated: Short stories with exercises.
"The manuscript for this book was received from the East African Literature Bureau."

1236
_______ Kisanduku cha dhahabu na hadithi nyingine. London, University of London Press [1966, c1951] 32 p. CSt
Title translated: The box of gold and other stories.
"The manuscript of this book was received from the East African Literature Bureau."

1237
_______ Mamba na kima na hadithi nyingine. London, University of London Press [1951] 32 p. DHU
Title translated: The crocodile and the monkey and other stories.
"The manuscript of this book was received from the East African Literature Bureau."

1238
_______ Mvulana na nguruwe na hadithi nyingine. London, University of London Press [1965, c1951] 31 p. CSt
Title translated: The boy and his pig and other stories.
"The manuscript of this book was received from the East African Literature Bureau."

1239
_______ Ujiongezee maarifa. [Dar es Salaam] Eagle Press [1950–53] 8 v. illus. (Eagle booklets) DHU
Title translated: Increase your knowledge.

1240
East African Literature Bureau. Jifunze kusoma; kimetungwa na wajumbe wa Kamati ya Uandikaji (Literacy Workshop) kutoka Idara

ya Maendeleo ya Tanzania, the Christian Council of Tanzania, East African Literature Bureau kwa niaba ya Wizara ya Maendeleo na Utamaduni Tanzania. Dar es Salaam [1966–67] 3 v. illus. CSt
Translation of Learn to read.

1241
_______ Njia za kutunza pesa zako; kitabu cha watu wazima wanaojifunza kusoma. Nairobi, Eagle Press, 1960. 36 p. CSt
Title translated: How to look after your money; a family budget reader for adult literacy schemes.

1242
Haarer, A. E., *and* C. T. Todd. Keti na kusoma. [Nairobi] Nelson [1972+] illus. (Nelson's Swahili readers) DLC
First published 1957.
Title translated: Sit down and read.
"The publishers wish to acknowledge the assistance they have received from the East African Literature Bureau in the preparation of this series."
L.C. has kitabu cha 1–3.

1243
Highman, Charles S. Nyazo za mwendo wa binadamu. Arusha, Longmans [1966–67] 4 v. illus. CSt
Translation of Landmarks of world history.
"The translation from the original English into Swahili was done through the services of the East African Literature Bureau."
Contents: 1. Watu wa kale. Ancestors.—2. Dini ya Kikristo. The Christian faith.—3. Elimu mpya. The new learning.—4. Dunia ilivyo sasa. The world today.

1244
Hollingsworth, Lawrence W. Historia fupi ya pwani ya Afrika ya Mashariki. London, Macmillan, 1951. 183 p. illus., maps. 4PL 112
"This translation of a A Short history of the East coast of Africa ... was provided by the African Literature Bureau."
"The Swahili in which the book is written has been approved by the Inter-Territorial Language (Swahili) Committee for the East African Dependencies."

1245
Jennings, *Sir* William Ivor. Demokrasi katika Afrika. Nairobi, East African Literature Bureau, 1962. 123 p. DT30.J419
Translation of Democracy in Africa.

1246
Kästner, Erich. Emil na wapelelezi. Kimetafsiriwa kutoka Kiingereza na W. Frank. Nairobi, East African Literature Bureau [1973] 120 p. illus.
Title translated: Emil and the spies.
Translation of Emil and die Detektive.
L.C. received; not retained.

1247
Kamati ya Uandikaji. Jiendeleze. Kimetungwa na wajumbe wa Kamati ya Unadikaji (Literacy Workshop) kutoka Idara ya Maendeleo ya Tanzania, East African Literature Bureau kwa niaba ya Wizara ya Serikali za Mitaa na Maendeleo Vijijini, Tanzania. Nairobi, East African Literature Bureau [1968+] illus. PL8702.K35
Title translated: Let's improve ourselves.
L.C. has kitabu 1.

1248
Keltie, *Sir* John Scott, *and* Samuel C. Gilmour. Uvumbuzi wa nchi mpya (Adventures of exploration, book 1, "Finding the continents"—Keltie and Gilmour. Swahili version prepared by the staff of the Inter-territorial Language Committee) . Dar es Salaam, East African literature Bureau [1968] 116 p. illus. G80.K3718 1968
"First published 1933 by the Sheldon Press."

1249
Kenya Institute of Education. *General Methods Section.* TKK Kiswahili. [Nairobi,] Longman Kenya, 1967+] illus. PL8702.K4
Contents: book 1B. Kenya primary course.—book 1C. Ali na mpira wake.—book 1D. Twende shule.—book 2A. Idi na Asha ruhusani, book 2B. Asha apotea sokoni.—book 2C.

Idi apata ajali.—supplementary reader[s]: 1. Mtoto wa Sofia.—1 for primary 2. Kuku mnono apotea.—2. Rajabu na gari lake.—2 for primary 2. Watoto watukutu.—3 for primary 2. Likizo ya mwisho wa mwaka.

1250
Kombo, Salum M. Ustaarabu na maendeleo ya Mwafrika. Nairobi, Eagle Press, 1950. 60 p. DHU

"Kitabu hiki ndicho kilichofuzu kupata zawadi ya kwanza katika Mashindano ya Utungaji vitabu kwa lugha ya Kiswahili yaliyoongozwa na East African Inter-territorial Language Committee, katika mwaka 1947."

Title translated: The civilization and progress of the African people.

1251
_______ _______Nairobi, East African Literature Bureau [1966] 54 p. DT14.K63

1252
Kuanza kusoma, kimetungwa kwa usomaji wa watu wazima. [Prepared for Adult Literacy Section, Kenya Education Dept.] Nairobi, Eagle Press [1961+] illus. PL8702.K8

First published 1959.

Vol. 3 prepared by Helen M. Roberts.

Title translated: Beginning to read, prepared for adult literacy.

L.C. has kitabu 1, and 3.

See also item 1276

1253
Kusoma na kuandika pamoja na maazimio na mapendekizo; ripoti za UNESCO. [Nairobi] East African Literature Bureau [1967] 59 p. DLC

Title translated: Literacy as a factor in development.

"Papers presented to the world congress of ministers of education on the eradicating of illiteracy."

1254
Laubach, Frank C. Ujumbe wa Bwana Yesu. [Translated by Beryl Long] Dar es Salaam, East African Literature Bureau, 1961. 3 pts. illus. CtHC

"From the revised English version, 1957."

Title translated: The message of Jesus.

Contents: Pt. 1. Kitabu cha kwanza: Kuzaliwa kwa Yesu na matendo yake.—Pt. 2. Kitabu cha pili: Kufa kwa Yesu na kufufuka kwake.—Pt. 3. Kitabu cha tatu: Mithali za Yesu.

1255
Lemenye, Justin. Maisha ya sameni ole kivasis yaani Justin Lemenye. Kampala, Eagle Press, 1953. 71 p. illus. DHU

Title translated: The life of Justin Lemenye.

1256
Loogman, Alfons. Someni kwa furaha. London, New York, Nelson [1965+] 4 v. in 5. illus. (Nelson's Swahili readers) PL8702.L598

Title translated: Reading for pleasure.

"The publishers wish to acknowledge the assistance they have received from the East African Literature Bureau in the preparation of this series."

Kitabu cha kwanza wanting in L.C. set.

1257
Machauru, F. J. Twende tusome 1 na 2; maelezo kwa mwalimu. Nairobi, East African Literature Bureau, 1956. 15 p. MiEM

Title translated: Let us go and read, 1 and 2; suggestions to the teachers.

1258
Mason, H. Twende tusome; kitabu cha kujifunza kuandika. Nairobi, East African Literature Bureau, 1965. 24 p. MiEM

Title translated: Let us go and read.

"First lessons in handwriting to accompany the literacy primer Twende tusome."

1259
Mason, H., P. Yoder, *and* B. Long. Twende tusome; kitabu cha watu wazima. Dar es Salaam, East African Literature Bureau, 1965. 43 p. illus. MiEM

Title translated: Let us go and read; a primer for adult literacy.

1260
Mbotela, James J. Uhuru wa watumwa. Nairobi,

Eagle Press, 1951. 102 p. illus. DHU
Title translated: The freeing of the slaves.
Issued also in English.

1261
______ ______ [Nairobi, Nelson, 1970] 88 p. PL8704.M38U5 1970
"First published in 1934 by the Sheldon Press, London."

1262
Michuki, David N. Masomo ya Kiswahili; kitabu cha wanafunzi. [Nairobi, Jomo Kenyatta Foundation] 1976–69. 4 v. in 5. illus. PL8704.A2M5
Vols. 2–4 by D. N. Michuki and W. F. Cahill.
Title translated: Studies of Swahili; student's book.
"CDRC/L."
Prepared with help from staff members of the Curriculum Development and Research Centre, which became the Curriculum Development Dept. of the Kenya Institute of Education in 1968.
"The series is designed specifically for children who begin the study of Swahili as a second language in Standard 4."

1262a
______ ______ Kitabu cha mwalimu. [Nairobi, Jomo Kenyatta Foundation] 1966–69. 4 v. PL8704.A2M5 Suppl.
Title translated: Studies of Swahili; teacher's book.

1263
Mnyampala, Mathias E. Kisa cha mrina asali na wenzake wawili. Dar es Salaam, East African Literature Bureau [1968] 66 p. illus. (Hadithi za Tanzania, 2) PL8704.M58K5 1968
First published 1961.
Title translated: The adventures of a honey-gatherer and his two friends.

1264
Molière, Jean Baptiste Poquelin. Mchuuzi mwungwana. Umefasiriwa na A. Morrison. Dar es Salaam, East African Literature Bureau [1966] 75 p. CLU
First published 1960.
Translation of Le bourgeois gentilhomme.

1265
______ ______ Kampala, East African Literature Bureau [1970] 75 p. PQ1829.A67M6

1266
Mzirai, Robert R. K. Maandishi ya barua zetu. Tabora, T.M.P. Book Dept., 1967. 117 p. illus. PL8701.M9
On verso of t.p.: The writing of letters.
"First published by E.A.L.B. 1957. Reprinted by E.A.L.B. 1962."

1267
Omar, C. A. Shariff. Hadithi ya Hazina binti Sultani. Nairobi, Eagle Press, 1951. 30 p. illus. (Treasury of East African literature) DHU
Title translated: The tale of Hazina, the Sultan's daughter.

1268
______ ______ Nairobi, Oxford University Press, 1968. 47 p. illus. PL8704.04H3
"First published by the East African Literature Bureau 1950."

1269
______ Kisa cha Hasan-Li-Basir. Nairobi, Eagle Press, 1951. 30 p. illus. (Treasury of East African literature) DHU
Title translated: The adventures of Hasan-Li-Basir.
A tale from the Arabian nights.

1270
______ ______ Nairobi, Oxford University Press, 1964. 47 p. CSt

1271
Perrott, Daisy V. Safari za watangulizi. Dar es Salaam, East African Literature Bureau [1965–69; v. 1, 1969] 4 v. in 1. illus. DT361.P382
First published 1954.
Title translated: Journeys of early travellers.

"This series first appeared in the weekly Swahili pictorial magazine Tazama."

Contents: 1. Krapf na Rebman.—2. Speke.—3. Livingstone.—4. Thomson.

1272

——— Wavumbuzi vijana. London, New York, Longmans, Green [1958] 150 p. illus. CSt

"Kitabu hiki kikitumika pamoja na Kitabu cha 2 cha Geography, History and Civics kilichoandikwa na J. M. Popkin."

Title translated: Young explorers.

"This book is published in association with the East African Literature Bureau."

1273

Richards, Charles G. Kisa cha Yohana mjinga na utiivu wake. Dar es Salaam, Eagle Press, 1951. 14 p. DHU

Translation of Simple John.

1274

——— ——— Nairobi, Oxford University Press [1969, c1951] 17 p. illus. PZ90.S94R5 1969

"First published by East African Literature Bureau 1951. Revised edition 1961."

1275

Riwa, R. L. Hadithi za rafiki saba; hadithi tamu za zamani. Nairobi, Eagle Press, 1951. 45 p. illus. (Treasury of East African literature) DHU

Title translated: Tales told by seven friends.

1276

Roberts, Helen M. Kitabu cha kuhesabu kwa Kuanza kusoma. Prepared for the Kenya Broadcasting Corporation and the Literacy Centre of Kenya. Written . . . in connection with the Adult Literacy Television Script of the Kenya Broadcasting Corporation. Nairobi, East African Literature Bureau, 1963. 51 p. illus. DLC

Title translated: Arithmetic book; first lessons in arithmetic to accompany the adult literacy primer Kuanza kusoma.

See also item 1252.

1277

Tanzania. *Ministry of National Education.* Tujifunzi lugha yetu, kimeandikwa na Wizara ya Elimu ya Taifa, Tanzania. Dar es Salaam, Kimepigishwa chapa na Oxford University Press, 1969–71? illus. PL8702.T29

Title translated: Let's learn our language.

L.C. has kitabu cha 5–6, and 8.

1278

——— ——— Kiongozi cha mwalimu, kimeandikwa na Wizara ya Elimu ya Taifa. Dar es Salaam, Kimepigishwa, chapa na Oxford University Press, 1969+ PL8702.T29 Suppl.

Title translated: Let's learn our language; teacher's guide.

L.C. has 5–6.

1279

Tazama. v. 1+ Apr. 9, 1952+ Nairobi, East African Literature Bureau, in cooperation with the East African Standard. weekly.

Title translated: Look.

Publication transferred from the East African Literature Bureau to the East African Standard, Jan. 1, 1956.

NN received early issues; not retained; vols. for 1957–59 held by Makerere University Library.

1280

Twende tusome; kitabu cha pili cha kujifunza kuandika. Nairobi, East African Literature Bureau, 1962. 32 p. MiEM

"Prepared by the staff of the Community Development Division of Tanzania."

Title translated: Let us go and read.

1281

Ulenge, Yussuf. Nguzo ya maji na hadithi nyingine. Nairobi, Eagle Press, 1951. 22 p. illus. (Treasury of East African literature) DHU

Title translated: The pillar of water and other stories.

1282

——— ——— Nairobi, Oxford University Press, 1966. 40 p. CSt

1283
Voltaire, François Marie Arouet de. Hadithi ya Zadig. Imefasiriwa na Abdula M. Abubakr. Nairobi, East African Literature Bureau [1966] 57 p. CSt
Translation of Zadig, ou la destinée, histoire orientale.

1284
Walford, Arthur S. Mazoezi na mafumbo: mazoezi 50 ya kuwasaidia wanafunzi katika kusoma. Nairobi, Oxford University Press [1963] 60 p. illus. PL8701.W3
First published 1951.
Title translated: Riddles and exercises: 50 excercises to help students in reading.
"This book is published by arrangement with the East African Literature Bureau, from whom the manuscript was received."

1285
Worthington, Frank. Sungura mjanja. Kimetafsiriwa na D. E. Diva. Nairobi, Oxford University Press [1971, c1965] 14 p. illus. DLC
"First published by the East African Literature Bureau 1961."
Title translated: Here is a rascal.

Swahili Study and Teaching

1286
Elphinstone, *Sir* Howard Graham, *bart.* The standard Swahili examination. [Rev. ed.] Nairobi, Eagle Press, 1950. 70 p. (Eagle language study series) DHU

1287
Gt. Brit. *Army. East African Force. Education Corps.* Kiswahili; a Ki-Swahili instruction book for the East Africa Command. Entebbe, Govt. Printer [1942?] 107 p. NjP
NjP catalogs under: The East African Army Education Corps.

1288
Gt. Brit. *Civil Service Commission.* Pamphlet containing the question papers of the interpretership tests in Swahili used at an examination . . . of officers of the army. London, Printed and published by H.M. Stationery Off. PL8702.G7
L.C. has June 1935; source for 1933: Col. Off. Lib. Cat.

1289
Halvorson, Marian. Kisomo cha watu wazima; maelezo kwa waalimu na wasimamizi. Vielelezo vimechorwa na Daniel Mazzuki. Nairobi, East African Literature Bureau [1967?] 67 p. illus. LC5225.R4H3
Title translated: Adult literacy; explanations for teachers and supervisors.
Text in Swahili.

1290
Mhina, George A., J. K. Kiimbila, *and* M. M. R. Alidina. Kichocheo cha uchunguzi. Dar es Salaam, Chuo cha Uchunguzi wa Kiswahili, 1971. 74 p. PL8701.M47
Title translated: Stirring up curiosity.
Essays on Swahili, with text in Swahili.

1291
——— Mwalimu wa Kiswahili [kimetungwa na] G. A. Mhina [na] J. K. Kiimbila. Dar es Salaam, Chuo cha Uchunguzi wa Lugha ya Kiswahili [1971] 105 p. PL8701.M48
Title translated: The Swahili teacher.
Text in Swahili.

1292
Tanganyika. Guide and aid to Swahili examinations. Dar es Salaam, Govt. Printer, 1954. 93 p.
Source: Dar es Salaam Lib. Bull. no. 88.

1293
——— Guide and aid to Swahili examinations; incorporating Elementary Swahili instructional course, by P. W. Mollard, and Lower Swahili examination vocabulary, by P. H. W. Haile. [Dar es Salaam, Govt. Printer, 1962] 100 p. WvU

1294
——— ——— [Dar es Salaam, Printed by the Govt. Printer, 1964] 97 p. MiEM

1295
Tanganyika. *Dept. of Education.* A guide and aid to Swahili examinations. Dar es Salaam, Printed by the Govt. Printer [1929] 80 p. PL8702.T25

"... for the guidance of the newly-joined officer of the Tanganyika Government Service in his reading for the Government examinations in Swahili."

1296
Uganda. A guide and aid to Swahili and Luganda examinations. Entebbe, Printed by the Govt. Printer [1930] 152 p. PL8702.U34

1297
Wilson, P. M. English Swahili; [classified vocabulary] Nairobi, East African Literature Bureau [1967?] 30 p. PL8703.W5

Contents: Agricultural terms.—Engineering terms.—Fishing terms.—Household terms.—Medical terms.—Veterinary terms.

1298
——— Simplified Swahili. [Tengeru, Ministry of Agriculture Training Centre, 1966] 264 p.

Source: Dar es Salaam Lib. Bull. no. 90.

1299
——— ——— Nairobi, East African Literature Bureau [1970] 561 p. PL8702.W56

1300
——— Swahili picture vocabulary. Nairobi, East African Literature Bureau [1972] 71 p. illus. PL8703.W53

". . . intended for use in conjunction with Simplified Swahili . . ."

1301
Zanzibar. Guide to Swahili examinations. [Zanzibar? 192–?]
DLC-Micro 23940 reel 2 octavo 103

Collation of the original: 51 p.

Colonial Office Library East Africa pamphlet octavo 103.

Law

1302
Ali bin Hemedi, *el Buhuri.* Mirathi, a handbook of the Mahomedan law of inheritance, with appendices on wills and gifts and an introduction, translation and notes, by Sheik Ali bin Hemedi el Buhuri, Kathi of Tanga. Translation and notes by P. E. Mitchell, Administrative Officer, Tanganyika Territory. [Nairobi, Reprinted for the Govt. Printer by D. L. Patel Press, pref. 1923, 1949] 65, 59 p. DLC-LL

Text in English and Swahili.

1303
Brownwood, David O. Selected East African cases on commercial law. Prepared for use in courses at Kenya Institute of Administration. [Lower Kabete, Kenya Institute of Administration] 1968. 134 p. DLC-LL

1304
Butterfield, Harry R., *comp.* Index digest of the reported cases determined by the Court of Appeal for Eastern Africa and on appeal therefrom by the Judicial Committee of the Privy Council, 1900–1952. Nairobi, Printed by the Govt. Printer, 1954. 135 p. DLC-LL

At head of title: Colony and Protectorate of Kenya.

Based on John H. Vaughan's Index-digest of the reported cases determined by the Court of Appeal for Eastern Africa and on appeal therefrom by the Judicial Committee of the Privy Council, 1900 to 1938.

1305
Byamugisha, Joseph B. Insurance law in East Africa. Nairobi, East African Literature Bureau [1973] xv, 218 p. DLC

1306
Conference on Public Policy, *2d, University College, Nairobi, 1963.* Conferences on public policy, 1963/4: East African federation; [papers] [Nairobi? 1964?] HC517.E2C6 1963

The following papers concern law:

[no. 15] De Smith, S. A. Integration of legal systems in a new federation. 15 leaves.

Later revised as Integration of legal systems, published in Colin Leys' Federation in East Africa; opportunities and problems (Nairobi, London, Oxford University Press, 1965 [i.e. 1966] HC517.E2L4) p. [158]-171.

[no. 18] Ghai, Yash. Some legal aspects of an East African federation. 9 leaves.

Later revised with the same title and published in Colin Leys' Federation in East Africa; opportunities and problems (Nairobi, London, Oxford University Press, 1965 [i.e. 1966] HC517.E2L4) p. [172]-182.

Court of Appeal for East Africa.

Note: The Court of Appeal for Eastern Africa was created by the Eastern African Protectorates (Court of Appeal) Order in Council in 1902 with "power and jurisdiction within the territories known as the East Africa, Uganda, and British Central Africa Protectorates." It was located at Zanzibar. For administrative purposes, the court was attached to the Kenya government. In December 1961, the court was transferred to the East African Common Services Organization. In December 1962, the secretary of state for the colonies relinquished responsibility for the terms and conditions of the judges and the staff, and the court was reconstituted as the Court of Appeal for Eastern Africa. In December 1967, with the Treaty for East African Co-operation coming into force, the name of the court was shortened to its present form. The court sits in the major cities in East Africa. Judges are appointed by the East African Authority. During its existence, the court has been responsible for appeals from Aden (until 1967), British Somaliland (until June 1960), St. Helena (until June 1965), and the Seychelles (until June 1965).

1307
Annual report. 1962+ [Nairobi, Govt. Printer] DLC-LL

At head of title: East African Court of Appeal.

Supersedes a publication with the same title (item 1323) issued by the Court of Appeal for Eastern Africa of Gt. Brit.

Vols. for 1962–67 issued by the agency under its earlier name: Court of Appeal for Eastern Africa.

L.C. has 1962+

1308
______ Court of Appeal for East Africa rules, 1972. [Nairobi, Printed by the Govt. Printer, 1972] p. 295–344. DLC-LL

"Special issue, Kenya Gazette supplement no. 66, 7th Oct. 1972."

Came into effect June 1, 1973.

1309
______ Digest of decisions of the court. 1962+ [Nairobi?] monthly. DLC-LL

Supersedes the Monthly bulletin of criminal [and civil] appeals (item 1327) issued by the Court of Appeal for Eastern Africa of Gt. Brit.

Title varies: 1962, Bulletin of decisions of the court marked for reporting.

Vols. for 1962–67 issued by the agency under an earlier name: Court of Appeals for Eastern Africa.

L.C. has Sept. 1971+ (scattered issues wanting); MH-L and NNC-L have more complete holdings.

1310
Durand, Philip P. Working with the laws of Kenya and law reports in East Africa. Lower Kabete, Publications Committee, Kenya Institute of Administration, 1969. 39 leaves. DLC-LL

1311
East Africa High Commission. Official gazette. v. 1–14; Jan. 31, 1948–Nov. 30, 1961. [Nairobi, Printed by the High Commission Printer] monthly. DLC-LL

Superseded by a publication with the same title (item 1313) issued by the East African Common Services Organization.

Supplements containing acts, subsidiary

legislation, and bills, accompany some numbers.

L.C. has 1948–61 (scattered issues wanting).

1312
East Africa High Commission. *East African Literature Bureau.* Registration of private companies, the filing of returns and the duties of private companies and their directors. Kuandikisha makampuni ya kizuio kutayarisha ripoti inayotakiwa na wajibu wa makampuni ya kizuio na wa wakuu wa makampuni hayo. [2d ed.] Dar es Salaam, Eagle Press, East African Literature Bureau, 1958. 29 p. MH-L

Cover title: The registration & duties of private companies. Kuandikisha makampuni ya kizuio na wajibu wake.

"The first edition of this book was published by the Kenya Information Office, Nairobi."

Text in English and Swahili on opposite pages.

1313
East African Common Services Organization. Official gazette. v. 1–7; Feb. 1962-Dec. 1967. [Nairobi, Printed by the East African Common Services Organization Printer] monthly (irregular) DLC-LL

Running title: E.A.C.S.O. gazette.

Supersedes a publication with the same title (item 1311) issued by the East Africa High Commission.

Superseded by a publication with the same title issued by the East African Community.

Supplements containing acts, subsidiary legislation, and bills, accompany most numbers.

L.C. has 1962–67.

1314
East African Community. Official gazette. v. 1+ Dec. 14, 1967+ [Nairobi, East African Community Printer] monthly (irregular) DLC-LL

Supersedes a publication with the same title issued by the East African Common Services Organization.

Supplements, containing acts, subsidiary legislation, and bills, accompany most numbers.

L.C. has Dec. 14, 1967+ (scattered issues wanting).

1315
East African Industrial Court. The East African Industrial Court: a report and a review of Court's activities. Nairobi, East African Literature Bureau, 1973. 94 p. *(Its* Special bulletin 1968–1969) DLC

1316
Eastern Africa law review. v. 1+ Apr. 1968+ Dar es Salaam, Faculty of Law, University of East Africa. 3 no. a year. K5.A8

Currently issued by the Faculty of Law of the University of Dar es Salaam.

"A journal of law and development."

L.C. has Apr. 1968+

1317
Elphinstone, *Sir* Howard Graham, *bart.* Africans and the law. Nairobi, Eagle Press, 1951. 75 p. DHU

1318
Errington, Kathleen, *comp.* A digest of the East African and Kenya law reports, 1897–1952. Nairobi, Printed by the Govt. Printer, 1953+ DLC

At head of title: Colony and Protectorate of Kenya.

1319
Gt. Brit. *Commission on Administration of Justice in Kenya, Uganda and Tanganyika Territory in Criminal Matters.* Report of the Commission of Inquiry into the Administration of Justice in Kenya, Uganda and the Tanganyika Territory in Criminal Matters, May, 1933, and correspondence arising out of the report. [London, H.M. Stationery Off., 1934] 160 p. fold. map. JQ2945.A8A6 1933

H. Grattan Bushe, chairman.

1320
______ ______ London, H.M. Stationery Off., 1934. 160 p. fold. map ([Parliament. Papers by command] Cmd. 4623) DLC-LL

H. Grattan Bushe, chairman.

1321
______ ______ 1. Minutes of evidence (with index) 2. Memoranda submitted to the Commission. London, H.M. Stationery Off., 1934. 221 p. ([Gt. Brit.] Colonial Office. Colonial no. 96) DLC-LL

1322
Gt. Brit. *Commonwealth Relations Office.* Tanganyika. Hearing by the Judicial Committee of the Privy Council of appeals from the Court of Appeal for Eastern Africa on appeal from a court or judge in Tanganyika. Exchange of letters between the Government of the United Kingdom of Great Britain and Northern Ireland and the Government of Tanganyika. London, H.M. Stationery Off., 1963. 3 p. ([Gt. Brit. Parliament. Papers by command] Cmnd. 2031) J301.K6 1962/63 v. 38

Procedure for appeal upon Tanganyika's becoming a republic.

1323
Gt. Brit. *Court of Appeal for Eastern Africa.* Annual report. -1961. [Nairobi, Govt. Printer] DLC-LL

At head of title: -1961, East African Court of Appeal.

Superseded by a publication with the same title (item 1307) issued by the Court of Appeal for Eastern Africa.

L.C. has 1958–61.

1324
______ Eastern African Court of Appeal orders in council and rules. Dar es Salaam, Govt. Printer, 1954. 57 p. MH-L

Amendment, 1956, Rules of court, inserted.

1325
______ Eastern African Court of Appeals, Tanganyika. Rules of court commendment 1956. [Dar es Salaam? 1956?]

Cited in Exchange list no. 6, Mar. 1972, issued by the Tanganyika Library Service.

1326
______ Law reports containing decisions of H.M. Court of Appeal for Eastern Africa and the Judicial Committee of the Privy Council on appeal from that court. v. 1–23; 1934–56. [Nairobi, Govt. Printer] annual. DLC-LL

Supersedes in part the Law reports of Kenya (item 1330).

Superseded by the Eastern Africa law reports.

Reprinted in Nairobi by the East African Literature Bureau in 1970.

L.C. has 1934–56.

1327
______ Monthly bulletin of decisions of criminal [and civil] appeals. no. 1–92; Jan. 1954–Dec. 1961. [Nairobi?] NNC-L

Superseded by the Bulletin of decisions of the court marked for reporting (item 1309) issued by the Court of Appeal for Eastern Africa.

1328
Kenya Colony and Protectorate. Proposals for the re-organisation of the Eastern African Court of Appeal. [Nairobi? 1950] 8 p.

Source: Col. Off. Lib. Cat.

1329
Kenya Colony and Protectorate. *Legislative Council. Committee on Extending Certain Provisions of Law to the East Africa High Commission.* Report of a select committee of Legislative Council appointed to consider a bill to make provision for extending certain provisions of law to the East Africa High Commission and its purposes. [Nairobi? 195–?] 2 p.

J. D. Rankine, chairman.

Source: Col. Off. Lib. Cat.

1330
Law reports of Kenya, containing cases determined by the Supreme Court of the Colony and Protectorate of Kenya. v. [1]–29; 1897/1905–1956. [Nairobi, Govt. Printer] DLC-LL

Frequency varies.

At head of title: 1897/1905–1919/21, East Africa Protectorate; 1922/23–1953, Colony and Protectorate of Kenya.

Title varies: 1897/1905, Law reports containing cases determined by the High Court of Mombasa, and by the Appeal Court at Zanzibar, and by the Judicial Committee of the Privy Council on appeal from that court.—1906/8–1919/21, Law reports containing cases determined by the High Court of East Africa, and by the Court of Appeal for Eastern Africa, and by the Judicial Committee of the Privy Council on appeal from that court.—1922/23, Law reports containing cases determined by the Supreme Court, Kenya Colony and Protectorate, and by the Judicial Committee of the Privy Council on appeal from that court.

Other slight variations in title.

On spine, 1897/1905–1954: East Africa law reports.

Superseded in part in 1934 by the Law reports containing decisions of H.M. Court of Appeals for Eastern Africa and the Judicial Committee of the Privy Council on appeal from that court (item 1326) issued by the Court of Appeals for Eastern Africa of Gt. Brit.

Vols. for 1897/1905–1915/16 include "appendices containing notes on native customs, appeal court rules, legal practitioners' rules, high court rules, circulars, etc."

L.C. has 1897/1905–1956.

1331

Oluyede, Peter. Administrative law in East Africa. Nairobi, East Africa Literature Bureau, 1973. xxi, 255 p. DLC-LL

Appendices include The preamble and some of the articles of the Treaty for East African Cooperation.

1332

Tanganyika. Proposals for the re-organization of the Eastern African Court of Appeal. Dar es Salaam [1947] 6 p.

Source: BM Cat., 1968.

1333

Wilkinson, R. Michael, *and* Pauline Ssenkiko. Decisions of the Court of Appeal for East Africa and the High Court of Uganda on quantum of damages for personal injuries, false imprisonment and defamation. [2d ed.] [Kampala? Uganda] 1972. 10, 72 leaves. MH-L

1334

Zanzibar. *Legislative Council.* Proposals for the re-organisation of the Eastern African Court of Appeal. *(Its* Sessional paper no. 4 of 1950) *In* Zanzibar. *Legislative Council.* Papers laid before the Legislative Council, 1950. Zanzibar, Printed by the Govt. Printer, 1951. p. 6–10. J733.J52 1950

Law Enforcement

1335

Amri, Daudi. Polisi na raia; au, The police and the public. Kampala, Eagle Press, 1951. 32 p. illus. DHU

Text in English and Swahili.

1336

Conference of Governors of British East African Territories. *Statistical Dept.* Analysis of crime statistics, Kenya Colony and Protectorate. Prepared under the direction of A. Walter, Statistician to the Conference of East African Governors, and Director of the Meteorological Service. [Nairobi? 1932?] 23 p. (*Its* Memoir no. 5) MiEM

1337

Conference of Law Officers of the East African Dependencies, *Nairobi, 1926.* Report. Nairobi, Printed at the Govt. Press, 1926.

DLC-Micro 23940 reel 9 folio 117

Collation of the original: 43 p.

W. C. Huggard, Attorney General, Kenya, chairman.

Colonial Office Library East Africa pamphlet folio 117.

1338

Conference of Law Officers of East African Dependencies, *Nairobi, 1933.* Report, March 1933. [Nairobi, Govt. Printer, 1933?] 71 p.

T. D. H. Bruce, chairman.

Source: Col. Off. Lib. Cat.

1339

Great Britain. Draft model penal code for the

East African dependencies. [n.p., n.d.] 68 p.
Source: Dar es Salaam Lib. Bull. no. 92.

1340
Gt. Brit. *Colonial Office.* Training of police officers of the West and East African colonies and protectorates with the Royal Irish Constabulary. [London] Printed for the use of the Colonial Office, 1908. *(Its* African no. 902) DLC-Micro 03759

Collation of the original: 5 p.

[Gt. Brit.] Public Record Office. C.O. 879/98.

1341
Paterson, Alexander. Report on a visit to the prisons of Kenya, Uganda, Tanganyika, Zanzibar, Aden, and Somaliland, by Mr. Alexander Paterson, His Majesty's Commissioner of Prisons for England and Wales, during 1939. [London? 1939] DLC-Micro 23940 reel 14 folio 402

Collation of the original: 42 leaves.

Colonial Office Library East Africa pamphlet folio 402.

"Comments on Mr. Paterson's report on penal administration in the East African dependencies," (5 leaves) by various East African government officials for the period 1940–41, is appended to the report.

1342
——— Report on a visit to the prisons of Kenya, Uganda, Tanganyika, Zanzibar, Aden, and Somaliland during 1939, by Alexander Paterson, His Majesty's Commissioner of Prisons for England and Wales. [Morija, Basutoland, Morija Printing Works, 1944] 48 p. IEN

Laws, Statutes, etc.

1343
East Africa High Commission. Acts and subsidiary legislation. 1948–61. [Nairobi, Printed by the High Commission Printer] annual DLC-LL

Title varies: 1948–49, Acts.

Superseded by a publication with the same title (item 1345) issued by the East African Common Services Organization.

Each issue cumulates the acts and subsidiary legislation issued in the supplements to the agency's Official gazette (item 1311).

L.C. has 1948–61.

1344
East Africa High Commisison. The laws of the High Commisison in force on the 31st December, 1951. Rev. ed., prepared under the authority of the Revised Edition of the Laws Act, 1953, by Charles D. Newbold, Commissioner for the Revision of the Laws. Nairobi, Printed and published by the High Commission Printer [1953] xvi, 955 p. DLC-LL

1345
East African Common Services Organization. Acts and subsidiary legislation. 1962-67. [Nairobi, Printed by the East African Common Services Organization Printer] annual. DLC-LL

Supersedes a publication with the same title (item 1343) issued by the East Africa High Commission.

Each issue cumulates the acts and subsidiary legislation issued throughout the year in the supplements to the agency's Official gazette (item 1313).

L.C. has 1962–67.

1346
East African Community. *Laws, statutes, etc.* East African Community legistlation. 1966+ [Nairobi, Kenya?] annual.

Vols. for 1966–Mar. 1970 cited in May 12, 1972 letter from L.C. Office, Nairobi, Kenya.

1347
——— Laws of the East African Community. By B. C. W. Lutta and D. S. Mangat. Rev. ed. Nairobi, Printed by the East African Community Printer, 1970. 5 v. DLC

1348
London. *Commonwealth Institute.* The mining laws of the British Empire and of foreign countries. V. 8. East Africa: pt. 1. Tanganyika, Kenya, Nyasaland, Zanzibar. London, H.M. Stationery Off, 1927. 277 p. TN215.L66 v. 8

Issued by the agency under an earlier name: Imperial Institute.

Prepared by Gilbert Stone.

Libraries

1349
Hockey, S. W. Development of library services in East Africa; a report submitted to the governments of East Africa. [n.p.] 1960 [i.e. 1964] 1 v. (unpaged) Z857.E3H6 1964

Medicine and Health

1350
Cancer in Africa; a selection of papers given at the East African Medical Research Council scientific conference in Nairobi in January 1967. Edited by Peter Clifford, C. Allen Linsell [and] Geoffrey L. Timms. [Nairobi] East African medical journal; [distributed in U.S. by Northwestern University Press, Evanston, Ill., 1968] xxvii, 458 p. illus., maps. RC279.A38C3

Prior to 1967, scientific conference reports are in the East African medical journal (R98. E3).

1351
Conference on Co-ordination of General Medical Research in East African Territories. [Proceedings] [1st–2d] 1933–36. Nairobi, Printed and published by the Govt. Printer. irregular. R653.B7C62

At head of title: Conference of Governors of British East African Territories.

A Research conference of the Conference of Governors of British East African Territories.

L.C. has 1st.–2d, 1934–36.

1352
East Africa High Commission. Report of a board of enquiry on the accounts and books of the East African Medical Survey, Mwanza, Tanganyika with particular reference to capital expenditure, 21st–26th September, 1954. [n.p., 195–?] 1 v. (various pagings)

Source: Col. Off. Lib. Cat.

East Africa High Commission. *East African Bureau of Research in Medicine and Hygiene.*

Note: The bureau was created July 1, 1949, to oversee medical activities and research in East Africa. The primary contribution of the bureau was the establishment of the Standing Advisory Committee for Medical Research in East Africa in 1952 to promote liaison between the Medical Research Council, the Colonial Medical Research Committee in Great Britain, and the medical research organizations in East Africa. The head of the bureau became secretary of the committee. The bureau's function was to implement the liaison activities decided upon by the committee. In 1955 the bureau was succeeded by the East African Council for Medical Research. At that time, the committee was replaced by the East African Medical Research Scientific Advisory Committee.

1353
Annual report. 1949–54. [Nairobi?]
Superseded by a publication with the same title (item 1355) issued by the East African Council for Medical Research of the East Africa High Commission.
Source: SCOLMA, Mar. 1969.

1354
_______ Digest of the annual reports of the medical research organsations. 1951–53. Nairobi. annual. DNLM
Title varies: 1951, Digest of the activities of the medical research organisations of the East Africa High Commission.
Each issue contains summaries of annual reports of the following organizations: East African Bureau of Research in Medicine and Hygiene, East African Interterritorial Leprosy Specialist, East African Malaria Unit, East African Medical Survey, East African Virus Research Institute, and Filariasis Research Unit.
DNLM has 1951–53.

1355
East Africa High Commission. *East African Council for Medical Research.* Annual report. 1954/55–1960/61. [Nairobi, Printed by the Govt. Printer] R854.A4E3
Report year ends June 30.
Supersedes the Annual report (item 1353) issued by the East African Bureau of Research in Medicine and Hygiene of the East Africa High Commission.
Superseded by the Annual report (item 1360) issued by East African Council for Medical Research.
Each issue contains summary reports for: East African Institute for Medical Research, East African Institute of Malaria and Vector-Borne Diseases, East African Leprosy Research Centre, East African Trypanosomiasis Research Organization, and East African Virus Research Institute.
L.C. has 1955/56, 1959/60; DNLM has 1956/57–1959/60.

1356
East Africa High Commission. *Filariasis Research Unit.* Annual report. no. 1–5; 1949–53. Nairobi, Printed by the Govt. Printer. RC142.5.E3
Title varies: 1949–50, Departmental annual report.
Final report, 1954, is included in the Annual report (item 1358) issued by the East African Medical Survey and Research Institute.
Later information on filariasis is included in the Annual report (item 1358) issued by the East African Medical Survey and Research Institute.
L.C. has 1949–53; DNLM has 1950–53.

1357
East African Common Services Organization. Periodicals in the East African Institute for Medical Research Library. Mwanza, Tanganyika, 1963. 25 leaves. (Catalogue no. 1)
Source: Dar es Salaam Lib. Bull. no 76.

East African Institute for Medical Research.
Note: In 1949, East African Medical Survey was created by the East Africa High Commission as an interterritorial medical survey located at Malya, Tanganyika. In October 1949, the survey was moved to Mwanza, Tanganyika, to share facilities with the Filariasis Research Unit, established June 1, 1949. On June 1, 1954, the Filariasis Research Unit was merged into the survey, and the organization was renamed the East African Medical Survey and Research Institute. In 1957, the present name was adopted. The institute's research is primarily concerned with schistosomiasis, hookworm, and filariasis.

1358
Annual report. 1949+ Mwanza, Tanzania. illus. R862.E27E27b
Report year for 1949–53, 1966+ ends Dec. 31; for 1954/55–1964/65 ends June 30.
Title varies: 1949, Departmental annual report.—1957/58–1959/60, Report.
Issued by the agency under earlier names: 1949–53, East African Medical Survey; 1954/55–1955/56, East African Medical Survey and Research Intitute.
Vol. for 1954/55 includes the Final report of the Filariasis Research Unit of the East Africa High Commission.
Vols. for 1967+ include the Progress report

on the project of WHO/Tanzania bilharziasis pilot control and training project at Mwanza.

Each issue contains a list of the agency's publications.

L.C. catalogs 1949–1961–62 under: East Africa High Commission. *East African Medical Survey*. Departmental report, with the call no.: RA407.5.A4A3

L.C. has 1949+

1359
East African journal of medical research. v. 1+ 1974+ [Nairobi, East African Literature Bureau] illus. quarterly. DNLM

"The journal of the East African Medical Research Council."

". . . devoted to medical and biomedical science research."

DNLM has 1974+

East African Medical Research Council.

Note: By Legal Notice no. 1 of 1955, the East African Council for Medical Research succeeded the East African Bureau of Research in Medicine and Hygiene as the coordinating body for medical research in East Africa. At the same time, the East African Medical Research Scientific Advisory Committee replaced the Standing Advisory Committee for Medical Research. The Scientific Advisory Committee made financial recommendations on medical research programs to the council. After 1964 the committee apparently ceased to function. The council began to use its present form of name also after 1964. The following organizations submit annual reports to the council: East African Institute of Malaria and Vector-Borne Diseases, East African Institute for Medical Research, East African Leprosy Research Centre, East African Trypanosomiasis Research Organization, East African Tuberculosis Investigation Centre, East African Virus Research Institute, and the Tropical Pesticides Research Institute. The council undertakes regional research into human diseases, and animal diseases where relevant, with emphasis on the major endemic communicable diseases.

1360
Annual report. 1961/62+ Arusha. illus. R854.A4E33

At head of title: East African Common Services Organisation.

Supresedes the Annual report (item 1355) issued by the East African Council for Medical Research of the East Africa High Commission.

Vols. for 1961/62– issued by the agency under its earlier name: East African Council for Medical Research.

L.C. has 1961/62, 1965–66.

1361
_______ Disorders of the kidney and urinary tract; diabetes in Africa. Scientific conference, 23rd, 24th and 25th January 1963, in the lecture theatre of the Princess Margaret Medical Training Centre, Dar es Salaam. Programme. Nairobi, 1963. 1 v. (various pagings) MiEM

Includes summaries of papers.

1361a
_______ The use and abuse of drugs and chemicals in tropical Africa: proceedings of the 1973 annual scientific conference of the East African Medical Research Council. Editors: A. F. Banshawe, G. Maina [and] E. N. Mngola. Nairobi, East African Literature Bureau, 1974. xvii, 672 p. DLC

1362
East African Tuberculosis Investigation Centre. Annual report. [Nairobi] R854.A4E33

At head of title: East African Medical Research Council.

Information on the Centre's research and surveys is included in the Annual report (item 1360) issued by the East African Medical Research Council.

L.C. has 1971.

East African Virus Research Institute.

Note: In late 1936, the International Health Division of the Rockefeller Foundation, the Colonial Office of Great Britain, and the Uganda government established the Yellow Fever Research Institute at the laboratory of the defunct Human Trypanosomiasis Research Institute in Entebbe, Uganda. The Rockefeller Foundation terminated its connection with the institute on December 31, 1949. Brief summaries of the activities of the Yellow Fever Research Institute are contained in the annual report, 1937–49, of the International Health Division of the Rockefeller Foundation. On January 1, 1950, the present name of the Institute was adopted. Research activities were concentrated on virus diseases. The East Africa High Commission formally took control of the East African Virus Research Institute on April 1, 1950.

1363
Report. no. 1+ 1950+ [Entebbe] annual. QR360.E6

Report year for 1950–53, 1963/64+ ends Dec. 31; for 1954/55–1962/63 ends June 30.

At head of title, 1950–1960/61: East Africa High Commission; 1961/62–1966: East African Common Services Organization; 1967+ East East African Community.

Title varies: 1950–53, Annual report.

Vols. for 1950–53 issued by the agency under its earlier name: Virus Research Institute.

Each issue includes a list of the agency's publications.

L.C. catalogs under: Entebbe, Uganda. Virus Research Institute.

L.C. has 1950+

1364
Frank, M. K., *comp.* Bibliography of East African literature on *Bilharziasis* (including that of Malawi, Rhodesia, Sudan, and Zambia) presents material published between 1933 and 1964. Mwanza, Tanzania, East African Institute for Medical Research [1965?] 16 leaves. Z6664.S33F7

1365
Frankl, Paul. Venereal diseases; a guide for African students and medical assistants. Nairobi, Eagle Press, East African Literature Bureau, 1958. 43 p. illus. DNLM

1366
Gt. Brit. *Admiralty.* Hygiene and disease in eastern tropical Africa. The protection of aircraft from the attacks of insects. Issued as a supplement to the Handbook of German East Africa. Prepared on behalf of the Admiralty and the War Office. [London] Admiralty War Staff, Intelligence Division, 1916. 58 p. illus., fold. map, plan, plates. ICJ

At head of title: For official use only.

On cover: I.D. 1055A.

1367
______ ______ London, H. M. Stationery Off., 1923. 58 p. illus., fold. map. RA943.G7 1923

At head of title: I.D. 1055A

1368
Gt. Brit. *Colonial Office.* Africa. Blackwater fever in the tropical African dependencies. Reports for 1912. London, Printed under the authority of H.M. Stationery Off. by Darling, 1914. 65 p. charts (part fold.), 6 maps (5 fold.) ([Gt. Brit. Parliament. Papers by command] Cd. 7211) RC165.A1G7 1912a

Includes information on blackwater fever for the East African Protectorate and Uganda.

1369
______ Africa. Blackwater fever in the tropical African dependencies. Reports for 1913. London, Printed under the authority of H.M. Stationery Off. by Darling, 1915. 96 p. map. ([Gt. Brit. Parliament. Papers by command] Cd. 7792) RC165.A1G7 1913

Includes information on blackwater fever for the East Africa Protectorate and Uganda.

1370
______ Africa. Reports on blackwater fever in the tropical African dependencies. London, H.M. Stationery Off., printed by Darling, 1912. 45 p. charts (part fold.), fold. maps. ([Gt. Brit. Parliament. Papers by command] Cd. 6514) RC165.A1G7

Covers period Jan. 24, 1911–Aug. 10, 1912.

Includes information on blackwater fever for the East Africa Protectorate and Uganda.

1371
______ Information regarding appointments for nursing sisters in the East African depend-

encies: Kenya, Uganda, Nyasaland, Zanzibar, Tanganyika Territory, and Northern Rhodesia. 7th ed. [London] Colonial Office, 1930. (*Its* African (East) no. 1086) DLC-Micro 03759

Collation of the original: 13 p.

[Gt. Brit.] Public Record Office. C.O. 879/120.

1372

Gt. Brit. *Ministry of Information*. An East African Rehabilitation Centre, Nairobi, Kenya Colony. [Nairobi? Ministry of Information, East Africa Command, and Kenya Medical Dept., 1944] 16 p.

Source: Royal Comm. Soc. Cat.

1373

Hints on the preservation of health in eastern Africa. London, Crown Agents for the Colonies [192–?] DLC-Micro 23940 reel 2 octavo 141

Collation of the original: 22 p. illus.

Colonial Office Library East Africa pamphlet octavo 141.

1374

International Symposium on Preventive Myocardiology and Cardiac Metabolism, *Nairobi, 1971*. Papers and abstracts. Editor: Hilary P. Ojiambo. [Nairobi, 1971, 1971] 31 p. DNLM

Sponsored by the East African Medical Research Council and organized by the International Study Group for Research in Cardiac Metabolism.

See also item 1376.

1375

King George VI Hospital, *Nairobi*. Elementary notes for nurses, on nursing procedures, hygiene, anatomy and physiology. Prepared by the Sister Tutors of the Medical Training Centre, King George VI Hospital. Nairobi, East African Literature Bureau, 1956. 143 p. illus. DNLM

1376

Myocardiology in Africa. Nairobi, East African Literature Bureau [for the East African Medical Research Bureau, 1974+] DLC

L.C. has v. 1, Proceedings of the International Symposium on Preventive Cardiology and Cardiac Metabolism.

See also item 1374.

1377

The parasitoses of man and animals in Africa; scientific conference 1972. [Dar es Salaam] 1972. 1 v. (unpaged) DLC

At head of title: East African Community.

Scientific conference held at Central Pathology Laboratory, Dar es Salaam, 24th–29th January, 1972. Organized by the East African Medical Research Council in collaboration with the Faculty of Medicine of the University of Dar es Salaam.

1377a

Parasitoses of man and animals in Africa: proceedings of the 1972 annual scientific conference of the East African Medical Research Council, Dar es Salaam. Editors: C. Andersen [and] W. L. Kilama. Nairobi, East African Literature Bureau [1974] 513 p. DLC

1378

Simpson, W. J. Report on sanitary matters in the East Africa Protectorate, Uganda, and Zanzibar. [London] Printed for the use of the Colonial Office, 1915. ([Gt. Brit.] Colonial Office. African no. 1025) DLC-Micro 03759

Collation of the original: 98 p. illus., 7 maps, plans, plates.

[Gt. Brit.] Public Record Office. C.O. 879/115.

Includes information on malaria, plague, tuberculosis, cerebro-spinal meningitis in Nairobi, Mombasa, Kisumu, Kampala, Jinja, Zanzibar Town, etc.

1379

Twining, Helen Mary Twining, *Baroness*. Camp officers' handbook, prepared by Lady Twining, in association with the Ross Institute of Tropical Hygiene, London School of Hygiene and Tropical Medicine. Nairobi, East African Literature Bureau, 1962. 137 p. illus. WvU

Leprosy

East Africa High Commission. *East African Interterritorial Leprosy Specialist.*

Note: In 1947, the Colonial Office of Great Britain appointed Dr. James Ross Innes interterritorial leprosy specialist, with headquarters in Nairobi, Kenya. On January 1, 1950, the East Africa High Commission assumed responsibility for the leprosy specialist. Areas surveyed included Kenya, Tanganyika, and Uganda, and later Northern Rhodesia, Nyasaland, Zanzibar, and Pemba. On September 23, 1953, the East African Interterritorial Leprosy Specialist was succeeded by the East African Leprosy Research Centre.

1380

Annual report. 1950–53. Nairobi, Govt. Printer. RC154.8.E3A32

Vol. for 1953 issued by the agency under a variant name: East African Interterritorial Leprologist.

Superseded by a publication with the same title issued by the East African Leprosy Research Centre.

L.C. has 1951–53; DNLM has 1950–53.

East African Leprosy Research Centre.

Note: On request of the East African Interterritorial Leprosy Specialist, the East Africa Central Legislative Assembly approved the creation of the Leprosy Research Centre as a non-self-contained service of the East Africa High Commission on September 23, 1953. The centre is located at Alupe, Kenya, on the border near Busia, Uganda. At the suggestion of the British Empire Leprosy Relief Association, which provided funds for the centre from 1953 to 1964, the name of John Lowe [1895–1955] medical secretary of the British Empire Leprosy Relief Association, was added to the centre's name for the period 1955 to ca. 1966. Currently the centre is financed by the East African Community.

1381

Annual report. 1954/55+ [Alupe, Kenya] RC154.8.E3E3

Report year for 1954/55–1962/63 ends June 30; for 1963/64+ ends Dec. 31.

Report for 1964/65 covers period July 1964–Dec. 1965.

Supersedes a publication with the same title issued by the East African Interterritorial Leprosy Specialist of the East African High Commision.

Vols. for 1955/56–1966? issued by the agency under a variant name: East African Leprosy Research Centre (John Lowe Memorial).

L.C. has 1954/55–1966, 1969–70.

1382

——— Bulletin. v. 1+ [Alupe, Kenya? 1969?+]

Source for v. 1, no. 1–6, and v. 2, no. 2: Makerere Lib. Bull. no. 87.

1383

Kinnear Brown, J. A. No more leprosy. [Rev. ed.] Kampala, Eagle Press, 1956. 20 p. illus., map. IEN

Malaria

East African Institute of Malaria and Vector-Borne Diseases.

Note: The East African Malaria Unit was created a non-self-contained service of the East Africa High Commission on January 1, 1950, with funds provided by the Colonial Development and Welfare Fund, with recurrent expenses to be shared by Kenya, Tanganyika, Uganda, Zanzibar, and British Somaliland. Permanent headquarters were established at Amani, Tanganyika, with a field station in nearby Muheza, Tanganyika. In 1955, the present name of the institute was adopted. Research at the institute has concentrated on a control scheme for the Pare Taveta area of northern Tanzania.

1384

Annual report. 1950+ [Amani] RA639.5.E3a

Report year for 1950–53, 1963/64+ ends Dec. 31; for 1954/55–1962/63 ends June 30.

Vols. for 1950–53 issued by the agency under its earlier name: East African Malaria Unit.

Each issue contains a list of the agency's publications.
L.C. has 1951+

1385
_______ Bulletin no. 1–17? 1951–59? [Amani?]
No more published?
The following numbers are identified in the agency's Annual report, 1958/59–1959/60:
no. 1. Therapeutics of malaria. 1951.
no. 2. Insecticides and public health. 1951. Revised ed. issued in 1958.
no. 3. Mosquito liquid larvacides. 1951. Revised ed. issued in 1959.
no. 4. Drug prevention of malaria. 1955.
no. 5. Recent advances in knowledge of adult malaria vectors. 1955.
no. 6. Anti-malarial drainage. 1959.
no. 7. The toxity of dieldrin vapour to *Anopheles gambiae* adults. 1959.
no. 8. Drain maintenance. 1959.
no. 9. Dry larvicides. 1959
no. 10. Maintenance of spraying equipment. 1959.
no. 11. Organization of anopheline control. 1959.
no. 12. Elementary mapping. Revised ed. issued in 1959.
no. 13. Diagnosis of malaria. 1959.
no. 14. Toxic hazards of pesticides in public health. 1959.
no. 15. Biology of adult anopheline mosquitoes. Revised ed. issued in 1959.
no. 16. Irrigation and disease. 1959.
no. 17. Management of insecticide poisoning. 1959.

1386
_______ Report on the Pare-Taveta Malaria Scheme, 1954–1959 [by] East African Institute of Malaria and Vector-Borne Diseases in collaboration with Colonial Pesticides Research Unit. Dar es Salaam, Printed by the Govt. Printer, 1960. 90 p. map. DLC

1387
Gray, Robert F. [Interim report on the Pare-Taveta Malaria Scheme] [Tanga, Tanganyika] 1956. 11 leaves. NNNAM
Project of the East African Institute of Malaria and Vector-Borne Diseases, Pare-Taveta Malaria Scheme.

1388
Gt. Brit. *Army. East African Force.* Provisional malaria map of East Africa. Reproduced . . . by E. A. Survey Group, May 1943 for D.M.S. from information supplied by malariologist, East Africa Command. [Nairobi?] 1943. 4 col. maps. 49 x 71 cm. or smaller. G8500.E5 1943.G7
Scale 1:2,000,000; 1 inch to 31.56 miles.
Contents: Abyssinia.—Kenya Colony.—Tanganyika.—Mozambique.

1389
James, Sydney P. Report on a visit to Kenya and Uganda to advise on antimalarial measures. [London, Crown Agents for the Colonies, 1929] 48 p. 4RA 306

1390
Pringle, G., *and* Y. G. Matola. Report on the Pare-Taveta vital statistics survey, 1962–1966. Nairobi, 1967. 47 p. illus. DLC
At head of title: East African Common Services Organization.

Medical Education

1391
Houghton, M. [Report of a visit in 1957 to Kenya, Uganda, Tanganyika and Zanzibar to inquire into the nursing training schools of East Africa] [London? Colonial Office? 1957] 4 parts in 1 v.
Source: Col. Off. Lib. Cat.

Medical Personnel

1392
East African medical service list. [London, Waterlow]
Two no. a year, 1914–27, 1930–32; annual, 1928–29, 1933.
Prepared in the Colonial Office.
Source for 1914–15, 1923–33: Col. Off. Lib. Cat.

Nutrition

1393
Eastern African Conference on Nutrition and Child Feeding, *Nairobi, 1969*. Proceedings. Washington; for sale by the Supt. of Docs., U.S. Govt. Print. Off. [1969] xxii, 311 p. port. TX345.E25 1969

"Sponsored by the Republic of Kenya and the United States of America Agency for International Development."

Includes country reports for Botswana, Ethiopia, Kenya, Lesotho, Malawi, Somalia, Swaziland, Tanzania, Uganda, U.S.A., and Zambia.

1394
Gt. Brit. *Economic Advisory Council. Committee on Nutrition in the Colonial Empire*. First report. London, H.M. Stationery Off., 1939. 2 v. ([Gt. Brit. Parliament. Papers by command] Cmd. 6050–6051) TX360.G7A6 1939

De La Warr, chairman.

Includes information on nutrition for Kenya, Tanganyika, Uganda, and Zanzibar.

Public Health

1395
Carman, John A. The East African home doctor. Kampala, East African Literature Bureau, 1957. 149 p. illus. DNLM

1396
East African Medical Research Council. Health and disease in Africa—the community approach; proceedings of the East African Medical Research Council scientific conference, 1970. Editor: G. Clifford Gould. Kampala, East African Literature Bureau [1971] 372 p. illus. RC961.5.E17 1970

1397
Threadgold, Nesta, *and* Hebe Welbourn. Health in the home. Nairobi, Eagle Press, 1957. 87 p. DHU

1398
——— ——— Nairobi, East Africa Literature Bureau [1972] 87 p. DLC

Sleeping Sickness

1399
Bax, S. Napier. Report on a visit to Uganda and Kenya, made at the request of the Standing Committee on Tsetse and Trypanosomiasis Research, by S. Napier Bax, Acting Director of Tsetse Research, Tanganyika Territory. [Shinyanga, Tanganyika? 1944?] DLC-Micro 23940 reel 13 folio 367

Collation of the original: 67 p. 2 maps (1 fold.)

Colonial Office Library East Africa pamphlet folio 367.

1400
——— ——— Addendum. [Shinyanga, Tanganyika, 1944] DLC-Micro 23940 reel 13 folio 367

Collation of the original: 16 p.

Colonial Office Library East Africa pamphlet folio 367.

1401
Buxton, Patrick A. Trypanosomiasis in Eastern Africa, 1947. [Prepared for the Tsetse Fly and Trypanosomiasis Committee] [London] Published for the Colonial Office by H.M. Stationery Off., 1948. 44 p. RC246.B85

An overall survey of tsetse control in Kenya, Tanganyika, and Uganda, with reference to local administration.

1402
Conference on Co-ordination of Tsetse and Trypanosomiasis Research and Control in East Africa. [Proceedings] [1st–3d] 1933–43. Nairobi, Printed by the Govt. Printer. irregular. RC246.C6

At head of title: Conference of Governors of British East African Territories.

Issued under earlier names: 1st, Entebbe, Uganda, Nov. 22–25, 1933: Conference on Tsetse and Trypanosomiasis (Animal and Human) Research; 2d, Entebbe, Uganda, Jan.

29–31, 1936: Conference on Co-ordination of Testse and Trypanosomiasis (Animal and Human) Research in East Africa.

A Research conference of the Conference of Governors of British East African Territories.

L.C. has 1st–3d, 1933–43; DNAL has 2d, 1936.

East African Trypanosomiasis Research Organization.

Note: The East African Tsetse and Trypanosomiasis Research and Reclamation Organization was established by the East Africa High Commission in 1948 by the merger of the Tsetse Research Institute, Shinyanga, Tanganyika, the Trypanosomiasis Research Station, Tinde, Tanganyika, and the East African Tsetse Reclamation Department, Nairobi. In March 1956, the organization moved from Nairobi to new facilities at Tororo, Uganda. At that time, the name of the organization was shortened to its present form and the activities concentrated on basic research in human and animal trypanosomiasis.

1403
Annual report. 1948+ [Tororo, Uganda] illus. RC186.T8E32

Report year for 1948–53, 1963/64+ ends Dec. 31; for 1954/55–1962/63 ends June 30.

Title varies: 1954/55–1969, Report.

Vols. for 1948–1954/55 issued by the agency under its earlier name: East African Tsetse and Trypanosomiasis Research and Reclamation Organization.

Each issue includes a list of the agency's publications.

L.C. catalogs under: East Africa High Commission. *East African Trypanosomiasis Research Organization.*

L.C. has 1949+; DNLM has 1948+

1404
_______ Notes for field studies of tsetse flies in East Africa. [2d ed.] Nairobi [195-?] 1 v. (various pagings) illus.

Issued by the agency under its earlier name: East African Tsetse and Trypanosomiasis Research and Reclamation Organization.

Source: Col. Off. Lib. Cat.

1405
_______ Sleeping sickness survey in Musoma District, Tanzania. [Tororo, Uganda? 197-?]

Source: Makerere Lib. Bull. no. 87.

Entebbe. Human Trypanosomiasis Research Institute.

Note: From 1927 to 1930, the institute constituted part of the Laboratory Service Division of the Medical Department of Uganda. In July 1930, the secretary of state for the colonies established the institute on a permanent basis independent of the Medical Department of Uganda. The institute was financed by contributions from Kenya, Nyasaland, Tanganyika, and Uganda until 1936, when its facilities were taken over by the Yellow Fever Research Institute.

1406
Annual report. 1931–35. Entebbe, Printed by the Govt. Printer. RC246.E7

At head of title: Uganda Protectorate.

Supersedes the agency's Report, in the Annual report, 1927–30, issued by the Laboratory Services Division of the Medical Dept. of Uganda.

Ceased publication with 1935.

L.C. has 1934–35; DNLM has 1932, and 1935.

1407
Gt. Brit. *Colonial Office. Sleeping Sickness Committee.* Report of the inter-departmental committee on sleeping sickness. London, Printed under authority of H.M. Stationery Off. by Eyre and Spottiswoode, 1914. 26 p. ([Gt. Brit. Parliament. Papars by command] Cd. 7350) RC246.G7

Earl of Desart, chairman.

Bound with:

1408
_______ Minutes of evidence taken by the departmental committee on sleeping sickness. London, Printed under authority of H.M. Stationery Off. by Eyre and Spottiswoode, 1914. 330 p. ([Gt. Brit. Parliament. Papers by command] Cd. 7349) RC246.G7

Includes information on the East Africa

Protectorate, German East Africa, and Uganda.

1409

Gt. Brit. *Economic Advisory Council. Tsetse Fly Committee.* East Africa Sub-committee of the Tsetse Fly Committee. Report. London, H.M. Stationery Off., 1935. 56 p. ([Gt. Brit. Parliament. Papers by command] Cmd. 4951) SF807.G7 1935

Francis Hemming, chairman of the sub-committee.

Includes information on the work of the Human Trypanosomiasis Research Institute, Entebbe, Uganda.

1410

Gt. Brit. *Treaties, etc., 1901–1910 (Edward VII).* Agreement and protocol between the United Kingdom and Germany with regard to sleeping sickness. Signed at London, October 27, 1908. London, Printed for H.M. Stationery Off. by Harrison, 1908. 4 p. ([Gt. Brit. Foreign Office] Treaty series, 1908, no. 28) JX636 1892 1908 no. 28

[Gt. Brit. Parliament. Papers by command] Cd. 4319.

Text in English and German in parallel columns.

Includes information on British and German East Africa.

1411

Potts, William H., *comp.* Distribution of tsetse species in Africa. [Map compiled and drawn by Directorate of Colonial Surveys from information collated by W. H. Potts, Chief Entomologist, East Africa [sic] Tsetse and Trypanosomiasis Research and Reclamation Organization] [London?] 1953–54. map on 3 sheets.

Cited in the Annual report, 1954/55, issued by the East African Tsetse and Trypanosomiasis Research and Reclamation Organization.

1412

Royal Society of London. *Sleeping Sickness Commission.* Reports of the Sleeping Sickness Commission of the Royal Society. no. 1–17. London, H.M. Stationery Off., 1903–19. illus., maps (part col.), plates (part col.) RC246.R88

Some of the agency's reports are reprinted from the Proceedings, series B, issued by the Royal Society of London.

L.C. has 1903–19.

The following parts concern East Africa:

no. 1 [pt.] 1. Castellani, Aldo. Presence of trypanosoma in sleeping sickness. Aug. 1903. p. 3–10.

Reprinted from Royal Society of London. Proceedings. v. 71, 1903. London. p. 501–8.

no. 1 [pt.] 2. Bruce, David, *and* David Nabarro. Progress report on sleeping sickness in Uganda. Aug. 1903. p. 11–88.

no. 2 [pt.] 3. Christy, Cuthbert. The distribution of sleeping sickness, *Filaria perstans,* etc., in east equatorial Africa. Nov. 1903. p. 3–8.

no. 3 [pt.] 5. Low, George C., *and* Aldo Castellani. Report on sleeping sickness from its clinical aspects. Nov. 1903. p. 14–63.

no. 3 [pt.] 6. Christy, Cuthbert. The epidemiology and etiology of sleeping sickness in equatorial east Africa, with clinical observations. Nov. 1903. p. 3–32.

no. 3 [pt.] 7. Theobald, Fred V. Report on a collection of mosquitoes and other flies from equatorial east Africa and the Nile provinces of Uganda. Nov. 1903. p. 33–42.

no. 4 [pt.] 8. Bruce, David, David Nabarro, *and* E. D. W. Greig. Further report on sleeping sickness in Uganda. Nov. 1903. p. 3–87.

no. 5 [pt.] 9. Austen, Ernest E. A provisional list of diptera. July 1905. p. 3–7.

Describes the diptera of Uganda.

no. 5 [pt.] 10. Nabarro, David, *and* E. D. W. Greig. Further observations on the trypanosomiasis (human and animal) in Uganda. July 1905. p. 8–[48]

no. 6 [pt.] 11. Greig, E. D. W., *and* A. C. H. Gray. Continuation report on sleeping sickness in Uganda. Aug. 1905. p. 1–273.

no. 6 [pt.] 12. Greig, E. D. W. Report on sleeping sickness in the Nile valley. Aug. 1905. p. 273–78.

no. 6 [pt.] 14. Gray, A. C. H., *and* F. M. G. Tulloch. The multiplication of *Trypanosoma gambiense* in the alimentary canal of *Glossina palpalis.* Aug. 1905. p. 282–87.

no. 8 [pt.] 16. ______ Continuation report on sleeping sickness in Uganda. Feb. 1907. p. 3–80.

no. 8 [pt.] 17. Ross, P. H. Report on experiments to ascertain the ability of tsetse flies to convey *Trypanosoma gambiense* from infected to clean monkeys, and on an intra-corpuscular stage of the trypanosoma. Feb. 1907. p. 80–85.

no. 8 [pt.] 18. Hodges, A. D. P. Report on sleeping sickness in Unyoro and the Nile valley. Feb. 1907. p. 86–99.

no. 8 [pt.] 19. Adams, E. B. Account of tour by Mr. Speke and Dr. Adams in northern Unyoro and on the Victoria Nile. Feb. 1907. p. 100–5.

no. 8 [pt.] 20. Minchin, E. A. Report on the anatomy of the tsetse fly (*Glossina palpalis*). Feb. 1907. p. 106–22.

Reprinted from Royal Society of London. Proceedings. Series B. v. 76, 1905. London. p. 531–47.

no. 8 [pt.] 21 Minchin, E. A., A. C. H. Gray, *and* F. M. G. Tulloch. *Glossina palpalis* in its relation to *Trypanosoma gambiense* and other trypanosomes (preliminary report). Feb. 1907. p. 531–47.

Reprinted from Royal Society of London. Proceedings Series B. v. 78, 1906. London. p. 242–58.

no. 8 [pt.] 22 Minchin, E. A. On the occurrence of encystation in *Trypanosoma grayi* novy, with remarks on the method of infection in trypanosomes generally. Feb. 1907. p. 137–42.

Reprinted from Royal Society of London. Proceedings Series B. v. 79, 1907. London. p. 35–40.

no. 9 [pt.] 23. Hodges, A. D. P. Reports on sleeping sickness in Uganda from January 1st to June 30th, 1906. 1908. p. 3–62.

no. 9 [pt.] 24. Gray, A. C. H. Report on the sleeping sickness camps, Uganda, from December 1906 to January 1908. 1908. p. 62–96.

no. 10 [pt.] 30. Bruce, David, A. E. Hamerton, *and* H. R. Bateman. A trypanosome from Zanzibar. 1910. p. 12–27.

Reprinted from Royal Society of London. Proceedings Series B. v. 81, 1909. London. p. 14–30.

no. 10 [pt.] 31. Bruce, David, *and others.* *Trypanosoma ingens.* 1910. p. 27–29.

Reprinted from Royal Society of London. Proceedings Series B. v. 81, 1909. London. p. 323–24.

no. 10 [pt.] 34. ______ A note on the occurrence of a trypanosome in the African elephant. 1910. p. 54–56.

Reprinted from Royal Society of London. Proceedings Series B. v. 81, 1909. London. p. 414–16.

no. 10 [pt.] 35. ______ Sleeping sickness in Uganda. Duration of the infectivity of the *Glossina palpalis* after the removal of the lake-shore population. 1910. p. 56–63.

Reprinted from Royal Society of London. Proceedings Series B. v. 82, 1909. London. p. 56–63.

no. 10 [pt.] 36. ______ *Glossina palpalis* as a carrier of *Trypanosoma vivax* in Uganda. 1910. p. 63–66.

Reprinted from Royal Society of London. Proceedings Series B. v. 82, 1909. London. p. 63–66.

no. 10 [pt.] 38. Minchin, E. A. Report on a collection of blood-parasites made by the Sleeping Sickness Commission 1908–09 in Uganda. 1910. p. 73–86.

no. 10 [pt.] 39. Bruce, David, *and others.* Amakebe: a disease of calves in Uganda. 1910. p. 86–103.

no. 11. ______ Sleeping sickness and other diseases of man and animals in Uganda during the years 1908–9–10. 1911. p. [1]–275.

no. 12 [pt.] 2. Mott, Frederick W. Note upon the examination, with negative results, of the central nervous system in a case of cured human trypanosomiasis. 1912. p. 9–13.

Reprinted from Royal Society of London. Proceedings Series B. v. 83, 1910. London. p. 235–38.

no. 12 [pt.] 4. Bruce, David. The morphology of *Trypanosoma gambiense (Dutton).* 1912. p. 19–25.

Reprinted from Royal Society of London. Proceedings. Series B. v. 84, 1911. London. p. 327–32.

no. 12 [pt.] 6. Fraser, A. D. The relation of wild animals to trypanosomiasis. 1912. p. 26–36.

no. 12 [pt.] 7. Fraser, A. D., and H. Lyndhurst Duke. The development of trypanosomes in *Glossina palpalis.* 1912. p. 36–56.

no. 12 [pt.] 8. ______ An antelope trypanosome. 1912. p. 56–63.

no. 12 [pt.] 9. ______ Duration of the infectivity of the *Glossina palpalis* after the removal of the lake-shore population. 1912. p. 63–75.

no. 12 [pt.] 10. ______ Various experiments. 1912. p. 75–78.

no. 12 [pt.] 12. Carpenter, G. D. Hale. Progress report on investigations into the bionomics of *Glossina palpalis,* July 27, 1910 to August 5, 1911. 1912. p. 79–111.

no. 12 [pt.] 13. Duke, H. Lyndhurst. The transmission of *Trypanosoma nanum* (Laveran). 1912. p. 111–17.

Reprinted from Royal Society of London. Proceedings. Series B. v. 85, 1912. London. p. 5–9.

no. 12 [pt.] 14. ______ Antelope and their relation to trypanosomiasis. 1912. p. 117–32.

Reprinted from Royal Society of London. Proceedings. Series B. v. 85, 1912. London. p. 156–69.

no. 12 [pt.] 15. Robertson, Muriel. Notes on some flagellate infections found in certain hemiptera in Uganda. 1912. p. 132–44.

Reprinted from Royal Society of London. Proceedings. Series B. v. 85, 1912. London. p. 234–40.

no. 13 [pt.] 1 Duke, H. Lyndhurst. Antelope as resevoir for *Trypanosoma gambiense.* 1913. p. 1–12.

Reprinted from Royal Society of London. Proceedings. Series B. v. 85, 1912. London. 299–311.

no. 13 [pt.] 3. ______ Observations on fowls and ducks in Uganda with relations to *Trypanosoma gallinarum* and *Trypanosoma gambiense.* 1913. p. 21–27.

Reprinted from Royal Society of London. Proceedings. Series B. v. 85, 1912. London. p. 378–84.

no. 13 [pt.] 4. ______ Further observations on the recovery of *Trypanosoma gambiense* from *Tragelaphus spekei* on the islands of Lake Victoria Nyanza. 1913. p. 27–30.

Reprinted from Royal Society of London. Proceedings. Series B. v. 85, 1912. London. p. 483–86.

no. 13 [pt.] 8. ______ The sleeping sickness reservoir on the islands of Lake Victoria Nyanza. 1913. p. 54–57.

no. 13 [pt.] 10. ______ A trypanosome from British East Africa showing posterior-nuclear forms. 1913. p. 67–89.

no. 13 [pt.] 14. Robertson, Muriel. Notes on the life-history of *Trypanosoma gambiense,* with a brief reference to the cycles of *Trypanosoma nanum* and *Trypanosoma pecorum* in *Glossina palpalis.* 1913. p. 119–42.

Reprinted from Royal Society of London. Philosophical transactions. Series B. v. 203, 1913. London. p. 161–84.

no. 14 [pt.] 1. Carpenter, G. D. Hale. Second report on bionomics of *Glossina fuscipes (palpalis)* of Uganda. 1913. p. 1–37.

no. 14 [pt.] 2. Duke, H. Lyndhurst. Some trypanosomes recovered from wild game in western Uganda. 1913. p. 37–59.

no. 14 [pt.] 3. Fraser, A. D., *and* H. Lyndhurst Duke. Antelope infested with *Trypanosoma gambiense.* 1913. p. 60–67.

Reprinted from Royal Society of London. Proceedings. Series B. v. 84, 1912. London. p. 484–92.

no. 17 Carpenter, G. D. Hale. Third, fourth and fifth reports on the bionomics of *Glossina palpalis* on Lake Victoria. 1919. p. 1–101.

Military

1413
Askari. Nairobi, East African Command headquarters. weekly.
Title translated: Soldier.
Text in Swahili.
Source for no. 77–247; Oct. 6, 1943–Jan. 9, 1947 (scattered issues wanting): SCOLMA, Mar. 1969.

1414
Askari. Jan. 1963+ Nairobi, Quality Publications on behalf of King's African Rifles. 2 no. a year.
Supersedes the Journal (item 1448) issued by the King's African Rifles.
Source for 1963+: SCOLMA, Mar. 1969.

1415
East Africa command fortnightly review. no. 1–69? 1944–Sept. 1946? Nairobi, Directorate of Education & Welfare, H.Q. East Africa Command.
Supplements accompany some issues.
L.C. received no. 1–47,. 1944–45; apparently not retained; source for no. 40–69; Aug. 20, 1945–Sept. 27, 1946 (scattered issues): SCOLMA. Mar. 1969.

East Africa High Commission. *Royal East African Navy.*
Note: On July 1, 1950, the East African Naval Force was constituted as a non-self-contained service of the East Africa High Commission. The force received the facilities and resources of the former Kenya Royal Naval Volunteer Force, which was disbanded on June 30, 1950. On May 22, 1952, the name of the force was changed to Royal East African Navy. In 1961, the decision was made to disband the Navy, which was completed by September 1962.

1416
Annual report. 1950?–1961. [Nairobi, Printed by the Govt. Printer] VA680.E3
At the head of title, 1961: East African Common Services Organization.
The activities of the Navy for the period 1950–1962 are summarized in the Annual report of the East Africa High Commission (item 1569) issued by the Colonial Office of Gt. Brit.
L.C. has 1953, 1957–61.

1417
East Africans at war. [Nairobi, Ministry of Information, 1944] 79 p. DLC

1418
Gandar Dower, Kenneth C. Askaris at war in Abyssinia. Nairobi, Produced for East Africa Command by the Ministry of Information, East Africa [1945?]
DLC-Micro 23940 reel 7 octavo 349
Collation of the original: 55 p. fold. map., ports.
Colonial Office Library East Africa pamphlet octavo 349.
Issued also in Swahili (item 1423).

1419
——— The King's African Rifles in Madagascar. Produced by the G.S.I., East Africa Command, in conjunction with the Ministry of Information. [Nairobi, 194?–] 64 p. illus., maps, ports. NN

1420
Gt. Brit. *Admiralty.* Naval and military despatches relating to operations in the war . . . With list of honours and rewards conferred. London, Published under the authority of H.M. Stationery Off. by Harrison, 1914–19. 10 v. fold map. D544.G7
Partial contents: VI. Lieutenant-General the Hon. J. C. Smuts. Dated 30th April, 1916. Operations in East Africa.—VII. Lieutenant-General the Hon. J. C. Smuts. 1. Dated 27th October, 1916. Operations in East Africa from 21st March, 1916. 2. Dated 28th February, 1917. Operations in East Africa from 28th October, 1916 to 20th January, 1917.—VIII. Lieutenant-General A. R. Hoskins. Dated 30th May, 1917. Operations in East Africa, 20th

January to 30th May, 1917.—Lieutenant-General Sir J. L. Van Deventer. Dated 21st January, 1918. Operations in East Africa, 30th May to 1st December, 1917.—IX. Lieutenant-General Sir J. L. Van Deventer: 1. Dated 30th September, 1918. Operations in East Africa, December 1st, 1917 to September 30th, 1918.—X. Lieutenant-General Sir J. L. Van Deventer. Dated 20th January, 1919. Operations in East Africa from 1st September to 12th November, 1918.

1421
Gt. Brit. *Army. East Africa Command.* East Africa Command. Exhibition of army art and photography at the Memorial Hall . . . Nairobi, August 25th to September 3rd 1944. Official catalogue. Nairobi [1944] 8 p.
Source: BM Cat., 1965.

1422
——— The infantry of East Africa Command, 1890–1944. [Nairobi, 1944?] 40 p. (chiefly illus.), fold. map. NN

1423
Gt. Brit. *Army. East African Force.* Askari vitani kwa Abyssinia. Kitabu hiki kimewaandikwa askari wa Afrika mashariki na Ministry of Information, East Africa, pia na wakubwa wa East Africa Command. Nairobi, Kimepigwa chapa na East African Standard [1945?] 56 p. illus., fold. col. map, ports. NN
Title translated: Askaris at war in Ethiopia.
Text in Swahili.
Issued also in English (item 1418).

1424
——— Kabete training map. Compiled, drawn and printed by E.A. Survey Group. [Nairobi?] 1942. (*Its* E.A.F. no. 871) DLC-G&M
Scale 1:10,000.
"Compiled from cadastral surveys furnished by Dept. of Lands & Settlement, Nairobi."

1425
——— South East Africa military communications map. 1st ed. [Nairobi?] 1942. map on 2 sheets. (*Its* E.A.F. no. 704) DLC-G&M
Scale 1:3,000,000.
Compiled, drawn and printed by E.A. Survey Group.
Shows Tanganyika, southern Kenya, and southern Uganda.
See also item 1435.

1426
——— The story of the East Africa electrical and mechanical engineers. Issued for the East Africa Command by the Ministry of Information, East Africa. Nairobi [1943?] 23 p. illus. NN

1427
——— The story of the East African Army Education Corps [by F. G. Sellwood, officer commanding E.A.A.E.C.] [Nairobi, 1943] 10 p. illus. NN
"Issued for the East Africa Command by the Ministry of Information, East Africa."

1428
Gt. Brit. *Army. East African Force. O.C.T.U.* Buruji. Oct. 1941. [Nairobi]
Title translated: Bugle.
Text in Swahili?
Source: BM Cat., 1965.

1429
Gt. Brit. *Army East African Force. Ordnance Corps.* Ordnance factories. Kenya Colony. [Nakuru] East Africa Army, Ordnance Corps [1944?] 1 v. (chiefly illus.) NN

1430
Gt. Brit. *Colonial Office.* Correspondence between the Secretary of State for the Colonies and the governors of Kenya, Uganda, and Tanganyika concerning the financial arrangements applicable on the transfer of the local East African forces from the control of the War Office to that of the East African territories. London, H.M. Stationery Off., 1957. [4] p. ([Gt. Brit. Brit. Parliament. Papers by command] Cmnd. 281) J301.K6 1956/57 v. 26

1431
Gt. Brit. *Commonwealth War Graves Commission*. The war dead of the commonwealth. The register of names of those who fell in the 1939–1945 war and are buried in Tanganyika and Uganda. London, 1961. 50 p. NN-Sc
Index numbers on cover: Tanganyika 1–11, Uganda 1–6.

1432
Gt. Brit. *Ministry of Information*. A spear for freedom. [Photography by Capt. A. G. Dickson, Cameroon Highlanders, of the East Africa Intelligence Corps. Nottingham, Printed for H.M. Stationery Off. by T. Forman, 1939?] [48] p. illus. UA857.B7A53
Stamped on cover: "Specimen of British war literature supplied for record purposes only."
Broshure for recruiting Africans to join the East African Military Labour Force.
L.C. also has on microfilm (23940, reel 6, octavo 316).

1433
_______ A spear for freedom; Mkuki na bunduki; Ntungo ya ufulu; Efumu ya ddembe. [Photography and design by Capt. A. G. Dickson, Cameron Highlanders, of the East Africa Intelligence Corps] Nairobi, The Ministry of Information (E.A. Command) [1942] 90 p. (chiefly illus.) UA857.B7A5 1942
Parallel texts in English, Swahili, Nyanja, and Ganda.
An expanded version of the above item.

1434
Gt. Brit. *Treasury*. Copy of a Treasury minute dated 16th April 1958, relative to the gift of the inshore minesweeper, H.M.S. Bassingham, to the governments of East Africa. London, H.M. Stationery Off., 1958. [2] p. ([Gt. Brit. Parliament. Papers by command] Cmnd. 418) J301.K6 1957/58 v. 24

1435
Gt. Brit. *War Office*. Military communications map: South East Africa. 1st ed. [London?] 1942. (*Its* Geographical Section, General Staff no. 4322) DLC-G&M
Scale 1:3,000,000.
"Copied from a map compiled and drawn by E. Africa Survey Group, January, 1952."
Shows Tanganyika, Zanzibar, southern Kenya, and southern Uganda.
See also item 1425.

1436
Hordern, Charles, *comp*. Military operations, East Africa. Founded on a draft by the late Major H. Fitz M. Stacke. Sketch maps by the compiler. London, H.M. Stationery Off., 1941+ maps. (History of the great war based on official documents, by direction of the Historical Section of the Committee of Imperial Defense) D576.G3H64
On cover: Official history of the war.
Maps on lining-papers.
Contents: 1. Aug. 1914–Sept. 1916.

1437
Jambo. v. 1–4; Jan. 1942–Nov.? 1945. [Nairobi, East Africa Command] 4 v. illus. monthly. D731.J35
Ceased publication with Nov.? 1945 issue.
Text in English.
L.C. has Jan. 1942–Sept. 1945 (scattered issues wanting).

1438
Kenya Colony and Protectorate. Administration of the East African Land Forces. Nairobi, Printed by the Govt. Printer, 1957. [1] p. (Kenya Colony and Protectorate. [Legislative Council] Sessional paper no. 105 of 1956/57) J731.H62 no. 105 of 1956/57

1439
_______ Reorganization of the King's African Rifles. [Nairobi? 1938?] (Kenya Colony and Protectorate. [Legislative Council] Sessional paper no. 1 of 1938)
Source: Kenya debates, Aug. 5, 1938.

1440
Kenya Colony and Protectorate. *Governor, 1922–1925 (Coryndon)*. Presentations of the colours

to the 3rd and 5th Battalions of the King's African Rifles by His Excellency Sir Robert T. Coryndon, at Nairobi, Kenya Colony, on Saturday, January 26th, 1924, at 9 a.m. [Nairobi? Govt. Printer? 1924?]
DLC-Micro 23940 reel 1 octavo 67
Collation of the original: [3] p.
Colonial Office Library East Africa pamphlet octavo 67.

1441
_______ Text of speech delivered by His Excellency the Governor and Commander-in-Chief on the presentation of the colours to the 3rd and 5th Battalions, King's African Rifles at the Parade at Nairobi, Kenya Colony, Saturday, 26th January, 1924. [Nairobi? Govt. Printer? 1924?]
DLC-Micro 23940 reel 1 octavo 66
Collation of the original: [3] p.
Colonial Office Library East Africa pamphlet octavo 66.

King's African Rifles.
Note: On January 1, 1902, the King's African Rifles was created by the Foreign Office of Great Britain by the merger of the Central Africa Regiment, the East Africa Rifles, and the Uganda Rifles. The Rifles were the local militia for the East Africa Protectorate (later Kenya), Nyasaland, Uganda, and Zanzibar. During its history the KAR participated in many campaigns, notably, the Somaliland campaign (1900–1914), the invasion of German East Africa (1916), the defeat of the Italians in Ethiopia and Somalia, the occupation of Madagascar, and the reconquest of Burma from the Japanese (1939–45). In the early 1950's, the KAR also took part in the anti-Mau Mau campaign in Kenya. Upon the independence of Kenya on December 12, 1963, Tanganyika on December 9, 1961, and Uganda on October 9, 1962, battalions of the KAR were reconstituted as the national militia of the three countries. For additional historical and bibliographical information see Hubert Moyse-Bartlett's *The King's African Rifles; a study in the military history of East and Central Africa, 1890–1945* (Aldershot, Gale & Polden, 1956. xix, 727 p. illus., maps (DT351.M6)).

1442
A comparative table of the draft King's African Rifles ordinances drawn up on the model of the ordinance prepared by the Inspector-general of the King's African Rifles. [London] Printed for the use of the Colonial Office, 1910. ([Gt. Brit.] Colonial Office. African no. 949) DLC-Micro 03759
Collation of the original: 60 p.
[Gt. Brit.] Public Record Office. C.O. 879/104.

1443
_______ Conditions of service for British warrant & non-commissioned officers, March 1908. 2d ed. [London] Printed for the use of the Colonial Office, 1908. ([Gt. Brit.] Colonial Office. African no. 784) DLC-Micro 03759
Collation of the original: 5 p.
[Gt. Brit.] Public Record Office. C.O. 879/88.

1444
_______ Conditions of service for officers, October, 1905. 1st ed. [London] Printed for the use of the Colonial Office, 1905. ([Gt. Brit.] Colonial Office. African no. 783)
DLC-Micro 03759
Collation of the original: 18 p.
[Gt. Brit.] Public Record Office. C.O. 879/88.

1445
_______ Conditions of service for officers, November, 1906. London, 1906. 18 p.
Source: War Off. Cat.

1446
_______ Draft of the King's African Rifles Ordinance, 190 . [London] Printed for the use of the Colonial Office, 1908. ([Gt. Brit.] Colonial Office. African no. 919) DLC-Micro 03759
Collation of the original: 23 p.
[Gt. Brit.] Public Record Office. C.O. 879/99.
Includes the constitution and government of the King's African Rifles.

1447
_______ Draft of the King's African Rifles Ordinance, 1910; to be enacted by the East African protectorates. [London] Printed for the use of the Colonial Office, 1910. ([Gt. Brit.] Colonial Office. African no. 955) DLC-Micro 03759
Collation of the original: 32 p.
[Gt. Brit.] Public Record Office. C.O. 879/105.

1448
_______ Journal. July 1956–1962. [Nairobi?] Dangerfield ltd. for the Regimental Committee of the King's African Rifles. 2 no. a year.
Superseded by Askari (item 1414).
Source for July 1956–1962: SCOLMA, Mar. 1969.

1449
_______ King's African Rifles reserve forces rules. [London?] 1912.
Source: Col. Off. Lib. Cat.

1450
_______ List of officers, October 11, 1907. 4th ed. [London] Printed for the use of the Colonial Office, 1907. ([Gt. Brit.] Colonial Office. African no. 786) DLC-Micro 03759
Collation of the original: 13 p.
[Gt. Brit.] Public Record Office. C.O. 879/88.

1451
_______ Regulations for Indian contingents, August, 1908. 2d ed. [London] Printed for the use of the Colonial Office, 1908. ([Gt. Brit. Colonial Office] African no. 855) DLC-Micro 03759
Collation of the original: 42 p.
[Gt. Brit.] Public Record Office. C.O. 879/93.

1452
_______ Regulations for the King's African Rifles. *Provisional*. London, 1905. 52 p.
Source: War Off. Cat.

1453
_______ Regulations for the King's African Rifles. London, Printed by Waterlow, 1908. 92 p. NN
"Amendments," 3 leaves, inserted.
NN catalogs under: Gt. Brit. *Army. King's African Rifles.*

1454
_______ Regulations for the King's African Rifles. London, 1925.
Source: Col. Off. Lib. Cat.

1455
_______ Standing orders of 3rd and 5th Batts. King's African Rifles. [London?] 1924.
Source: Col. Off. Lib. Cat.

1456
Salmon, E. Marling. Beyond the call of duty; African deeds of bravery in wartime. London, Macmillan, 1952. 49 p. illus. NN–Sc
"The MS for this book was received from the East African Literature Bureau, at whose request it was written."

1457
Tanganyika. Administration of East African land forces. Dar es Salaam, 1957. 2 p. (Tanganyika. Legislative Council. Government paper, 1957, no. 3) MBU

1458
Uganda. Sessional paper on the administration of the East African land forces. Entebbe. Printed by the Govt. Printer [1958] 2 p. (Uganda. [Legislative Counsil] Sessional paper no. 3 of 1957/58) J732.H6 no. 3 of 1957/58

Politics and Government

1459

East Africa High Commission. *East Africa Central Legislative Assembly*. Membership list. [Nairobi?] irregular.

Source for no. 6: Makerere Lib. Bull. no. 39.

1460

_______ Proceedings; official report. v. 1–14, no. 2; Apr. 6/9, 1948-Nov. 8/16, 1961. Nairobi [Govt. Printer] JQ2945.A75

Vols. for 1948–61 called also 1st–4th Assembly.

Superseded by the Proceedings of the debates; official report (item 1464) issued by the Central Legislative Assembly of the East African Common Services Organization.

Each volume contains papers laid on the table, committee reports, bills debated, estimates and appropriations passed.

L.C. has Apr. 6/9, 1948–Nov. 8/16, 1961.

1461

_______ Standing rules and orders. Nairobi, Printed by the Govt. Printer, 1948. 22, ii p. JQ2945.A75A5

1462

East Africa High Commission. *East Africa Central Legislative Assembly. Select Committee Appointed to Review Standing Rules and Orders.* Report. [Nairobi? 1957?]

Source: E.A.H.C. proceedings, Dec. 3, 1957.

1463

East Africa High Commission. *East Africa Central Legislative Assembly. Select Committee on Standing Rules and Orders.* Report. [Nairobi? Govt. Printer?] 1948.

Source: E.A.H.C. proceedings, Apr. 8, 1948.

1464

East African Common Services Organization. *Central Legislative Assembly.* Proceedings of the debates; official report. v. 1–6, no. 3; May 22, 1962–Nov. 1967. Nairobi. J730.H24

Vols. for 1962–67 called also 1st–18th? Meeting.

Supersedes the Proceedings; official report (item 1460) issued by the East Africa Central Legislative Assembly of the East Africa High Commission.

Superseded by the Proceedings of the East African Legislative Assembly debates (item 1466) issued by the East African Legislative Assembly.

Each volume contains papers laid on the table, committee reports, bills debated, estimates, and appropriations passed.

L.C. has May 22, 1962–Nov. 23, 1965, Nov. 22, 1966/Jan. 26, 1967.

1465

East African Common Services Organization. *Central Legislative Assembly. Select Committee Appointed to Consider the Privileges and Allowances in Respect of Members.* Report. [Nairobi?] 1962.

Source: E.A.C.S.O. debates, May 25, 1962.

1466

East African Legislative Assembly. Proceedings of the East African Legislative Assembly debates. v. 1+ 21st May/30th May 1968+ [Arusha, East African Authority, etc.] irregular. J730.H25

"Official report."

Supersedes the Proceedings of the debates; official report (item 1464) issued by the Central Legislative Assembly of the East African Common Services Organization.

On cover, May 21/30, 1968+: East African Community.

Vols. for May 21/30, 1968+ are the proceedings of the first+ meetings.

Each volume contains papers laid on the table, committee reports, bills debated, estimates and appropriations passed.

L.C. has May 21/30, 1968–May 13/29, 1969; Aug. 1970+

Administration, Civil Service, etc.

The following entries (items 1467–1553) are arranged chronologically.

1903–47

1467
Gt. Brit. *Foreign Office*. Information with regard to civil appointments in the African protectorates. [London? 1903?]
DLC-Micro 23940 reel 11 folio 234
Collation of the original: 8 p.
Colonial Office Library East Africa pamphlet folio 234.
Includes information on the East Africa Protectorate and Uganda.

1468
——— Memorandum showing position of the four African protectorates administered by the Foreign Office in June 1903, arranged in chronological order of date of administration. London, Printed for H.M. Stationery Off. by Harrison, 1903. 9 p. (*Its* Africa no. 9 (1903))
J301.K6 1903 v. 45
[Gt. Brit. Parliament. Papers by command] Cd. 1635.
Includes information on the East Africa Protectorate and Uganda.

1469
Gt. Brit. *Colonial Office*. Table of precedence in East African protectorates. [London] Printed for the use of the Colonial Office [1904?] (*Its* African no. 876)
DLC-Micro 03759
Collation of the original: 2 p.
[Gt. Brit.] Public Record Office. C.O. 879/95.

1470
Gt. Brit. *Foreign Office*. Memorandum on the state of the African protectorates administered under the Foreign Office. London, Printed for H.M. Stationery Off. by Harrison, 1904. 9 p. (*Its* Africa no. 10 (1904)) J301.K6 1904 v. 62
[Gt. Brit. Parliament. Papers by command] Cd. 2163.
Includes information on the East Africa Protectorate and Uganda.

1471
——— ——— London, Printed for H.M. Stationery Off. by Harrison, 1905. 5 p. (*Its* Africa no. 3 (1905)) J301.K6 1905 v. 55
[Gt. Brit. Parliament. Papers by command] Cd. 2408.
Includes information on the East Africa Protectorate and Uganda.

1472
Gt. Brit. *Colonial Office*. Regulations for the employment of officers in the East Africa, Uganda, and Somaliland protectorates. 5th ed. [London] Printed for the use of the Colonial Office, 1907. (*Its* African no. 775)
DLC-Micro 03759
Collation of the original: [9] p.
At head of title: Provisional.
[Gt. Brit.] Public Record Office. C.O. 879/87.

1473
African Tropical Service Committee. Report of the departmental committee appointed to consider questions connected with the qualifications, selection, and training of officers appointed to the civil services of the West and East African colonies and protectorates. [London] Printed for the use of the Colonial Office, 1908. ([Gt. Brit.] Colonial Office. African no. 903.) DLC-Micro 03759
Collation of the original: 12 p.
[Gt. Brit.] Public Record Office. C.O. 879/98.

1474
Gt. Brit. *Colonial Office*. East Africa, correspondence, May, 1909, to July, 1912 relating to the administration of the East African protectorates. [London] Printed for the use of the Colonial Office, 1913. (*Its* African no. 954, confidential) DLC-Micro 03759
Collation of the original: 249 p.
[Gt. Brit.] Public Record Office. C.O. 879/105.

Includes Governor E. P. C. Girouard's proposal to amalgamate Uganda into "British East Africa" with one administration in Nairobi (p. 22–54) and his Report upon the British East Africa Protectorate (p. 57–140, 146–153, and 170–208) with detailed information on land tenure, "native taxation," and "native courts" in the East Africa Protectorate.

Includes also information on the military situation in the Northern Frontier District of the East Africa Protectorate (p. 211–219) and additional data on the police and the military, e.g., Memorandum by the Inspector-general, King's African Rifles, on the military situation in the East Africa Protectorate and Uganda (p. 225–246) by G. Thesiger.

1475

_______ Notes for officers appointed to East Africa. London, Printed by Waterlow, 1909.
DLC-Micro 23940 reel 1 octavo 26

Collation of the original: 61 p.

Colonial Office Library East Africa pamphlet octavo 28.

Includes information on the East Africa Protectorate and Uganda.

1476

_______ Leave and passage rules for civil officers serving in the East Africa, Uganda, and Nyasaland protectorates. 2d ed. [London, 1911] (*Its* African no. 974) DLC-Micro 03759

Collation of the original: 2 p.

[Gt. Brit.] Public Record Office. C.O. 879/108.

1477

_______ Regulations relating to pensions and gratuities to be made to European officers in respect of their having served in the British protectorates in East Africa, Uganda, Somaliland, and Nyasaland. 3d ed. [London] Printed for the use of the Colonial Office, 1911. (*Its* African no. 839) DLC-Micro 03759

Collation of the original: 6 p.

[Gt. Brit.] Public Record Office. C.O. 879/92.

1478

_______ Notes for officers appointed to East Africa and Uganda. London, Printed by Waterlow, 1912.
DLC-Micro 23940 reel 1 octavo 27

Collation of the original: 72 p. illus.

Colonial Office Library East Africa pamphlet octavo 28.

1479

_______ Regulations for the employment of officers in the East Africa, Uganda, Nyasaland, and Somaliland protectorates. 2d ed. [London] Printed for the use of the Colonial Office, 1912. (*Its* African no. 973) DLC-Micro 03759

Collation of the original: 8 p.

[Gt. Brit.] Public Record Office. C.O. 879/108.

1480

Uganda. Terms of service for members of the non-European clerical staff of the Uganda and East Africa protectorates. [Entebbe?] Govt. Press, 1912. DLC-Micro 23940 reel 8 folio 33

Collation of the original: 8 p.

Colonial Office Library East Africa pamphlet folio 33.

1481

Gt. Brit. *Colonial Office*. Notes for officers appointed to East Africa and Uganda. [London?] 1914.

Source: Col. Off. Lib. Cat.

1482

_______ East Africa, papers, May 1919 to December 1920, relating to the revision of salaries in the East African dependencies. [London] Printed for the use of the Colonial Office, 1923. (*Its* African no. 1077, confidential)
DLC-Micro 03759

Collation of the original: 121 p.

[Gt. Brit.] Public Record Office. C.O. 879/119.

Includes information for the East Africa Protectorate, Tanganyika, Uganda, and Zanzibar.

1483

_______ Notes for officers appointed to Kenya

and Uganda. [London?] Crown Agents for the Colonies, 1921. 47 p. illus.
Source: Royal Comm. Soc. Cat.

1484
——— East African dependencies staff list; alphabetical list of officers. [London, H.M. Stationery Off.]
Source for 1922–32: Col. Off. Lib. Cat.

1485
——— Notes for officers appointed to Kenya and Uganda. London, Crown Agents for the Colonies, 1927. 24 p. CaBVaU

1486
Kenya Colony and Protectorate. Memorandum embodying proposals for encouraging the settlement in Kenya of retiring East African civil servants. [Nairobi? Govt. Printer? 1928?] DLC-Micro 23940 reel 11 folio 241
Collation of the original: 3 p.
Typed at head of title: Scheme as amended in Legislative Council and passed May, 1928.
Colonial Office Library East Africa pamphlet folio 241.
Includes information only on European civil servants.

1487
Gt. Brit. *Colonial Office.* Notes for officers appointed to Kenya and Uganda. London, Crown Agents for the Colonies, 1929. DLC-Micro 23940 reel 2 octavo 142
Collation of the original: 24 p.
Colonial Office Library East Africa pamphlet octavo 142.

1488
——— Memorandum on native policy in East Africa. London, H.M. Stationery Off., 1930. 15 p. ([Gt. Brit. Parliament. Papers by command] Cmd. 3573) DT429.A3 1930

1489
——— East Africa. Vital statistics of European officials. Returns. –1945? London, Crown Agents for the Colonies. annual. JQ2945.A4A32
No more published?
L.C. has 1939, 1942–45; NNAM has 1912 cataloged under Kenya Colony and Protectorate. *Medical Dept.;* source for 1930–45: Col. Off. Lib. Cat.

1490
Conference of Governors of British East African Territories. Conference of advisors on native affairs. [Nairobi, 1933] 1 v. (various pagings) CaQML
"Papers circulated in connection with the conference."

1948–61

1491
Gt. Brit. *Commission on the Civil Services of Kenya, Tanganyika, Uganda and Zanzibar.* Report, 1947–48. London, H.M. Stationery Off., 1948. 243 p. ([Gt. Brit.] Colonial Office. Colonial no. 223) JQ1892.A52
Maurice Holmes, chairman.
Includes background information and salary scales for Kenya, Tanganyika, Uganda, Zanzibar, the East Africa High Commission, and the East African Railways and Harbours Administration.

The following entries (items 1492-1508) are arranged alphabetically and concern the implementation of the recommendations in the commission's report.

1492
East Africa High Commission. The Report of the Commission on the Civil Services of Kenya, Tanganyika, Uganda and Zanzibar: memorandum prepared by the pricipal executive officers of the East Africa High Commission for submission to the Standing Committee on Finance of the East African Central Legislative Assembly. Nairobi, Printed by the Govt. Printer [1948] DLC-Micro 23940 reel 7 octavo 387
Collation of the original: 23 p.
Colonial Office Library East Africa pamphlet octavo 387.

1493
______ Report of the East African Salaries Commission terms and conditions of service for the High Commission's service, excluding the E.A. Railways & Harbours Administration. Nairobi, 1948. 38 p. (H.C. circular no. 14)
G. R. Sandford, administrator.
Source: Col. Off. Lib. Cat.

1494
East African Railways and Harbours Administration. Proposals for the implementation of the recommendations of the East African Salaries Commission. [Nairobi? 1948?] ([East Africa High Commission] White paper no. 1, 1948)
Source: E.A.H.C. proceedings, Aug. 31, 1948.

1495
East African Railways and Harbours Administration. *Kenya and Uganda Section.* Report of the East African Salaries Commission. [Nairobi, 1948] (*Its* Special notice, no. 942)
DLC-Micro 23940 reel 8 octavo 399
Collation of the original: 54 p.
Colonial Office Library East Africa pamphlet octavo 399.
"For the information and guidance of servants of the Administration only and not for publication."

1496
East African Railways and Harbours Administration. *Tanganyika Section.* Report of the East African Salaries Commission. [Dar es Salaam?] 1948. (*Its* White paper no. 1 of 1948)
DLC-Micro 23940 reel 7 octavo 391
Collation of the original: 32 p.
Colonial Office Library East Africa pamphlet octavo 391.
"Special notice to staff dated 9th November, 1948."

1497
Kenya Colony and Protectorate. Proposals for the implementation of the recommendations of the East African Salaries Commission [by J. F. C. Troughton] Nairobi, Govt. Printer, 1948. 42 p. (Kenya Colony and Protectorate. [Legislative Council] Sessional paper no. 2 of 1948)
Source: Col. Off. Lib. Cat.

1498
Kenya Colony and Protectorate. *Secretariat.* Report of the East African Salaries Commission: leave, tours of service, passages. Nairobi, 1948. (*Its* Circular no. 70, 1948) MiEM
Collation of the original: 4 p.
MiEM catalogs under: Kenya. *National Archives.* Secretariat circulars. (Film 9044, reel 4).

1499
______ Report of the East African Salaries Commission: minor employees. Nairobi, 1948. (*Its* Circular no. 69, 1948) MiEM
Collation of the original: 6 p.
MiEM catalogs under: Kenya. *National Archives.* Secretariat circulars. (Film 9044, reel 4).

1500
______ Report of the East African Salaries Commission, 1947–48: conversion to new salary scales and conditions of service. Nairobi, 1948. (*Its* Circular no. 68, 1948) MiEM
Collation of the original: 102 p.
MiEM catalogs under: Kenya. *National Archives.* Secretariat circulars. (Film 9044, reel 4).

1501
Tanganyika. Report of the Commission on the Civil Services of Tanganyika, Kenya, Uganda and Zanzibar. [Dar es Salaam?] 1948. 27 p. (Tanganyika. Legislative Council. Sessional paper, 1948, no. 4) J801.H62 1948 no. 4

1502
______ ______ [Dar es Salaam? 1948] (Tanganyika. Legislative Council. Sessional paper, 1948, no. 8)
Source: Col. Off. Lib. Cat.

1503
______ Salary scales and conditions of service revised as the result of the Report of the East African Salaries Commission, 1947–48. Dar es Salaam, Printed by the Govt. Printer, 1948. 54 p. (*Its* Government circular no. 12 of 1948)
JQ3516.Z2T35 1948

1504
Uganda. Proposals for the implementation of the

recommendations contained in the Report of the Commission of the Civil Services of Kenya, Tanganyika, Uganda and Zanzibar, 1948–48. Entebbe, Printed by the Govt. Printer, 1948. 25 p. (Uganda. Legislative Council. Sessional paper no. 3 of 1948) J732.H6 no. 3 of 1948

1505

_______ Supplement to Sessional paper no. 3 of 1948 on proposals for the implementation of the recommendations contained in Colonial no. 223. Entebbe, Printed by the Govt. Printer, 1948. 14 p. (Uganda. Legislative Council. Sessional paper no. 3a of 1948)
J732.H6 no. 3a of 1948

1506

Zanzibar. Proposals for the implementation of the recommendations contained in the Report of the Commission on the Civil Services of Kenya, Tanganyika, Uganda and Zanzibar, 1947–48. (Zanzibar. Legislative Council. Sessional paper no. 6 of 1948) *In* Zanzibar. *Legislative Council.* Papers laid before the Legislative Council, 1948. Zanzibar, Printed by the Govt. Printer, 1948. p. 11–26. J733.J52 1948

1507

_______ Proposals in respect of the recommendations of the Commission on the Civil Services of Kenya, Tanganyika, Uganda and Zanzibar. Zanzibar, Printed at the Govt. Print. Press, 1948. 9 p. JV1076.Z37

"This Sessional paper is published simultaneously with the Report of the Commission; its object is to set out the proposals that His Highness' Government will make to the Legislative Council for the implementation of the recommendations of the Commission."

L.C. also has on microfilm (23940, reel 7, octavo 388).

1508

Zanzibar. *Legislative Council.* Proposals for the implementation of the recommendations contained in the Report of the Commission on the Civil Services of Kenya, Tanganyika, Uganda and Zanzibar, 1947–48. (*Its* Sessional paper no. 9 of 1948) *In* Zanzibar. *Legislative Council.* Papers laid before the Legislative Council, 1948. Zanzibar, Printed by the Govt. Printer, 1948. p. 30–31. J733.J52 1948

1509

East Africa High Commission. Service regulations [Nairobi?]

Source for 1949–57: Col. Off. Lib. Cat.

1510

East Africa High Commission. Staff list. Nairobi. annual. DLC

Superseded by a publication with the same title (item 1540) issued by the East African Common Services Organization.

L.C. has 1955, 1958–60; source for 1948–61: Col. Off. Lib. Cat.

1511

Hailey, William Malcolm Hailey, *Baron.* Native administration in the British African territories. pt. 1. East Africa: Uganda, Kenya, Tanganyika. pt. 2. . . . Zanzibar . . . London, H.M. Stationery Off., 1950. JQ1890.H28 pt. 1–2

At head of title: Colonial Office.

1512

Gt. Brit. *Colonial Office. African Studies Branch.* The construction and composition of governmental organs of the British African territories including similar notes on Southern Rhodesia, Zanzibar and the High Commission territories at the 1st of January, 1951. [London?] 1951. [38] p.

Contents: pt. 1. East Africa.—pt. 2. Central Africa.

Source: Col. Off. Lib. Cat.

1513

Kebaso, John K. Jinsi Afrika Mashariki inavyowiwa deni kubwa na Utawala wa Dola ya Kiingereza. East Africa owes much to British rule. Kampala, Eagle Press, 1953. [47] p. (Mawazo ya wenzanu. Your friends are thinking series) DLC

Text in English and Swahili.

1514
Gt. Brit. *Commission on the Civil Services of the East African Territories and the East Africa High Commission.* Report, 1953–54. [London?] 1954. 2 v. JQ2945.A65A53

David J. Lidbury, chairman.

Includes background information on cost of living and detailed salary scales for Kenya, Tanganyika, Uganda, Zanzibar, East Africa High Commission non-self-contained services, East African Railways and Harbours Administration, and East African Posts and Telecommunications Administration.

The following entries (items 1515–31) are arranged alphabetically, and concern the implementation of the recommendations in the commission's report.

1515
East Africa High Commission. Report of the East African Salaries Commission 1953–54: terms and conditions of service for the non-self-contained services of the East Africa High Commission. Nairobi, 1954. 17 p. (*Its* Circular no. 69 of 1954)

Source: Col. Off. Lib. Cat.

1516
______ The Report of the Salaries Commission on the Civil Services of the East African Territories and the East Africa High Commission (non-self-contained services). Memorandum prepared by the principal executive officers of the East Africa High Commission for submission to the Standing Committee on Finance of the East Africa Central Legislative Assembly. Nairobi, Govt. Printer, 1954. 32 p. IEN

1517
East Africa High Commission. *East Africa Central Legislative Assembly. Standing Committee on Finance.* Report on the Report of the Commission on the Civil Services of the East African Territories and the East Africa High Commission, 1953–54. [Nairobi? 1954?]

Source: E.A.H.C. proceedings, Dec. 16, 1954.

1518
East African Posts and Telecommunications Administration. Proposals for the implementation of the recommendations contained in the Report of the Commission on the Civil Services of the East African Territories and the East Africa High Commission, 1953–54. Nairobi, Govt. Printer, 1954. 24 p. ([East Africa High Commission] White paper no. 2, 1954)

Source: Col. Off. Lib. Cat.

1519
East African Railways and Harbours Administration. Proposals for the implementation of the recommendations contained in the Report of the Commission on the Civil Services of the East African Territories and the East Africa High Commission, 1953–54. Nairobi, Govt. Printer, 1954. 34 p. ([East Africa High Commission] White paper no. 1, 1954)

Source: Col. Off. Lib. Cat.

1520
______ Report of the East African Salaries Commission, 1953/54: introduction of new salary scales and conditions of service. Nairobi, General Manager's Office, 1955. 45[?] p. (*Its* Special notice no. 1)

Source: Col. Off. Lib. Cat.

1521
Kenya Colony and Protectorate. Proposals for the implementation of the recommendations contained in the Report of the Commission on the Civil Services of the East African Territories and the East Africa High Commission, 1953–54. Nairobi, Printed by the Govt. Printer, 1954. 51 p. (Kenya Colony and Protectorate. [Legislative Council] Sessional paper no. 17 of 1954) J731.H62 no. 17 of 1954

"The intention of this Paper is to set out in general terms the extent to which the Government proposes to advise the Legislative Council to reject or revise the Commission's recommendations and also to explain the manner in which the majority of the major proposals will be implemented."

1522
Kenya Colony and Protectorate. *Secretariat.* Re-

vision of salaries and terms of service. Nairobi, 1953. 2 v.
On cover: Salaries Commission 1953.
Source: Col. Off. Lib. Cat.

1523
Tanganyika. Report of the Commission on the Civil Services of the East African Territories and the East Africa High Commission, 1953–54. Dar es Salaam, Printed by the Govt. Printer, 1954. 45 p. (Tanganyika. Legislative Council. Sessional paper no. 3, 1954)
J801.H62 1954 no. 3

1524
——— ——— Dar es Salaam, Printed by the Govt. Printer, 1954. 4 p. (Tanganyika. Legislative Council. Sessional paper no. 4, 1954)
J801.H62 1954 no. 4

1525
Uganda. Proposals for the implementation of the recommendations contained in the Report of the Commission of the Civil Services of the East African Territories and the East Africa High Commission, 1953–54. Entebbe, Govt. Printer, 1954. 68 p. [(Uganda. Legislative Council. Sessional paper no. 1 of 1954)]
JQ2945.A65U33

1526
——— Supplementary proposals for the implementation of the recomendations contained in Report of the Commission on the Civil Services of the East African Territories and the East Africa High Commission, 1953–54. Entebbe, Printed by the Govt. Printer, 1954. 15 p. (Uganda. [Legislative Council] Sessional paper no. la of 1954) J732.H6 no. la of 1954

1527
Zanzibar. *Grading Team Appointed to Examine Clerical and Non-Clerical Posts.* Report. Zanzibar, 1955. 37 p. MBU
S. R. Tubbe, chairman.
Report based on the recommendations in the Report of the Commission on the Civil Services of the East African Territories and the East Africa High Commission, 1953–54.

1528
Zanzibar. *Legislative Council.* Further proposals for the implementation and modification of the recommendations contained in the Report of the Commission on the Civil Services of the East African Territories and the East Africa High Commission, 1953–54. Zanzibar, 1954. 5 p. (*Its* Sessional paper no. 9 of 1954) MBU
MBU catalogs under: Zanzibar. *British Resident.*

1529
——— ——— (*Its* Sessional paper no. 9 of 1954) *In* Zanzibar. *Legislative Council.* Papers laid before the Legislative Council, 1954. Zanzibar, Printed by the Govt. Printer, 1955. p. 49–52. J733.J52 1954

1530
Zanzibar. *Legislative Council.* Proposals for the implementation and modification of the recommendations contained in the Report of the Commission on the Civil Services of the East African Territories and the East Africa High Commission, 1953–54. Zanzibar, 1954. 30 p. (*Its* Sessional paper no. 7 of 1954) MBU
Issued as a Supplement to the Official gazette, v. 58, no. 3592, of Zanzibar.
MBU catalogs under: Zanzibar. *British Resident.*

1531
——— ——— (*Its* Sessional paper no. 7 of 1954) *In* Zanzibar. *Legislative Council.* Papers laid before the Legislative Council, 1954. Zanzibar, Printed by the Govt. Printer, 1955. p. 24–43. J733.J52 1954

1532
Gt. Brit. *Commission on the Public Services of the East African Territories and the East Africa High Commission.* Report, 1960. Entebbe, Uganda, Printed by the Govt. Printer, 1960. 209 p. JQ2945.A691A5
Sir Gilbert Flemming, chairman.

The commission examined the salary and pension scales of the government employees of the East Africa High Commission, Kenya, Tanganyika (expatriates only), Uganda, and Zanzibar.

The following entries (items 1533–35) are arranged alphabetically, and concern the implementation of the recommendations in the commission's report.

1533
East African Railways and Harbours Administration. Proposals for the implementation of the recommendations contained in the Report of the Commission on the Public Services of the East African Territories and the East Africa High Commission, 1960. [Nairobi?] Govt. Printer, 1961. 20 p. ([East Africa High Commission. East Africa Central Legislative Assembly] Sessional paper no. 2 of 1961)
Source: Col. Off. Lib. Cat.

1534
_______ Report of the East African Salaries Commission, 1960. Introduction of new salary scales and conditions of service. Nairobi, General Manager's Office, 1961. 21 p. (*Its* Special notice no. 1 of 1961)
Source: Col. Off. Lib. Cat.

1535
Uganda. Proposals for the implementation of the recommendations contained in the Report of the Commission on the Public Services of the East African Territories and the East Africa High Commission, 1960. Entebbe, Printed by the Govt. Printer [1961] 27 p. (Uganda. [Legislative Council] Sessional paper no. 4 of 1961)
J732.H6 no. 4 of 1961

1536
Ramage, Richard O. Report on the localisation of the civil service in the non-self-contained services of the East Africa High Commission and in the East African Posts and Telecommunications Administration, by Sir Richard Ramage. [Nairobi, 1961] 117 p. DLC

At head of title: East Africa High Commission.

The following entry concerns the implementation of the recommendations in Ramage's report.

1537
East Africa High Commission. *East Africa Central Legislative Assembly.* Localisation of the civil service in the non-self-contained services of the East Africa High Commission and in the East African Posts and Telecommunications Administration. [Nairobi?] Govt. Printer, Kenya, 1961. 17 p. (*Its* Sessional paper no. 5 of 1961)
At head of title: East Africa High Commission.
Source: Col. Off. Lib. Cat.

1962–66

1538
Africanization Commission. Report of the Africanization of the public services of the East African Common Services Organization. [Nairobi, 1963] 105, [52] p. JQ2945.A67A62
Cover title: Report of the Africanization Commission.
J. O. Udoji, chairman.

The following entry concerns the implementation of the recommendations in the commission's report.

1539
East African Common Services Organization. Memorandum by the Authority [on] the Report of the Africanization Commission, 1963. [Nairobi, Printed by the English Press, 1963] 30 p. (E.A. Common Services Organization. [Central Legislative Assembly] Sessional paper no. 1 of 1963) JQ2945.A67E17

1540
East African Common Services Organization. Staff list. 1963?–1967. [Nairobi] annual.
JQ2945.A4E3

At head of title: "For official use only."

Supersedes a publication with the same title (item 1510) issued by the East Africa High Commission.

Superseded by a publication with the same title (item 1547) issued by the East African Community.

L.C. has 1963, 1965–67; source for 1963–64: Col. Off. Lib. Cat.

1541
East African Common Services Organization. *Local Civil Service Salaries Commission.* Report of the commission on the Kenya civil service, the Kenya teaching services, the East African Posts and Telecommunications Administrations [sic] and the general fund services of the East African Common Services Organization. [Nairobi, Printed by the Govt. Printer] 1963. 2 v. JQ2945.A65A4 1963

Lewis J. Pratt, chairman.

At head of title: Government of Kenya.

The following entries (items 1542–43) concern the implementation of the recommendations in the commission's report.

1542
Kenya. Proposals by the Government of Kenya for the implementation of the recommendations contained in the Report of the commission on the Kenya civil service, the Kenya teaching service, the East African Posts and Telecommunications Administration and the general fund services of the East African Common Services Organization. [Nairobi, Printed by the Govt. Printer] 1964. 23 p. (Kenya. [National Assembly] Sessional paper no. 2 of 1963/64) DLC

1543
——— The teaching service. Proposals by the Government of Kenya for the implementation of the recommendations contained in chapter XXVII of the Report of the commission on the Kenya civil service, the Kenya teaching service, the East African Posts and Telecommunications Administration and the general fund services of the East African Common Services Organization. [Nairobi, Printed by the Govt. Printer] 1964. 9 p. (Kenya. [National Assembly] Sessional paper no. 4 of 1963/64) DLC

1544
Conference on Public Policy, *2d, University College, Nairobi, 1963.* Conferences on public policy, 1963/4: East African federation; [paper no. 6] Staffing and training the federal civil service [by] A. L. Adu. [Nairobi? 1964?] 5 leaves. HC517.E2C6 1963 no. 6

Concerns the staffing of the East African Common Services Organization.

1545
Gt. Brit. *Treaties, etc., 1952– (Elizabeth II).* Public officers' agreement between Her Majesty's Government in the United Kingdom and the governments of Kenya, Tanganyika and Uganda and the East African Common Services Organisation. London, H.M. Stationery Off., 1964. [6] p. ([Gt. Brit. Parliament. Papers by command] Cmnd. 2244) J301.K6 1963/64 v. 33

At head of title: Department of Technical Co-operation.

"This Agreement may be cited as the Public Officers' (East African Common Services Organisation) Agreement, 1961. Done in quintuplicate at Nairobi this eighteenth day of November, 1963."

1546
East African Common Services Organization. *O. & M. Division.* Keep smiling; a manual for personal secretaries. [Nairobi, 1966] 29 p. illus. HF5547.E2

1967–74

1547
East African Community. Staff list. 1968+ Nairobi. annual?

Supersedes a publication with the same title (item 1540) issued by the East African Common Services Organization.

Source: Col. Off. Lib. Cat.

1548
Nyagah, S. The politicalization of administration in East Africa; a comparative analysis of Kenya and Tanzania. Lower Kabete, Kenya Institute of Administration, 1968. 32 p. (Kenya Institute of Administration. K.I.A. occasional papers, no. 1) JQ2945.A55 1968

1549
United Nations. *Development Programme*. Administrative improvement and training: project of the East African Community/United Nations Development Programme. [Arusha? East African Community? 1969?] 27 leaves. DLC

1550
Gt. Brit. *Central Office of Information. Reference Division*. Britain and the process of decolonisation [London, H.M. Stationery Off., 1970] 49 p. ([Gt. Brit.] Central Office of Information. Reference pamphlet 91) JV1060.A517 1970b

"Prepared for British Information Services."

Includes information on Kenya, Tanzania, and Uganda.

1551
Gt. Brit. *Treaties, etc., 1952– (Elizabeth II)*. Exchange of notes between the Government of the United Kingdom of Great Britain and Northern Ireland and the East African Community concerning officers designated by the Government of the United Kingdom in service of the East African Community. The Overseas Service (East African Community) Agreement, 1971. Nairobi/Arusha, March 5, 1971. The Agreement entered into force on April 1, 1971. London, H.M. Stationery Off., 1973, 8 p. ([Gt. Brit. Foreign Office] Treaty series, 1973, no. 84]

[Gt. Brit. Parliament. Papers by command] Cmnd. 5361.

Cited in Government publications, 1973, issued by the Stationery Office of Gt. Brit.

1552
East African Community. *Salaries Review Commission*. East African Community (General Fund Services) Salaries Review Commission [report] Arusha, Tanzania, 1972. 85 p. DLC

1553
United Nations. *Development Programme*. Assistance to the East African Community Management Institute. [Arusha? 1974] 45 leaves. DLC

At head of title: Project of the East African Community.

Conformed copy.

East African Cooperation

The following entries (items 1554–1600) are arranged chronologically.

1926–47

1554
Conference of Governors of British East African Territories. Summary of proceedings, 1926. London, Waterflow [1926?] 51 p. CtY

Note: The following note appears in the Catalogue of the Library of the Colonial Office of Great Britain, v. 7, p. 58: "Minutes of meetings and documents submitted to the 1926 conference are confidential, and are filed . . . in Confidential Cupboard."

Minutes and proceedings, and minutes and memoranda of the 1926 Conference are held by the Public Record Office, Chancery Lane, London WC1, in Class CO 962, with the proceedings and memoranda of subsequent meetings, held in 1930, 1932, 1933 (February and October), 1934, 1935 (January and April), 1936, 1937, 1938, 1939 (June and November), 1940, 1941, and 1942 (January and November).—Information supplied by Library and Records Dept., Foreign and Commonwealth Office, Nov. 15, 1974.

1555
Gt. Brit. *Colonial Office*. Future policy in regard to eastern Africa. London, H.M. Stationery Off., 1927. 7 p. ([Gt. Brit. Parliament. Papers by command] Cmd. 2904) DT434.E2G7 1927

1556
Gt. Brit. *Commission on Closer Union of Dependencies in Eastern and Central Africa.* Report. London, H.M. Stationery Off., 1929. 354 p. 5 fold. maps. ([Gt. Brit. Parliament. Papers by command] Cmd. 3234)
DT431.A5 1929

E. Hilton Young, chairman.

Recommended the appointment of a high commissioner for Kenya, Uganda, and Tanganyika, to promote a regional approach to customs, transportation, research, etc.

1557
Gt. Brit. *Colonial Office.* Report of Sir Samuel Wilson . . . on his visit to East Africa, 1929. London, H.M. Stationery Off., 1929. 38 p. ([Gt. Brit. Parliament. Papers by command] Cmd. 3378 JQ2947.A694 1929

Samuel Wilson was requested by the Secretary of State for the Colonies to visit Kenya, Tanganyika, and Uganda, to discuss with the local governments and communities the recommendations of the Hilton Young commission for the closer union of Kenya, Tanganyika, and Uganda. He recommends the appointment of a high commissioner, with full control, legislative and administrative, of the essential economic services.

1558
Great Britain. Statement of the conclusions of His Majesty's Government in the United Kingdom as regards closer union in East Africa. [London, H.M. Stationery Off., 1930] 19 p.
JQ1883 1930.A55

Issued also by the Colonial Office of Gt. Brit. in the series of British parliamentary reports and papers:

1559
Gt. Brit. *Colonial Office.* Statement of the conclusions of His Majesty's Government in the United Kingdom as regards closer union in East Africa. London, H.M. Stationery Off., 1930. 19 p. ([Gt. Brit. Parliament. Papers by command] Cmd. 3574) JQ2947.A694 1930

1560
Kenya Colony and Protectorate. *Governor, 1925–1930 (Grigg).* Despatch from Sir Edward Grigg, Governor of Kenya, to the Secretary of State for the Colonies on the subject of the closer union proposals. Nairobi, Govt. Printer, 1930. 171 p.

Source: Col. Off. Lib. Cat.

1561
______ Despatch from Sir Edward Grigg, High Commissioner for Transport, Kenya and Uganda, to the Secretary of State for the Colonies on the subject of the closer union proposals. Nairobi, Govt. Printer, 1930. 21 p.

Source: Col. Off. Lib. Cat.

1562
Gt. Brit. *Parliament. Joint Select Committee on Closer Union in East Africa.* Report, together with the Proceedings of the committee. [Minutes of evidence and Appendices] London, H.M. Stationery Off., 1931. 3 v. ([Gt. Brit. Parliament, 1931. H. of C. Repts. and papers] 156) JQ2947.A55 1931

At head of title: Joint committee on closer union in East Africa.

Vol. 1 issued also as H. of L. Papers and bills (184) Parliament, 1931; v. 2–3 as H. of L. Papers and bills (29) Parliament, 1930.

Lord Stanley of Alderley, chairman, Dec. 4, 1930–July 3, 1931; Earl of Onslow, chairman, July 10–Sept. 30, 1931.

L.C. has an additional copy with the above entry under: JQ2947.A55 1931a

1563
Gt. Brit. *Colonial Office.* Papers relating to the question of the closer union of Kenya, Uganda, and the Tanganyika Territory. London, H.M. Stationery Off., 1931. 130 p. map. (*Its* Colonial no. 57) DT431.A5 1931

Includes despatches from the governors of Kenya, Tanganyika, and Uganda for the period 1927–30.

1564
______ Correspondence (1931–1932) arising from the Report of the Joint Select Committee on Closer Union in East Africa. [London, H.M. Stationery Off., 1932] 60 p.
JQ2947.A694 1932a

1565
______ ______ London, H.M. Stationery Off., 1932. 60 p. ([Gt. Brit. Parliament. Papers by command] Cmd. 4141) JQ2947.A694 1932
Includes correspondence from the Secretary of State for the Colonies, and Despatches from the governors of Kenya, Tanganyika, and Uganda.

1566
Tanganyika. A despatch received from the Secretary of State for the Colonies in connexion with the Memorandum on closer union which was prepared at an East African unofficial conference held at Arusha on the 15th and 16th of March, 1935, and other memoranda on the subject. [Dar es Salaam? 1935?] (Tanganyika. Legislative Council. Sessional paper, 1935, no. 3)
Source: Tanganyika debates, Nov. 12, 1935.

1567
Gt. Brit. *Colonial Office.* Inter-territorial organisation in East Africa. London, H.M. Stationery Off., 1945. 11, [1] p. (*Its* Colonial no. 191) JQ2945.A5 1945

1568
______ ______ Revised proposals. London, H.M. Stationery Off., 1947. 14, [2] p. (*Its* Colonial no. 210) JQ2945.A5 1947

1948–61

1569
Gt. Brit. *Colonial Office.* Annual report of the East Africa High Commission. 1948–60. London, H.M. Stationery Off., 1949–61. illus. (*Its* Colonial no. 245, 263, 279, 289, 297, 305, 316, 326, 331) JQ2945.A4A34
Superseded by the Annual report (item 1581) issued by the East African Common Services Organization.
L.C. has 1948–60.

1570
East Africa High Commission. *Administrator.* Review by the administrator of the services under his control. [Nairobi] 1951. 29 p.
Speech made in the East Africa Central Legislative Assembly on Wednesday, Oct. 3, 1951.
Source: Col. Off. Lib. Cat.

1571
East Africa High Commission. *East Africa Central Legislative Assembly.* Interterritorial co-operation: work of the East Africa Central Legislative Assembly. [Nairobi?] 1952. 107 p. ([East Africa High Commission] Despatch no. 1/52) DLC
Signed (p. 78): P. E. Mitchell, chairman, East Africa High Commission.
Surveys the development of the High Commission and its departments.
"Appendix 'B': List of publications produced by High Commission departments and services and individual officers of the High Commission during the period, 1st January, 1948, to 31st December, 1951."

1572
East Africa High Commission. Press releases. [Nairobi?] irregular. DHU
DHU has 1957–58 (scattered issues).

1573
Gt. Brit. *British Information Services.* Regional co-operation in British East Africa. [New York] 1959. 13 p. map. DLC

1574
East Africa High Commission. This is the High Commission: the story in words and pictures, of how the East Africa High Commission works for everyone in East Africa. 3d ed. [Nairobi, Govt. Printer, 1960] 24 p. illus. IEN

1575
Gt. Brit. *Colonial Office.* The future of East Africa High Commission services; report of the London discussions, June, 1961. London, H.M. Stationery Off., 1961. 15 p. ([Gt. Brit. Parliament. Papers by command] Cmnd. 1433) JQ2945.A55 1961

1961–66

1576
Gt. Brit. *Treaties, etc., 1952– (Elizabeth II).* United Kingdom of Great Britain and Northern Ireland (on behalf of Kenya and Uganda) and Tanganyika: Agreement for the establishment of the East African Common Services Organization (with annexed constitution of the said organization). Signed at Dar es Salaam on 9 December 1961. *In* United Nations. Treaty series. v. 437. New York, 1963. p. 47–109. JX170.U35 1962 v. 437 no. 6299

Amended by agreements of Oct. 10, 1962, and Nov. 21/22/24, 1962.

Entered into force on Dec. 11, 1961.

Text in English and French on opposite pages.

1577
Tanganyika. *Treaties, etc. Great Britain (on behalf of Kenya and Uganda), Dec. 9, 1961.* An Agreement between . . . Tanganyika . . . Kenya and . . . Uganda for the establishment of the East African Common Services Organization. [Nairobi?] Kenya, Govt. Printer [1961] 39 p.

Source: Col. Off. Lib. Cat.

1578
——— ——— Secretary of State's letters ratifying the agreement. [London? 1961?]

Source: Col. Off. Lib. Cat.

1579
——— ——— [Amendment] agreement.

Source: Col. Off. Lib. Cat.

1580
——— ——— [Amendment no. 2]

Source: Col. Off. Lib. Cat.

1581
East African Common Services Organization. Annual report. 1961–67. [Nairobi] illus. JQ2945.A58E25

Supersedes the Annual report of the East Africa High Commission (item 1569) issued by the Colonial Office of Gt. Brit.

Superseded by a publication with the same title (item 1596) issued by the East African Community.

L.C. has 1961–67.

1582
East African Common Services Organization. East African Common Services Organization. [Nairobi, 1962?] [9] p. illus. DS

1583
——— ——— [Nairobi, Printed by the Govt. Printer, Kenya, 1964] 16 p. illus. DLC

Includes brief descriptions of the various services of the East African Common Services Organization.

1584
Meetings and discussions on the proposed East Africa federation. [Dar es Salaam, Information Services of the United Republic of Tanganyika and Zanzibar, Ministry of Information and Tourism, 1964] 29 p. DT421.M43

1585
Conference on Public Policy, *2d, University College, Nairobi, 1963.* Conferences on public policy, 1963/4: East African federation; [papers] [Nairobi? 1964?] 19 pieces in 2 v. HC517.E2C6 1963

Some pieces have subtitle: Federation and its problems.

Sponsored by the University of East Africa at the University College, Nairobi, November 1963.

Revisions of some papers were issued later in Colin Leys' Federation in East Africa; opportunities and problems, edited by Colin Leys and Peter Robson. Nairobi, London, Oxford University Press, 1965 [i.e. 1966] 244 p. (HC517.E2L4)

Individual papers held by L.C. are listed in this bibliography under their respective subjects, and may be identified by consulting the index to this guide under Conference on Public Policy, 2d, University College, Nairobi (1963).

The following papers concern the political

aspects of East African cooperation:

[no. 13] Nye, Joseph S. The extent and viability of East African co-operation. 13 leaves.

Later revised with the same title and published in Colin Leys' Federation in East Africa; opportunities and problems (Nairobi, London, Oxford University Press, 1965 [i.e. 1966] HE517.E2L4) p. [41]-55.

[no. 17] Macmahon, Arthur W. The opportunities of federation; some structural problems. [20] leaves.

[no. 19] Banfield, Jane. The structure and administration of the East Africa High Commission and the East African Common Services Organization. 9 leaves.

Later revised as The structure and administration of the East African Common Services Organization, published in Colin Leys' Federation in East Africa; opportunities and problems (Nairobi, London, Oxford University Press, 1965 [i.e. 1966] HC517.E2L4) p. [30]-40.

1586

Kenya. Statement by the Kenya Government on the East African Federation. [Nairobi, 1965?] 1 p. (Kenya. [National Assembly] Sessional paper no. 1 of 1964/65)

Corrected to read: Sessional paper no. 5 of 1963/65.

Information received from L.C. Office, Nairobi, Kenya; (publication not held by DLC).

1587

East African Common Services Organization. The East African Common Services Organization. Nairobi, Information Division, Secretary General's Office, 1965. 9 leaves. DLC

Brief history of the organization and its departments.

1588

——— How E.A.C.S.O. serves you. [Nairobi, Information Division, Secretary General's Office, 1965?] 16 p. (chiefly illus.) DLC

1589

EACSO news. v. 1-3, no. 6? Mar. 1965-Oct. 1967? Nairobi, Information Division of The Office of the Secretary General, East African Common Services Organization. monthly. DLC

Superseded by The Community; a magazine of the East African Community (item 1593).

L.C. has Mar. 1965, July-Aug., and Oct. 1967.

1590

Uganda. An agreement between the Government of the United Republic of Tanzania, the Government of Uganda and the Government of Kenya. Entebbe [Govt. Printer] 1966. 2 p.

Source: Royal Comm. Soc. Cat.

1967–74

1591

Kenya. *Treaties, etc. June 6, 1967.* Treaty for East African co-operation. Nairobi, Printed on behalf of the East African Common Services Organization by the Govt. Printer . . . Kenya, 1967. 125 p. JX191 1967.VI.6

"Signed at Kampala, Uganda, on 6th June 1967, on behalf of the governments of the United Republic of Tanzania, the sovereign State of Uganda, and the Republic of Kenya. Coming into force: 1st December, 1967."

See item 1598 for the 1970 ed. of the Treaty.

1592

Uganda. *Laws, statutes, etc.* The East African Community Act, 1967 [an act to provide for giving effect to certain provisions of the Treaty for East African Co-operation and for purposes connected therewith] Entebbe, Printed by the Govt. Printer [1967] 157 p. IEN

"Treaty for East African Co-operation."

1593

The Community; East African Community monthly magazine. v. 1+ 1967+ Nairobi, Information Division, East African Community. illus. HC517.E2C58

Supersedes EACSO news (item 1589).

L.C. has 1967+

1594

East African Community. Handbook. [Nairobi? 1967?] 41 p. illus. MBU

1595
East African Community. *Information Division.* Press releases. 1967?+ [Arusha?] irregular.

The following years are cited on p. 40 of the Annual report, 1972, issued by the East African Community: 1968 (204 issues), 1969 (208 issues), 1971 (209 issues), and 1972 (567 issues).

1596
East African Community. Annual report. 1968+ [Arusha, Tanzania] illus. JQ2945.A58E25

Supersedes a publication with the same title (item 1581) issued by the East African Common Services Organization.

Each issue includes summaries of the activities of the organizations, councils, departments, etc. of the Community, e.g. the East African Development Bank, the East African Industrial Court, the East African Negotiating Team [on the admission of other eastern African countries to the Community], the Community Service Commission, the Inter-university Committee for East Africa, the East African Examinations Council, and the East African Tuberculosis Investigation Centre.

L.C. has 1968+

1597
East African Community. *Information Division.* Fifty facts about the East African Community. [Nairobi, 1969?] [16] p. DLC

1598
Kenya. *Treaties, etc. June 6, 1967.* Treaty for East African co-operation. [Rev. ed. 1970] [Nairobi] East African Community [1972] 176 p. JX191 1967a.V16

Signed June 6, 1967, by the governments of Kenya, Tanzania, and Uganda.

1599
East African Community. *Information Division.* The East African Community: a handbook [Arusha, Tanzania] 1972. 138 p. illus. map. HC517.E2E27 1972

1600
______ Some facts on the E.A. Community. [Arusha?] 1972.

Cited in the agency's Annual report, 1972.

Science and Technology

1601
Annesley, G. Scientific and technical periodicals held in the principal libraries of British East Africa, June, 1949. [Nairobi?] Printed by the Metreorological Dept. [1949] 74 p. (East Africa High Commission. Paper no. 2) Z7403.A4

At head of title: East Africa High Commission.

Botany

1602
Burtt, Bernard D. A field key to the savanna genera and species of trees, shrubs and climbing plants of Tanganyika. Dar es Salaam, Printed by the Govt. Printer, 1939–53. 2v. MnU

At head of title of v. 1: Tsetse Research Department, Tanganyika Territory; of v. 2: East African Tsetse Research Organization.

Vol. 2 rev. and ed. by P. E. Glover and C. H. N. Jackson.

1603
______ ______ 2d ed. rev. by J. R. Welch. Dar es Salaam, Printed by the Govt. Printer, 1957+ DNAL

At head of title: East African Trypanosomiasis Research Organization.

Contents: pt. 1. Genera and some species.

1604
Flora of tropical East Africa. [London, etc.] Pub-

lished on behalf of the East African Community by the Crown Agents for Oversea Governments and Administrations, 1952+ illus. QK401.F55

When complete, this work will be the basic source of information about the characteristics, distribution and habitats of vascular plants native to Kenya, Tanzania, and Uganda. Each family, genus, and species is fully described, and most are illustrated by black and white plates. Expected date of completion for the 210 unnumbered parts is 1985. Additions and corrections to individual parts of this work are included regularly in Kew bulletin.

Contents: [1] Foreword and preface.– [2] Ranunculaceae.–[3] Oleaceae.–[4] Marantaceae.–[5] Onagraceae.–[6] Trapaceae.–[7] Hypericaceae.–[8] Pedaliaceae.–[9] Turnereceae. –[10] Chenopodiaceae.–[11] Cornaceae.–[12] Caricaceae.–[13] Primulaceae.–[14] Melianthaceae.–[15] Resedaceae.–[16] Droseraceae.–[17] Leguminosae, sub-family Mimosoideae.–[18] Buxaceae.–[19] Fumeriaceae (sic) [i.e. Fumariaceae]–[20] Papaveraceae.–[21] Taccaceae.– [22] Theaceae.–[23] Aizoaceae.–[24] Alangiaceae.–[25] Alismataceae.–[26] Butomaceae. [27] Canellaceae.–[28] Caryophyllaceae.–[29] Connaraceae.–[30] Convolvulaceae.–[31] Gymnospermae.–[32] Loganiaceae.–[33] Menispermaceae.–[34] Orobanchaceae.–[35] Polygonaceae.–[36] Rhizophoraceae.–[37] Rosaceae.–[38] Linaceae.–[39] Berberidaceae.–[40] Juncaceae.–[41] Pittosporaceae.–[42] Tamaricaceae.–[43] Tecophilaeaceae.–[44] Ulmaceae.–[45] Cucurbitaceae.–[46] Leguminsoae, subfamily Caesalpinioideae.–[47] Araliaceae.– [48] Basellaceae.–[49] Cactaceae.–[50] Malpighiaceae.–[51] Opiliaceae.–[52] Salvadoraceae.–[53] Sonneratiaceae.–[54] Dilleniaceae.– [55] Orchidaceae, pt. 1.–[56] Icacinaceae.–[57] Scytopetalaceae.–[58] Aquifoliaceae.–[59] Monimiaceae.–[60] Pontederiaceae.–[61] Elatinaceae.–[62] Caprifoliaceae.–[63] Brexiaceae.– [64] Dipsacaceae.–[65] Sapotaceae.–[66] Valerianaceae.–[67] Sphenocleaceae.–[68] Lecythidaceae.–[69] Annonaceae.–[70] Cabombaceae.–[71] Capparidaceae.–[72] Escalloniaceae. –[73] Flagellariaceae.–[74] Geraniaceae.–[75] Gramineae, pt. 1.–[76] Haloragaceae.–[77] Hamamelidaceae.–[78] Juncaginaceae.–[79] Leguminosae, subfamily Papilionoideae 1.–[80] Leguminosae, subfamily Papilionoideae 2.– [81] Lentibulariaceae.–[82] Montiniaceae.– [83] Oxalidaceae.–[84] Phytolaccaceae.–[85] Plantaginaceae.–[86] Rhamnaceae.–[87] Typhaceae.–[88] Combretaceae.–Glossary of botanical terms, reprinted from the Flora of west tropical Africa, by R. W. J. Hutchinson and J. M. Dalziel. 2d ed., rev. by R. W. J. Keay. London, Crown Agents for Oversea Governments, 1954. 12 p. illus.

1605

Glover, Phillip E. A glossary of botanical-Kipsigis names from the Mau-Mara region of Kenya, by P. E. Glover, assisted by J. Stewart, B. Fumerton and Kipkemo arap Marindany [with] descriptions of the meanings of the Kipsigis words and their derivations, by Earl J. Andersen. [Nairobi, East African Agriculture and Forestry Research Organization, 1967] 276 p. QK13.G56

Cover title: A botanical-Kipsigis glossary from Mau-Mara, Kenya.

1606

Greenway, Percy J. Report of a botanical survey of the indigenous & exotic plants in cultivation at the East African Agricultural Research Station, Amani, Tanganyika Territory. [Amani, Tanganyika?] 1934. NSyU

Collation of the original: 511 leaves. illus.

"Period of field work: September 1928 to January 1933."

NSyU has on microfilm (Amani records, film 2071, reel 6.)

1607

______ A Swahili-botanical-English dictionary of plant names. [2d ed.] Dar es Salaam, Printed by the Govt. Printer, 1940. 308 p. QK9.G68 1940

At head of title: East African Agricultural Research Station, Amani, Tanganyika Territory.

First published in 1937.

1608

______ A Swahili dictionary of plant names. Dar es Salaam, Printed by the Govt. Printer,

1937. xvi, 112 p. DNAL

At the head of title: East African Agricultural Research Station, Amani, Tanganyika Territory.

1609
Kew, Eng. Royal Botanic Gardens. East African pasture plants. London, The Crown Agents for the Colonies [1926–27] 2 v. illus. QK401.K4

Contents: 1–2. East African grasses, by C. E. Hubbard.

1610
Moomaw, James C. A study of the plant ecology of the coast region of Kenya Colony, British East Africa. [Nairobi, Printed by the Govt. Printer, 1960] 54 p. illus., 2 fold. charts (in pocket) DNAL

"Kenya Department of Agriculture and East African Agriculture and Forestry Research Organization co-operating with the United States Educational Commission in the United Kingdom."

Chemistry

1611
Dandy, A. J., *comp.* University examination papers in chemistry. Nairobi, East Africa Literature Bureau [1971] 248 p.

"First and final years examination papers at the Makerere University, and universities of Dar es Salaam and Nairobi."

L.C. received; not retained.

Geology

1612
Dixey, Frank. Colonial geological surveys, 1947–56; a review of progress during the past ten years. London, H.M. Stationery Off., 1957. 129 p. illus., maps (part fold., part col.) (Colonial geology and mineral resources. Supplement series, bull. suppl. no. 2) QE261.D5

Includes information on the geological surveys of Kenya, Tanganyika, and Uganda.

1613
_______ The East African rift system. London, H.M. Stationery Off., 1956. 71 p. illus., maps. (Colonial geology and mineral resources. Supplement series, bull. suppl. no. 1) QE320.D5

1614
East-Central Regional Committee for Geology, *Dar-es-Salaam, 1956.* [Pamphlets reprinted from first meeting] Dar-es-Salaam, 1956.

The following numbers are held by the Col. Off Lib. Cat.:

no. 1. Handley, J. R. F. Banded ironstones and associated rocks.

no. 2. _______ An unusual 'Vesicular' ironstone (Nzegite) from the Nyanzian system of Tanganyika.

no. 3. Aitken, W. G. The Jurassis-Cretaceous junction in Tanganyika.

no. 4. James, T. C. The nature of rift-faulting in Tanganyika.

no. 5. Haldemann, E. G. A note on structural features and erosion in eastern and southern Tanganyika.

no. 6. Quennell, A. M. Metallogenic epochs in East and Central Africa.

no. 7. King, A. J. Notes on the seismicity of the Lake Nyasa and Lake Rukwa areas.

1615
Inter-territorial Geological Conference, *5th, Dodoma, Tanganyika, 1952.* Proceedings of a conference held at Dodoma on 13th, 14th, 15th, and 16th May, 1952. Nairobi, East Africa High Commission [1952?] (East Africa High Commission. Paper no. 5) DLC-Micro 40822

Collation of the original: 88 p.

Contents: List of delegates and visitors. —Conclusions.—Minutes.—Text of Circular savingram no. 141/52 of 15th February from the Colonial Office to colonial governments on the subject of the establishment of seismographic stations.—Extract from a letter from Dr. P. L. Willmore of the Department of Geodesy and Geophysics, University of Cambridge, to Dr. S. H. Shaw of the Directorate of Colonial Geological Surveys about the cost of establishing seismographic stations.—Record of an informal inter-territorial meeting of geophysicists held in Nairobi on 5th and 6th

March, 1952.—Report of a sub-committee on the 1:2,000,000 geographical map of East Africa.—Report of a sub-committee on geological symbols.—List of papers presented to the conference and summary of the discussion arising therefrom.

Abstracts of papers presented at the conference are included in Fifth East African Inter-territorial Geological Conference, 1952, abstracts of papers. *In* Colonial geology and mineral resources, v. 3; 1952. p. 234-248.

See also item 1619.

1616
Inter-territorial Geological Conference, *6th, Entebbe, Uganda, 1953.* Sixth Inter-territorial Geological Conference, Entebbe, May 19th–22nd, 1953. Nairobi, [1953] 39 p. (East Africa High Commission. Paper no. 7) DLC

1617
Makowiecki, L. Z., A. J. King, *and* C. R. Cratchley. A comparison of selected geophysical methods in mineral exploration; results of an aerial and ground survey in East Africa. London, H. M. Stationery Off., 1971. 80 p. illus. (2 fold. col. in pocket) (Geophysical paper no. 3) QC801.G3835 no. 3

"This paper describes work in East Africa sponsored by Overseas Geological Surveys. The fieldwork was carried out between December 1959 and June 1962; the airborne surveys were flown by contractors, and the ground surveys were made by the authors, two of whom at the time were with Overseas Geological Surveys and the third with the Geological Survey Division, Tanzania. The paper compares the three airborne techniques employed, in the light of the results obtained over two mineralized areas in East Africa [the Gieta Goldfield in Tanzania and the Migori Gold Belt in Kenya] An abridged account of the results has been published in 1965 in Geological Survey of Canada Paper 65–6, 'Some guides to mineral exploration', edited by F. R. W. Neale."

1618
Overseas geology and mineral resources. v. 1+ 1950+ London, H.M. Stationery Off. illus., fold. maps (part col.) quarterly (irregular) TN57.058

Supersedes in part the Bulletin issued by the Imperial Institute, London, of Gt. Brit.

Bulletin of the Overseas Geological Surveys (called Colonial Geological Surveys, 1950–56) and issued by its Mineral Resources Division.

Title varies: v. 1–6, Colonial geology and mineral resources.

Includes reports from the geological surveys of Kenya, Tanganyika, and Uganda.

L.C. has 1950+

1619
Tanganyika. *Geological Survey Dept.* Geological map of East Africa. Dar es Salaam, 1954. col. map 95 x 72 cm. DLC-G&M

Scale 1:2,000,000.

Prepared on behalf of the Inter-territorial Geological Conference, 1952, from information supplied by the use of geological surveys of Kenya, Uganda, and Tanganyika.

See also item 1615.

1620
Uganda. *Geological Survey.* Preliminary account of the tin deposits of northwestern Karagwe [Tanganyika Territory] and southern Ankole [Uganda Protectorate] by A. D. Combe. [Entebbe?] 1926. 36 p.

Cited in the Royal Empire Society's Overseas office publications, v. 1, no. 1.

Hydrology

1621
Barrett, Raymond. UNDP/WHO hydrometeorological survey of the catchments of lakes Victoria, Kioga, and Albert. [Nairobi, 1967] 4 leaves. GB800.B3

"WRA/1/42/2."

At head of title: Water Development Department, P.O. Box 30521, Nairobi."

"This five-year project is being undertaken by the governments of Kenya, Sudan, Uganda, United Arab Republic, and the United Republic of Tanzania with the assistance of the United Nations Development Programme (Special Fund) with the World Meteorologi-

cal Agency acting as the executing agency."
See also item 1628a.

1622
Brooks, Charles E. P. Variations in the levels of Central African lakes, Victoria and Albert. Pub. by the authority of the Meteorological Committee. London, H.M. Stationery Off., 1923. p. 337–344. ([Gt. Brit.] Meteorological Office. Geophysical memoirs, no. 20) QC801.G7 no. 20

At head of title: Air Ministry.

Official publication no. 220j.

1623
Debenham, Frank. Report on the water resources of the Bechuanaland Protectorate, Northern Rhodesia, the Nyasaland Protectorate, Tanganyika Territory, Kenya and the Uganda Protectorate. London, H.M. Stationery Off., 1948. 84 p. plates, maps. ([Gt. Brit. Colonial Office] Colonial research publications [no. 2]) DI-GS

1624
East Africa High Commission. *East African Agriculture and Forestry Research Organization.* Progress report on East African catchment area research. no. 1–8? Kikuyu, Kenya, Aug. 1958–Sept. 1959? illus. irregular. CU

"Compiled by Dr. H. C. Pereira from contributions by collaborating officers of all departments."

Title varies: no. 3–6, Progress reports on East African catchment area research.—no. 7, East African catchment area research.

No more published?

The following numbers have been identified:

no. 1. Water-use of bamboo forest and softwoods at Kinale in the Aberdares. [1958?]

Cited in H. C. Pereira's Study of the streamflow effects of land use change in catchment areas, published in Proceedings (item 1626) issued by the Formal Conference of Hydrologists of the British East and Central African Territories on Hydrology and Water Resources, 3d, Kampala, 1958, p. 11.

The following numbers are held by CU:

no. 2. Effects of conversion of bamboo forest to softwood plantations. 1958. 8, 11 leaves.

Contents: The land use problem [in the southern part of the Aberdare range]—Rainfall assessment on small catchment areas, by J. S. G. McCulloch.

no. 3. Effects of tea plantation development in the southwest Mau rain forest. 1958. 16 leaves.

no. 4. Effects of African peasant agriculture on steep hillsides. 1958. 9 leaves.

The experiment was conducted in Mbeya District, Tanganyika.

See also no. 6 below.

no. 5. Effects of grazing on torrential streamflow in Karamoja District, Uganda. 1958. 7 leaves.

no. 6. Effects of African peasant agriculture on steep hillsides (ii). 1959. 7 leaves.

See also no. 4 above.

no. 7. Conversion of rain forest to tea plantation, August 1958–August 1959. 1959. 4 leaves.

A comparative study of catchment areas in Kenya.

no. 8. Effects of conversion of bamboo forest to softwood plantations (ii) September 1958 to September 1959. 1959. 14 leaves.

Includes information on the Nairobi city water supply.

See also no. 2 above.

1625
East African Literature Bureau. Maji na mali; kimetungwa kwa msaada wa wenge ujuzi wa mali na ukulima wafanya kazi Kenya na Tanganyika. Nairobi, 1956. 10 p. illus. WU

Title translated: Water and property.

Text in Swahili.

1626
Formal Conference of Hydrologists of the British East and Central African Territories on Hydrology and Water Resources. Proceedings. 1st–3d; 1950–58. Nairobi, Printed by the Govt. Printer. illus. irregular. GB651.F6

Vol. for 1950 issued as Paper no. 3 of the East Africa High Commission.

At head of title 1950 and 1958: East Africa High Commission.

Vol. for 1954 published in Salisbury, Southern Rhodesia.

Superseded in part by Papers and communications issued by the Inter-African Conference on Hydrology, *Nairobi, 1961*.

Includes information on Kenya, Northern and Southern Rhodesia, Nyasaland, Tanganyika, and Uganda.

L.C. has 3d, Kampala, 1958; source for 1st, Nairobi, 1950, and 2d, Salisbury, 1954: Col. Off. Lib. Cat.

1627

Garstin, *Sir* William E. Despatch from His Majesty's agent and consul-general at Cairo, inclosing a report by Sir William Garstin, Undersecretary of State for Public Works in Egypt, upon the basin of the upper Nile. London, Printed for H.M. Stationery Off. by Harrison, 1904. 243 p. illus. ([Gt. Brit. Foreign Office] Egypt no. 2 (1904)) TC517.N6G3

[Gt. Brit. Parliament. Papers by command] Cd. 2165.

Another edition was printed at Cairo with the title: Report upon the basin of the upper Nile with proposals for the improvement of that river.

Includes a detailed description of the lakes and rivers of the upper Nile basin in the East Africa Protectorate and Uganda.

1628

Gt. Brit. *Directorate of Overseas Surveys*. General map: water resources [of eastern Africa] [Tolworth, Surrey? 195–?] (*Its* D.O.S. (Misc.) 11 (A)) DLC-G&M

Scale 1:6,000,000.

Shows eastern Africa from the Horn to the Limpopo.

1628a

Hydrometeorological Survey of the Catchments of Lakes Victoria, Kyoga and Albert. Undertaken by the governments of Kenya, Sudan, Uganda, United Arab Republic and United Republic of Tanzania. Assisted by United Nations Development Programme and World Meteorological Organization. Inauguration, 22nd March 1968, Entebbe, Uganda. [Kampala, Printed by Consolidated Printers Ltd., 1968] 83 p. illus., maps, ports. GB811.E27H9

See also item 1621.

1629

Richards, E. V. Report on the hydro-electric resources of East Africa. London [Crown Agents for the Colonies] 1947.

DLC-Micro 23940 reel 13 folio 387

Collation of the original: 61 p. illus., 12 maps.

Colonial Office Library East Africa pamphlet folio 387.

Includes information on hydro-electric potential for Kenya, Tanganyika, and Uganda.

1630

Woodhead, Terence. Studies of potential evaporation in Kenya. Nairobi, East African Agriculture and Forestry Research Organisation, 1968. 69 leaves. 7 fold. col. maps.

QC915.W75

At head of title: Government of Kenya, Ministry of Natural Resources, Water Development Department.

1631

——— Studies of potential evaporation in Tanzania. Nairobi, East African Agriculture and Forestry Research Organisation, 1968. 60 p. 7 fold. col. maps. DLC

At head of title: East African Common Services Organization in co-operation with the Water Development and Irrigation Division, Ministry of Lands, Settlement and Water Development, Government of Tanzania.

Meteorology

British East African Meteorological Service.

Note: The British East African Meteorological Service was created by the Conference of Governors of British East African Territories on January 1, 1929, with headquarters in Nairobi, Kenya. The area of responsibility included Kenya, Northern Rhodesia, Tanganyika, Uganda, and Zanzibar. In December 1937, service for Northern Rhodesia was transferred to Salisbury, Southern Rhodesia. The Seychelles Islands were part of the area of service from January 1942. From January 18, 1943 to 1947, the service was a branch of the Meteorological Office of the Air Ministry of Great Britain. The service became a department within the East Africa High Commission in 1948.

1632
Atmospheric pressure in millibars from 1931 to 1936, at Tabora. [Nairobi? 1937?]
Cited in the agency's Annual report, 1937.

1633
_______ Atmospheric pressure in millibars from 1932 to 1935, at Kampala. [Nairobi? 1937?]
Cited in the agency's Annual report, 1937.

1634
_______ Atmospheric pressure in millibars from 1931 to 1936, at Zanzibar. [Nairobi? 1937?]
Cited in the agency's Annual report, 1937.

1635
_______ Atmospheric pressure in millibars from 1933 to 1936, at Kabete. [Nairobi? 1937?]
Cited in the agency's Annual report, 1937.

1636
_______ Bulletin of daily rainfall in Zanzibar Protectorate. 1933/37–1946. Nairobi. annual. DAS
Title varies: 1933/37, Bulletins.
Absorbed by the Summary of rainfall (item 1682) issued by the East African Meteorological Dept. of the East Africa High Commission.
DAS has 1933/37–1946.

1637
_______ Coded weather reports for April 1937–April 1939. Nairobi [1940?] 1 v. (various pagings) DAS

1638
_______ Cyclone tracks in the south Indian Ocean. Prepared by Lieut. (Sp.) J. T. Huddart . . . for use of the Royal Navy. Nairobi, 1942. 16 leaves. DAS

1639
_______ Daily synoptic reports. [Nairobi?]
Reports for July 1937–Aug. 1938 cited in the agency's Annual report, 1937–38.

1640
_______ Mean and extreme values of certain meteorological elements for selected stations in East Africa. Nairobi [1947] [13] leaves. DAS

1641
_______ Meteorological report for Northern Rhodesia. 1906/24–1936/37. [Nairobi?] annual. QC991.R5A35
Report year ends June 30.
Cover title, 1906/24–1926/27: Meteorological report.
At head of title, 1906/24–1930/31: Northern Rhodesia.
Title varies: 1906/24, Meteorological report and statistical survey.—1924/25–1930/31, Meteorological report and statistics.
Vols. for 1904/24–1930/31 issued by the Survey Dept. of Northern Rhodesia.
Later information is included in Climatological summaries, Northern Rhodesia, July 1938–June 1948 issued by the Federal Dept. of Meteorological Services of Rhodesia and Nyasaland.
L.C. catalogs under: Rhodesia, Northern. *Survey Dept.* Meteorological report and statistics.
L.C. has 1906/24–1931/32; DAS has 1906/24–1936/37.

1642
_______ Monthly frequency tables. [Nairobi] DAS
Each issue contains summaries of observations of horizontal visibility, height of base of low cloud, and speed and direction of surface and upper winds for Kenya, Tanganyika, Uganda, and Zanzibar.
DAS has 1937–48 (scattered issues wanting).

1643
_______ Non-technical notes. no. 1+ Nairobi [1936+] NN
The following number is held by NN:

no. 1. Reply to the query: What has the Meteorological Service done? [1936]

1644

_______ Note on the observation of cyclonic sea swell on the coasts of islands in the Indian Ocean, by A. Walter. [Nairobi? 1947?]

Cited in the agency's Annual report, 1939/47.

1645

_______ Note on the office printing methods in use in the British East African Meteorological Service. [Nairobi? 1937?]

Cited in the agency's Annual report, 1937.

1646

_______ Notes on forecasting in East Africa, by J.R. Clackson. [Nairobi? 1947?]

Cited in the agency's Annual report, 1939/47.

1647

_______ Observers' manuals. no. 1–20? [Nairobi? 1939?–1947?] irregular.

Continued by a publication with the same title (item 1676) issued by the East African Meteorological Dept. of the East Africa High Commission.

The following numbers are cited in the agency's Annual report, 1939/47, with additional information supplied from the E.A.M.-D. list of meteorological publications, 1972, issued by the East African Meteorological Dept. of the East African Community:

no. 1. Rainfall observations. [1939?] 5 p.

Revised editions were issued in 1957, and in 1967.

no. 1a. Uangalizi wa mvua. 1968. 6 p.

Swahili translation of no. 1.

no. 2. Temperature observations. 7 p.

A revised edition was issued in 1960.

no. 3. Meteorological observations for part-time observers.

no. 4. Meteorological observations for full-time observers.

no. 5. Instructions for pilot balloon observations. 13 p.

no. 6. Aviation weather reports.

no. 7. International code for aviation weather reports.

no. 8. Reports of sudden changes in meteorological conditions.

no. 9. Tables for deriving relative humidity from dry bulb and departure of wet bulb.

no. 10. Tables for deriving dew point from dry bulb and departure of wet bulb (sea-level).

no. 12. Tables for deriving dew point from dry bulb and departure of wet bulb (1200 gdm.).

no. 13. Tables for deriving north and east components. 20 p.

no. 14. Codes for reporting meteorological observations.

no. 15. Tables for reduction of pressure to sea-level.

no. 16. Tables for reduction of pressure to 1200 gdm.

no. 17. Previ code for short period forecasts.

no. 18. Weather forecasts for aircraft in flight.

no. 19. Instructions and tables for the Bilham humidity slide rule.

no. 20. Instructions and tables for sunrise and sunset computations. 6 p.

1648

_______ Preliminary results of a magnetic survey in Uganda Protectorate, by A. Walter. [Nairobi? 1947?]

Cited in the agency's Annual report, 1939/47.

1649

_______ Rainfall at certain stations in East Africa. Jan. 1932?–Jan. 1939? [London?] weekly. DAS

At head of title: H.M. Eastern African Dependencies Trade and Information Office.

No more published?

DAS has Jan. 1932–Jan. 1933, Jan. 1936–Jan. 1939 (scattered issues wanting).

1650

_______ Report on a journey by air over the British East African territories, October 23rd-November 5th, 1931. [Nairobi? 1931] 7 p. CtY

"Under the direction of A. Walter, Statistician to the Conference of East African Governors, and Director of the Meteorological Service."

CtY catalogs under: Kenya Colony and Protectorate. *Meteorological Service.*

1651
_______ Report on a journey through East and Central Africa in connection with the organisation of the British East African Meteorological Service, September-October, 1930. Under the direction of A. Walter, Statistician to the Conference of East African Governors, and Director of the Meteorological Service. [Nairobi, 1932] DLC-Micro 23940 reel 11 folio 233

Collation of the original: 20 p. map.

At head of title: British East African Meteorological Service.

Colonial Office Library East Africa pamphlet folio 233.

The trip included visits to Kenya, Northern Rhodesia, Tanganyika, and Uganda.

1652
_______ Report on arrangements for the supply of weather information for East Africa in connection with the aviation services. [Nairobi? 1931?]

Prepared by A. Walter, director.

Cited in the agency's Annual report, 1931.

1653
_______ Results of meteorological observations made at Kabete, first order station, Kenya. Jan. 1931-May, 1932? [Nairobi] monthly. DAS

No more published?

DAS has Jan. 1931-May 1932 (Feb.-Apr. 1932 wanting).

1654
_______ Results of meteorological observations made at the Kololo Hill, Kampala, first order station, Uganda. May 1931-Mar. 1932? [Nairobi] monthly. DAS

No more published?

DAS has May 1931–Feb. 1932.

1655
_______ Results of meteorological observations made at the Chukwani Palace, first order station, Zanzibar Protectorate. May 1931-Apr. 1932? [Nairobi] monthly. DAS

No more published?

DAS has May 1931-Apr. 1932.

1656
_______ Terms and conditions of service for the Asian staff. Nairobi, 1939.
DLC-Micro 23940 reel 12 folio 328

Collation of the original: 10 p. forms.

Colonial Office Library East Africa pamphlet folio 328.

1657
_______ Upper wind frequencies; tables of frequencies of the speed and direction of upper winds determined by pilot balloon observations at stations in British East Africa during the period 1927–43, prepared under the direction of A. Walter. Nairobi [1946] 149 leaves. DAS

1658
Dagg, M., *and* F. J. Wangati. Climatic characteristics of the principal regions in East Africa. [Muguga?] 1964.

Paper prepared for the Specialist Meeting on Crops in Areas of Low or Erratic Rainfall, Muguga, Kenya, June 1, 1964.

Source: E.A.A.F.R.O., 1964.

1659
Davies, David A. East Africa's weather service. Foreword by Robert Scott. Nairobi, Published for the East African Meteorological Dept. by the Eagle Press [1952] 32 p. illus.
QC875.E23D3

1660
East Africa High Commission. *East African Meteorological Dept.* Annual rainfall totals at selected stations in East Africa over a period of 30 years (1920–1949). [Nairobi? 1950?]

Cited in the agency's Annual report, 1950.

1661
_______ Annual report. 1929–1959/60. [Nairobi]

illus., maps. QC857.A33E224

Report year for 1929–53 ends Dec. 31; for 1954/55–1959/60 ends June 30

Reports for 1939/47 issued in combined form.

Vols. for 1929–38 issued by the agency under its earlier name: British East African Meteorological Service.

Superseded by a publication with the same title (item 1692) issued by the East African Meteorological Dept. of the East African Common Services Organization.

Each issue includes a list of the agency's publications.

L.C. has 1939/47–1959/60; DAS has 1929–1959/60 (1935 wanting).

1662

——— Aviation meteorological codes. [Nairobi?] 1961.

Cited in the agency's Annual report, 1960/61.

1663

——— Bulletin of monthly values of atmospheric pressure, temperature and humidity with total rainfall. [Nairobi] monthly. DAS

Running title: Monthly mean of certain meteorological elements at selected stations.

Each issue contains data for Kenya, Seychelles, Tanganyika, Uganda, and Zanzibar.

DAS has 1937–51.

1664

——— Bulletin of weekly rainfall in Kenya Colony. [Nairobi] DAS

DAS has Nov. 30, 1948-Dec. 27, 1955.

1665

——— Collected climatological statistics for East African stations. Nairobi [1950] 44 p. DAS

1666

——— The daily rainfall of East Africa. 1930-Oct. 1961. Nairobi. monthly. QC925.6.A32

Title varies: 1930-Apr. 1956, Bulletin of daily rainfall.

Vols. for 1930-Apr. 1956 issued in 3 parts: pt. 1. Kenya Colony.—pt. 2. Tanganyika Territory.—pt. 3. Uganda Protectorate.

Superseded by a publication with the same title (item 1696) issued by the East African Meteorological Dept. of the East African Common Services Organization.

Vols. for May 1956-Oct. 1961 include data for Kenya, Seychelles, Tanganyika, Uganda, and Zanzibar.

L.C. has 1954–61; DAS has 1930–61.

1667

——— Frequencies of surface wind speeds and directions. Nairobi, 1961. 3 v. DAS

Contents: pt. 1. Kenya (including Seychelles).—pt. 2. Uganda.—pt. 3. Tanganyika and Zanzibar.

Each part contains comprehensive summaries of surface wind observations for five-year periods.

1668

——— The frequency of total cloud amounts at stations in East Africa. [Nairobi] 1959. 1. v. (various pagings) QC924.A53A52

Reprinted in 1965.

1669

——— Highest rainfall totals at selected stations in East Africa. [Nairobi? 1950?]

Cited in the agency's Annual report, 1950.

1670

——— Hourly values of radiation on a horizontal surface at Kabete, Kenya, February 1938-April 1943. [Nairobi? 1949?]

Cited in the agency's Annual report, 1949.

1671

——— Lowest rainfall totals at selected stations in East Africa. [Nairobi? 1950?]

Cited in the agency's Annual report, 1950.

1672

——— Mean monthly evaporation at selected stations in East Africa. [Nairobi? 1950?]

Cited in the agency's Annual report, 1950.

1673

_______ Mean temperature and dew point temperature (F°) at various pressure surfaces above Nairobi at about 0600 G.m.t. 1948/49–1950. [Nairobi] annual. DAS

Vols. for 1948/49 issued in combined form.
No more published.
DAS has 1948/49–1950.

1674

_______ Memoirs. v. [1]–3, no. 9. Nairobi, 1929–61. illus., maps. irregular. QC925.6.A33E2

Vol. 1 issued by the agency under its earlier name: British East African Meteorological Service.

Continued by a publication with the same title (item 1701) issued by the East African Meteorological Dept. of the East African Common Services Organization.

L.C. has v. 2, no. 4, 7–v. 3, no. 9; DAS has v. [1]–3, no. 9.

The following numbers have been identified:

v. [1] no. 1. Walter, A. Notes on the inauguration of a joint meteorological service for British East African territories. 1929. 5 p.

v. [1] no. 2. _______ Notes on the storm on Victoria Nyanza, May 18th–19th, 1930. [1930?] 2 p.

v. [1] no. 3. _______ Note on the construction of a portable generator for hydrogen gas required for filling pilot and sounding balloons. [1930] 6 p.

v. 2, no. 1. _______ Observations of atmospheric pressure in East Africa. pt. 1. Results from first order stations. 1948. 87 p.

v. 2, no. 2. Grinsted, W. A., *and* M. Adams. A note on the measurement of rainfall, with special reference to East African conditions. 1948. [10] p.

v. 2, no. 3. Forsdyke, A. G. Synoptic analysis in the western Indian Ocean. [1944] 11 p.

v. 2, no. 4 _______ Cloud forecasting by means of tephigram, with particular reference to turbulence cloud. 1943. 12 p.

v. 2, no. 5. Henderson, J. P. Some aspects of climate in Uganda, with special reference to rainfall. 1949. 16 p.

v. 2, no. 6. Davies, D. A. A comparison of the climate of the Orissa/Bihar district of India with that of East Africa, with particular reference to the lac insect. 1950. 6 p.

v. 2, no. 7. _______ Report on effect on local rainfall likely to follow the replacement of forest area of the West Mau reserve by tea plantations. 1950. 5 p.

v. 2, no. 8. _______ A note on the climate of Kenya in relation to the cultivation of ramie. 1951. 4 p.

v. 2, no. 9, _______ Report on experiments at Kongwa on artificial stimulation of rain, January-April, 1951. 1951. 31 p.

v. 2, no. 10. _______ Report on experiments at Kongwa on artificial control of rainfall, January-April, 1952. 1952. 14 p.

v. 2, no. 11. Grundy, F. The use of cetyl alcohol in solution to reduce evaporation from reservoirs. Report on an experiment on Malya reservoir in Tanganyika Territory in August 1957. 1958. 11 leaves.

v. 2, no. 12. Brazell, J. H. Rainfall at Tabora, Tanganyika. 1958. 4 p.

Includes data for 1894–1956.

v. 3, no. 1. Sansom, H. W., *comp.* The Lindi cyclone, 15 April 1952; a survey of its meteorological history and behaviour. 1953. 16 p.

v. 3, no. 2. _______ The climate of East Africa based on Thornthwaite's classification. 1954. 49 p.

v. 3, no. 3. Davies, D. A., H. W. Sansom, *and* G. Singh Rana. Report on experiments on artificial control of rainfall at Amboseli, Kenya, and Dodoma, Tanganyika, 1953–54. 1955. 21 p.

v. 3, no. 4. Sansom, H. W., D. J. Bargman, *and* G. England. Report on experiments on artificial stimulation of rainfall at Mityana, September-December 1954. 1955. 6 p.

v. 3, no. 5. Griffiths, J. F. An initial investigation of the annual rainfall in East Africa. 1958. 12 p.

v. 3, no. 6. Brazell, J. H., *and* C. M. Taylor. Artificial stimulation of rainfall in East Africa by means of rockets. 1959. 6 p.

v. 3, no. 7. McCallum, D. The relationship between maximum rainfall intensity and time. 1959. 6 p.

v. 3, no. 8. Johnson, D. H., *and* H. T. Mörth. Some trans-equatorial contour analyses. 1961. 32 p.

v. 3, no. 9. _______ Forecasting research in East Africa. 1961. 57 p.

"This paper was originally prepared for

presentation at the joint Munitalp/World Meteorological Organization Symposium in Nairobi in December, 1959, and is to be published in the final report of that meeting which will be entitled 'Proceedings of the Symposium on Tropical Meteorology, Nairobi, 1959.' "

1675
——— Meteorological Analysis Centre and Meteorological Communication Centre: programme for the future. Nairobi, 1961. 39 leaves. illus., 3 fold. plans. QC991.E3A5

1676
——— Observers' manuals. no. 21?–24? [Nairobi? 1948?–1960?] irregular.

Supersedes and continues the numbering of a publication with the same title (item 1647) issued by the British East African Meteorological Service.

Continued by a publication with the same title (item 1725) issued by the East African Meteorological Dept. of the East African Community.

The following numbers have been identified:

no. 21. Meteorological glossary. 1948. 8 p.
Cited in the agency's Annual report, 1948.
no. 22. Instructions for the preparation and despatch of climatological returns.
Cited in the agency's Annual report, 1948.
no. 24. Dew point and relative humidity tables (degrees Celsius). 1959. 21 p.
Cited in List of publications, 1970, issued by the East African Meteorological Dept. of the East African Community.

1677
——— Phases of the moon and eclipses, 1950. [Nairobi? 1950?]

Cited in the agency's Annual report, 1949.

1678
——— Rainfall at selected stations in East Africa. 1956?–1961? [Nairobi] weekly. DAS

Supersedes the agency's Weekly notes and weather forecasts (item 1691)?

Superseded by a publication with the same title (item 1708) issued by the East African Meteorological Dept. of the East African Common Services Organization.

Each issue includes data for Kenya, Tanganyika, Uganda, and Zanzibar.

DAS has Apr. 1, 1956–Dec. 31, 1958.

1679
——— Relations between the meteorological and hydrological services in British East Africa, by D. A. Davies. [Nairobi] 1951. 1 leaf. DAS

1680
——— Selected meteorological data for East Africa. [Nairobi? 1950?]

Cited in the agency's Annual report, 1950.

1681
——— Summary of meteorological observations, Mahé Seychelles. 1952?–1955. Nairobi. annual. DLC

Superseded by the agency's The weather of East Africa (item 1690).

L.C. and DAS have 1955; source for 1952–55: Col. Off. Lib. Cat.

1682
——— Summary of rainfall. 1930–60. Nairobi. annual. QC925.6.A3

Absorbed Bulletin of daily rainfall in Zanzibar Protectorate (item 1636) issued by the British East African Meteorological Service.

Title varies: 1956–58, Summary of rainfall in East Africa.

Vols. for 1930–47 issued by the agency under its earlier name: British East African Meteorological Service.

Issued in parts: pt. 1. 1930–55, Kenya Colony; 1959–60, Kenya and Seychelles.—pt. 2. 1934–55, Tanganyika Territory; 1959–60, Uganda.—pt. 3. 1932–55, Uganda Protectorate; 1959–60, Tanganyika and Zanzibar.—pt. 4. 1947–55, Zanzibar bulletin of daily rainfall.

Superseded by a publication with the same title (item 1709) issued by the East African Meteorological Dept. of the East African Common Services Organization.

L.C. has 1930–32, 1936–37, 1950–60; DAS 1930–60.

1683
_______ Summary of rainfall in Seychelles. Nairobi.
Later information is included in the agency's Summary of rainfall. DLC
L.C. has 1955.

1684
_______ Summary of rainfall records. Jan. 1930-Apr. 1956. Nairobi. monthly. DAS
Vols. for 1930–47 issued by the agency under its earlier name: British East African Meteorological Service.
Issued in parts: pt. 1. Kenya (Jan. 1930-Apr. 1956).—pt. 2. Tanganyika (Apr. 1931-Apr. 1956.—pt. 3. Uganda (Apr. 1931—Apr. 1956).
DAS has Jan. 1930-Apr. 1956 (scattered issues wanting).

1685
_______ Summary of upper winds as measured by radar methods at Nairobi. Jan. 1948-Dec. 1950. [Nairobi?] irregular. DAS
DAS has Jan. 1948-Dec. 1950.

1686
_______ Technical memorandum. no. 1–8. [Nairobi] 1952–57. irregular. DAS
Continued by a publication with the same title (item 1711) issued by the East African Meteorological Dept. of the East African Common Services Organization.
The following numbers are held by DAS:
no. 1. Sansom, H. W. The trend of rainfall in East Africa. 1952. 6 p.
no. 2. Nicholls, K. V. W. Some mathematical fragments and formulae. 1952. 1 v. (unpaged)
no. 3. Sansom, H. W. The maximum possible rainfall in East Africa. 1953. 17 p.
no. 4. Henderson, J. P. Some notes on earth tremors in East Africa. 1953. 23 p.
no. 5. Sansom, H. W. The measurement of evaporation in East Africa. 1954. 7 p.
no. 6. Davies, D. A. Artificial inducement of precipitation in the tropics. 1954. 11 p.
no. 7. Thompson, B. W. Some reflections on equatorial and tropical forecasting. 1957. 14 p.
no. 8. _______ The diurnal variation of precipitation in British East Africa. 1957. 70 p.
See also item 1711 (no. 10) and item 1727.

1687
_______ 10% probability map of annual rainfall of East Africa. [Nairobi] 1961. map on 2 sheets. DLC-G&M
Scale 1:2,000,000.
"The map shows the annual isohyets which are the likely minima in a ten-year period. This may be expressed differently as the amounts that should be exceeded nine years in ten."

1688
_______ 20% probability map of annual rainfall of East Africa. [Nairobi] 1961. map on 2 sheets. DLC-G&M
Scale 1:2,000,000.
"This map shows the annual isohyets which are the likely minima in a five-year period. This may be expressed differently as the amounts that should be exceeded four years in five."

1689
_______ Upper air data for Nairobi; summaries of radio-sonde observations of temperature and humidity and of radar wind measurements at standard pressure levels, 1948–55. [Nairobi] 1960. 45 p. (chiefly tables)
QC879.59.K4E2 1960
See also item 1713.

1690
_______ The weather of East Africa. 1937–60. Nairobi. annual. QC991.E3A3
Title varies: 1937–48, 1950–55, Summary of meteorological observations.—1949, Summaries of meteorological observations at selected stations in East Africa.
Vols. for 1937–47 issued by the agency under its earlier name: British East African Meteorological Service.
Issued in parts: pt. 1. Kenya (1937–48, 1950–55).—pt. 2. Tanganyika (1938?–48, 1950–55).—pt. 3. Uganda (1939–48, 1950–55).—pt. 4. Zanzibar (1938?—48, 1950–55).
Superseded by a publication with the same title (item 1714) issued by the East African Meteorological Dept. of the East African Common Services Organization.
Vols. for 1956–60 include weather informa-

tion for Kenya, Tanganyika, Zanzibar and Pemba, Seychelles, and Uganda.

Earlier meteorological observations are included in the blue books of Kenya, Tanganyika, Uganda, and Zanzibar.

L.C. has 1948–60; DAS has 1937–60 (scattered issues wanting).

1691

_______ Weekly notes and weather forecast. Nairobi. DAS

Superseded by the agency's Rainfall at selected stations in East Africa (item 1678)?

Each issue contains data for Kenya, Tanganyika, Uganda, and Zanzibar.

DAS has Dec. 1, 1948–Dec. 21, 1955 (scattered issues wanting).

1692

East African Common Services Organization. *East African Meteorological Dept.* Annual report. 1960/61–1966/67. [Nairobi] illus. QC857.A33E224

Report year ends June 30.

Supersedes a publication with the same title (item 1661) issued by the East African Meteorological Dept. of the East Africa High Commission.

Superseded by a publication with the same title (item 1715) issued by the East African Meteorological Dept. of the East African Community.

L.C. has 1960/61–1966/67.

1693

_______ The behaviour of raingauges and Appendix 1: Investigations of the behaviour of an aero-dynamic shield for a raingauge, by L. Poncelet. Translated from the French by E. F. Lawes. Nairobi, 1963. 51, 10 p.

Translation of *Sur le comportement des pluviomètres,* and *Suite 1. Comportement expérimental d'un écran de protection aérodynamique pour pluviomètre. In* Brussels. *Institut royal météorologique de Belgique.* Publications. Publicaties. Série A, no 10, 1959, p. 1–58; no 26, 1962, p. 1–14.

Cited in the agency's List of publications and bibliography. Rev. Jan. 1966.

1694

_______ Catalogue of publications. Rev. June 1964. Nairobi [1964] 7 p. DLC

1965 ed.: List of publications and bibliography (item 1697).

1695

_______ Collected climatological statistics for East African stations. Nairobi, 1964. 3 v. DLC

Contents: pt. 1. Kenya and Seychelles.—pt. 2. Uganda.—pt. 3. Tanganyika and Zanzibar.

1696

_______ The daily rainfall. Nov. 1961–1968. Nairobi. monthly. QC925.6.A32

Supersedes The daily rainfall of East Africa (item 1666) issued by the East African Meteorological Dept. of the East Africa High Commission.

Title varies: Nov. 1961–July 1962, 1963, The daily rainfall of East Africa.

Vols. for Aug. 1962–1968 issued in 3 parts: pt. 1. Kenya (called 1962 Kenya and Seychelles).—pt. 2. Uganda.—pt. Tanzania (called 1962–63 Tanganyika and Zanzibar).

No more published.

Daily rainfall in Tanzania, 1964, cataloged separately in L.C. (QC925.6.T34E25).

L.C. has 1961–64 (scattered issues wanting); DAS has 1961–68.

1697

_______ List of publications and bibliography. Rev. Apr. 1965. Nairobi, 1965. 14 p. DLC

1964 ed.: Catalogue of publications (item 1694).

1698

_______ _______ Rev. Jan. 1966. Nairobi, 1966. 18 p. DLC

1699

_______ _______ Rev. Jan. 1967. [Nairobi, 1967] 16 p. DLC

1970 ed.: Lits of publications 1970 (item 1718) issued by the East African Meteorological Dept. of the East African Community.

1700

_______ Mean monthly and annual rainfall for stations in the western half of Kenya having eight or more years of records. [Nairobi? 1962?]

Cited in the agency's Annual report, 1962/63.

1701

_______ Memoirs. v. 3, no. 10-v. 4, no. 4. Nairobi, 1963–67. illus., maps. irregular. DLC

Supersedes and continues the numbering of a publication with the same title (item 1674) issued by the East African Meteorological Dept. of the East Africa High Commission.

Continued by a publication with the same title (item 1721) issued by the East African Meteorological Dept. of the East African Community.

L.C. and DAS have v. 3, no. 10–v 4, no. 4.

The following numbers have been identified:

v. 3, no. 10. Griffiths, J. F., *and* G. F. Hemming. A rainfall map of eastern Africa and southern Arabia. 1963. 42 p.

v. 4, no. 1. Sansom, H.W. A hail suppression experiment at Kericho, first progress report. 1965. 9 p.

"This report was originally prepared for presentation at the First National Symposium on Hail Suppression, held at Dillon, Colorado, 14–16 October 1965."

v. 4, no. 2. Mörth, H. T. Investigation into the meteorological aspects of the variations in the level of Lake Victoria. 1967. 10 p.

v. 4, no. 3. Sissons, J. An analysis of clear air turbulence reports over Africa and adjacent ocean areas south of latitude 15° North. 1967. 19 p.

v. 4, no. 4. Neave, C. F. Tropical storm "Lily," 19th April-3rd May 1966; an account of its history and behaviour. 1967. 8 p.

QC947.N4

1702

_______ Meteorological data recorded at agricultural, hydrological, and other research stations in Tanzania. 1963/65–1966/67. Nairobi.

QC991.T35E37a

Reports for 1963/65, and 1966/67, issued in combined form.

Superseded by a publication with the same title (item 1723) issued by the East African Meteorological Dept. of the East African Community.

L.C. has 1963/65–1966/67.

1703

_______ Meteorological data recorded at agricultural, hydrological, and other research stations in Uganda. 1963/65–1966/67. Nairobi.

QC991.U3E37a

Reports for 1963/65, and 1966/67, issued in combined form.

Superseded by a publication with the same title (item 1724) issued by the East African Meteorological Dept. of the East African Community.

L.C. has 1963/65–1966/67.

1704

_______ Monthly and annual rainfall in Kenya during the 30 years, 1931 to 1960. Nairobi, 1966. 172 p. QC925.6.K4E38

1705

_______ Monthly and annual rainfall in Tanganyika and Zanzibar during the 30 years, 1931–1960. Nairobi, 1966. 4, 97, 8 p.

QC925.6.T3E38

Caption title: Monthly and annual rainfall in Tanzania during the 30 years, 1931–1960.

1706

_______ Monthly and annual rainfall in Uganda during the 30 years, 1931 to 1960. Nairobi, 1965. 33 p. QC925.6.U4E38

1707

_______ On the causes of aridity of north-eastern Africa, by Hermann Flöhn. Translated by H. T. Mörth. [Nairobi?] 1966. 18 p.

Translation of *Uber die Ursachen der Ariditüt Nordost-Afrikas. In* Würzburger geographische Arbeiten, Heft 12, 1964, p. 25–41.

Cited in the agency's Annual report, 1966/67.

1708

_______ Rainfall at selected stations in East Africa. 1961?–1967? [Nairobi?]

Supersedes a publication with the same title (item 1678) issued by the East African Meteorological Dept. of the East Africa High Commission.

Superseded by a publication with the same title (item 1728) issued by the East African Meteorological Dept. of the East African Community.

Source for Apr./June 1966: Makerere Lib. Bull. no. 63.

1709

_______ Summary of rainfall. 1961–66. Nairobi. annual. QC925.6.A3

Supersedes a publication with the same title (item 1682) issued by the East African Meteorological Dept. of the East Africa High Commission.

Issued in parts: pt. 1. Kenya (called 1960–61 Kenya and Seychelles).—pt. 2. Uganda.—pt. 3. Tanzania (called 1960–64 Tanganyika and Zanzibar).

Vols. for 1964–66 are unnumbered parts with the word "parts" no longer appearing.

Superseded by a publication with the same title (item 1729) issued by the East African Meteorological Dept. of the East African Community.

L.C. and DAS have 1961–66.

1710

_______ Sunshine and radiation data at stations in East Africa. [Nairobi, 1962?] 19 p. MiEM

1711

_______ Technical memorandum. no. 9–11. Nairobi, 1963–66. irregular. DLC

Supersedes and continues the numbering of a publication with the same title (item 1686) issued by the East African Meteorological Dept. of the East Africa High Commission.

Continued by a publication with the same title (item 1730) issued by the East African Meteorological Dept. of the East African Community.

The following numbers are held by L.C. and DAS:

no. 9. Sansom, H. W. A moisture/humidity index as an aid to local forecasting in East Africa. 1963. 8 p.

no. 10. Tables showing the diurnal variation of precipitation in East Africa and Seychelles. 1965. 49 p.

"Supplement to Technical memorandum no. 8, 1957."

no. 11. Lumb, F. E. The use of persistence as a means of estimating the probability of low stratus at Nairobi Airport up to 24 hours ahead. 1966. 13 p.

1712

_______ Temperature data for stations in East Africa. Nairobi, 1959–62. 3 v. DAS

Contents: pt. 1. Kenya.—pt. 2. Uganda.—pt. 3. Tanganyika and Zanzibar.

Each part contains a summary of temperature measurements available in the agency's archives.

1713

_______ Upper air data for Nairobi; summaries of radio-sonde observations of temperature and humidity and of radar wind measurements at standard pressure levels, 1957–1962. [Nairobi] 1963. 1 v. (various pagings) DLC

See also item 1689.

1714

_______ The weather of East Africa. 1961–66. Nairobi. annual. QC991.E3A3

Supersedes a publication with the same title (item 1690) issued by the East African Meteorological Dept. of the East Africa High Commission.

Superseded by a publication with the same title (item 1737) issued by the East African Meteorological Dept. of the East African Community.

Includes weather information for Kenya, Tanzania, and Uganda.

L.C. and DAS have 1961–66.

East African Community. *East African Meteorological Dept.*

Note: In 1948, the British East African Meteorological Service became the East African Meteorological Department within the East

Africa High Commission. In December 1961, the department came under the commission's successor, the East African Common Service Organization. The Seychelles Islands in the Indian Ocean were part of the area of service from 1942 until June 30, 1964. Under the Treaty for East African Co-operation the department became part of the East African Community in 1967 and it currently provides meteorological information for Kenya, Tanzania, and Uganda.

1715
Annual report. 1967/68+ [Nairobi] illus. DLC
Report year ends June 30.
Supersedes a publication with the same title (item 1692) issued by the East African Meteorological Dept. of the East African Common Services Organization.
L.C. has 1967/68+

1716
_______ E.A.M.D. list of meteorological publications, 1972. [Nairobi, 1972] 14 p. DLC
1970 ed.: List of publications 1970 (item 1718).

1717
_______ East African observer's handbook. [Nairobi?] 1970.
Handbook of standard precedures for surface weather observing and recording of climatological data.
Includes amendment service.
Cited in the agency's E.A.M.D. list of meteorological publications, 1972.

1718
_______ List of publications 1970. [Nairobi? 1970] 16 p. DLC
1967 ed.: List of publications and bibliography (item 1699) issued by the East African Meteorological Dept. of the East African Common Services Organization.
1972 ed.: E.A.M.D. list of meteorological publications (item 1716).

1719
_______ Mean annual rainfall map of East Africa (based on all available data at 1966). Isohyets compiled by the Meteorological Dept. of the East African Community and drawn by Survey of Kenya. [Nairobi?] East African Community, c1971. col. map 95 x 73 cm. on 2 sheets 64 x 83 cm. G8401.C883 1966.E3
Scale 1:2,000,000.
Rainfall shown by isohyets and gradient tints.
"Base map compiled and drawn in the Drawing Office of the Geological Survey Dept., Dodoma, Tanzania, from information supplied by the Geological Surveys of Kenya, Uganda, and Tanzania. Partial revision by Survey of Kenya, 1971."

1720
_______ Mean monthly rainfall map of East Africa . . . (based on all available data at 1966). Isohyets compiled by the Meteorological Dept. of the East African Community and drawn by Survey of Kenya. [Nairobi?] c1971. 12 col. maps 118 x 72 cm. on 24 sheets 64 x 90 cm. G8401.C883 s2000.E3
Scale 1:2,000,000.
Rainfall shown by isohyets and gradient tints.
Issued as 12 separate monthly maps.
"Base map compiled and drawn in the Drawing Office of the Geological Survey Department, Dodoma, Tanzania, from information supplied by the Geological Surveys of Kenya, Uganda, and Tanzania. Partial revision by Survey of Kenya 1971."

1721
_______ Memoirs. v. 4, no. 5+ Nairobi, 1968+ illus., maps. irregular.
Supersedes and continues the numbering of a publication with the same title (item 1701) issued by the East African Meteorological Dept. of the East African Common Services Organization.
The following numbers are held by L.C.:
v .4, no. 5. Brinkman, S. E., P. Wurzel, *and* R. Jaetzold. Meteorological observations on Mount Kenya. 1968. 44 p. DLC
v. 4, no. 6. Hay, R. F. M. Analysis of time series of monthly rainfall in the region of Dar es Salaam. 1974. 21 p. QC925.6T32D374

1722

_______ Meteorological data recorded at agricultural, hydrological, and other research stations in Kenya. 1963/65+ Nairobi. annual.
QC991.K4E37a

Reports for 1963/65, and for 1966/67, issued in combined form.

L.C. has 1963/65+

1723

_______ Meteorological data recorded at agricultural, hydrological, and synoptic stations in Tanzania. 1968+ Nairobi. annual.
QC991.T35E38a

Supersedes a publication with the same title (item 1702) issued by the East African Meteorological Dept. of the East African Common Services Organization.

L.C. has 1968+

1724

_______ Meteorological data recorded at agricultural, hydrological and synoptic stations in Uganda. 1968+ Nairobi. annual.
QC991.U3E38a

Supersedes a publication with the same title (item 1703) issued by the East African Meteorological Dept. of the East African Common Services Organization.

L.C. has 1969+

1725

_______ Observers' manuals. no. 25+ [Nairobi? 1970?+] irregular.

Supresedes and continues the numbering of a publication with the same title (item 1676) issued by the East African Meteorological Dept. of the East Africa High Commission.

The following number is cited in the agency's List of publications, 1970:

no. 25. Dew point and relative humidity tables for use with screen readings (degrees Celsius). 1970. 13 p.

1726

_______ Pamphlet series. no. 1+ [Nairobi] 1938+ irregular. DAS

The following numbers are held by DAS:

no. 1. A note on the climate of East Africa, with special reference to rainfall and temperature. [1948] 6 p.

no. 2. The climate of Nairobi City. [1956] 4 p.

Revised in 1967.

First published in 1938 under title: Note on the climate of Nairobi Township; revised ed. 1952 has title: A note on the weather at Nairobi.

no. 3. A note on the weather at Dar es Salaam. [1947?] 4 p.

Revised in 1966.

no. 4. A note on the climate of East Africa, with special reference to flying conditions. [1948] 4 p.

no. 5. A note on the weather at Entebbe and Kampala. [1948] 6 p.

Revised in 1967.

no. 6. Weather forecast areas. [1948] 4 p. illus., map.

no. 6. Aviation barometry. [1957] 4 p.

No. 6 repeats numbering.

no. 7. The weather of East Africa. [1957] 11 p. illus., map.

no. 8. Climatic seasons of East Africa. [1962] 3 p. illus., maps.

1727

_______ Patterns of diurnal rainfall in East Africa. [Nairobi, 197–?]

Earlier information is included in the Technical memorandum no. 8 (item 1686) issued by the East African Meteorological Dept. of the East Africa High Commission, and in the Technical memorandum no. 10 (item 1711) issued by the East African Meteorological Dept. of the East African Common Services Organization.

Cited in the agency's E.A.M.D. list of publications, 1972.

1728

_______ Rainfall at selected stations in East Africa. [Nairobi] weekly.

Supersedes a publication with the same title (item 1708) issued by the East African Meteorological Dept. of the East African Common Services Organization.

Lists 50 stations in Kenya, 24 stations in Uganda, and 30 stations in Tanzania.

Cited in the agency's E.A.M.D. of meteorological publications, 1972.

1729

_______ Summary of rainfall. 1967+ Nairobi. annual. QC925.6.A3

Supersedes a publication with the same title (item 1709) issued by the East African Meteorological Dept. of the East African Common Services Organization.

Issued in unnumbered parts: Kenya.—Tanzania.—Uganda.

L.C. and DAS have 1967+

1730

_______ Technical memorandum. no. 12+ Nairobi, 1968+ irregular. DLC

Supersedes and continues the numbering of a publication with the same title (item 1711) issued by the East African Metrological Dept. of the East African Common Services Organization.

L.C. has no. 16–23; DAS has no. 12–15.

The following numbers have been identified:

no. 12. Findlater, J. The month to month variation of mean winds at low level over eastern Africa. 1968. 27 p.

no. 13. Fremming, D. Notes on an easterly disturbance affecting East Africa, 5–7 Sept. 1967. 1970. 3, [10] p.

no. 14. Tomsett, J.E. Average monthly and annual rainfall maps of East Africa. 1969. 20 leaves.

no. 15. Lawes, E. F. Some confidence limits of expected rainfall. 1969. 44 p.

no. 16. Lumb, F. E. Probable maximum precipitation (PMP) in East Africa for durations up to 24 hours. 1971. 4 leaves, charts (3 fold.)

no. 17. Taylor, C. M., *and* E. F. Lawes. Rainfall intensity–duration–frequency data for stations in East Africa. 1971. 30 p. 1 fold. chart.

no. 18. Pant, P. S., *and* E. M. Rwandusya. Climates of East Africa. 1971. 13 p.

no. 19. Mörth, H. T. A study of the areal and temporal distributions of rainfall anomalies in East Africa. 1973. 4 p. maps.

Paper read at the Symposium on Tropical Meteorology, Honolulu, Hawaii, 1970.

no. 20. Kovacs, G., *and* M. T. Mörth. The use of rainfall data in estimating actual and maximum probable river discharge (Tana/Kenya). 1974. 8 p.

Paper read at the Symposium on Tropical Meteorology, Honolulu, Hawaii, 1970.

no. 21. Gichuiya, S. N. Easterly disturbances in the south-east monsoon. 1947. 7 p.

Paper read at the Symposium on Tropical Meteorology, Honolulu, Hawaii, 1970.

no. 22. Sansom, H. W., *and* S. Gichuiya. Hailstorms in the Kericho area. 1971. 6 p. charts (3 fold.)

Paper submitted to the American Meteorological Society Conference on Thunderstorm Phenomena, Chicago, April 1969.

no. 23. Lawes, E. F. An analysis of short duration rainfall intensities. 1974. 43 p.

1731

_______ Temperature data at stations in East Africa for the year 1970 (Kenya, Tanzania, and Uganda). [Nairobi? 1970 or 1971]

Cited in the agency's Annual report, 1970/71.

1732

_______ Uganda region. Statement of rainfall. [Nairobi?] weekly.

Source for May 30/June 5, 1973: Makerere Lib. Bull. no. 91.

1733

_______ Uganda region. Weather summary. [Nairobi?] monthly.

Source for Mar. and Apr. 1972: Makerere Lib. Bull. no. 91.

1734

_______ Upper air data for Dar es Salaam: summaries of radio-sonde observations and radar-wind measurements at standard pressure levels with tropopause data during 1965, 1966, and 1967; monthly means of radar wind measurements, from 1961–1967. [Nairobi] Meteorological Dept. of the East African Community, 1968. 16 p. QC879.59.T33E28

1735

_______ Upper air data for Entebbe, summaries

of radio-sonde observations and radar-wind measurements at standard pressure levels with tropopause data during the period 1966–69 (monthly means of radar wind measurments from 1961 to 1967). [Nairobi?] 1971. 10 p.
Cited in the agency's E.A.M.D. list of meteorological publications, 1972.

1736
_______ Weather messages, 2d ed. [Nairobi?] 1970.
Handbook of standard procedures for coding, decoding and plotting of weather messages.
Includes amendment service.
Cited in the agency's E.A.M.D. list of meteorological publications, 1972.

1737
_______ The weather of East Africa. 1967+ Nairobi. annual. DLC
Supersedes a publication with the same title (item 1714) issued by the East African Meteorological Dept. of the East African Common Services Orgnization.
Includes weather information for Kenya, Tanzania, and Uganda.
L.C. and DAS have 1967+

1738
Gt. Brit. *Army. East African Force.* East Africa: annual rainfall. 2d ed. [Nairobi?] 1941. *(Its* E.A.F. no. 505) map. DLC-G&M
Scale 1:6,000,000.
"Drawn and printed by E.A. Survey Group."
"Meteorological information compiled by B.E. Africa Meteorological Services from service records, Italian rainfall map dated 1939, and Nile basin, v. 1, 1931, published by Govt. Press, Cairo."

1739
Gt. Brit. *Meteorological Office.* Climatological observations at colonial and foreign stations. I. Tropical Africa, 1900–1901–1902, with summaries for previous years and frontispiece map. Tables prepared by E. G. Ravenstein. Published by the authority of the Meteorological Council. London, Printed for H.M. Stationery Off. by Darling, 1904. 54 p. col. map. *([Its* Official publication, no. 165]) QC991.A1G7
Includes data from meteorological stations in the East Africa Protectorate and Uganda. The bibliography (p. 49–54) lists individual stations with years of observations taken for the period 1893–1901.
See also item 1742.

1740
Kenya Colony and Protectorate. Memorandum on the formation of a joint meterological service for eastern Africa. [Nairobi? 1928]
DLC-Micro 23940 reel 10 folio 171
Collation of the original: 4 p.
Colonial Office Library East Africa pamphlet folio 171.
Includes the estimate of cost to Egypt, Kenya, Northern Rhodesia, Nyasaland, Tanganyika, Uganda, and Zanzibar.

1741
Maximum likely 24-hour rainfall at selected stations in Uganda. [Kampala, 1971] [71] p. DLC
Introductory matter signed P. A. Byarugaba, Director, E.A. Meteorological Dept. (Uganda Region).
Tables.

1742
Ravenstein, Ernest G. Report on meteorological observations in British East Africa for 1893. London, George Philip, 1894. 12 p DAS
"Published by authority of the Directors of the Imperial British East Africa Company."
Includes a summary of data for the period 1891–92.
Summarized in Appendix 17 of British East Africa; or IBEA; a history of the formation and work of the Imperial British East Africa Company (item 1100) compiled by P. L. McDermott.
Information for the period 1892–1901 is included in the Reports of the Committee Appointed to Inquire into the Climatological and Hydrographical Conditions of Tropical Africa, chaired by Ernest G. Ravenstein, and published in Reports, 62d–71st, issued by the British Association for the Advancement of Science.
See also item 1739.

1743
Specialist Meeting on Applied Meteorology in East Africa, *4th, Nairobi, 1968.* Proceedings of the fourth specialist meeting on applied meteorology in East Africa. Held at the University College, Nairobi, Kenya, 26–27 Nov. 1968. [Nairobi, East African Agriculture and Forestry Research Organization and the East African Meteorology Dept., 1968?] 1 v. (various pagings) DAS

Individual papers presented at the meeting were issued also separately.

DAS catalogs under: East African Community. Proceedings of the fourth specialist meeting on applied meteorology in East Africa.

1744
Tanganyika. *Geological Survey Dept.* Annual rainfall, East Africa 1:2,000,000, the probability of obtaining less than 30 inches of rain a year. Dodoma, 1955. map. DLC-G&M

Scale 1:2,000,000.

"From information supplied by J. Glover & P. Robinson, East African Agriculture & Forestry Research Organization, Muguga, Kenya."

1745
——— East Africa, 1:2,000,000, the probabilities of obtaining less than 20 inches of rain a year. Dodoma, 1955. map. DLC-G&M

Scale 1:2,000,000.

"From information supplied by J. Glover & P. Robinson, E.A.A.F.R.O., Muguga, Kenya."

1746
——— Mean annual rainfall map of East Africa, based on all available data at 1955. Dodoma, 1959. map on 2 sheets. DLC-G&M

Scale 1:2,000,000.

". . . from information supplied by the Geological Surveys of Kenya, Uganda, and Tanganyika."

"Rainfall information compiled by the Meteorological Department of the East Africa High Commission and drawn by the Survey of Kenya."

Zoology

1747
Hofmann, R. R. The ruminant stomach: stomach structure and feeding habits of East African game ruminants. [Nairobi] East African Literature Bureau [1973] 354 p. illus. (East African monographs in biology, v. 2) DLC

1748
Kayanja, F. I. B. Reproduction in antelopes; reproduction in the female impala (Aepyceros melampus Lichtenstein, 1812). [Nairobi] East African Literature Bureau [1972] 111 p. illus. (East African monographs in biology, v. 1) QL737.U53K39

Entomology

1749
Carcasson, Robert H. P. New and little-known African Lepidoptera. Nairobi, Coryndon Memorial Museum, 1961. 23 p. illus., 5 plates. Coryndon Memorial Museum, *Nairobi.* Occasional papers, no. 7) DT421.C622 no. 7

1750
——— Some new African Lepidoptera. Nairobi, Coryndon Memorial Museum, 1958. [9] p. illus., plate. (Coryndon Memorial Museum, *Nairobi.* Occasional papers, no. 5) DT421.C622 no. 5

1751
——— The Sphingidae (Hawk moths) of eastern Africa. [Kampala, University of East Africa] 1968. 2 v. illus., plates.

Source: Dar es Salaam Lib. Bull. no. 102.

1752
Coryndon Memorial Museum, *Nairobi.* Reports on new and little known insects from East Africa. Nairobi, 1956. 43 p. illus., 4 plates. *(Its* Occasional papers, no. 4) DT421.C622 no. 4

Contents: Some new species of East African Neuroptera and Trichoptera, by D. E. Kimmins.—Some new species of Lepidoptera from eastern Africa, by E. C. G. Pinhey.—Some dragonflies of East and Central Africa and a rarity from Mauritius, by E. C. G. Pinhey.—A new moth from East Africa, by A. L. H. Townsend.

1753
Eastop, Victor F. A study of the Aphididae (Homoptera) of East Africa. London, H. M. Stationery Off., 1958. 126 p. illus. ([Colonial research publications]) QL523.A6E2

At head of title: Colonial Office.

Includes information on aphids for Kenya, Tanganyika, Uganda, and Zanzibar.

1754
Fraser, F. C. Notes on African Gomphidae; and Three new species of Odonata, by E. C. G. Pinhey. Nairobi, Coryndon Memorial Museum, 1952. [16] p. illus. (Coryndon Memorial Museum, *Nairobi*. Occassional papers, no. 3) DT421.C622 no. 3

Contents: Notes on African Gomphidae with descriptions of four new species and a new genus (order Odonata), by F. C. Fraser.—Three new species of Odonata from eastern Africa, by E. C. G. Pinhey.

1755
Pinhey, Elliot C. G. A survey of the dragonflies (order Odonata) of eastern Africa. London, Printed by order of the Trustees of the British Museum, 1961. 214 p. QL513.O2P54

Includes information on the dragonflies of Kenya, Tanganyika, Uganda, and Zanzibar.

1756
Ruwenzori expedition, *1934–5*. London, Printed by order of the Trustees of the British Museum, 1939–53. 3 v. in 4. illus. QH195.R9R67

At head of title: British museum (Natural history).

"The main object of the expedition being to study the flora and insect fauna of Eastern Ruwenzori . . . In order to obtain material for comparative purposes brief expeditions were also arranged to three other mountainous districts—the Birunga range in south-west Uganda; Mount Elgon, on the Kenya-Uganda border; and the Aberdare range, north-east of Nairobi; also to two lowland forest areas, the Kalinzu forest, near Lake Edward, and the Budongo forest, near Masindi."

Contents: v. 1. no. 1. Introduction, with list of localities.—no. 2–3. Simuliidae, by E. G. Gibbins. Mosquitoes, by F. W. Edwards and E. G. Gibbins.—no. 4. Psychodidae, by A. L. Tonnoir.—no. 5. Ceratopogonidae, by J. W. S. Macfie.—no. 6. Bibionidae, by D. E. Hardy.—v. 2. no. 1–2. Stratiomyiidae, von E. Lindner. Rhagionidae, Tabanidae, Asilidae, Bombyliidae, by H. Oldroyd.—no. 3. Muscidae: Muscinae and Stomoxydinae, by F. van Emden.—no. 4. Muscidae: B. Coenosiinae, by F. van Emden.—no. 5. Empididae: A. Hybotinae, Ocydromiinae, Clinocerinae and Hemerodromiinae, by C. G. Jones.—no. 6. Muscidae: C. Scatophaginae, Anthomyiinae, Lispinae, Fanniinae and Phaoniinae, by F. I. van Emden.—no. 7. Chloropidae [by] C. W. Sabrosky.—no. 8. Brachypterous Sphaeroceridae, by O. W. Richards.—v. 3. no. 1. Trichoptera, by M. E. Mosely.—no. 2. Siphonaptera, by K. Jordan.—no. 3. Rhopalocera, by A. G. Gabriel.—no. 4. Heterocera: Lymantriidae, by C. L. Collenette.—no. 5. Ephemeroptera and Neuroptera, by D. E. Kimmins.—no. 6–10. Coleoptera. Carabidae, par R. Jeannel. Staphylinidae, von M. Bernhauer. Hydrophilidae, by J. Balfour-Browne. Lycidae, von R. Kleine.—no. 11–13. Coleoptera. Chrysomelidae, by G. E. Bryant. Cerambycidae, by E. A. J. Duffy. Carabidae, par P. Basilewsky.

1757
Ruwenzori expedition, *1952*. London, Trustees of the British Museum (Natural History), 1968 [i.e. 1958+] illus. (British Museum (Natural History). Publication 671) QH195.R9R68

"This will deal principally with the material collected during the 1952 expedition but it is proposed that if possible it will include papers on any un-worked material remaining from the previous expedition. Volume 1 will cover the Lepidoptera, volume 2 other orders of insects, and volume 3 the Arachnida and Myriapoda."

The following numbers are held by L.C.:

Vol. 1, no. 1. Evans, G. O., *and* D. S.

Fletcher. Introduction with list of localities. [n.d.] vii p.

Vol. 1, no. 2–3. Kiriakoff, S. G. Arctiidae (except Nolinae), Thyretidae and Notodontidae. 1958. 53 p.

Vol. 1, no. 4. Fletcher, David S. Arctiidae, Nolinae. 1958. 55–67 p.

Vol. 1, no. 5. Collenette, Cyril L. Lymantriidae. 1958. 69–75 p.

Vol. 1, no. 6. Fletcher, David S. Geometridae. 1958. 77–176 p.

Vol. 1, no. 7. _______ Noctuidae. 1961. 177–323 p.

Vol. 1, no. 8. _______ Cossidae, Metarbelidae, Psychidae, Limacodidae, Drepanidae, Uraniidae, Lasiocampidae, Eupterotidae, Bombycidae, Saturniidae, Sphingidae. 1968. 325–369 p. (British Museum (Natural History). Publication no. 669)

Ruwenzori expedition, 1952. Index to volume 1. 1968. 372–380 p.

Bound with vol. 1, no. 1.

Vol. 2, no. 11. Condé, B. Protura. 1961. 69–79 p.

Text in French.

Vol. 2, no. 12. Bradley, John D. Microlepidoptera. 81–148 p.

Herpetology

1758

Skinner, Hugh A. Snakes and us: an introduction to East African herpetology. [Nairobi] East African Literature Bureau [1973] xvi, 146 p. illus. QL666.O6S46

Ichthyology

1759

Greenwood, Peter H. The Cichlid fishes of Lake Victoria, East Africa: the biology and evolution of a species flock. London, British Museum (Natural History), 1974. 134 p., illus., 2 col. maps. (British Museum (Natural History). Bulletin: Zoology. Supplement 6) QL638.C55G74

Ornithology

1760

Archbold, Mary E. Ndege zetu. [London] Longmans, Published in association with the East African Literature Bureau [1959] 111, [12] p. illus. PPiD

Title translated: Our birds.

Text in Swahili.

"The Swahili in which this book is written has been approved by the East African Swahili Committee."

1761

Dyson, William G., *and* Michael D. Gwynne. A check list of birds of the Muguga area, Kenya, 1967. [Muguga? East African Agriculture and Forestry Research Organization, 1967] 20 leaves. DLC

Sociology

1762
Askwith, Tom G. Progress through self-help; principles and practices in community development. Nairobi, East African Literature Bureau, Eagle Press, 1960. 33 p. illus. DHU

1763
Chinn, Wilfred H. Tour of British East and Central African territories. [London?] Colonial Office, 1951. 8 p.

Mr. Chinn was Adviser on Social Welfare to the Secretary of State for the Colonies.

Source: Col. Off. Lib. Cat.

Population

The following entries (items 1764–89) **on** *population are arranged by geographic area. This section includes only censuses and studies issued by the East African Statistical Department during the period 1924–1961 for the East Africa High Commission and its predecessor, the Conference of Governors of British East African Territories. After 1961, censuses were taken on a national basis by statistical units in Kenya, Tanzania, and Uganda. The following entries, with the exception of the East African entries, together with earlier and later censuses, will appear in subject guides to official publications of Kenya, Tanzania, and Uganda.*

East Africa

1764
East Africa High Commission. *East African Statistical Dept.* East African census of population, 1948: preliminary estimates of the civil non-native population, Kenya, Tanganyika and Uganda. [Nairobi?] 1948. [24] p.

Source: Col. Off. Lib. Cat.

1765
Tanganyika. *Dept. of Lands and Surveys.* [African population distribution, East Africa, 1948] 8 maps. [Dodoma?] 1958. DLC-G&M

Scale not given.

Accompanying text, p. 5–12.

Contents: Map 1. African population distribution, East Africa, 1948, drawn by A. Serubiri. —Map 2. Main tribal groups of East Africa, drawn by J. K. Mbazira.—Map 5. Tribes of Kenya, subtribes of Kikuyu, Embu and Meru, drawn by J. K. Mbazira.—Map 6. Tribes of Kenya, drawn by A. Serubiri.—Map 7. Rural population of Zanzibar Island, 1931, drawn by A. Serubiri.—Map 8. Rural population of Pemba Island, 1931, drawn by A. Serubiri.

Kenya

1766
Conference of Governors of British East African Territories. *Statistical Section.* Report on the non-native population [of Kenya] from an analysis of information obtained from the issue of series V ration books by the Commodity Distribution Board during January 1947. [Nairobi] 1947. 21 p. NNUN

Issued by the agency under a variant name: Conference of East African Governors.

1767
East Africa High Commission. *East African Statistical Dept.* African population of Kenya Colony and Protectorate (geographical and tribal studies). [London? H.M. Stationery Off.] 1952. 4 p.

Source: Royal Comm. Soc. Cat.

1768
_______ African population of Kenya Colony and Protectorate; geographical and tribal studies. [Nairobi] 1952. 38 p. CSt-H

1769
_______ African population of Kenya Colony and Protectorate; geographical and tribal studies (source: East African population census, 1948). [Nairobi] 1950. 57 leaves.
HA1977.K4A5 1948a

African population by district and tribal affiliation.

1770
_______ _______ [Nairobi] 1953. 58 p.
HA1977.K4A5 1948b

Reprint of 1950 edition.

1771
_______ Kenya Colony and Protectorate: East Africa population census; racial distribution of civil population by district. Nairobi, 1950. 2 p.
NjP

1772
_______ Report on migration [for the] Colony and Protectorate of Kenya. [1st-4th] 1946–1949/53. [Nairobi] annual. JV8975.K4E33

Reports for 1949/53 issued in combined form.

Vol. for 1946 issued by the Conference of Governors of British East African Territories.

Earlier statistics and information is included in Statistics of migration (item 1774) issued by the Native Registration and Statistical Departments of Kenya Colony and Protectorate.

Later statistics and information is included in the Annual report issued by the Dept. of Immigration of Kenya Colony and Protectorate.

L.C. has 1946–1949/53.

1773
East Africa High Commission. *East African Statistical Dept. Kenya Unit.* Kenya; sample population census of Nairobi, 1957/58, an experiment in sampling methods. [Nairobi?] 1958. 17 p. HA1978.N3E3 1958

Includes comparative statistics for the 1948 and the 1958 censuses.

1774
Kenya Colony and Protectorate. *Native Registration and Statistical Departments.* [Statistics of migration] 1924/30–1939. [Nairobi?] annual (irregular) MiEM

Reports for 1924/30 issued in combined form.

Suspended 1933.

Title varies: 1924/30–1934, Statistics of migration through the port of Mombasa.

Vols. for 1924/30–1934 issued as Memoir no. 3, and 7 of the Dept. of Statistical Research of British East Africa (called Statistical Dept. of the Conference of Governors of British East African Territories by L.C. and other American libraries).

MiEM has 1924/30–1931; source for 1924/30–1939 (1935 wanting): Col. Off. Lib. Cat.

Tanganyika

1775
East Africa High Commission. *East African Statistical Dept.* African population of Tanganyika Territory; geographical and tribal studies (source: East African population census, 1948). [Nairobi] 1950. 88 p. HB3669.T3E33

African population by district and tribal affiliation.

1776
_______ _______ [Nairobi] 1950 [i.e.] 1953. 89 p. IEN

1777
_______ East African population census 1948 [Tanganyika]. Nairobi, 1949. 47 p.

Source: Dar es Salaam Lib. Bull. no. 88.

1778
_______ General African census, August 1957, tribal analysis. Tanganyika population census, 1957. [Nairobi] 1958. 2 v. HA2131.A5 1957

Contents: pt. 1. Territorial, provincial, district.—pt. 2. Territorial census areas.

1779
_______ Population density [of Africans, Asians, and Europeans in Tanganyika] [Dar es Salaam?] 1955. map. DLC-G&M

Scale 1:3,000,000.

"Compiled from the Statistical abstract, 1938/52, and from information supplied by the Land Tenure Adviser, August, 1955."

Text on verso.

Includes provincial and district statistics for Africans at 1948, and non-Africans at 1952.

1780
_______ Report on the census of the non-African population [of Tanganyika] taken on the night of 13th February 1952. [Dar es Salaam, Govt, Printer, 1954] 51 p. DLC

At head of title: Tanganyika.

1781
_______ Tanganyika African population census, 1957; analysis by sex and age for province, district, and territorial census areas. [Nairobi?] 1958. [21] leaves. HA1977.T3A53 1957

1782
_______ Tanganyika population census, 1957; analysis of total population, certain analyses by race and sex, geographical area, age, religion, and nationality. [Nairobi?] 1958. [10] leaves. HA1977.T3A53 1957a

1783
East Africa High Commission. *East African Statistical Dept. Tanganyika Office.* Report on the census of the non-African population taken on the night of 20th–21st February, 1957. Dar es Salaam, Printed by the Govt. Printer, 1958. 63 p. HA2132.E25

At head of title: Tanganyika.

Uganda

1784
East Africa High Commission. *East African Statistical Dept.* African population of Uganda Protectorate; geographical and tribal studies (source: East African population census, 1948). [Nairobi] 1950. 59 leaves. HA1977.U35A5 1948

African population by district and tribal affiliation.

1785
_______ _______ Rev. [Nairobi] 1953. 59 p. HA1977.U35A5 1953

At head of title: NPU (T) 1.

1786
_______ Uganda general African census 1959. [Nairobi] 1960. 2 v. in 6. HA1977.U35A56

Contents. v. 1. Age sex analysis. Population by sex & age-group for Protectorate, provinces, districts counties, divisions & parishes.—v. 2. Tribal analysis.—pt. 1. Tribal analysis for Protectorate, provinces, districts & counties.—pt. 2. Tribal analysis for Buganda Province, districts, counties & divisions.—pt. 3. Tribal analysis for Eastern Province, districts, counties & divisions.—pt. 4. Tribal analysis for Northern Province, districts, counties & divisions—pt. 5. Tribal analysis for Western Province, districts, counties & divisions.

1787
East Africa High Commission. *East African Statistical Dept. Uganda Unit.* Non-African population census, 1959. Nairobi, 1959. [5] leaves. CSt-H

CSt-H catalogs under: Uganda. Non-African population census, 1959.

1788
_______ Uganda census, 1959: African population. [Entebbe? Uganda] Statistics Branch, Ministry of Economic Affairs [1961] 103 p. illus., fold. col map. HB3666.U4A56

At head of title: Uganda Protectorate.

"The 1959 Census of Uganda was analysed and this report drafted by the Uganda Unit of the East African Statistical Department, before that Department was reorganised on 1st July, 1961. Owing to delay in publication this report is issued under the imprint of the Statistics Division, Ministry of Economic Affairs, Uganda."

A comparative analysis of census data by district, county, and town, with tribal affiliation, age, education, religion, infant mortality, and fertility rates. Also includes statistics for the African population by district, 1948.

1789
——— Uganda census, 1959; non-African population. [Entebbe, 1960] 110 p.
HB3666.U4A56 1960
At head of title: Uganda Protectorate.

Race Relations

South Asians

1790
Great Britain. East India (Indians in East Africa). Correspondence regarding the position of Indians in East Africa (Kenya and Uganda). London, H.M. Stationery Off., 1921. 10 p. ([Gt. Brit. Parliament. Papers by command] Cmd. 1311) J301.K6 1921 v. 26
Contents: Letter from the Government of India to His Majesty's Secretary of State for India, no. 33, dated 21st October 1920.—From His Majesty's Secretary of State for India to the Government of India, dated 24th December 1920.

Social Groups

Families and Marriage

1791
Banks, A. W. Mume mmoja, mke mmoja; kwa nini kuwe na desturi ya mwanamume kukoa mke mmoja tu? Nairobi, East African Literature Bureau [1964] 30 p. CSt
Title translated: One husband, one wife: why monogamy?
Text in Swahili.

1792
——— Yohanna na Mariamu; ndoa imefanyiwa mipango. Dar es Salaam, East African Literature Bureau, 1961. 31 p. CSt
Title translated: John and Mary; a marriage has been arranged.
Text in Swahili.

1793
Brown, Winifred. The partnership of Christian marriage. Nairobi, East African Literature Bureau, 1963. 81 p. DLC

1794
el-Busaidy, Hamed bin Saleh. Ndoa na talaka. Nairobi, East African Literature Bureau, 1968. 45 p. DLC-LL
Title translated: Marriage and divorce.
Text in Swahili.

1794a
Gt. Brit. *Colonial Office.* Correspondence relating to the welfare of women in tropical Africa, 1935–37. London, H.M. Stationery Off., 1938. 35 p. ([Gt. Brit. Parliament. Papers by command] Cmd. 5784) HQ1019.A3G7 1937
Includes information on forced marriages in Kenya, Tanganyika, and Uganda.

Sports

1795
Thornton, R. S. Maelezo ya mchezo wa mpira. Nairobi, Eagle Press, 1951. 39 p. illus. DHU
Title translated: A guide to the rules of football.
Text in Swahili.

1796
_______ _______ [Rev. ed.] Tabora [Tanzania] T.M.P. Book Dept., 1967. 31 p. illus. GV943.T53
"First published in 1951 by E.A.L.B."

Wildlife Conservation

1797
Bere, Rennie M. The wild mammals of Uganda and neighboring regions of East Africa. [London] Longmans [1962] 148 p. illus. (East African natural history series) QL731 B35
"This book is published in association with the East African Literature Bureau."

1798
British East and Central African Fauna Conference. Fauna of British East and Central Africa; proceedings. 1947?+ Nairobi, etc. biennial (irregular) SK351.B65
Vol. for 1959 called also 6th.
Vols. for 1947 and 1952 were issued as East Africa High Commission Paper no. 1, 4.
At head of title 1947?–1956? East Africa High Commission; 1959, Northern Rhodesia.
Each issue includes information on wildlife in Kenya, Tanganyika, Uganda, Nyasaland, Northern and Southern Rhodesia.
L.C. has 1947, 1952 ,1956, and 1959.

1799
Copley, Hugh. Wanyama wa porini wa Afrika ya mashariki. Nairobi, Eagle Press, 1953. 59 p. illus. DHU
Title translated: Game animals of East Africa.
Text in Swahili.

1800
East African Agriculture and Forestry Research Organization. Survey of current wildlife research projects in East Africa. no. 1?+ 1966?+ [Muguga, Kenya?] (*Its* AF/584/05)
Source for no. 4, 1969 (83 projects), and no. 5, 1970 (105 projects): Zumer.

1801
Gt. Brit. *Foreign Office*. Africa. Correspondence relating to the preservation of wild animals in Africa. London, Printed for H.M. Stationery Off. by Darling, 1906. xxiii, 391 p. 4 fold. maps. ([Gt. Brit. Parliament. Papers by command] Cd. 3189) SK571.A4 1906
Includes detailed correspondence on the protection of wild animals in German East Africa, the East Africa Protectorate, Uganda, and Zanzibar, for the period 1896–1906.

1802
_______ Africa. Further correspondence relating to the preservation of wild animals in Africa. London, Printed for H.M. Stationery Off. by Darling, 1909. 100 p. fold. map. ([Gt. Brit. Parliament. Papers by command] Cd. 4472) SK571.A4 1909
"In continuation of [Cd. 3189] November, 1906."
Includes correspondence on the protection of wild animals in the East Africa Protectorate and Uganda for 1906–8.

1803
_______ _______ London, Printed for H.M. Stationery Off. by Darling, 1910. 118 p. 2 maps (1 fold.) ([Gt. Brit. Parliament. Papers by command] Cd. 5136) SK571.A4 1910

"In continuation of [Cd. 4472] January, 1909."
Includes correspondence on the protection of wild life in the East Africa Protectorate and Uganda for 1908–10.

1804
——— ——— London, H.M. Stationery Off., printed by Darling, 1911. 33 p. 2 maps (1 fold.) ([Gt. Brit. Parliament. Papers by command] Cd. 5775) SK571.A4 1911
"In continuation of [Cd. 5136] June, 1910."
Includes correspondence on the protection of wild animals in the East Africa Protectorate and Uganda for 1910–11.

1805
——— ——— London, H.M. Stationery Off., printed by Darling, 1913. 55 p. ([Gt. Brit. Parliament. Papers by command] Cd. 6671) SK571.A4 1913
"In continuation of [Cd. 6671] July, 1911."
Includes correspondence on the protection of wild animals in the East Africa Protectorate and Uganda for 1911–12.

1806
Kenya. *Survey of Kenya.* East Africa: National parks and game reserves. [Nairobi] 1963. col. map 46 x 67 cm. G8401.G52 1963.K4
Not drawn to scale.
Oriented with north to the upper right.
Relief shown by shading and spot heights.
"Crown copyright."
Includes illus., location map, and index to parks and reserves.

1807
——— ——— Compiled, drawn and printed by Survey of Kenya, 1963. [Nairobi, 1970] col. map 46 x 67 cm. G8401.G52 1963.K41
Not drawn to scale.
Oriented with north to the upper right.
Relief shown by shading and spot heights.
"1,000/7/70."
"C[opyright by] Kenya Government."
Includes illus., location map, and index to parks and reserves.

1808
Payne, W. J. A. Report on a visit to the Ngorongoro Conservation Area. [Maguga?] 1962.
Source: E.A.A.F.R.O., 1962.

1809
Talbot, Lee M. A survey of past and present wildlife research in East Africa. [Muguga?] 1964.
Paper prepared for the Second Symposium of the East African Academy of Science, June, 1964.
Reprinted in East African wildlife journal, v. 3, Aug. 1965, p. 61–85.
Source: E.A.A.F.R.O., 1964.

1810
Uganda Railway. Game regulations. Nairobi, 1916. 4 p.
Source: Royal Empire Soc. Cat.

1811
Wildlife Conference for Eastern Africa, *1st, Nairobi, 1969.* First Wildlife Conference for Eastern Africa, March/April, 1969. [Nairobi, 1969?] 120 leaves. S964.A32W48 1969
"Held under the auspices of the Government of the Republic of Kenya and the Board of Trustees of Kenya National Parks."

1812
Worthington, Edgar B. The wild resources of East and Central Africa; a report following a visit to Kenya, Uganda, Tanganyika, Northern and Southern Rhodesia, and Nyasaland in February and March 1960. London, H.M. Stationery Off., 1961. 26 p. ([Gt. Brit. Colonial Office. Colonial no. 352]) JV33.G7A5 no. 352

Index

A

'Abd al-Rahman ibn Abi Bakr, 1171
Abdallah bin Hemedi 'lAjjemy, 1162-63
Abdul Karim bin Jamaliddini. *See* Jamaliddini, Abdul Karim bin
Abdulla, Muhammed Said, 1164
Abedi, K. Amri, 1165–66, 1204
Abeid, R. K., 1214
Aberdare mountains, Kenya
  insects, 1756
  land, 1624 (2)
Abridged annual trade statistics of Kenya, Uganda, and Tanganyika, 287, 301
Abridged annual trade statistics of Tanganyika, Uganda, and Kenya, 301, 310
Abridged annual trade statistics of Tanzania, Uganda, and Kenya, 310
Abu Sufyan, 1171
Abubakr, Abdulla M., 1167, 1283
Abubakr Siddik, Khalifa, 1167
Accounting, 923
  study and teaching, 867
Acts and subsidiary legislation, 1343, 1345
Adams, E. B., 1412 (8, pt. 19)
Adams, M., 1674 (v. 2, no. 2)
Adefris Bellehu, 123
Aden. Supreme Court, 1326
Adili na nduguze, 1215
Administration, civil service, etc., 1459–1553
Administration of criminal justice. *See* Criminal justice, administration of
Administrative law, 1331
Adu, A. L., 1544
Adult education, 807-8
Adult Literacy Organizing Centre, Nairobi, 890
Adviser on Literature for Africans, 804
Aerial photogrammetry, Tanganyika, 1000–1001
Aerial spraying against tsetse flies in East Africa, 134
Aerodromes. *See* Airports
Aeronautics, 354–55, 357, 366, 368
  accidents, 356, 364
  handbook, manuals, etc., 359–60

Aeronautics (cont.)
  law and legislation, 365
  See also Air lines; Meteorology in aeronautics
Aeronautics, commercial. *See* Air lines; *and* names of air lines, e.g., East African Airways Corporation
Aeronautics as a profession, 369
Afadhali mchawi, 1185
African Auxiliary Pioneer Corps. *See* Great Britain. Army. African Auxiliary Pioneer Corps
The African journal of tropical hydrobiology and fisheries, 156
African soldiers. *See* Askaris
African Tropical Service Committee, 1473
An African view of literature, 269
Africanization, 1538–39
Africanization Commission, 1538
Africans and the law, 1317
Agave, 47
  See also Sisal hemp
Agreement establishing an association between the European Economic Community and the United Republic of Tanzania, the Republic of Uganda, and the Republic of Kenya, 279–80, 308, 318
Agreement for the establishment of the East African Common Services Organization, 1576–80
Agricultural censuses
  Kenya, 98–105
  Tanganyika, 106–8
Agricultural chemistry, 223
Agricultural cooperatives, 114
Agricultural diseases and pests, 120–55
Agricultural education and extension, 57, 72–73, 91–97
Agricultural journal of British East Africa, 36
Agricultural libraries, 39–40, 65
Agricultural machinery
  Kenya, 55
  Tanganyika, 74–75
  Uganda, 74–75
Agricultural research, 30, 32, 36–38, 43, 46–47, 50–53, 58–60, 65, 67, 69, 83–84, 90, 765
  Kenya, 37
  Tanganyika, 37, 90

Agricultural research (cont.)
Uganda, 37
Agricultural Research Conference, Amani, Tanganyika (1931), 37
Agriculture, 11, 36–247
bibliography, 39–40, 794–95
dictionaries, Swahili, 1297
economic aspects, 45 (8)
information services, 46, 66, 68
Kenya, 11, 36, 48, 71, 76–79, 88, 98–105, 753, 767 (10)
statistics, 752
Tanganyika, 11, 70, 75–78, 88, 106–8, 203–8, 755, 767 (10), 1624 (4, 6)
Uganda, 11, 48, 56, 75–78, 88, 756, 767 (10)
Zanzibar, 88
See also Forage plants; *and* names of individual crops, e.g., Coffee; Cotton
Agriculture and Forestry Research Conference, Nairobi (1947), 38
Air lines, 352–53, 362–63, 365, 370, 372, 378–81
employees, 373
finance, 374–77
statistics, 764
time-tables, 363
See also names of air lines, e.g., East African Airways Corporation
Air lines, local service, 367
Air mail service, 415
Air travel, 352–81
Aircraft applications of insecticides in East Africa, 134
Airports, 358, 361, 371
Kenya, 358
Tanganyika, 358
Uganda, 358
Zanzibar, 358
Airways, 361
maps, 380
Aitken, W. G., 1614 (3)
al-Akida and Fort Jesus, Mombasa, 1182–83
Akilimali Snow-White, K. H. A., 1168–69a
Albert, lake. *See* Lake Albert
Alcohol, pelletizing of, 1121 (17)
Aldous, L. W., 767 (4)
Alexander, D. H., 830, 834
Ali, Seyyidha Huseni bin, 1174
Ali bin Hemedi, el Buhuri, 1302
Ali bin Said, Sultan of Zanzibar (1890–1893), 1059–60, 1105–6
Alidina, M. M. R., 1290
Allan, D. P., 767 (10)
Allen, J. W. T., 1162–63, 1171, 1173–75
Allen, Roland, 1171, 1173
Allen, Winifred E., 1225
Amakebe, 1412 (10 pt. 39)
Amani, Tanganyika. East African Agricultural Research Institute. *See* East African Agricultural Research Institute
Amani Library, 39–40
Amani memoirs, 59, 112, 226
Amani records, 1606
Amateur theatricals, 248–49, 262
American Meteorological Society Conference on Thunderstorm Phenomena, Chicago (April 1969), 1730 (22)
Amri, Daudi, 1335
Andersen, Earl J., 1605
Anderson, C., 1377a
Anderson, G. W., 767 (10)
Anderson, John, 212
Anglo-Belgian East African traffic convention, 281
See also Convention between Great Britain and Belgium with a view to facilitating Belgian traffic through the territories of East Africa
Anglo-German Agreement Relative to Africa and Heligoland (1890), 23, 1081, 1083
Anglo-German Boundary Commission, 998, 1014, 1090
Animal parasites. *See* Parasites
Annesley, G., 1601
Annual trade report of Kenya and Uganda, 328
Annual trade report of Kenya, Uganda, and Tanganyika, 288
Annual trade report of Tanganyika, Uganda, and Kenya, 302, 311
Annual trade report of Tanzania, Uganda, and Kenya, 311
Anthologies, 252, 275, 277
Anthracotheriidae, 1018 (4)
Anthropology. *See* Ethnology.
Anti-locust bulletin, 120
Anti-locust memoir, 121
Anti-Locust Research Centre, London. *See* London. Anti-Locust Research Centre.
Antrobus, R. L., 531
Aquatic biology, 156
Arabian nights. Swahili. Selections, 1269–70
Arboriculture. *See* Tree breeding.
Archaeology, 767 (2)

See also Bats, fossil; Erinaceidae, fossil
Archer, C. Kenneth, 41
Archbold, Mary E., 1760
Arid regions, 1707
Arithmetic, study and teaching in Swahili, 1276
Armed forces, 1474
administration, 1438, 1442, 1446–47, 1457–58
conditions of service, 1443–45
finances, 1430
regulations, 1452–55
regulations for South Asians, 1451
reserve forces rules, 1449
staff, 1450
See also Askaris; Bassingham (mine sweeper); European War (1914–1918); Great Britain. Army; King's African Rifles; Navy; World War (1939–1945)
Armitage, A. J., 75
Arnold, M. H., 47
Arnot, W. D., 191
Arrow, 783
The Arrow poisons, 258
The Arts, 248–78, 1421
See also Swahili literature
Ashall, C., 120 (25), 122
Asians in East Africa. *See* South Asians in East Africa
Askari, 1413–14
Askaris, 1413–14, 1418, 1425
Askwith, Tom G., 1762
Astronomy
juvenile literature, 883
See also Eclipses, lunar; Solar radiation
Athletic fields, 891
Atmosphere, upper
Dar es Salaam, Tanzania, 1734
Entebbe, Uganda, 1735
Nairobi, Kenya, 1734
See also Balloons—pilot; Balloons—sounding: Winds
Atmospheric pressure, 1674 (v. 2, no. 1)
Kabete, Kenya, 1635
Kenya, 1663
observers manuals, 1647 (15–16)
Seychelles, 1663
Tanganyika, 1632, 1663
Uganda, 1633, 1663
Zanzibar, 1634, 1663
Atmospheric turbulence, 1701 (v. 4, no. 3)
See also Storms
Atoms, juvenile literature, 878
Auckland, A. K., 47
Austaraa, Øystein, 171–72
Austen, Ernest E., 1412 (5, pt. 9)
Austin, J. R., Registrar of Co-operative Societies, Southern Cameroons, 109
Aviation. *See* Aeronautics

B

B. A. (Holdings), Ltd., 376
Bagshawe, A. F., 1361a
Baker, E. C., 1170
Bakhashweini, Muhammad bin Abdallah bin Mbarak, 1183
Balance of payments, 293, 763
Kenya, 753
Balance of trade, 325
Balfour, Sir Arthur, 319
Balfour-Browne, J., 1756 (v. 3, no. 6–10)
Ball, H., 1177
Balloons
pilot, 1674 (v. 1, no. 3)
sounding, 1674 (v. 1, no. 3)
Bamboo, 1125
Bandari zetu, 427
Banfield, Jane, 1585 (19)
Banks, A. W., 1791–92
Banks and banking, 894–916, 1117
central, 895
Kenya, 753, 894, 897, 901
statistics, 752, 761, 763–64, 896
Tanganyika, 755
Tanzania, 898, 902
Uganda, 756, 899, 903
Zanzibar, 900
See also Currency; Development banks
Bargash bin Said, Sultan of Zanzibar (1870–1888), 1033, 1038, 1078, 1094, 1099–1100, 1103
Bargman, D. J., 1674 (v. 3, no. 4)
Baring, Sir Evelyn, 14, 17
Barker, Ronald D., 1226
Barlow, F., 145
Barrett, Raymond, 1621
Basilewsky, P., 1756 (v. 3, no. 11–13)
Bassingham (mine sweeper), 1434
Bateman, H. R., 1412 (10, pt. 30)
Bates, Margaret, 1187
Bats, fossil, 1018 (13)
Bax, S. Napier, 1399–1400
Beans, 47
Bees, 85

Belfield, Henry C., 779, 781
Belshaw, D. G. R., 45, 93
Bere, Rennie M., 1797
Bernhauer, M., 1756 (v. 3, no. 6–10)
Beverton, R. J. H., 157
Bible stories, 890
Bibliographies, general, 27–28
Bilharziasis. *See* Schistosomiasis
Binaisa, G. L., 413
Binns, H. R., 236
Biology, 798, 802
  acquatic. *See* Acquatic biology
  See also Reproduction
Birds, 1760
  Muguga, Kenya, 1761
Blacker, J. G. C., 767 (3)
Blackwater fever
  East Africa Protectorate, 1368–70
  Uganda, 1368–70
Blumer, J. A. C., 238–49
Boer immigration, 773
Bonney, R. S. P., 628
Botany, 767 (9), 1602–10
  dictionaries, 1605, 1607–8
  Kenya, 1605, 1610
  See also Cinchona; Tree breeding; Trees
Boundaries, 999, 1002–3, 1013–14, 1079, 1084, 1086, 1088
  East Africa Protectorate, 1084, 1087–88, 1091
    maps, 1011
  Maps, 1011, 1090
  Uganda, 1091
  See also Spheres of influence
Bowring, C. C., 919
Bradley, John D., 1757 (v. 2, no. 12)
Brazell, J. H., 1674 (v. 2, no. 12; v. 3, no. 6)
Brenan, R. A. F., 1121 (17)
Brickmaking, 1121 (5–6, 14, 16)
Brinkman, S. E., 1721 (v. 4, no. 5)
British Broadcasting Corporation, 1214
British Commonwealth Forestry Conference
  6th, Canada (1952), 183
  7th, Australia and New Zealand (1957), 184
  8th, East Africa (1962), 150, 185, 187, 189, 192, 195
  9th, New Delhi, India (1968), 188
British East Africa; economic and commercial conditions in British East Africa (Kenya, Uganda, Tanganyika and Zanzibar), 717
British East Africa Company. *See* Imperial British East Africa Company
British East Africa Corporation, 772
British East African Association, 1094
  See also Imperial British East Africa Company
British East African Meteorological Service, 984, 1632–57, 1674 (v. 1), 1682, 1684, 1690
  about, 1643, 1645, 1650–52, 1674 (v. 1, no. 1), 1740
  See also East Africa High Commission. East African Meteorological Dept.; East African Common Services Organization. East African Meteorological Dept.; East African Community. East African Meteorological Dept.
British East and Central African Fauna Conference, 1798
British Expedition against the Turkana, 1474
British Information Services. *See* Great Britain. British Information Services
British Museum (Natural History), 1018, 1755–57, 1759
British Overseas Airways Corporation, 381
The British territories in East and Central Africa, 1945–1950, 5
Brooks, Charles E. P., 1622
Brown, Alice, 636
Brown, E. S., 42
Brown, L. H., 767 (10)
Brown, Winifred, 1793
Browne, J. Balfour. *See* Balfour-Browne, J.
Brownwood, David O., 1303
Bruce, David, 1412 (1, pt. 2; 4, pt. 8; 10, pt. 30–31, 34–36, 39; 11; 12, pt. 4)
Bruce, T. D. H., 1338
Brussels Conference relative to the African slave trade, 1059
Bryant, G. E., 1756, (v. 3, no. 11–13)
Bryce, V. K., 1227
Buchanan, John Williams, 1097
Budget estimates
  East Africa High Commission, 942, 944–45, 950
  East Africa Protectorate, 924–31, 933–34
    See also Budget estimates—Kenya
  East African Common Services Organization, 955
  East African Community, 957
  Kenya, 935
    See also Budget estimates—East Africa Protectorate
  Tanganyika, 934–35, 949
  Uganda, 924–31, 933–35

Budget estimates (cont.)
Uganda Railway, 924–25, 929
Zanzibar, 930–31, 933–35
Bodongo forest, Uganda
concessions, 773–77
insects, 175
el-Buhriy, Hemedi bin Abdallah, 1171–75
el Buhuri, Ali bin Hemedi. *See* Ali bin Hamedi, el Buhuri
Bull, A. F., 1228–29
Bulletin of entomological research, 134
Bulletins of statistical research, 725
Bunning, A. J. F., 347
Burnett, G. F., 120 (26)
Burtt, Bernard D., 1602–3
Buruji, 1428
el Busaidy, Hamed bin Saleh, 1794
Bush, R. E., 1215
Bushe, Henry Grattan, 1319–20
Business directories, 1116
Butler, Percy M., 1018 (11, 13, 18)
Butterfield, Harry R., 1304
Buxton, D. R., 120 (5)
Buxton, Patrick A., 1401
Byamugisha, Joseph B., 1305
Byarugaba, P. A., 1741
Byrne, Joseph A., 1564–65

C

Caddis-flies, 1752, 1756 (v. 3, no. 1)
Cahill, W. F., 1262
Calder, Angus, 275, 278
California Texas Oil Corp., 604
Callander, J. F., 846
Cameron, Sir Donald C., 1145, 1563
Cameron, M. A., 531
Cameroons, Southern. *See* Southern Cameroons
Campbell, A. J., 1121 (15–16)
Cancer, 1350
Capital
Kenya, 705, 707
Uganda, 756
Carcasson, Robert H. P., 1749–51
Cargo handling, 300
See also Shipping
Carman, John A., 1395
Carpenter, G. D., Hale, 1412, (12, pt. 12; 14, pt. 1; 17)
Carr-Saunders, Sir Alexander M., 834
Carry it home, 264
Carson, John B., 428
Carson, M. A., 635
Cartography, 1004–7
Castellani, Aldo, 1412 (1, pt. 1; 3, pt. 5)
Castor-oil, 1121 (3)
Cattle, 94–95, 213–16
Kenya, 213–15
Tanganyika, 213–15
Uganda, 213–15
Zanzibar, 213–15
Cattle diseases, 239, 246–47
Census
Kenya, 1764, 1769–71
maps, 1765 (1)
Nairobi, Kenya, 1773
Tananyika, 1764, 1777–78, 1780–83
Uganda, 1764, 1784–89
See also Population
Censuses, agricultural. *See* Agricultural censuses
Central Legislative Assembly. *See* East African Common Services Organization. Central Legislative Assembly
Chama cha Kiswahili, 1150
Chapman, R. F., 120 (33)
Chemistry
agricultural. *See* Agricultural chemistry
examinations, questions, etc., 1611
text-books (elementary), 863
Children
care and hygiene, 811–14
games, 784
management, 855, 861
nutrition, 1393
recreation. *See* Children—games; Creative activities and seat work
Chilvers, R. M., 164 (13)
Chilton, N., 809–10
Chinn, Winfred H., 1763
Christian Council of Tanganyika, 1240
Literacy Sub-committee, 1230
Christianity, 1243, 1254
See also Bible stories; Missions
Christy, Cuthbert, 1412 (2, pt. 3; 3, pt. 6)
Chum, Haji, 1221–22
Chuo cha Uchunguzi wa Lugha ya Kiswahili, 1149, 1154, 1156, 1172, 1184, 1191–92, 1199, 1213, 1218, 1290–91
See also East African Swahili Committee; Inter-territorial Language (Swahili) Committee to the East African Dependencies
Churchill, W. S., 429
Cichlidae, 160 (1), 1759

Cichlidae (cont.)
See also Tilapia
Cinchona, bibliography, 217
Civics, East African text-books (elementary), 889
Civil service, 1469, 1473, 1489, 1538–39
British East African Meteorological Service, 1656
East Africa High Commission, 1491–93, 1509, 1514–17, 1532, 1936–37
salaries, 1491–93, 1514, 1516–17, 1532
staff list, 1510
East Africa Protectorate, 1467, 1472, 1475, 1478–81
leave regulations, 1476
salaries, 1482
East African Common Services Organization, 1541–42, 1544–45
salaries, 1541
staff list, 1540
East African Community, 1549, 1551, 1553
salaries, 1552
staff list, 1547
East African Posts and Telecommunications Administration, 1514, 1518, 1536–37, 1541
salaries, 1514, 1518, 1541
East African Railways and Harbours Administration, 471, 496–97, 499, 509, 517–17a, 524, 569, 588, 593, 606–7, 625–27, 1137, 1491, 1494–96, 1514, 1519–20, 1533–34
salaries, 503, 517–17a, 572, 589–90, 1491, 1494–96, 1514, 1519–20, 1533–34
staff list, 498
Kenya, 1483, 1485, 1487, 1491–92, 1497, 1499–1500, 1514, 1521–22, 1532, 1541–43, 1545
leave regulations, 1498
salaries, 1491–92, 1497, 1499–1500, 1514, 1522, 1532, 1541–42
Tanganyika, 1491–92, 1501–3, 1514, 1523–24, 1532, 1545
salaries, 1482, 1491–92, 1501–3, 1514, 1523–24, 1532
Uganda, 1467, 1472, 1475, 1478-81, 1483, 1485, 1487, 1491–92, 1504–5, 1514, 1525–26, 1532, 1535, 1545
leave regulations, 1476
salaries, 1482, 1491–92, 1504–5, 1514, 1525–26, 1532, 1535
Zanzibar, 1491–92, 1506–8, 1514, 1527–32
salaries, 1482, 1491–92, 1506–8, 1514, 1527–32

Civil service (cont.)
See also Civil service pensions; Harbors—employees; Postal service—employees; Railroads—employees; Teachers
Civil service pensions
East Africa High Commission, 1532
East Africa Protectorate, 1477
East African Railways and Harbours Administration, 432, 517–17a
Kenya, 1486, 1532
Tanganyika, 1532
Uganda, 1477, 1532
Zanzibar, 1532
Clackson, J. R., 1646
Clarendon, Earl of, 1027
Clark, Sir Wilfred E. L. G., 1018 (1, 3, 5, 9)
Clarke, Edith R., 784
Clarke, Ron, 807
Clifford, Peter, 1350
Climatology, 24, 767 (7), 1658, 1674 (v. 2, no. 6; v. 3, no. 2), 1726 (1, 8), 1730 (18)
statistics, 1665, 1695
See also Arid regions; Crops and climate; Meteorology; Weather
Climbing plants, 1602–3
Clouds, 1642, 1668, 1674 (v. 2, no. 4)
Kenya, 1711 (11)
Clough, R. H., 92
Clove, 315
Coal, 770
Coates, E., 966
Cockburn, Helen, 91
Coffee, 41, 43, 47, 109–13, 722
diseases and pests, 112 (2)
Kenya, 71, 109, 1119 (11, 13)
Tanganyika, 109
Uganda, 109
Coffee research, 1118–20, 1126
Coffee trade, 109, 313, 323
Cohen, Andrew B., 14, 21
Cole, A. F. C., 1121 (17)
Cole, Sonia M., 1019
Coleoptera, 1756 (v. 3, no. 6–13)
Colet Birch, W., 1121 (6, 16)
Collective labor agreements, railroads, 559
Collenette, Cyril L., 1756 (v. 3, no. 4), 1757 (v. 1, no. 1, 4, 6–8)
Collister, Peter, 1023
Colonial concessions, 768–82
Colonial Empire [*picture sets*], 4
Colonial geology and mineral resources, 1618
Supplement series, bull. suppl., 1612–13

Colonial Medical Research Committee. *See* Great Britain. Colonial Medical Research Committee
Colonial Official Library East Africa pamphlet. See Index to Major Series
Colonial paper, 383
Colonial partition, 998, 1077–1106
Colonial research publications. See Great Britain. Colonial Office. *Colonial research publications*
Combe, A. D., 1620
Command papers, British. *See* Index to Major Series
Commerce and trade, 2, 10, 24, 36, 45 (8), 279–346, 717, 722, 767 (4)
Kenya, 24, 36, 287–88, 291, 301–3, 310–12, 320–21, 325, 328, 667–70, 753
statistics, 287–88, 291, 301–6, 310–12, 328, 752, 761, 763
Tanganyika, 287–88, 291, 301–3, 310–11, 317, 325, 755
Tanzania, 310–12
Uganda, 24, 287–88, 291, 301–3, 310–12, 320–21, 325, 328, 671–72, 756, 947
See also Balance of payments; Customs union; Tariff
Commercial aeronautics. *See* Air lines; *and* names of air lines, e.g., East African Airways Corporation
Commercial law, 1303, 1312
Commercial treaties
Belgium–Great Britain, 281, 322
European Economic Community–Kenya, 279–80, 308, 318
European Economic Community–Tanzania, 279–80, 308, 318
European Economic Community–Uganda, 279–80, 308, 318
France–Great Britain, 323
Great Britain–Belgium, 281, 322
Great Britain–France, 323
Kenya–European Economic Community, 279–80, 308, 318
Tanzania–European Economic Community, 279–80, 308, 318
Uganda–European Economic Community, 279–80, 308, 318
See also Treaties, etc.
Commission on Closer Union of Dependencies in Eastern and Central Africa. *See* Great Britain. Commission on Closer Union of Dependencies in Eastern and Central Africa
Commission on the Civil Services of Kenya, Tanganyika, Uganda and Zanzibar. *See* Great Britain. Commission on the Civil Services of Kenya, Tanganyika, Uganda and Zanzibar
Commission on the Civil Services of the East African Territories and the East Africa High Commission. *See* Great Britain. Commission on the Civil Services of the Eastern African Territories and the East Africa High Commission
Commission on the Desert Locust Control Organization. *See* East Africa High Commission. Commission on the Desert Locust Control Organization
Commission on the Most Suitable Structure for the Management, Direction and Financing of Research on an East African Basis. *See* East Africa High Commission. Commission on the Most Suitable Structure for the Management, Direction and Financing of Research on an East African Basis
Commission on the Public Services of the East African Territories and the East African High Commission. *See* Great Britain. Commission on the Public Services of the East African Territories and the East Africa High Commission
Commission To Inquire Into the Question of Native Labour in British East Africa, 779
Commissioner for the East African Pavilion, 41
Committee for the Standardization of the Swahili Language, 1145
Committee of Inquiry Appointed To Inquire Into the Causes of the Failure of K.A.G. and Other Vaccines Prepared at Kabete, 240
Committee on the Amalgamation of East African Railways, 779
Committee on the East African Slave Trade. *See* Great Britain. Committee on the East African Slave Trade
Commonwealth Agricultural Bureaux, 215
Commonwealth Bureau of Animal Breeding and Genetics, 215
Commonwealth Bureau of Plant Breeding and Genetics, 47
Commonwealth Economic Committee, 699
Commonwealth Shipping Committee, 430
Communications and transportation, 10, 24, 347–635

Communications and transportation (cont.)
Kenya, 11, 347, 349, 557–58, 753
maps, 986–91, 1015
military, 579–80
maps, 1425, 1435
statistics, 752, 761, 763
Tanganyika, 11, 347, 349, 468, 602–3, 755
Uganda, 11, 347, 349, 557–58, 699 (9), 756
See also Transportation
The Community; East African Community monthly magazine, 1593
Community development, 1762
See also Public welfare
Community health services, 1396
See also Public health
Competition, industrial, 1109
Concessions, colonial. *See* Colonial concessions
Condé, B., 1757 (v. 2, no. 11)
Conference of Directors of Education of Kenya, Tanganyika, Uganda and Zanzibar, held at Makerere (January 18th-19th, 1937), 785
Conference of Directors of Social and Economic Research Institutes in Africa, Nairobi (1971), 696
Conference of East African Agricultural and Soil Chemists, 2d, Zanzibar (1934), 223
Conference of East African Directors of Public Works
10th, Entebbe (1957), 697
12th, Nairobi (1959), 698
Conference of East African Soil Chemists, Amani, Tanganyika (1932), 230
Conference of Governors of British East African Territories, 38, 43, 58, 224, 237–38, 980, 1351, 1402, 1490, 1554
about, 10, 155
Committee Appointed To Consider a Revision of the Customs Tariff of Kenya, Uganda and Tanganyika Territory, 282
Committee Appointed To Prepare a Scheme for Post-War Local Air Serivces in East Africa, 352
Statistical Dept., 725–26, 749–50, 894, 960, 1336
about, 750
Memoir, 725–26, 894, 960, 1336
See also East Africa High Commission. East African Statistical Dept.; East African Common Services Organization. East African Statistical Dept.
Statistical Section, 1127, 1766
Conference of Law Officers of East African Dependencies, Nairobi (1933), 1338
Conference of Law Officers of the East African Dependencies, Nairobi (1926), 1337
Conference on African Land Tenure in East and Central Africa, Arusha, Tanganyika (1956), 209
Conference on Co-ordination of Agricultural Research (Coffee, Entomological and Mycological) and Plant Protection, 43
Conference on Co-ordination of Agricultural Research in the East African Territories, 43
Conference on Co-ordination of General Medical Research in East African Territories, 1351
Conference on Co-ordination of Tsetse and Trypanosomiasis (Animal and Human) Research in East Africa, 1402
Conference on Co-ordination of Tsetse and Trypanosomiasis Research and Control in East Africa, 1402
Conference on Co-ordination of Veterinary Research, 238
Conference on Crop Responses to Fertilisers and Manures, Muguga (1953), 44
Conference on Institutes of Education, Mombasa, Kenya (1964), 847
Conference on International Support for Research in East Africa, Nairobi (1964), 29
Conference on Muslim Education, Dar es Salaam (1958), 786
Conference on Public Policy
2d, University College, Nairobi (1963), 45, 283, 348, 741, 895, 1128, 1306, 1544, 1585
3d, Dar es Salaam (1964), 721
Conference on Rinderpest, 2d, Nairobi (1939), 239
Conference on Severe Local Storms, 6th, Chicago (1969). *See* American Meteorological Society Conference on Thunderstorm Phenomena, Chicago (April 1969)
Conference on Teacher Education for East Africa, 5th, Makerere University College (1967), 848
Conference on the University of East Africa, Nairobi (1967), 823–25
about, 823–26
Conference on Tsetse and Trypanosomiasis (Animal and Human) Research, 1402
Coniferae, 176 (29)
Construction industry
Kenya, statistics, 753

Construction industry (cont.)
statistics, 752
Tanganyika, 753
Uganda, employees, 1130
Convention between Great Britain and Belgium with a view to facilitating Belgian traffic through the territories of East Africa, 322
See also Anglo-Belgian East African traffic convention
Coode, Matthews, Fitzmaurice and Wilson (firm), 778
Cook, David J., 250
Cookery, study and teaching, 858–59
Cooney, Sean, 46
Cooperative societies, 114
Tanganyika, 755
Cooperatives, agricultural. *See* Agricultural cooperatives
Copley, Hugh, 1799
Cory, Hans, 1176
Coryndon, Sir Robert T., 1440–41
Coryndon Memorial Museum, Nairobi. *Occasional papers,* 1020–21, 1749–50, 1752, 1754
Cost and standard of living
Kenya, 753
Africans, 733
Europeans, 727–20, 732
South Asians, 728
statistics, 752
Tanganyika, 729, 735–36, 755
Uganda, 730–31, 738–39, 756, 947
Zanzibar, 740
See also Prices
Cotton, 41, 47, 86, 115–19, 319, 732, 773–74
Jubaland, East Africa Protectorate, 116–17
Tanganyika, 350
Uganda, 115–19
Cotton gins and ginning, 1136
Council for Agricultural Education for East Africa, 92
Court of Appeal for East Africa, 1307–9
about, 1307
See also Great Britain, Court of Appeal for Eastern Africa
Court rules, 1308, 1324
Tanganyika, 1325
Courts, 1307, 1323, 1328, 1332, 1334
East Africa Protectorate, 1474
industrial. *See* Labor courts
Tanganyika, 1322
See also Court of Appeal for East Africa; Great Britain. Court of Appeal for Eastern Africa;

Courts (cont).
East African Industrial Court
Cowie, Mervyn, 637
Cratchley, C. R., 1617
Creative activities and seat work, 872–73
Creech-Jones, A., 917
Crime and criminals, Kenya, 1336
Criminal justice, administration of, 1319–21
Criminal law, 1339
Crop improvement in East Africa, 47
Crop report, Kenya Colony, 71
Crop report, Tanganyika Territory, 70
Crops, 217–22
See also names of crops, e.g., Coffee; Cotton; Sugar
Crops and climate, 767 (8)
Kenya, 1674 (v. 2, no. 8)
Crown Agents' Office. *See* Great Britain. Crown Agents' Office
Currency, 917–19
See also Banks and banking
Curriculum Development and Research Centre, 1249, 1262
A Curse from God, 270
Customs and excise tariff, 329
Customs and excise tariff handbook, 295–98, 307
Customs union, 282–83, 324–27, 333, 336, 350, 1556
See also Balance of trade; East African Common Market
Cyclones, 1638, 1644, 1674 (v. 3, no. 1), 1701 (v. 4, no. 4)
Cypress, 1761 (11)

D

DDT (insecticide), 134 (2), 136, 139–40
Dagg, M., 195, 234, 1658
Dalziel, J. M., 1604
Damages, 1333
Dandy, A. J., 1611
Dar es Salaam, Tanzania
cost and standard of living, 729, 735
guide-books, 638, 647–48
University
Faculty of Medicine, 1377
Institute of Education. *Progress report,* 852–53
University College, 826
Faculty of Law, 1316
Institute of Education, 851
Library. *Library bulletin and accessions list,* 1177

Dar es Salaam, Tanzania (cont.)
weather, 1726 (3), 1734
Dare to die, 257
Daubney, R., 237
David, E. B., 836
Davies, David A., 1659, 1674 (v. 2, no. 6–10; v. 3, no. 3), 1679
Davis, P. R., 1018 (16)
Day after tomorrow, 272
Debates, legislative, 1460, 1464, 1466
Debenham, Frank, 1623
Debts, public. *See* Public debts
Defoe, Daniel, 1231–33
Defoliation, 171–72
De La Warr, Herbrand Edward Dundonald Brassey Sackville, 9th Earl, 831, 1394
Delegated legislation, 1343, 1345–46
Demography. *See* Population
Desai, N. C., 863
Desart, Hamilton John Agmondesham, 5th Earl of, 1407
Description and travel, 617, 622–23, 636–95
Kenya, 617, 623, 639, 643–46, 656–58, 666–70, 678–79, 694
gazetteers, 997
guide-books, 680–90
See also Mombasa region, Kenya—guide-books; Nairobi, Kenya—guide-books
maps, 640–42
Tanganyika, 639, 643–46, 666, 675, 691
gazetteers, 997
maps, 630
See also Dar es Salaam—guide-books
Uganda, 639, 643–46, 664, 666, 671–72, 679, 694
gazetteers, 997
guide-books, 680–86, 688–90
maps, 630
See also Kampala, Uganda
Zanzibar, 639, 643–46, 666, 674
See also Tourist trade
Desert locust, 120 (4, 9, 25, 31), 121 (1), 122–29, 131
Desert Locust Control Organization for Eastern Africa, 123–27
about, 123–24, 128–29
Desert locust situation report, 125
De Smith, S. A., 1306 (15)
Development banks, 747–48, 764, 904–5, 913–14, 1596
Dhana, 251
Diabetes, 1361
Dickson, Capt. A. G., 1432–33
Dictation (office practice), 871
Digest decisions of the court, 1309
Digest of the annual reports of the medical research organizations, 1354
Diptera, 1412 (5, pt. 9)
See also Mosquitoes
Directories, business. *See* Business directories
Diseases, 1366–67, 1379, 1385 (16), 1396
See also names of diseases, e.g., Blackwater fever; Cancer; Diabetes; Filaria and filariasis; Hookworm disease; Leprosy; Malaria; Plague; Schistosomiasis; Trypanosomiasis; Tuberculosis
Diseases and pests, agricultural. *See* Agricultural diseases and pests
Diva, David E., 95, 1234–39, 1285
Diwani ya Shabaan, 1216–17
Dixey, Frank, 1612–13
Doggett, H., 47
Domestic relations (Islamic law), 1794–95
Dow, Hugh, 11
Dower, Kenneth C. Gandar. *See* Gandar Dower, Kenneth C.
Dowson, W. J., 219
Dragonflies, 1752–1755
See also Odonata
Drama. *See* East African literature (English)—drama; Swahili drama
Draper, C. C., 1386
Drugs, 1361a
Duckham, Alec N., 48
Duffy, E. A. J., 1756 (v. 3, no. 11–13)
Duke, H. Lyndhurst, 1412 (12, pt. 13–14; 13, pt. 1, 3–4, 8, 10; 14, pt. 2–3)
Dunlop, R. Y., 815
Durand, Philip P., 1310
Dynamos, portable, 1674 (v. 1, no. 3)
Dyson, William G., 173–74, 176 (16–17, 26–29), 1761

E

EAAFRO newsletter, 49
E.A.C.S.O. gazette, 1313
EACSO news, 1589
EAFFRO occasional papers, 164
EALB students' book writing scheme, 254, 259, 265, 270, 274–75
EAR & H magazine, 606

E.A. Survey Group. *See* Great Britain. Army. East African Survey Group
Eagle language study series, 1286
Earthquakes, 1686 (1)
See also Seismometry
East Africa (general), 1–26, 335
East Africa: gateway to safari, 637
East Africa Central Legislative Assembly. *See* East Africa High Commission. East Africa Central Legislative Assembly.
East Africa Command. *See* Great Britain. Army. East Africa Command
East Africa command fortnightly review, 1415
East Africa Commission (1925). *See* Great Britain. East Africa Commission
East Africa High Commission
about, 1567–75, 1585
Administrator, 12, 354, 1570
Audit Dept., 435
Auditor-General, 943
budget, 943
Circular, 1515
Commission on the Desert Locust Control Organization, 129
Commission on the Most Suitable Structure for the Management, Direction and Financing of Research on an East African Basis, 31
Commissioner for Transport, 355, 436–40, 459
Committee of Inquiry Appointed Consequent Upon a Resolution Dated 24th April, 1952, of the East Africa Central Legislative Assembly. *See* East Africa High Commission. Mombasa Committee of Equiry
Committee of Inquiry Appointed To Inquire Into the Causes of the Failure of K.A.G., and Other Vaccines Prepared at Kabete, 240
Committee of Inquiry Into the Working of the Port of Mombasa. *See* East Africa High Commission. Mombasa Committee of Enquiry
Court of Inquiry Into the Accident to Dakota VP-KKH (on 18th May, 1955), 356
Dept. of Economic Co-ordination, 742, 1107
Desert Locust Control, 131
Desert Locust Survey, 131, 149
Despatch, 1571
Directorate of Civil Aviation, East Africa, 354–55, 357–60
about, 345–55, 357

East Africa High Commission (cont.)
See also East African Common Services Organization. Directorate of Civil Aviation
East Africa Central Legislative Assembly, 128, 442, 627, 1459–61, 1537, 1571
about, 1571
debates, 1460
membership lists, 1459
rules and practice, 1461–63
Select Committee Appointed To Review Standing Rules and Orders, 1462
about, 1463
Select Committee on the East African Income Tax (Management) Bill, 961
Sessional paper, 128, 442, 627, 1533, 1537
Standing Committee on Finance, 1517
See also East African Common Services Organization. Central Legislative Assembly; East African Community. East African Legislative Assembly
East African Agriculture and Fisheries Research Council, 52
East African Agriculture and Forestry Research Organization, 53–54, 175, 1624
See also East African Agriculture and Forestry Research Organization
East African Bureau of Research in Medicine and Hygiene, 1353–54
about, 1360
East African Council for Medical Research, 1355
See also East African Medical Research Council
East African Customs and Excise Dept., 287–91
about, 324, 327
See also East African Common Services Organization. East African Customs and Excise; East African Community. East African Customs and Excise Dept.
East African Fisheries Research Organization, 158, 166
East African Hides and Leather Bureau, 1108
East African Hides, Tanning and Allied Industries Bureau, 1108
about, 700, 1108
East African Income Tax Dept., 962–64
See also East African Income Tax Dept.
East African Industrial Council, 1109–10
about, 700, 742

East Africa High Commission (cont.)
East African Inland Fisheries Research Organization, 158
East African Institute for Medical Research. *See* East African Institute for Medical Research
East African Interterritorial Leprosy Specialist, 1354, 1380
See also East African Leprosy Research Centre
East African Literature Bureau, 787–90, 1310
Advisory Council, 791
See also East African Literature Bureau
East African Malaria Unit, 1354, 1384
East African Medical Survey, 1354
about, 1352, 1358
East African Medical Survey and Research Institute, 1358
East African Meteorological Dept., 1659–91, 1746
See also British East African Meteorological Service; East African Common Services Organization. East African Meteorological Dept.; East African Community. East African Meteorological Dept.
East African Office, London, 2, 292, 335, 792
See also East African Common Services Organization. East African Office, London
East African Production and Supply Council, 700
East African Revenue Advisory Board, 965
East African Statistical Dept., 98, 100, 106, 293, 701–4, 727–33, 739, 751–53, 920, 1129–34, 1764, 1767–72, 1775–81, 1784–86
about, 751
East African Unit, 294
about, 751
Kenya Unit, 55, 99, 101–5, 705–7, 733–34, 1111, 1773
about, 751
Tanganyika Office, 107–8, 708, 735–36, 754–55, 949, 951, 1112–14, 1783
about 751
Uganda Unit, 56, 709–11, 737–39, 756, 947–48, 1135–36, 1787–89
about, 751
See also Conference of Governors of British East African Territories. Statistical Dept.; East African Common Services Organization. East African Statistical Dept., East African Community. East African Statistical Dept.

East Africa High Commission (cont.)
East African Trypanosomiasis Research Organization. *See* East African Trypanosomiasis Research Organization
East African Veterinary Research Organization, 241
See also East African Veterinary Research Organization
Filariasis Research Unit, 1354, 1356, 1358
finance, 946, 952
Inter-territorial Committee on Ground Services for Civil Aviation in East Africa, 361
Laws, statutes, etc., 944
Maize and Produce Control, 1115
Meteorological Analysis Centre, 1675
Mombassa Committee of Enquiry, 441
about, 441–44
Official gazette, 1311
officials and employees. *See* Civil service—East Africa High Commission
Paper, 35, 1601, 1615–16, 1626, 1798
Posts and Telegraphs Dept., 382
Advisory Board, 383
See also East African Posts and Telecommunications Administration; East African Posts and Telecommunications Corporation
Royal East African Navy, 1416
Staff list, 1510
White paper, 1494, 1518
East Africa information digest, 2
East Africa law reports, 1330
East Africa laws of income tax, 978
East Africa Protectorate (general), 22, 24–26
Currency Committee, *Report,* 919
Governor
1909–1912 (Girouard), 1474
1912–1919 (Belfield), 779, 781
Land Office, 998
See also Kenya (general)
East Africa Royal Commission. *See* Great Brittain. East Africa Royal Commission
East Africa tackles the land problem, 57, 73
East Africa to-day, 3
East Africa Tourist Travel Association, 338–41, 636, 638–65, 675, 677–78, 691–93
about, 338–42
Formation Committee, 342
East Africa University. *See* University of East Africa

East African Academy of Science Symposium, 2d (1964), 1809
East African Advisory Council on Agriculture, Animal Industry, and Forestry, 52
East African Agricultural and Fisheries Research Council. *See* East Africa High Commission. East African Agricultural and Fisheries Research Council
East African agricultural and forestry journal, 58
East African Agricultural Diploma Manpower Survey, 1964/65, 92
East African agricultural journal of Kenya, Tanganyika and Zanzibar, 58
East African Agricultural Manpower Survey (1963), 93
East African Agricultural Research Institute, 59–60, 217
East African Agricultural Research Station, 61–64, 83, 226–29, 1606–8, 1610
  about, 10, 53–54, 59–60, 90
East African Agriculture and Forestry Research Organization, 44, 49, 52, 65–68, 80, 82, 84, 113, 133, 173, 176–77, 183, 188, 192, 233–34, 1605, 1630–31, 1743–45, 1761, 1800
  about, 34, 42, 49–50, 52, 54, 69, 183, 765
  Forestry Division, 178–80
    about, 185
  Plant Quarantine Station, 130
  Soil Survey Division, 225
  Sorghum and Millet Division, 231
  See also East Africa High Commission. East African Agriculture and Forestry Research Organization
East African Airways Corporation, 362–63, 373, 380–81, 666
  about, 352, 362, 365, 370, 374–77, 381, 764
East African and Uganda diary, 26
East African Army Education Corps, 1427
East African Bureau of Research in Medicine and Hygiene. *See* East Africa High Commission, East African Bureau of Research in Medicine and Health
East African Cargo Handling Services Ltd., 300
East African Commission of Inquiry on Income Tax, 966–69
East African Common Market, 45 (8), 283 (7), 952
East African Common Services Organization
  about, 1575–83, 1585, 1587–90

East African Common Services Organization (cont.)
  Accident Investigation Branch, 364
  Africanization Commission. *See* Africanization Commission
  Audit Dept., 447
  Auditor-General, 954
  budget, 954
  Central Legislative Assembly, 492, 517a, 1464, 1539
    allowances, 1465
    debates, 1464
    privileges and immunities, 1465
    Sessional paper, 492, 517a, 1539
    Select Committee Appointed To Consider The Privileges and Allowances in Respect of Members, 1465
    See also East Africa High Commission. East Africa Central Legislative Assembly; East African Community. East African Legislative Assembly
  Commission on the Constitutional Position of East African Airways, 365
  Desert Locust Survey, 131
  Directorate of Civil Aviation, 366
    about, 366
    See also East Africa High Commission. Directorate of Civil Aviation, East Africa.
  East African Customs and Excise, 301–3
    See also East Africa High Commission. East African Customs and Excise Dept.; East African Community. East African Customs and Excise Dept.
  East African Meteorological Dept., 1692–1714
    about, 1692
    See also British East African Meteorological Service; East Africa High Commission. East African Meteorological Dept.; East African Community. East African Meteorological Dept.
  East African Metric Commission, 712
  East African Office, London, 304
    See also East African High Commission. East African Office, London.
  East African Statistical Dept., 305–6, 351, 713, 740, 757–62, 896–900, 921
    See also Conference of Governors of British East African Territories. Statistical Dept.; East African High Commission. East African Statistical Dept.; East Africa High Commission. East African Statistical Dept.; East African Community. East

East African Common Services Organization (cont.)
African Statistical Dept.
Information Division, 1587–89
Laws, statutes, etc., 955
Local Civil Services Salaries Commission, 1541
about, 1541–43
O. & M. Division, 1546
Official gazette, 1313
Staff list, 1540
East African Community
about, 1591–1600
Auditor General, 958
budget, 958
Catalogue of publications, 1970/71, 28
Common Market and Economic Affairs Secretariat, 714, 743
Directorate of Civil Aviation, 368–69
about, 368
See also East Africa High Commission. Directorate of Civil Aviation, East Africa
East African Customs and Excise Dept., 310–12a
See also East African High Commission. East African Customs and Excise Dept.; East African Common Services Organization. East African Customs and Excise
East African Legislative Assembly, 1466
debates, 1466
Select Committee on the Reorganization of the East African Railways Board of Directors, 448
Select Committee to Examine the Difficulties Faced by the East African Airways Corporation, 370
Select Committee To Inquire Into the Harbours Operations, 449
See also East Africa High Commission. East Africa Central Legislative Assembly; East African Common Services Organization. Central Legislative Assembly
East African Meteorological Dept., 1715–37, 1741, 1743
about, 1715
see also British East African Meteorological Service; East Africa High Commission. East African Meteorological Dept., East African Common Services Organization. East African Meteorological Dept.
East African Statistical Dept., 371, 763–64, 901–3, 922

East African Community (cont.)
See also Conference of Governors of British East African Terroritories. Statistical Dept., East Africa High Commission. East African Statistical Dept.; East African Common Services Organization. East African Statistical Dept.
finance, 959
Information Division, 1593, 1559, 1557, 1599–1600
Laws, statutes, etc., 970, 1346–47
Management Institute, 1553
Salaries Review Commission, 1552
Treaties, etc., International Bank for Reconstruction and Development (May 1970), 450
See also Treaty for East African co-operation
The East African Community Act, 1967, 1592
East African cooperation, 1554–1600
East African Council for Medical Research, 1360
See also East Africa High Commission. East African Council for Medical Research
East African Currency Board, 917–18
East African customs and excise tariffs, 309
The East African customs regulations, 1954, 284
East African Development Bank, 904–5, 913, 1117
about, 747–48, 764, 904, 913–14, 1117, 1596
East African Directorate of Civil Aviation. *See* East Africa High Commission. Directorate of Civil Aviation, East Africa; East African Common Services Organization. Directorate of Civil Aviation; East African Community. Directorate of Civil Aviation
East African Economic and Fiscal Commission. *See* Great Britain. East African Economic and Fiscal Commission
East African economic and statistical bulletin, 752
East African Estates, ltd., 780
East African Examinations Council, 827–29
about, 827, 1596
The East African excise regulations, 1954, 285
East African External Telecommunications Company, 384
East African federation, 1555–66, 1570–71, 1584–87, 1589–90
See also Customs union; East African Negotiating Team; Economic integration; *Treaty for East African co-operation*
East African Force. *See* Great Britain. Army. East African Force

East African Freshwater Fisheries Research Organization, 52, 156, 163–64, 170
  about, 52, 69, 164 (2), 765
East African Governors' Conference. *See* Conference of Governors of British East African Territories
East African grasses, 1609
East African groundnut scheme, 199–208
East African Guaranteed Loan Committee. *See* Great Britain. Colonial Office. East African Guaranteed Loan Committee
East African Harbours Corporation, 427, 451–57, 524, 606
  about, 449, 560–61, 764
  budget, 451a–52
  See also East African Railways and Harbours Administration
East African Herbicide Conference, 4th, Arusha (1970), 132
East African Herbicide Conference on Soil-Applied Herbicides in East Africa, 3d, Nairobi (1964), 133
East African Hides and Allied Industries Bureau. *See* East Africa High Commission. East African Hides, Tanning and Allied Industries Bureau
East African Income Tax Dept., 971–73
  See also East Africa High Commission. East African Income Tax Dept.
East African Industrial Court, 1315
  about, 1315, 1596
East African Industrial Research Board, 1118, 1121 (10–16), 1126
East African Industrial Research Organization, 1118–21
East African Industries Technical Advisory Committee, 1121 (1–9), 1122
East African Institute for Medical Research, 1355, 1364
  about, 1360
East African Institute of Malaria and Vector-Borne Diseases, 1355, 1384–87
  about, 1360, 1384
East African Institute of Social Research. *See* Kampala, Uganda. Makerere University College. East African Institute of Social Research
East African Interterritorial Leprologist. *See* East Africa High Commission. East African Interterritorial Leprosy Specialist
East African journal of literature and society, 256
East African journal of medical research, 1359
East African Legislative Assembly, 1466
East African Leprosy Research Centre, 1355, 1381–82
  about, 1360, 1381
  See also East Africa High Commission. East African Interterritorial Leprosy Specialist
East African Literature Bureau, 181, 248–78, 343, 793–95, 1240–41, 1625
  about, 787, 791, 793, 804
  See also East Africa High Commission. East African Literature Bureau
East African literature (English), 248–49, 251–62, 264–78
  bibliography, 787, 789–90, 794–95
  drama, 248–49, 251, 255, 262, 273
  fiction, 251–53, 257–61, 265–68, 270, 272, 274
  history and criticism, 256, 269, 277–78
  poetry, 251–52, 264, 271, 276
East African Literature Service, 46, 66, 68
East African Malaria Unit. *See* East Africa High Commission. East African Malaria Unit
East African Marine Fisheries Research Organization, 52, 156, 165
  about, 52, 69, 765
East African medical journal, 1350
East African Medical Research Council, 1350, 1359–62, 1374, 1377–77a, 1396
  See also East Africa High Commission. East African Council for Medical Research
East African Medical Research Advisory Committee, 1360
East African medical service list, 1392
East African Medical Survey. *See* East Africa High Commission. East African Medical Survey
East African Medical Survey and Research Institute. *See* East Africa High Commission. East African Medical Survey and Research Institute
East African Military Labour Service. *See* Great Britain. East African Military Labour Service
East African monographs in biology, 1747–48
East African natural history series, 1797
East African Natural Resources Research Council, 69, 765
East African Negotiating Team, 1596

East African Office, London. *See* East Africa High Commission. East African Office, London
East African pavilion, 41, 316
East African Posts and Telecommunications Administration, 385–403, 414, 424–26, 906–9, 1518
  about, 383, 425–26
  budget, 385, 387–88, 391
  See also East Africa High Commission. Posts and Telegraphs Dept.
East African Posts and Telecommunications Corporation, 404–6a, 414 423–24, 910–12
  about, 404, 417–418, 764
  budget, 404–5
  Regional Director, Kenya, 407–8
  Regional Director, Tanzania, 409–10
  Regional Director, Uganda, 411–12
  Salaries Review Commission, 413
  Stamp Bureau, 414
East African Railways and Harbours Administration, 443–45, 458–509, 517a, 559, 604, 606–7, 627, 630, 715, 982, 1494, 1533–34
  about, 12, 440, 446, 609
  budget, 435, 447, 463
  General Manager, 12, 440
  Kenya and Uganda Section, 510–11, 1495
  Memorandum, 472
  officials and employees. *See* Civil service—East African Railways and Harbours Administration
  Railway Administration
    Dar es Salaam District, 512
    Mwanza District, 513
    Tabora District, 514
    Tanga District, 515
  Special notice, 496, 1520, 1534
  Tanganyika Section, 516, 1496
  Tanzania Road Service, 631–32
  See also East African Harbours Corporation; East African Railways Corporation
The East African Railways and Harbours Administration Act, 1950, 431
East African Railways and Harbours Commission, 517
East African Railways Corporation, 518–21, 606–7
  about, 448, 562–63, 764
  Salaries and Terms of Service Review Commission, 523
  See also East African Railways and Harbours Administration
East African Rangeland Committee, 80
An East African Rehabilitation Centre, Nairobi, Kenya Colony, 1372
East African Revenue Advisory Board. *See* East Africa High Commission. East African Revenue Advisory Board
East African Rice Mission. *See* Great Britain. East African Rice Mission
East African Scientific and Industrial Research Organization, 34
The East African scientific literature service, 46
East African Specialist Committee Meeting for Forest Research, 10th, Nairobi (1971), 174, 178, 180
East African Specialist Committee on Sugar Cane Research, 233
East African Specialist Entomology and Insecticides Committee Meeting, 15th, Nairobi (1971), 179
East African Standing Committee on the Metric System, 714
East African statistical digest, 304
East African Substitutes Committee, 1123
East African Swahili Committee, 1139–44, 1151–53, 1157–58, 1160–61, 1173, 1175, 1219
  about, 1143, 1158
  Bulletin, 1158
  Journal, 1158
    Supplement, 1175, 1181, 1201–2, 1217
  See also Chuo cha Uchunguzi wa Lugha ya Kiswahili; Inter-territorial Language (Swahili) Committee to the East African Dependencies
East African tax cases, 974
East African Timber Advisory Board, 197
  about, 700, 742
  Meeting, 14th, Moshi (1957), 182
East African Transport Policy Board, 349
East African Trypanosomiasis Research Organization, 52, 1355, 1360, 1403–5, 1603
  about, 52, 69, 765, 1360
  See also Entebbe, Uganda. Human Trypanosomiasis Research Institute
East African Tsetse and Trypanosomiasis Research Organization, 34, 1403
East African Tsetse Research Organization, 1602
East African Veterinary Research Organization, 52, 242
  about, 34, 53, 69, 236, 241–42, 765
  See also East Africa High Commission. East

African Veterinary Research Organization
East African Virus Research Institute, 1345–55, 1363
about, 1360
East African War Supplies Board. Timber Control, 193
East Africans at war, 1417
East-Central Regional Committee for Geology, Dar es Salaam (1956), 1614
East Coast fever, 247
East Indians in East Africa. *See* South Asians in East Africa
Eastell, Roger, 604
Eastern Africa law review, 1316
Eastern African Conference on Nutrition and Child Feeding, Nairobi (1969), 1393
Eastern African Dependencies Trade and Information Office, 70–71, 110–11, 115, 218, 313–17, 667–72, 679, 1649
about, 314
Eastop, Victor F., 1753
Ebrahim, G. J., 811–14
Eclipses, lunar, 1677
Economic and statistical review, 761, 763
Economic assistance, 721, 745
American, 744
British, 718–19, 745
Economic conditions, 715, 723, 952, 1109–10
Kenya, 702, 716–17, 953
See also Capital—Kenya
Tanganyika, 708, 716–17
Uganda, 703–4, 711, 716–17
See also Capital—Uganda
Zanzibar, 713, 716–17
See also Cost and standard of living; Prices
Economic conditions in Africa, 717
Economic development, 283 (10)
See also East African Development Bank
Economic indicators
Kenya, 718–19, 724
Tanzania, 718–19
Uganda, 718–19, 724
Economic integration, 45 (8), 283, 741–43, 1557
See also Development banks.
Economic policy, 700, 720, 1109
Economic research, 32, 724
Economics, 11, 33, 283 (10), 304, 696–782, 905
bibliography, 701
Kenya, 11, 699 (11)
statistics, 752, 761, 763
Tanganyika, 11, 602–3

Economics (cont.)
text-books, 869–70
Uganda, 11, 699 (9)
See also Finance; Public finance
Economist Intelligence Unit, ltd., London, 715
Education, 5, 10–11, 33, 783–893, 1427
curricula, biology, 798, 802
European, tuition, 792
higher, 823–40, 842, 844–45, 1596
study and teaching, 828–29
Tanzania, 826
Uganda, 831, 838
See also Nursing schools
Kenya, 11, 753, 796
Muslim, 786, 800
secondary, 806
South Asians, 803
Tanganyika, 11, 755, 803
Uganda, 11, 756, 796, 803, 1159
Zanzibar, 803
See also Agricultural education and extension; Health education; Illiteracy Education Conference, Dar es Salaam, Tanganyika Territory (1925), 1145
Education of adults. *See* Adult Education
Educational publishing, 787, 791, 793, 804
Educational research, 801
Edwards, F. W., 1756 (v. 1, no. 2–3)
Eels, 168 (6)
Egerton Agricultural College, Njoro, Kenya, 92
Elder, H. Y., 164 (1)
Electric engineers, 1426
Elgon, Mount. *See* Mount Elgon
Ellis, A. J., 805
Ellis, Peggy E., 1920 (25)
Elphinstone, Sir Howard Graham, Bart., 1286, 1317
Elton, F., 1036
Embu (ethnic group), 1765 (5)
Emigration and immigration
Kenya, 733, 1772, 1774
See also Boer immigration; Population—Kenya
The Empire Exhibition, Glasgow (1938), 316
The Empire Exhibition, South Africa (1936), 41
Employees, government. *See* Civil service
Employees' magazines, handbooks, etc., 373, 424, 524, 606–7
Energy sources. *See* Power resources
Engineering, dictionaries, Swahili, 1297
England, G., 1674 (v. 3, no. 4)
English language

English language (cont.)
dictionaries, Swahili, 1147, 1156, 1297
study and teaching
African students, 783, 886
bibliography, 787–90, 794–95
English literature. *See* East African literature (English)
Entebbe, Uganda
Human Trypanosomiasis Research Institute, 1406
about, 1363, 1406, 1409
See also East African Trypanosomiasis Research Organization
weather, 1726 (5), 1735
Entomology, 1749–57
See also Insects, injurious and beneficial
Entwistle, A. R., 864
The Epic of the Battle of Uhud, 1222
Erinaceidae, fossil, 1018 (11)
Erosion, 88, 224
Errington, Kathleen, 1318
Estimates, budget. *See* Budget estimates
Ethnology, 24
bibliography, 787–90, 794–95
See also names of ethnic groups, e.g., Kikuyu (ethnic group); Kilindi (ethnic group)
Eucalyptus, 176 (9, 13)
Europe, history, juvenile literature, 888
European Economic Community, 279–80, 308, 318
European War (1914–1918), campaign in German East Africa, 1420, 1436
See also King's African Rifles
Evans, A., 891
Evans, G. O., 1757 (v. 1, no. 1)
Evaporation (meteorology), 1672, 1674 (v. 2, no. 11), 1686 (5)
Evaporative power
Kenya, 1630
Tanzania, 1631
Examinations, 827
Exploring East Africa, 644–46
Export-Import Bank of the United States, 377

F

Faces at crossroads; a 'Currents' anthology, 275
Fairey Air Surveys Limited, 1000–1001
Farming. *See* Agriculture
Farsi, S. S., 1178
Farsy, Muhammad Saleh, 1179
Fasili johari ya mashairi, 1201
Father and son (motion picture) 72
Fauna of British East and Central Africa; proceedings, 1798
Fernie, L. M., 47
Fertilizers and manures, 44
Fibers, 772
See also Cotton; Sisal hemp
Fiction. *See* East African literature—fiction; Swahili fiction
Filaria and filariasis, 1354–56, 1358
See also Trypanosomiasis
Filariasis Research Unit. *See* East Africa High Commission. Filariasis Research Unit
Filmstrips, 1, 57
See also Moving-pictures
Finance, 5, 11, 304, 894–980
Kenya, 11, 753, 980
Tanganyika, 11, 980
Uganda, 11, 699 (9), 980
Finance, public. *See* Public finance
Findlater, J., 1730 (12)
Fish, Geoffrey R., 168 (10)
Fisheries, 34, 52, 69, 156–70
bibliography, 164 (4)
dictionaries, Swahili, 1297
Kenya, 164 (1, 10), 168 (6, 21)
Lake Victoria, 156–63, 164 (5, 8, 11, 13), 166–67, 168 (10)
Tanzania, 164 (6, 9), 168 (2)
Uganda, 164 (5, 8, 11), 758
Fisheries research, 155–58, 163–65, 168, 765
See also East African Freshwater Fisheries Research Organization; East African Marine Fisheries Research Organization
Fishes, 168 (8)
Lake Victoria, 1759
See also Cichlidae; Eels; Tilapia
Fitzgerald, D. F. Vesey-. *See* Vesey-Fitzgerald, D. F.
Flemming, Sir Gilbert, 532
Fletcher, David S., 1757 (v. 1, no. 1, 4, 6–8)
Floating islands in Lake Victoria, 87
Flöhn, Herman, 1707
Flora. *See* Botany
Flora of tropical East Africa, 1604
Food crop varieties available for distribution, 61
Football. *See* Soccer
Forage plants, 1609
See also Beans; Maize; Peas; Sorghum; Soybeans

Forced labor, Uganda, 779
Forest insects, 171–72, 176 (7, 9, 13), 179, 182, 186–87, 189–90, 193–94, 198
catalogs and collections, 186
Tanganyika, 190
Forest nurseries, 176 (1–2), 15)
See also Tree breeding
Forest soils, 176 (3)
Forestry, 58, 65, 171–98
bibliography, 175
Kenya, 753, 767 (11), 774–77, 779–80, 1674 (v. 2, no. 7)
water use, 1624 (1–3, 7–8)
libraries, 39–40
maps, 766–67
statistics, 752
Tanganyika, 190, 755, 767 (11), 782
Tanzania, 171–72
Uganda, 171, 756, 767 (11), 770–71, 773–82
See also names of forests, e.g., Budongo forest, Uganda; Mabira forest, Uganda; Mwele forest, East Africa Protectorate
Forestry research, 38, 50–52, 58, 67, 69, 173–80, 183–85, 188, 765
See also East African Agriculture and Forestry Research Organization
Forestry technical note, 176
Forests and climate, 184, 192
Forland, K. S., 863
Formal Conference of Hydrologists of the British East and Central African Territories on Hydrology and Water Resources, 1626
Forsdyke, A. G., 1674 (v. 2, no. 3–4)
Fort Portal, Uganda, cost and standard of living, 738
Fossil mammals of Africa, 1018
Foster, Captain, 24
The fourth trial (2 plays), 255
Frank, M. K., 1364
Frank, W., 122, 1246
Frankl, Paul, 1365
Fraser, A. D., 1414 (12, pt. 6–10; 14, pt. 3)
Fraser, F. C., 1754
Frazer, A. C., 28
Fremming, D., 1730 (13)
French, M. H., 1121 (7)
Frere, Sir Bartle, 1032
Frost, Winifred E., 168 (6)
Fuggles-Couchman, N. R., 75
Fumerton, B., 1605
Fumo Liyongo, 1192, 1219
Fungicides, 153
Furnaces, 1121 (11)

G

Gabriel, A. G., 1756 (v. 3, no. 3)
Gacii, P., 878–83
Game, 1799, 1810
See also Wildlife conservation
Gammexane, 140
Gandar Dower, Kenneth C., 1418–19
Ganzel, Eddie, 1180
Gardner, J. C. M., 176 (7), 182
Garrod, D. J., 159, 160 (2), 166
Garstin, Sir William E., 1627
Gateways of Eastern Africa, 524
Gazettes, 1311, 1313–14
Gee, J. M., 164 (5, 8, 11)
Gentry, Alan W., 1018 (20, 22)
Geography and maps, 981–1017
text-books (elementary), 889
Geological research, 1612, 1615–16
Geological surveys
Kenya, 1612, 1618
Migori gold belt, 1617
Tanganyika, 1612, 1618
Tanzania, Gieta goldfield, 1617
Uganda, 1612, 1618
Geology, 767 (5), 1612–20
maps, 766–67, 1619
Tanganyika, 1614 (2–5)
See also Magnetism, terrestrial
Geophysics, 1617
The German conquest of the Swahili coast, 1891 A.D., 1175
German Foundation for Developing Countries, 913
Germans in East Africa, 1175
Ghai, Dharam, 283 (7), 696
Ghai, Yash, 1306 (18)
Gibb (Sir Alexander) and Partners, 602–3
Gibb, Roger, 525–26
Gibbins, E. G., 1756 (v. 1, no. 2–3)
Gibson, I. A. S., 176 (23–25)
Gichuiya, S. N., 1730 (21–22)
Giffen, Edmund, 830, 834
Gilbert, M. P., 164 (5, 8)
Gilmour, Samuel C., 1248
Girouard, Edward P. C., 1474
Glass manufacture, 1109, 1121 (1)

Glover, J., 1121 (10), 1744–45
Glover, Phillip E., 1602, 1605
Goats, diseases, 245
Goldstucker, L., 1121 (10)
Gomphidae, 1754
Goodship, H. E., 595
Gould, G. Clifford, 1396
Government. See Politics and government
Gowers, William F., 1159, 1563–65
Gracey, T., 533
Graham, Michael, 167
Grain storage, 222
  Kenya, 222
  Tanganyika, 222
  Uganda, 222
Grant, Julius, 1124
Grants (university). *See* Scholarships
Grasses, 1609
Gray, A. C. H., 112 (6 pt. 11, 14; 8 pt. 16, 21; 9, pt. 24)
Gray, Robert F., 1387
Great Britain
  Admiralty, 1366–67, 1420
  Air Ministry, 372, 415, 1003, 1622
    See also Great Britain. Ministry of Aviation
  Army
    African Auxiliary Pioneer Corps, 1432–33
    Corps of Royal Engineers, 600
    East Africa Command, 983, 1372, 1413, 1418–19, 1421–23, 1426–27, 1437
      about, 1413, 1415, 1421–22
      Directorate of Education and Welfare, 1415
    East African Force, 984–95, 997, 1003, 1388, 1423–27, 1738
      Education Corps, 1287
      O.C.T.U., 1428
      Ordnance Corps, 1429
    East African Survey Group, 984, 993–94, 996, 1388, 1424–25, 1435, 1738
      medals, badges, decorations, etc., 1420
      Middle East Forces, 997
      registers of dead, 1431
      See also World War (1939-1945)
  Board of Education, 796
  Board of Inland Revenue, 975
  Board of Trade, 319
  British Information Services, 1, 72, 199, 1550, 1573
  Central Office of Information, 3–4, 6, 8, 57, 73
    Reference Division, 1550

Great Britain (cont.)
Centre for Overseas Pest Research, 120–21
Civil Service Commission, 1288
Colonial Advisory Council of Agriculture and Animal Health, 88–89, 246
Colonial Advisory Council of Agriculture, Animal Health and Forestry, *Publication*, 74–75, 213–14, 232
Colonial Medical Research Committee, 1353
Colonial Office
  1904–25: 116–19, 212, 281, 528, 530, 770–81, 919, 924–36; 1076, 1340, 1368–70, 1469, 1472–79, 1481–83
  1926–47: 797, 941, 999, 1138, 1321, 1371, 1401, 1484–85, 1487, 1555, 1557, 1559, 1563–65, 1567–68, 1794a
  1948–74: 1, 5–9, 13–15, 72, 76–78, 168, 200, 211, 222, 235, 244, 602, 716, 1137, 14030, 1511, 1576, 1623, 1753, 1763
  Advisory Committee on Education in the Colonies, 798–99, 802, 838
  African no. . .; African no. . . ., confidential; African (East) no. . . ., confidential. See Index to Major Series
  African Studies Branch, 1512
  Colonial Forest Resources Development Dept., 196
  Colonial Insecticide Research Unit, 134–45, 152
  Colonial no. See Index to Major Series
  Colonial Pesticides Research Institute, 152, 1386
  Colonial research publications, 222, 235, 634, 1137, 1623, 1753
  Committee on Private Enterprise in British Tropical Africa, 350
  East African Guaranteed Loan Committee, 938
  Library. *East Africa pamphlet. See Colonial Office Library East Africa pamphlet folio* and *Colonial Office Library East Africa pamphlet octavo* in the Index to Major Series
  Sleeping Sickness Committee, 1407–8
Colonial Survey Committee, 999
Commercial Relations and Exports Dept., 717
Commission on Administration of Justice in Kenya, Uganda and Tanganyika Territory in Criminal Matters, 1319–21
Commission on Closer Union of Dependencies in Eastern and Central Africa, 1556
  about, 1556–57

Great Britain (cont.)
Commission on Higher Education in East Africa (1937), 831
Commission on the Civil Services of Kenya, Tanganyika, Uganda and Zanzibar, 1491
about, 1491–1508
Commission on the Civil Services of the East African Territories and the East Africa High Commission, 1514
about, 1514–31
Commission on the Public Services of the East African Territories and the East Africa High Commission, 1532
about, 1532–35
Committee on Industry and Trade, 319
Committee on the East African Slave Trade, 1027
Commonwealth Relations Office, 1322
Commonwealth War Graves Commision, 1431
Court of Appeal for Eastern Africa, 974, 1304, 1307, 1309, 1323–27, 1330
about, 1307, 1322–23, 1328, 1332, 1334
See also Court of Appeal for East Africa
Crown Agents for Oversea Governments and Administration, 1000–1001, 1604
Crown Agents for the Colonies, 1389, 1485, 1489, 1609, 1629
Crown Agents' Office, 531, 676, 805
Dept. of Technical Co-operation, 344–46, 1545
Directorate of Colonial Surveys. *See* Great Britain. Directorate of Overseas Surveys
Directorate of Military Survey, 1002–3
Directorate of Overseas Geological Survey, 1618
Directorate of Overseas Surveys, 225, 766, 1004–11, 1411, 1628
East Africa Commission, 10
East Africa Royal Commission, 11, 1008–11
about, 11–21, 1008–11
East African Currency Board. *See* East African Currency Board
East African Economic and Fiscal Commission, 952
about, 952–53
East African Military Labour Service, 1432–33
East African Rice Mission, 220
Economic Advisory Council
Committee on Nutrition in the Colonial Empire, 1394
Tsetse Fly Committee 1409
Empire Market Board, 320
Fact-Finding Mission To Study Muslim Education in East Africa, 800

Great Britain (cont.)
Foreign Office
1872–85: 674, 1034–51
1886–99: 537–40, 545, 547–49, 1052–57, 1060–70, 1079–82, 1092
1900–13: 243, 321, 533–36, 541–44, 546, 550–52, 768–69, 1071–75, 1467–68, 1470–71, 1801–5
1953: 744
Africa no. . . . See Index to Major Series
Historical Section, 22–23
Slave trade no. . . . See Index to Major Series
Imperial Mineral Resources Bureau, 1348
Inter-departmental Committee on the Apportionment of the East African War Expenditure, 936
Joint Select Committee on Closer Union in East Africa. *See* Great Britain. Parliament. Joint Select Committee on Closer Union in East Africa
Meteorological Office, 1622, 1739
Ministry of Aviation, 364
See also Great Britain. Air Ministry
Ministry of Food, 201–3
Ministry of Information, 1372, 1417–19, 1423, 1426–27
Ministry of Overseas Development. Statistics Division, 718–19
Office of Commonwealth Relations, 1511
Ordnance Survey Office, 227, 1090
Parliament
House of Commons
Select Committee on Overseas Aid. Subcommittee E, 745
Select Committee on Slave Trade (East Coast of Africa), 1029
House of Lords. *Papers and bills,* 1562
Joint Select Committee on Closer Union in East Africa, 1562
about, 1562–66
Papers by command. See Index to Major Series
Privy Council. Judicial Committee, 1304, 1322, 1326, 1330
Public Record Office. *C.O. 879/–. See* Index to Major Series
Treasury, 746
about, 1049–52, 1434
Treaties, etc.
1837–1901 (Victoria), 1033, 1038, 1058–59, 1077–78, 1083–84, 1086–88, 1093
1901–1910 (Edward VII), 1089, 1091, 1410

Great Britain (cont.)
1952– (Elizabeth II), 554, 976–77, 1322, 1545, 1551, 1576–80
Uganda Railway Committee, 534
War Office, 1366–67, 1420, 1435
General Staff, 1012–14
Geographical Section, 555, 992, 1003, 1015–16, 1435
Intelligence Division, 24–25, 556, 1085
Working Party on Higher Education in East Africa (1955), 834
about, 834–35
Working Party on Higher Education in East Africa, (1959), 832
Gregory, R. M., 865
Green, D. H., 133
Green, Robert, 252
Greenway, Percy J., 1606–8
Greenwood, Peter H., 1759
Greig, E. D. W., 1412 (4, pt. 8; 5, pt. 10; 6, pt. 11–12)
Griffith, Arthur L., 175, 176 (8–15), 183–85
Griffiths, J. F., 767 (7), 1674 (v. 3, no. 5), 1701 (v. 3, no. 10)
Griffiths, V. L., 800
Grigg, Sir Edward M., 529, 1560–61, 1563
Grinsted, W. A., 1674 (v. 2, no. 2)
Gross domestic product
Uganda, 711, 756
Zanzibar, 713
Gross national product, Tanganyika, 708
Groundnut scheme, 199–208
Grundy, 1674 (v. 2, no. 11)
A Guide to creative writing, 263
Guinness, Walter, 936
Gunn, D. L., 120 (4)
Gurney, H. L. G., 352
Gurney, Russell, 1029
Gurr, Andrew, 278
Gutherie, E. J., 47
Gutkind, A. E., 1139–42
Gwynne, Michael D., 80–81, 1761

H

Haarer, A. E., 1242
Hadaway, A. B., 140, 145
Hadithi za Tanganyika, 1226, 1231–32
Hadithi za Tanzania, 1263
Hail, 1701 (v. 4, no. 1)
Kenya, 1730 (22)
Haile, P. H. W., 1293–94
Hailey, William Malcolm Hailey, Baron, 1511
Haji Chum. *See* Chum, Haji
Haldemann, E. G., 1614 (5)
Halmashauri ya Kiswahili ya Afrika Mashariki. *See* East African Swahili Committee
Halvorson, Marian, 1289
Hamed bin Saleh el-Busaidy. *See* el-Busaidy, Hamed bin Saleh
Hamed bin Thwain, Sultan of Zanzibar (1893–1896), 1087
Hamerton, A. E., 1412 (10, pt. 30)
Hamid ibn Muhammad, called Tipoo Tib, 1181
Hammond, F. D., 528
Hamoud bin Muhammad, Sultan of Zanzibar (1896–1902), 1088
Hamp, A. E., 596
Hand of chance, 274
Handbook for East Africa, Uganda and Zanzibar, 26
Handbook of British East Africa, including Zanzibar, Uganda, and the territory of the Imperial British East Africa Company, 24
A Handbook of German East Africa, 1366–67
Handicraft, 866, 872–73
Handley, J. R. F., 1614 (1–2)
Harbors, 427, 440, 445–46, 451, 454, 458–59, 466, 472, 564, 568, 585, 620, 624
accounts, bookkeeping, etc., 465
Dar es Salaam, Tanzania 433–34, 461–62, 478
distances, etc., 500–501, 505, 621
employees, 471, 496–99, 509, 524, 569, 588, 593, 606–7, 626–27, 1137, 1491, 1496, 1514, 1519–20, 1533–34
salaries, pensions, etc., 432, 503, 517–17a, 572, 582, 589–90, 1491, 1494–96, 1514, 1519–20, 1933–34
estimates, 463, 468–69, 510, 566–67, 575
finance, 435–36, 447, 451a–52, 455, 560–61, 568
Mombasa, Kenya, 441–45, 479–80, 554, 581, 770–71, 776–78
maps, 479
Mtwara, Tanzania 436, 609
port charges, 456–57, 478, 573, 591
Tanzania, 504
regulations, 453, 574
statistics, 764
Tanga, Tanzania, 554
See also Cargo handling; East African Harbours Corporation; East African Railways and Harbours Administration; Tides, tables

Hardinge, Sir Arthur, 1068
Hardy, D. E., 1756 (v. 1, no. 6)
Harres, Hans, 517
Harries, Lyndon, 1220
Harrison, M. N., 47
Hastie, Catherine, 866
Hawk moth, 1751
Hawkins, F., 221
Hawkins (D. A.) ltd., Nairobi, 675
Hawridge, D. G., 801
Hay, R. F. M., 1721 (v. 4, no. 6)
Heady, Harold F., 82
Health. *See* Medicine and health
Health, public. *See* Public health
Health and disease in Africa—the community approach, 1396
Health education, 72, 809–22, 1397–98
  bibliography, 787, 789–90, 794–95
  See also Children—care and hygiene
Heart disease, 1374
Heat, juvenile literature, 880
Hekaya za kuburudisha, 1214
Heligoland, 1081, 1083
Hemedi bin Abdallah el-Buhriy. *See* el-Buhriy, Hemedi bin Abdallah
Hemming, Francis, 1409
Hemming, G. F., 1701 (v. 3, no. 10)
Hemp. *See* Ramie
Henderson, J. P., 1674 (v. 2, no. 5), 1686 (4)
Herbicides, 132–33, 146, 153–55
Herpetology, 1758
Hicks, Ursula, 956
Hides and skins, 1108
  See also Tanning
Higham, Charles S., 1243
The Higher College of East Africa (1938), 833
Higher education, 823–45
Higher education in East Africa (1958), 834, 837
Hilal, A. M. A., 1214
Hill, A. Glendon, 83
Hill, Mervyn F., 557–58, 605
Hinaway, Mbarak Ali, 1182–83
Hinchey, J., 961
Hinga, E., 253–54
Hints on the preservation of health in eastern Africa, 1373
Hisi yetu, 1184
History, 33, 767 (1), 1018–1106, 1244, 1271
  bibliography, 90, 787–90, 794–95
  East Africa Protectorate, 21–24, 1099, 1474

History (cont.)
  Tanganyika, 317, 1162–63, 1175, 1188
  Tanzania, poetry, 1187, 1196, 1206
  text-books, (elementary), 889
  Uganda, 24, 1099
  Zanzibar, 24, 1099
  See also Discovery and exploration
The history of Abudrrahman and Sufian, 1171
The history of Prince Hussein son of Ali, 1174
History of the great war based on official documents, 1436
Hockey, S. W., 1349
Hocking, K. S., 140
Hocombe, S. D., 146
Hodge, Edward R. Vere-. *See* Vere-Hodge, Edward R.
Hodge, A. D. P., 1412 (8, pt. 18; 9, pt. 23)
Hoes, 1121 (2)
Hofmann, R. R., 1747
Hollingsworth, Lawrence W., 1244
Holmes, Maurice, 1491
Home economics, 855–62
  dictionaries, Swahili, 1297
  study and teaching, 865
Honoré, E. J., 767 (11)
Hooijer, Dirk A., 1018 (21)
Hookworm disease, 820, 1358
Hopwood, Francis J. S., 210
Hordern, Charles, 1436
Hornby, H. E., 239, 244
Hoskins, A. R., 1420
Hotels, directories, 649–50, 652–54
Houghton, M., 1391
Household budgets. *See* Cost and standard of living
Howland, P., 176 (8, 11–15)
Hoy, Harry E., 1017
Hubbard, Charles E., 1609
Hubbard, H. E., 75
Huddart, J. T., 1638
Huggard, W. C., 1337
Human Trypanosomiasis Research Institute. *See* Entebbe, Uganda. Human Trypanosomiasis Research Institute
Hume, Violet R., 855
Humidity, 1711 (9)
  Kenya, 1663, 1689, 1713
  observers' manuals, 1647 (9–11, 19), 1674 (24), 1725 (25)
  Seychelles, 1663
  Tanganyika, 1663

Humidity (cont.)
Uganda, 1663
Zanzibar, 1663
Humphrey, Norman, 94–95
al-Husayn ibn 'Ali, 1174
Hussey, E. R. J., 785
Hutchinson, R. W. J., 1604
Hutt, A. M. Bruce, 12
Huxley, Julian S., 802
Hydén, Göran, 114
Hydro-electric power. *See* Water-power
Hydrography, 168 (9, 12), 169
maps, 986–89, 991, 1015
Hydrology, 1621–31, 1679
East Africa Protectorate, 1627
Kenya, 1626, 1730 (20)
Aberdare mountains, 1624 (1–2)
Lake Victoria, 168 (10)
maps, 766–67, 1628
Tanganyika, 1626
Uganda, 1626–27
Karamoja District, 1624 (5)
See also Evaporation (meteorology); Rain and rainfall; Water-supply; *and* names of lakes and rivers, e.g., Lake Victoria; Tana River, Kenya
Hydrometeorological survey of the catchments of lakes Victoria, Kyoga and Albert, 1621, 1628a
Hygiene. *See* Public health
Hyslop, Graham, 1185–86

I

Ichthyology, 1759
See also Lethrinus; Tilapia
Illiteracy, 1253
Imbuga, F. D., 255
Impala, 1748
Imperial Airways Ltd., 372, 414
Imperial British East Africa Company, 538, 1094–95, 1097–98, 1742
about, 1092–1106
charter, 538, 1095–96, 1099–1100
staff, 1100
treaties, 1094, 1098–1100, 1103–6
Imperial Shipping Committee, 430
In a brown mantle, 268
Income
Kenya, 702, 706, 753
statistics, 752, 761, 763

Income (cont.)
Uganda, 703–4, 709–10, 947
Income tax, 961–78
India, 1790
Indian Ocean
cyclones, 1638, 1644
weather, 1674 (v. 2, no. 3)
Indians in East Africa. *See* South Asians in East Africa
Industrial competition. *See* Competition, industrial
Industrial courts. *See* Labor courts
Industrial relations, 425–26, 559, 625–27
Industrial research, 32, 1118, 1120, 1122
bibliography, 1120
Industry, 767 (4), 1107–26
Kenya, 1111
statistics, 753
Tanganyika, 1112–14
statistics, 755
Uganda, statistics, 756
See also Construction industry; Soda industry
Information for sportsmen and travellers in East Africa, 676
Innes, D., 75
Innes, Dr. James Ross, 1380
Insecticides, 134–45, 149, 152–53, 155, 1385 (3, 7, 9–10, 17)
physiological effect, 1385 (2, 14)
Insectivora, fossil, 1018 (13)
Insects, 1756–57
See also Names of insects and insect orders, e.g., Caddis-flies; Coleoptera; Diptera; Lepidoptera; Moths, Neuroptera; Odonata
Insects, injurious and beneficial, 43, 86, 147–48, 1366
See also Desert locust; Forest insects; Lac-insects; Locusts; Mosquitoes; Plant-lice; Tsetse-flies
Insurance, 763, 920–22
Insurance law, 1305
Inter-African Conference on Hydrology, Nairobi (1961), 1626
Internal revenue law, 285
International Bank for Reconstruction and Development, 417–18, 450
International Conference on Special Problems of Development Banks in Eastern Africa, Kampala, Uganda (1969), 913
International Study Conference on the Current and Future Problems of Acridology, 123

International Study Group for Research in Cardiac Metabolism, 1374
International Symposium on Preventive Myocardiology and Cardiac Metabolism, Nairobi (1971), 1374, 1376
Inter-territorial Committee on Ground Services for Civil Aviation in East Africa, 361
Inter-territorial Conference on Hydrology and Water Resources, 1st, Nairobi (1950), 1626
Inter-territorial Geological Conference
5th, Dodoma, Tanganyika (1952), 1615, 1619
6th, Entebbe, Uganda (1953), 1616
Inter-territorial Hides and Skins Advisory Committee, 1108
Inter-territorial Language (Swahili) Committee to the East African Dependencies, 1146–48, 1158, 1198, 1248, 1250
about, 1158
See also Chuo cha Uchunguzi wa Lugha ya Kiswahili; East African Swahili Committee
Inter-territorial organisation in East Africa, 1567–68
Inter-university Committee for East Africa, 1596
Introducing East Africa, 4, 6–9
Introducing East and Central Africa (filmstrip), 1
Invoices, 289, 330
Irrigation and disease, 1385 (16)
Islamic law, 1302
See also Domestic relations (Islamic law)

J

Jaafar, Kadhi Kassim bin, 1172
Jackson, C. H. N., 1602
Jackson, Richard H., 939
Jaetzold, R., 1721 (v. 4, no. 5)
Jahadhmy, A. A., 1199
Jamaliddini, Abdul Karim bin, 1187
Jambo, 1437
Jambo news, 373
James, Sydney P., 1389
James, T. C., 1614 (4)
Jeannel, R., 1756 (v. 3, no. 6–10)
Jeeranjee and Co., 614
Jennings, Sir William Ivor, 1245
Jerome, Abraham, 720
Jews, colonization, 770
Jinja, Uganda, cost and standard of living, 730
Johari za Kiswahili, 1168–69a, 1171, 1174–75, 1181, 1196, 1200, 1204–5, 1220–22
Johnson, D. H., 1674 (v. 3, no. 8–9)
Johnson, Frederick, 1147–48
Johnston, H. B., 120 (5)
Johnston, W., 324
Joint Select Committee on Closer Union in East Africa. *See* Great Britain. Parliament. Joint Select Comimttee on Closer Union in East Africa
Joliso, 256
Jones, C. G., 1756 (v. 2, no. 5)
Jones, Tecwyn, 186–90
Jordan, K., 1756 (v. 3, no. 2)
Journal of African administration, special supplement, 209
Journal of Eastern African research and development, 33
Journal of the East African Railways and Harbours corporations, 606
Jubaland, East Africa Protectorate
concessions, 775
cotton, 116–17
Juba River, East Africa Protectorate
as boundary, 1084
concessions, 773
Judicial statistics, 1307, 1323
Kenya, 753
Tanganyika, 755
Uganda, 756
See also Courts
Judiciary. *See* Courts
Jury, S. J., 867
Just a moment, God! 252
Justice, administration of
Kenya, 1319–21
Tanganyika, 1319–21
Uganda, 1319–21

K

K.A.G. virus vaccine, 240
K.I.A. occasional papers, 1548
K.I.O., 656
Kabete Laboratory, 240
Kabete training map, 1424
Kabeya, John B., 1188
Kadhi Kassim bin Jaafar. *See* Jaafar, Kadhi Kassim bin
Kästner, Erich, 1246
Kalimugogo, Godfrey, 257

Kalinzu forest, Uganda, insects, 1756
Kamaliza, Minister for Labour of Tanganyika (ca. 1962), 1128
Kamati ya Uandikaji, 1240, 1247
Kamiti, S. M., 186
Kampala, Uganda, 677
 cost and standard of living, 731
 Makerere University College, 831, 833, 838
  East African Institute of Social Research, 1139–42
  Faculty of Agriculture, 47
  National Institute of Education. *Progress report,* 851
   See also Makerere University. National Institute of Education
 prices, 737
 weather, 1726 (5), 1633
Kampala agreement, 325
Karanja, M. K., 186
Karimi, Maitai, 258
Karoki, John, 259
Katalambula, Faraji H., 1189
Kauntze, W. H., 833
Kawuma, Ally Medi, 560
Kayanja, F. I. B., 1748
Kaye, J. W., 1024
Kazimi, Ali A., 803
Keay, R. W. J., 1604
Kebaso, John K., 1513
Keen, B. A., 54
Keltie, Sir John Scott, 1248
Kemoli, Arthur, 271
Kenia forest, East Africa Protectorate, concessions, 776–77
Kenya (general), 1, 6–9, 23, 667–70, 678
 Game Dept., 675
 Gazette, Supplement, 1308
 Laws, statutes, etc., 978
 Ministry of Power and Communications, 375–77, 418, 561–63
 Ministry of Tourism and Wildlife, 637
 National Assembly. *Sessional paper,* 374–77, 417–18, 560–63, 747–48, 1542–43, 1586
 National Archives, 1498–1500
 Survey of Kenya, 1002, 1719–20, 1806–7
 Treaties, etc. (June 6, 1967), 914, 1591, 1598
 Water Development Dept., 1621, 1630
Kenya and Uganda Railways and Harbours, 326, 564–93, 679–90
 First Department Committee on the Amount of Contribution to Renewals Funds Necessary To Allow for Depreciation of Wasting Assets, 595
 Second Departmental Committee on the Amount of Contribution to Renewals Funds Necessary To Allow for Renewing Wasting Assets, 596
Kenya Broadcasting Corporation, 1276
Kenya Colony and Protectorate
 Adult Literacy Section, 1252
 Audit Dept., 597–98, 915
 Commissioner of Customs, 324, 328
 Customs Dept., 329–32
 Dept. of Agriculture, 82, 221, 1610
  Bulletin, 219, 245
  Statistical Branch. *Crop report,* 71
 Dept. of Lands and Settlement, 1424
 Dept. of Veterinary Services, 85
 Forest Dept., 1125
 Governor
  1922–1925 (Coryndon), 1440–41
  1925–1930 (Sir E. W. M. Grigg), 529, 1560–61, 1563
  1931–1937 (Byrne), 1564–65
  1944–1952 (Mitchell), 15–16
  1952–1957 (Sir Evelyn Baring), 14, 17
 Legislative Council
  Sessional paper, 327, 599, 953, 967, 1438–39, 1497, 1521
  Committee on Extending Certain Provisions of Law to the East Africa High Commission, 1329
 Medical Dept., 1372, 1489
 Posts and Telegraphs Dept., 419–22, 916
  budget, 419
 Public Works Dept., 191
 Secretariat, 1498–1500, 1522
 Supreme Court, 974, 1326
 Survey Dept., 1746
 Tariff Committee, 333
Kenya crop report, 71
Kenya Institute of Administration, 1303, 1310, 1548
Kenya Institute of Education
 General Methods Section, 1249
  See also Curriculum Development and Research Centre
 Progress report, 851–53
Kenya National Parks, 675
Kenya National Parks' Trustees, 1811
Kenya Royal Naval Volunteer Force, 1416
Kerfoot, O., 192

Kerkham, R. K., 75
Kew, England, Royal Botanic Gardens, 1609
Kezilahabi, Euphrase, 1190
Khalifa Abubakr Siddik. *See* Siddik, Khalifa Abubakr
Khalifa bin Said, Sultan of Zanzibar (1888–1890), 1058, 1093, 1104
Kiango, S. D., 1184
Kidney diseases, 1361
Kifo cha penzi, 1207
Kiimbila, J. K., 1191, 1290–91
Kijuma, Muhammad, 1192, 1220
Kikuyu (ethnic group), 79, 1765 (5)
Kilama, W. L., 1377a
Kilindi (ethnic group), 1162–63
Kilindini harbor. *See* Harbors—Mombasa, Kenya
Kilombero railway project, 494
Kilombero sugar estate, 234
Kimenye, Barbara, 269
Kimmins, D. E., 1752, 1756 (v. 3, no. 5)
Kimweri, William, 1162–63
King, A. J., 1614 (7), 1617
King, M. C., 868
King George VI Hospital, Nairobi, 1375
Kingdon, Sir Donald, 240
Kings' African Rifles, 1414, 1442–55, 1474
  about, 1414, 1419, 1439, 1441, 1448
  conditions of services, 1443–45
  insignia, 1440
  ordinances, 1442, 1446–47
  regulations, 1452–55
  regulations for South Asians, 1451
  reserve forces rules, 1449
  staffs, 1450
Kingsbury, O. A., 869–70
Kinnaird, Mr., 1024
Kinnear, Brown, J. A., 1383
Kintu, a play, 262
Kipsikis dialect of Kalenjin, glossary of botanical terms, 1605
Kirby, A. F., 434
Kiriakoff, S. G., 1757 (v. 1, no. 2–3)
Kirk, John, 1039
Kirkpatrick, Thomas W., 112, 193
Kironde, E. C. N., 262
Kisses of fate, 254
Kiswahili, 1149
Kiswahili fasihi na ufanisi, 1150
Kleine, R., 1756 (v. 3, no. 6–10)
Knappert, Jan, 1177
Knitting, 860
Koenig, T. A., 1121 (17)
Koeune, Esther, 815–19, 856–59
Kombo, Salum M., 1250–51
Kongwa Working Party, 206
Kopoka, O. B., 1157 (1–2)
Kovacs, G., 1730 (20)
Kreditanstalt für Wiederaufbau, 913
Kuanza kusoma, 1252, 1276
Kuboja, Nacksso J., 1193
Kuria, Henry, 1194–95
Kurtz, Margaret A., 871
Kurwa na Doto; maelezo ya makazi katika kijiji cha Unguja yaani Zanzibar, 1179
Kusadikika, nchi iliyo angani, 1216
Kusoma na kuandika pamoja na maazimio na mapendekizo, 1253
Kyoga, lake, Uganda. *See* Lake Kyoga, Uganda

L

Laana ya Pandu, 1211
Labor, 10, 424–25, 559, 779, 1127–38
  Arab, 778
  Kenya, 1128, 1137–38
  Somali, 778–79
  South Asian, 778–79
  Tanganyika, 1128, 1138
  Uganda, 1128, 1138
  Zanzibar, 1138
Labor courts, 1315, 1596
Labor supply
  Kenya, 753, 778–79, 1131, 1133–34
  Tanganyika, 755, 1132
  Uganda, 756, 1135
  See also Construction industry—Uganda—employees; Cotton gins and ginning; Forced labor—Uganda
Lac-insects, 1674 (v. 2, no. 6)
Lacey, Gerald, 220
Lake Albert, hydrology, 1621–22, 1628a
Lake Kyoga, Uganda, 530
  hydrology, 1621, 1628a
Lake Magadi Railway, 772
Lake Magadi soda scheme, 770–71, 773–74, 776
Lake Nyasa, 1089
  seismicity, 1614 (7)
Lake Rukwa, Tanganyika, seismicity, 1614 (7)
Lake Tanganyika, 1089
Lake Victoria, 87, 530, 546, 617, 622–23, 673

Lake Victoria (cont.)
fishes, 1759
hydrology, 1621–22, 1628a, 1701 (v. 4, no. 2)
triangulation of southern shores, 1013
Lambermont, Baron, 1099–1100
Lambert, H. E., 1151–53, 1166, 1196, 1201, 1222
Lamprey, H. F., 767 (12)
Land, 10–11, 15
Kenya, Aberdare mountains, 1624 (2)
See also Public land concessions
Land and population in East Africa, 15–16
The land is ours, 259
Land settlement, 770
Kenya, 110, 781
Land tenure, 11, 209–12, 772–73
bibliography, 211
East Africa Protectorate, 209, 211–12, 778–79
Kenya, 11, 209, 211, 767 (10), 1008
maps, 1011
Tanganyika, 11, 209, 211, 767 (10), 1008
Uganda, 11, 209–12, 767 (10), 776, 779–80, 1008
Zanzibar, 211, 779
Langdale-Brown, I., 767 (9)
Language and linguistics, 24, 33, 1139–1301
bibliography, 1139–42
See also English language; Swahili language
Laubach, Frank C., 1254
Law, 1302–48
See also Domestic relations (Islamic law); Labor courts; Railroad law; Tariff—law; *and* subdivision Laws, statutes, etc. under names of countries, e.g., Kenya—Laws, statutes, etc.
Law, administrative. *See* Administrative law
Law and politics, 1306, 1316
Law enforcement, 1335–42
Law officers. *See* Police
Law reports, digests, etc., 1309, 1318, 1326–27, 1330
indexes, 1304
Law reports of Kenya, 1330
Lawes, E. F., 1693, 1739 (15, 17, 23)
Laws of the East African Community, 1347
The Laws of the High Commission in force on the 31st December, 1951, 1344
Laws, statutes, etc., 1343–48
Leakey, C. L. A., 47
Leakey, L. S. B., 767 (2), 1018 (1, 14), 1020–21
Leakey, Margaret, 1022
Legal research, 1310
Legislation, 1343, 1345–46
Legislative bodies, 1460, 1464, 1466
allowances, 1465
debates, 1460, 1464, 1466
membership lists, 1459
privileges and immunities, 1465
See also names of legislative bodies, e.g., East Africa High Commission. East Africa Central Legislative Assembly; East African Common Services Organization. Central Legislative Assembly
Lemenye, Justin, 1255
Lemon-grass, 1120
Le Pelley, R. H., 147
Lepidoptera, 171–72, 1749–50, 1752, 1757 (v. 1)
Leprosy, 1354–55, 1360, 1380–83
Leslie, J. R., 383
Lesso, Zuberi H., 1197
Lethrinus, 168 (15)
Let's make a play, 262
Letter-writing, Swahili, 1230, 1266
Levin, L. S., 666
Lewis, Arthur J., 847
Libraries, 787, 1349, 1601
See also Agricultural libraries
Lidbury, David J., 1514
Lieb, L. V., 847, 849
Light, juvenile literature, 881
Lily (cyclone), 1701 (v. 4, no. 4)
Lime-kilns, 1121 (13, 15)
Limnopithecus macinnesi, 1018 (3)
The Lindi cyclone, 15 April 1952, 1674 (v. 3, no. 1)
Lindner, E., 1756 (v. 2, no. 1–2)
Linguistics. *See* Language and linguistics
Linsell, C. Allen, 1350
List of food crop varieties available for distribution, 62–63
Literacy Centre of Kenya, 1276
Literates, writing for. *See* Readers for new literates
Literature, 33, 250, 804
See also East African literature (English); Swahili literature
Literature and society, 250, 256, 269
Livestock, 213–16
bibliography, 215
Livingston, H. G., 84
Livingstone, David, 674, 1271
Liyong, Taban lo, 260–61
Llewelyn, D. A. B., 1126

Loans
American, 554, 744
British, 563
British guarantee of, 746
International Bank for Reconstruction and Development, 450, 560–63, 747–48
Kenya guarantee of, 347–77, 417–18, 560–63, 747–48
Swedish, 747
Local Civil Service Salaries Commission. *See* East African Common Services Organization. Local Civil Service Salaries Commission
Local service air lines. *See* Air lines, local service
Lockwood, J. F., 832, 834
Locomotives, 464, 551
See also Railroads—rolling-stock
Locusts, 120–29, 131, 149, 151
Kenya, 120 (4, 25), 151
Tanganyika, 120 (15, 20, 26, 33), 151
Logan, W. E. M., 767 (11)
Loggin, G. N., 613
London
Anti-Locust Research Centre, 120–21, 149
Commonwealth Institute, 1348
London School of Hygiene and Tropical Medicine, 1379
Long, B., 1259
Long, Beryl, 1254
Loogman, Alfons, 1256
Low, George C., 1412 (3, pt. 5)
Lowe, John, 1381
Lowe, Rosemary H. M., 160 (1)
Lowe-McConnell, Rosemary H., 168 (2)
Lowestoft, Eng. Fisheries Laboratory, 157
Lugard, Frederick John Dealtry, Baron, 538, 1099–1101
Lumb, F. E., 1711 (11), 1730 (16)
Lunan, M., 767 (10)
Lutta, B. C. W., 1347
Lyth, Nora, 860

M

Mabira forest, Uganda, concessions, 770–71, 773, 776–79
McCallum, D., 1674 (v. 3, no. 7)
McCoy-Hill, M., 194
McCulloch, J. S. G., 192, 195, 767 (8), 1624 (2)
McDermott, P. L., 1099–1100
McDonnell Douglas Corporation, 377
Macfie, J. W. S., 1756 (v. 1, no. 5)
Machauru, F. J., 1257
Machinery, agricultural. *See* Agricultural machinery
MacInnes, Donald G., 1018 (4, 6, 10, 12)
Mackay, James A., 423
McKenzie, Bruce, 45 (1)
Mackenzie, G. S., 1097
Mackenzie, George, 1106
McKenzie, John C., 872–73
Mackenzie, Muir, 1096
Mackenzie concession, 774–75
McKilliam, K. R., 874
Mackinder, H. J., 430
Mackinnon, William, 1094
Macmahon, Arthur W., 1585 (17)
McNeil, R. T., 875
Macpherson, Margaret, 262
Madan, Arthur C., 1147
Magadi soda scheme. *See* Lake Magadi soda scheme
Magnetism, terrestrial
maps, 984–85
Uganda, 1648
Maina, G., 1361a
Maize, 47, 97, 1115
Kenya, 71, 218
Maize stalk borer, 135, 142
Maji Maji uprising (1905–7), 1187
Makerere University. National Institute of Education. *Program report,* 852–53
Makerere University College. *See* Kampala, Uganda. Makerere University College
Makowiecki, L. Z., 1617
Malaria, 1354–55, 1378, 1384–90
diagnosis, 1385 (13)
Kenya, 1389
maps, 1388
prevention, 1385 (4)
Tanganyika, maps, 1388
Tanzania, 1384, 1386–87, 1390
Uganda, 1389
See also Cinchona; Mosquitoes
Malet, Sir E., 1082
Maletnlema, T. N., 861
Malindi, East African Protectorate, concessions, 774–75
Malipo duniani hesabu ahera, 1214
Mammals, 1797
See also Impala; Ruminatia
Mambo leo, 1198

Mamuya, S. J., 820
Man, prehistoric, 1019
See also Primates, fossil
Management Institute. *See* East African Community. Management Institute
Mance, Sir H. Osborne, 349
Manda concession, 1099–1100
Mandao, Martha, 821
Mangat, D. S., 1347
Mangua, Charles, 269
Mann, Erica, 85
Mann, I., 85
Mann, M. J., 164 (10, 12)
Manone, Carl J., 848, 850–53
Mantsur, S., 234
Maps, 766–67, 981, 1017
ethnic groups, 995
indexes, 983, 997
military, 986–87, 991, 1015
training, 1424
topographic, 987–93, 996, 1002–3, 1015–16
See also Boundaries; *and* under specific subjects, e.g., Railroads—maps
Marindany, Kipkemo arap, 1605
Marriage, 1791–93
forced, 1794a
See also Domestic relations (Islamic law)
Martin, C. J., 334, 1131
Martin, D. L., 203
Maryam na siku ya mwanzo ya Dakhalia, 1214
Masai (ethnic group), land rights, 772
Mashairi ya Mambo leo, 1198
Mashairi yangu, 1223–24
Mason, H., 1258–59
Mason, Ian L., 215
Massell, Benton F., 741
Matano, Hyder M., 855
Maternal and infant welfare, 812–14
Mathes, H., 164 (9)
Mathews, D. O., 640–41
Matola, S., 1199
Matola, Y. G., 1390
Matson, A. T., 767 (1), 1094
Maule, J. P., 215
Maximum likely 24-hour rainfall at selected stations in Uganda, 1741
May, W. B., 176 (1, 3, 15)
al-Mazrui, Abdallah bin Mas'ud bin Salim, 1183
Mazzuki, Daniel, 1289
Mbale, Uganda, cost and standard of living, 739
Mbarak Ali Hinawy. *See* Hinawy, Ali Mbarak
Mbazira, J. K., 1765
Mbojo: simba-mtu, 1193
Mbotela, James J., 1260–61
Mboya, T. J., 1128
Mechanical drawing, study and teaching, 893
Mechanical engineers, 1426
Mechanics, juvenile literature, 879
Medical education, 1391
Medical geography, 1350, 1366–67
Medical parasitology, 809–10, 1377
See also Hookworm disease
Medical personnel, 1392
Medical research, 30, 32, 1350–51, 1353–55, 1358–60
costs, 1352
periodicals, 1359
See also Myocardiology; Tuberculosis research
Medicine and health, 10–11, 1350–1412
dictionaries, Swahili, 1297
Kenya, 11
periodicals, 1357
Tanganyika, 11
Uganda, 11
See also Public health
Meetings and discussions on the proposed East Africa federation, 1584
Megapedetes pentadactylus, 1018 (12)
Meningitis, cerebro-spinal, 1378
Mentally ill, care and treatment, 822
Merrick, J. E. S., 333
Meru (ethnic group), 1765 (5)
Metal-work, 1109
Meteorological Analysis Centre. *See* East Africa High Commission. Meteorological Analysis Centre
Meteorology, 1632–1746
bibliography, 1694, 1697–99, 1716, 1718, 1739
East Africa Protectorate, observations, 1100, 1739, 1742
glossaries, vocabularies, etc., 1676 (21)
Kenya, observations, 753, 1653, 1690, 1714, 1721 (v. 4, no. 5), 1722, 1737
observers' manuals, 1647, 1676, 1717, 1725
Rhodesia, Northern, 1641
Seychelles, observations, 1681, 1690
Tanganyika, observations, 755, 1690
Tanzania, observations, 1702, 1714, 1723, 1737
Uganda, observations, 756, 1100, 1690, 1703, 1714, 1724, 1737, 1739, 1742
Zanzibar, observations, 1655, 1690
See also Climatology; Rain and rainfall

Meteorology in aeronautics, 1652, 1662, 1726 (4, 6)
observers' manuals, 1647 (5–7, 18)
Metric handbok for the consumer, 714
Metric system, 712, 714
Mettam, R. W. M., 245
Mgeni karibu, 1186
Mhina, George A., 1290–91
Mica, 780
Michuki, David N., 1262–62a
Military, 1413–58
See also Armed forces
Military engineers, 1426
Millar, Douglas J., 876–77
Milne, Geoffrey, 226–29
Minchin, E. A., 1412 (8, pt. 20–22; 10, pt. 38)
Mines and mineral resources, 41
Kenya, statistics, 753
maps, 766–67
statistics, 752
Tanganyika, statistics, 755
Uganda, statistics, 756
Mining law
Kenya, 1348
Tanganyika, 1348
Zanzibar, 1348
Mirambo, 1188
Mirathi, a handbook of the Mahomedan law of inheritance, 1302
Missions, 1032
Kenya, 775
Mitchell, P. E., 1302, 1571
Mitchell, Sir Philip E., 15–16, 433, 838
Mkabarah, J., 1212
Mkelle, Mohamed Burham, 1172
Mkunumbi, Kenya, poetry, 1220
Mngola, E. N., 1361a
Mnyampala, Mathias E., 1196, 1200–1204, 1263
Mörth, H. T., 1674 (v. 3, no. 8–9), 1701 (v. 4, no. 2), 1707, 1730 (19–20)
Mohamed, Jan, 637
Mohamed, S. A., 1214
Mohammedan law. *See* Islamic law
Molesworth, Sir Guilford, 549
Molière, Jean Baptiste Poquelin, 1264–65
Mollard, P. W., 1293–94
Molluscicides, 153
Mombasa Committee of Enquiry, 441–44
Mombasa region, Kenya
guide-books, 651, 657–58, 687
water-supply, 772–74
Mombasa, Victoria Lake Railway Survey, 545
Mombasa-Victoria (Uganda) Railway Committee, 540–44
Mongolia, ltd., 772
Monsoons, 1730 (21)
Monthly bulletin of decisions of criminal [and civil] appeals, 1327
Monthly desert locust situation report, 126
Moomaw, James C., 1610
Morant, V., 121 (2)
Moreau, R. E., 217
Morey, Hal, 604
Morgans, J. F. C., 168 (21)
Mortars, 1121 (8)
Mortimer, John 72
Mosely, M. E., 1756 (v. 3, no. 1)
Mosquitoes, 1385 (15), 1412 (3, pt. 7), 1756 (v. 1, no. 2–3)
extermination, 1385 (7–12)
Moths, 1751–52
Motor bus lines
fares, 490–91
Kenya, maps, 483–86
Tanganyika, maps, 483–86, 630, 635
Tanzania, 631–32
time-tables, 491, 507, 630
Uganda, maps, 483–86, 630
Motor oil filters, 1121 (4)
Motor vehicles, 351, 628–29
Kenya, 351
statistics, 351
Tanzania, 351
Uganda, 351
Mott, Frederick W., 1412 (12, pt. 2)
Mount Elgon, insects, 1756
Moving pictures, 41, 72, 604
See also Filmstrips
Mphahlele, Ezekiel, 263
Mtemi Mirambo; mtawala shujaa wa Kinyamwezi, 1188
Mtwanguo, A., 96
Mudie, Sir Francis, 129
Mugambi, Jesse N. K., 264
Muguga Arboretum, 176 (8, 12, 27–29)
Muhammad, Saleh, 1205
Muhammad bin Abdallah bin Mbarak Bakhashweini. *See* Bakhashweini, Muhammad bin Abdallah bin Mbarak
Muhammad Kijuma. *See* Kijuma, Muhammad
Mulika, 1154
Munitalp/World Meteorological Organization

Symposium, Nairobi (1959), 1674 (v. 3, no. 9)
Munitions, Kenya, 1429
Murray, John, 831
Murray, Stephen S., 235
Muruah, George K., 265
Musiba, Aristablus E., 1205a
Mwana Taabu, na michezo mingine ya kuigiza, 1207
Mwanga, King of Buganda (d. 1903), 1098–99
Mwaruka, Ramadhani, 1206
Mwaura, Joshua N., 266
Mwaura, Mike, 267
Mwele forest, East Africa Protectorate, concessions, 774–75, 777, 779–80
Mwenda kwao, 1213
Mwerevu mjinga, 1207
Myocardiology, 1374, 1376
Mycology, 43, 86, 177
Mzee Khamis, leo wapi? 1214
Mzirai, Robert R. K., 1266

N

Nabarro, David, 1412 (1, pt. 2; 4, pt. 8; 5, pt. 10)
Nairobi, Kenya
  cost and standard of living
    African, 733
    European, 732
  guide-books, 659
  prices, 725
  Royal Technical College of East Africa, 835
  sample population census (1957/58), 1773
  water-supply, 1624 (8)
  weather, 1689, 1713, 1726 (2)
Nairobi Electric Light and Power Company, 776, 778, 780
Nakupenda, lakini . . ., 1194/95
Napier, John R., 1018 (16)
Nassor, F. H., 1214
Nassor, M. G., 1214
National agrarianism, 720
National Bank of Kenya, 375
National Museums of Kenya. Education Section, 1022
National parks and reserves, 1811–12
  Kenya, 661–62, 1812
  maps, 675, 766–67, 1806–7
  Tanganyika, 661–62, 691, 1808, 1812
  Uganda, 660–62, 692, 1811
Nationalism, 1245
Native policy. *See* Administration, civil service, etc.
Natural resources, 5, 765–82
Nautical terms, 1156
Navy, 1416, 1434
Nayer, P. N., 712
Nazareth, Peter, 268–69
Ndoa ya mzimuni, 1210
Ndoto ya mwendawazimu, 1180
Neale, F. R. W., 1617
Neatby, H., 856–57
Neave, C. F., 1701 (v. 4, no. 4)
Neuroptera, 1752, 1756 (v. 3, no. 5)
Never forgive father, 265
New literates, writing for. *See* Readers for new literates
Newall, H. W., 1155
Newbold, Charles D., 1344
Newell, B. S., 168 (9, 12), 169
Newman, Peter, 283 (10), 721
Ngali, Mwanyengela, 1207
Ngorongoro Conservation Area, 691, 1808
Ngubiah, Stephen N., 270
Ngugi, Gerishon, 1208–9
Ngugi wa Thiong'o. *See* Thiong'o, Ngugi Wa
Ng'weno, Hilary, 878–83
Nicholls, K. V. W., 1686 (2)
Nimelogwa nisiwe na mpenzi! mchezo wa kuigiza, 1208–9
North Sea Aerial & General Transport Ltd., 378
Northcott, Clarence W., 1137
Norton, R. E., 441
Not guilty; a comedy in one act for African actors, 248–49
Not just peanuts, 199
Ntende, E. K., 448
Nurru, Saidi M., 1210
Nurses and nursing, 1371, 1375
Nursing schools, 1391
Nutrition, 1393–94
  Kenya, 1393–94
  Tanganyika, 1394
  Tangania, 1393
  Uganda, 1393–94
  Zanzibar, 1394
Nyagah, S., 1548
Nyasa, lake. *See* Lake Nyasa
Nyasulu, Godfrey, 1211–12
Nye, I. W. B., 148
Nye, Joseph S., 1585 (13)

O

OQMG, 1017
O'Callaghan, F. L., 600
Oculi, Okello, 269
Odonata, 1752, 1754–55
Office practice, 1546
Official gazette, 1311, 1313–14
Official history of the [European] war [1914–1918], 1436
Official import and export list, 290
Officials and employees. *See* Civil service
Oils and fats, edible, 1123 (1)
Ojiambo, Hilary P., 1374, 1376
Okedi, John, 170
Oldroyd, H., 1756 (v. 2, no. 1–2)
Oliphant, F. M., 196
Oloya, J. J., 722–23
Oluyede, Peter, 1331
Omar, C. A., Shariff, 1267–70
Omari, Cuthbert K., 1213
Omari, Dunstan A., 523
Onama, Minister for Labour of Uganda (ca. 1962), 1128
Ongalo, M. E., 601
Onslow, Richard William Alan Onslow, 5th Earl of, 1562
Orde-Browne, Sir Granville St. John, 1138
Ordnance Corps. *See* Great Britain. Army. East African Force. Ordnance Corps
Ordnance factories. *See* Munitions
O'Reilly, M. P., 633
Ormsby-Gore, W., 10
Ornithology, 1760–61
Ouma, Joseph P., 343
Out of the jungle, 253
Overseas Consultants, inc., New York, 602–3
Overseas economic surveys, 717
Overseas Food Corporation, 204–6
  about, 200, 202, 208, 609
Overseas geology and mineral resources, 1618
The Overseas Service (East African Community) Agreement, 1551
Owino, F., 176 (26–27)
Oxley, Thomas A., 222
Oysters, 168 (14)

P

Paint, 1121 (6)
Paleontology, 1018
  Kenya, 1018 (9, 12)
Paleontology (cont.)
  Lake Victoria, 1018 (10)
  Miocene, 1018 (1, 4–7, 9, 11–13, 15, 18–19, 21)
  Pleistocene, 1018 (14, 18, 22)
  tertiary, 1018 (10)
Palestine and East Africa loans, 937–41
Pan-African Agricultural and Veterinary Conference, Pretoria (1929), 245, 247
Pant, P. S., 1730 (18)
Paper making and trade, 1121 (9), 1123 (2), 1125
  Kenya, 1124
  Uganda, 1124
Papyrus (the plant), 770
Parasites, 1377–77a, 1412 (10, pt. 38)
  See also Trypanosomiasis
Pare-Taveta Malaria Scheme, 1384, 1386–87, 1390
Partition, colonial. *See* Colonial partition
Paterson, Alexander, 1341–42
Paterson, D. N., 176 (17–22)
Patta concession, 1099–1100
Pavements. *See* Roads
Pavumapo palilie, na hadithi nyingine, 1214
Payne, W. J. A., 1808
Peanuts, 199–208
Peas, 221
Pelham-Johnson, M. F., 884–85
Pelorovis oldowayensis, 1018 (22)
Penal code. *See* Criminal law
Penpoint, 251
Pensions, civil service. *See* Civil service pensions
Pereira, H. C., 767 (8), 1624
Permanent way, 557–58, 604–5
Perren, G., 886
Perrott, Daisy V., 1271–72
Pesa moto, 1214
Philatelic bulletin, 414
Phillips, C. H., 797
Phiri, Desmond D., 887
Phosphates, 1120
Physical education and training
  text-books (primary), 864, 876–77
  text-books (secondary), 875
Physicians, directories, 1392
Physiography. *See* Geology
Pilot balloons. *See* Balloons—pilot
Pine, 176 (24–25, 27–28)
Pinhey, Elliot C. G., 1752, 1754–55
Pinto, F. F., 47
Place, James, 888

Plague, 1378
Plant-lice, 1753
Plant names, popular, 1607–8
  Narok region, Kenya, 1605
Plant quarantine, 43, 130, 150
Plants, effect of insecticides on, 136, 138, 143
Pleuropneumonia, 245
Poetry. *See* East African literature (English) — poetry; Swahili poetry
Police, 1335, 1337–38, 1340
Politics and government, 5, 10, 33, 1459–1600
  East Africa Protectorate, 1468, 1470–71, 1474
  Kenya, 1511, 1548, 1550, 1560
  Tanganyika, 1511, 1566
  Tanzania, 1548, 1550
  Uganda, 1468, 1470–71, 1474, 1511, 1550
  Zanzibar, 1511–12
  See also Boundaries; Spheres of influence
Pollitt, H. W. W., 634
Poncelet, L., 1693
Popkin, J. M., 889, 1272
Popov, G. B., 120 (31)
Popular science readers series, 878–83
Population, 11, 767 (3), 1764–89
  Kenya, 10, 753
    African, 1767–68
    maps, 1011
    "non-native," 1766
    See also Boer immigration; Emigration and immigration—Kenya
  maps, 766–67, 982, 1009–10
  statistics, 752, 761, 763
  Tanganyika, 10, 755
    African, 1775–76
    maps, 1779
  Uganda, 10, 756, 947
  Zanzibar, 1765 (7)
    Pemba, 1765 (8)
  See also Census
Portal, Gerald H., 1099–1100
Postage-stamps, 414, 423
Postal savings-banks, 916
  Kenya, 906–7, 910, 915
  Tanganyika, 907–8, 915
  Tanzania, 908, 911
  Uganda, 907, 909, 912, 915
Postal service, 385, 389, 398, 404, 415–16, 419, 421, 531
  directories
    Kenya, 392, 407
    Tanganyika, 393–94

Postal service (cont.)
    Tanzania, 409
    Uganda, 395, 411
  employees, 400, 1536–37
    salaries, pensions, etc., 1514, 1518, 1541
  guides, 396–97, 399, 406, 420
  rates, 399
  salaries, pensions, etc., 413
  statistics, 764
Postgen, 424
Posts and telecommunications, 382–426
Pottery, 1109, 1121 (10)
Potts, William H., 1411
Poultry, 91, 96
Power resources
  Kenya, 753
  statistics, 752
  Tanganyika, 755
  Uganda, 699 (9), 756
  See also Coal; Evaporative power; Water-power
Pozzuolanas, 1121 (8)
Pratt, Lewis J., 1541
Prehistory, 1018–22
  See also Archaeology
Preliminary studies in Swahili lexicon, 1156
Price indexes, 728, 734
  See also Cost and standard of living
Prices
  Kenya, 725–26, 753
  statistics, 752, 761, 763
  Tanganyika, 755
  Uganda, 737, 75
Primates, fossil, 1018 (1, 9)
  See also Man, prehistoric
Pringle, G., 1390
Pringle, Patrick, 605
Prins, Adriaan H. J., 1156
Printing, 1645
Prisons, 1341–42
Private enterprise in British tropical Africa, 350
Procedure (law). *See* Courts—Tanganyika
Proceedings of a conference of East African soil chemists, 230
Proceedings of the fourth specialist meeting on applied meteorology in East Africa, 1743
Proconsul africanus, 1018 (16)
Produce trade, 722, 741, 1115
Production and trade reports, 320
Programmed instruction, 801
Prospecting, geophysical methods, 1617
Prosser, Roy, 807
Public debts, 938–39, 941

Public finance, 923–59
East Africa Protectorate, 932
Kenya, 936, 953
statistics, 752, 761, 763
Tanganyika, 755, 932, 940, 949, 951
Uganda, 756, 932, 936, 947–48
Zanzibar, 932
Public health, 809–10, 1373, 1395–97
Kenya, 753
Tanganyika, 755
Uganda, 756
See also Children—care and hygiene; Health education; Nurses and nursing
Public land concessions, 768–82, 1099–1100
East Africa Protectorate, 768–81, 1099–1100
Kenya. *See* Public land concessions—East Africa Protectorate
Uganda, 768–82, 1099
See also British East African Association
Public Officers' (East African Common Services Organisation) Agreement, (1961), 1545
Public welfare, 5, 1763
See also Community development
Public works, 697–98
Publishing, educational. *See* Educational publishing
Pulp and Paper Research Co., ltd., 1124
Pulsations; an East African anthology of poetry, 271

Q

Quarterly economic and statistical bulletin, 752
Queen Elizabeth National Park, 692
Quennell, A. M., 1614 (6)
Quinine. *See* Cinchona
Quinquennial Advisory Committee, 836

R

R. M. S. 'Victoria,' 482
Race relations, South Asians, 1790
Radio relay systems, 386
Railroad bridges, 552
Railroad engineering, 600, 602–3
Railroad law, 431–32
Railroads, 348, 440, 443, 448, 459, 489, 493, 511, 568, 576, 583, 585, 587, 604, 620, 622–23, 773, 775
accounts, bookkeeping, etc., 465, 570–71

Railroads (cont.)
Central Africa link, 460, 493, 602–3
consolidation, 466, 529, 599, 608, 610, 779
distances, etc., 500–501, 505, 621
electrification, 476
employees, 471, 496–99, 509, 517–17a, 569, 588, 593, 606–7, 625–27, 1137, 1491, 1494–96, 1514, 1519–20, 1533–34
salaries, pensions, etc., 432, 503, 517–17a, 572, 582, 589–90, 1491, 1494–96, 1514, 1519–20, 1533–34
training, 446, 496, 624
estimates, 463, 468–69, 481, 510, 516, 519–20, 566–67, 575, 615–16, 923–25, 929
fares, 490–91
finance, 435–36, 446–47, 450, 525–26, 532, 536, 551, 553, 562–63, 568, 597–98, 609, 932
history, 428–29, 557–58, 587, 604–5
industrial, 487–88
Kenya, 476, 525–26, 528, 533–36, 538–50, 557–58, 577–78, 778–79
maps, 477, 483–86, 555
See also Lake Magadi Railway
maintenance and repair, 578
management, 489, 497, 509, 565
maps, 467, 471, 474, 483–86, 555, 601, 766, 982, 1101
rates, 490, 492, 500–501, 521–22, 525–26, 568, 584, 618, 741
rolling-stock, 475
See also Locomotives
statistics, 502, 764
Tanganyika, 436–37, 439, 466, 470, 494–95, 512–16, 525–28, 557–58, 602–3, 608–9
maps, 474, 483–86
time-tables, 491, 507, 592, 594, 619
Uganda, 438, 508, 525–26, 528, 557–58, 611–13, 775–76
maps, 467, 483–86, 555
valuation, 595–96
vocational guidance, 473
See also East African Railways and Harbours Administration; East African Railways Corporation
Railroads and harbors, 427–627
Rain and rainfall, 81, 1621, 1649, 1660, 1669, 1671, 1674 (v. 2, no. 2; v. 3, no. 5, 7), 1686 (1, 3, 8), 1708, 1711, 1727, 1730 (15–17, 19, 23)
Kenya, 1663–64, 1666, 1674 (v. 2, no. 7), 1678,

Rain and rainfall (cont.)
1682, 1684, 1696, 1700, 1704, 1709, 1728–29
maps, 1011
maps, 474, 766–67, 982, 1009–11, 1687–88, 1701 (v. 3, no. 10), 1719–20, 1730 (14), 1738, 1744–46
observers' manuals, 1647 (1–1a)
Seychelles, 1663, 1666, 1682–83, 1696, 1709, 1711
Tanganyika, 1663, 1666, 1678, 1682, 1684, 1696, 1705, 1709
Tabora, 1674 (v. 2, no. 12)
Tanzania, 1696, 1705, 1709, 1721, 1728–29
maps, 474
Uganda, 1663, 1666, 1674 (v. 2, no. 5), 1678, 1682, 1684, 1696, 1706, 1709, 1728–29, 1732, 1741
Zanzibar, 1636, 1663, 1666, 1678, 1682, 1696, 1705, 1709
Rainey, R. C., 120 (9, 26), 149
Rain gauges, 1693
Rain-making, 1674 (v. 3, no. 6), 1686 (6)
Kenya, 1674 (v. 3, no. 3)
Tanganyika, 1674 (v. 2, no. 9–10; v. 3, no. 3)
Uganda, 1674 (v. 3, no. 4)
Raisman, Jeremy, 952
Ramage, Sir Richard O., 1536
Ramie, 1674 (v. 2, no. 8)
see also Sisal hemp
Rana, G. Singh, 1674 (v. 3, no. 3)
Range research, 80, 82
Rankine, J. D., 1329
Ravenstein, Ernest G., 1099–1101, 1739, 1742
Readers for new literates, 804, 890
bibliography, 787–90, 794–95
See also Swahili language—readers
The rebels, 273
Red locust, 120 (15, 20, 26, 33), 121 (2)
Rees, P. M., 55
Regional economic integration. *See* Economic integration
Registration of private companies, the filing of returns and the duties of private companies and their directors, 1312
Rehabilitation, 1372
Religion, Tanganyika, census, 1782
The renegade, 267
Report on economic and commercial conditions in British East Africa, 717
Reproduction, 1748
Research, 10, 29–35, 1556, 1569, 1581, 1596
finance, 952

Research (cont.)
See also Agricultural research; Industrial research
Resorts, directories, 649–50, 652–54
Restaurants, directories, 649–50, 652–54
Restraint of trade, 286
Rhinoceros, fossil, 1018 (21)
Rice, 220, 1394
Richards, C. G., 804
Richards, Charles G., 1273–74
Richards, E. V., 1629
Richards, O. W., 120 (15), 1756 (v. 2, no. 8)
Ridgway, Robin, 604
Rigby, Christopher P., 1024
Rinderpest, 239
Tanganyika, 239, 246
Riwa, R. L., 1275
Road services. *See* Motor bus lines
Road research technical paper, 628, 633
Roads, 348, 628–35
earth, 628
gravel, 628
Kenya, 628, 634
maps, 766–67
Tanganyika, 634
Uganda, 628, 634
Zanzibar, 634
Robert, Shaaban, 1199, 1215–17
Roberts, Helen M., 890, 1252, 1276
Robertson, Muriel, 1412 (12, pt. 15; 13, pt. 14)
Robinson, Edward A. G., 724
Robinson, John B. D., 113, 113, 234
Robinson, P., 1744–45
Rockefeller Foundation. International Health Division, 1363
Rogers, P. F., 233
Ronaldshay. *See* Zetland, Lawrence John Lumley Dundas, 2d Marquis of
Rosa, J., 203
Rosa Mistika, 1190
Ross, F. E., 891
Ross, P. H., 1412 (8, pt. 17)
Ross Institute of Tropical Hygiene, 1379
Royal East African Navy. *See* East Africa High Commission. Royal East African Navy
Royal Engineers Institute, 600
Royal Irish Constabulary, 1340
Royal Society of London. Sleeping Sickness Commission, 1412
Royal Technical College of East Africa. *See* Nairobi. Royal Technical College of East Africa

Rubber, 770, 774, 777, 780
Rukwa, lake, Tanganyika. *See* Lake Rukwa, Tanganyika
Ruminantia, 1747
Russam, K., 633
Russell, Edward W., 766–67
Ruwenzori expedition (1934–5), 1756
Ruwenzori expedition (1952), 1757
Rwandusya, E. M., 1730 (18)

S

SPEAR, 606
Sabrosky, C. W., 1756 (v. 2, no. 7)
Safari, 693
Safari za watangulizi, 1271
Saggerson, E. P., 767 (5)
Said, M. M., 1214
Salmon, E. Marling, 1456
Sanford, Sir George R., 38, 361, 1493
Sangster, R. G., 767 (11)
Sanitation, 1378
Sansom, H. W., 1686 (1, 3, 5), 1674 (v. 3, no. 1–4), 1701 (v. 4, no. 1), 1711 (9), 1730 (22)
Sarufi na ufasaha, 1157
Savage, Robert J. G., 1018 (19)
Sayer, H. J., 149
Schauder, Leon, 72
Schistocerca gregaria Forskål. *See* Desert locust
Schistosomiasis, 1358
  bibliography, 1364
  Tanzania, 1358
Scholarships, 843
School grounds, 868
School management and organization, 846
Schools, exercises and recreation, 784
Schuster, Sir George, 938–39
Science, periodicals, bibliography, 1601
Science and technology, 1601–1761
Scientific expeditions, 1756–57
Scott, R. M., 767 (6)
Scott, Robert, 1659
Scouts and scouting, 892
Seed distribution, 61–64
Seiches, Lake Victoria, 168 (10)
Seismometry, 1615
  See also Earthquakes
Select Committee on the East African Income Tax (Management) Bill. *See* East Africa High Commission. East Africa Central Legislative Assembly. Select Committee on the East African Income Tax (Management) Bill
Sellwood, F. G., 1427
Selsjord, Mikael, 757–60, 762
Semghanga, Francis H. J., 1218
Sengo, T. S. Y., 1184
Serjeant, R. B., 800
Serubiri, A., 1765
Sesame, 47
Sewing, 884–85
Seychelles. Supreme Court, 1326
Shaw, S. H., 1615
Sheffield, F. M. L., 150
Shelley, Norman, 72
Shipping, 430
  Kenya, 479
    maps, 483–86
  maps, 483–86
  Tanzania, maps, 483–86
  Uganda, maps, 483–86
  See also Cargo handling
Shrubs, identification, Tanganyika, 1602–3
Siddik, Khalifa Abubakr, 1167
Sikilizeni mashairi, 1176
Sikio, 607
Sikupendi tena, 1212
Silk, 772
Simopithecus, 1021
Simpson, W. J., 1378
Simu ya kifo, 1189
Sincerity divorced, 254
Singh Rana, G. *See* Rana, G. Singh
Singing with the night, 276
Sisal hemp, 722
  See also Agave; Ramie
Sissons, J., 1701 (v. 4, no. 3)
Skinner, Hugh A., 1758
Sky is the limit, 266
Slater, Isobel, 216
Slave trade, 1023–76, 1099–1100, 1260–61
  South Asian involvement, 1041
  suppression, treaties, 1059
  Zanzibar, 1024, 1032, 1039–54, 1057–60, 1062–76
    suppression, treaties, 1033, 1038, 1058
Sleeping-sickness, 1399–1412
  See also Trypanosomiasis
Sleeping Sickness Commission. *See* Royal Society of London. Sleeping Sickness Commission
Sleeping Sickness Committee. *See* Great Britain. Colonial Office. Sleeping Sickness Committee

Smith, A., 87
Smith, A. M., 434
Smith, G. E., 998
Smith, J., 246
Smith, J. Stephen, 892
Smuts, J. C., 1420
Snapnews, 335
Snow-White, K. H. A. Akilimali. *See* Akilimali Snow-White, K. H. A.
Sociology, 33, 1762–94a
Soccer, 1795–96
Social groups, families and marriage, 1791–94a
Social service. *See* Public welfare
Soda industry, 770–74, 776
Soil chemistry, 223, 230
Soil-surveys, Kenya, 225
Soils, 223–30, 767 (6)
  Kenya, 226–27
  maps, 225–27, 766–67
  Tanganyika, 226–27, 229
  Uganda, 226–27
  Zanzibar, 226–27
Solar radiation, 1710
  observations, Kabete, Kenya, 1670
Soldiers, African. *See* Askaris
Sorghum, 47, 231–32
  Kenya, 232
  Tanganyika, 232
  Uganda, 232
Sorghum Mission to Certain British African Territories, 232
Sound, juvenile literature, 882
Sounding balloons. *See* Balloons—sounding
South and East African Combined Agricultural, Cotton, Entomological and Mycological Conference, Nairobi (1926), 86
South Asians in East Africa, 272, 614, 778–79, 803, 1032, 1451, 1656, 1790
Southern Cameroons. House of Assembly. *Sessional paper,* 109
Soy-beans, 47
Specialist Meeting on Applied Meteorology in East Africa, 4th, Nairobi (1968), 1743
Specialist Meeting on Coffee Research in East Africa, 1st, Nairobi (1966), 113
Specialist Meeting on Crops in Areas of Low or Erratic Rainfall, Mugua, Kenya (1964), 81, 1658
Spheres of influence
  British, 1077–84, 1089
  German, 1077–83, 1089

Spheres of influence (cont.)
  Italian, 1084
  maps, 1085
  See also Boundaries
Sports, 1795–96
Ssenkiko, Pauline, 1333
Stacke, Henry Fitz Maurice, 1436
Staff list, 1484, 1510, 1540, 1547
Standard of living. *See* Cost and standard of living
Standing Advisory Committee for Medical Research in East Africa, 1353, 1360
Standing Committee on Finance. *See* East Africa High Commission. East Africa Central Legislative Assembly. Standing Committee on Finance
Standing Committee on Tsetse and Trypanosomiasis Research, 1399–1400
Standing Veterinary Research Committee, 237
Standpoints on African literature; a critical anthology, 277
Stanley, Edward John Stanley, Baron, 1562
Starnes, O., 87
Statistical digest, 304
Statistical survey of the East African Community institutions, 764
Statistics, 304, 749–52, 759, 761–64
  Kenya, 753, 757
  Tanganyika, 754–55
  Tanzania, 758
  Uganda, 756, 760
  See also Conference of Governors of British East African Territories. Statistical Dept.; East Africa High Commission. East African Statistical Dept.; *and* under specific subjects, e.g., Commerce and trade —statistics
Steamboat lines, 416, 478, 530–31, 546, 550, 617, 620, 673
  fares, 490
  time-tables, 491, 507, 619
Steere, Edward, Bp., 1146
Stephens, J. H., 629
Stevens, N. F., 628
Stewart, J., 1605
Stock and stockbreeding. *See* Livestock
Stockdale, Frank A., 37, 88–89
Stock-ranges, 80, 82, 84
Stoddard, George D., 845
Stone, Sir Gilbert, 1348
Stordy, Robert, J., 243

Storey, H. H., 53
Stories, Bible. *See* Bible stories
Storms, Lake Victoria, 1674 (v. 1, no. 2)
Strachey, C., 1076
The structure of harmony, 1205
Stuart, B. E. St. L., 175, 176 (2, 5–6)
Studies in Swahili dialect, 1151–53, 1160–61
Studies on the ecology of coffee plantations in East Africa, 112
Students' book-writing schemes, 254, 259, 265, 270, 274–75
Study, method of, 887
Sturt, George, 72
Sugar, 233–34, 1107
  Tanzania, 234
Sugar cane, 233
Suleiman, M., 1214
Survey of current wildlife research projects in East Africa, 1800
Surveys, 1012
  East Africa Protectorate, 998
  Kenya, 1005
  Tanzania, 1005
  Uganda, 998, 1005
Swahili, 1158
Swahili biography, 1181, 1188, 1255
Swahili drama, 1185–86, 1194–95, 1207–9, 1212
Swahili fiction, 1164, 1170, 1179–80, 1184, 1189–91, 1205a, 1210–17
Swahili language, 1143–1301
  addresses, essays, lectures, 1290
  agricultural terms, 1297
  bibliography, 787–90, 794–95, 1139–42
  composition and exercises, 1287
  dialects
    Chi-chifundi, 1151
    Chi-jomvu, 1152
    Ki-mtang'ata, 1161
    Ki-ngare, 1152
    Ki-vumba, 1153
    Mombasa region, Kenya, 1152
    Pemba, 1160
    Southern Kenya coast, 1151, 1153
    Tanganyika coast, 1161
  dictionaries, English, 1148, 1156, 1607–8
  engineering terms, 1297
  examinations, questions, etc., 1286, 1288, 1292–96, 1301
  fishing terms, 1297
  glossaries, vocabularies, etc., 1297, 3100

Swahili language (cont.)
  grammar, 1146, 1150, 1157, 1228–29, 1298–99
  household terms, 1297
  letter-writing, 1230, 1266
  medical terms, 1297
  orthography and spelling, 1143, 1145
  periodicals, 1149, 1154, 1158, 1279
  readers and text-books, 1225–85
  reading (adult education), 1289
  study and teaching, 1286–1301
  terms and phrases, 1155
  Uganda, 1159
  versification, 1165–66, 1204
  veterinary terms, 1297
  writing, 1258
  See also East African Swahili Committee
Swahili linguistics, 1143–61
Swahili literature, 1162–1223
  periodicals, 1149, 1158
  translations from English, 1231–33, 1240, 1243–45, 1248, 1254, 1272–74
  translations from French, 1264–65, 1283
  translations from German, 1246
Swahili manuscripts, bibliography, 1177
Swahili poetry, 1160, 1165–66, 1168–69a, 1171–76, 1182–83, 1187, 1192, 1196–1203, 1205–6, 1218–24
Swahili proverbs, 1178
Swahili riddles, 1178, 1284
Swine, fossil, 1018 (14)
Symes, George S., 1564–65
Symposium of Tropical Meteorology, Honolulu, Hawaii (1970), 1730 (19–21)

T

TKK Kiswahili, 1249
T.P.R.I. miscellaneous report, 155
Tabora, Tanzania, weather, 1632, 1674 (v. 2, no. 12)
Tack, C. H., 197
Talbot, Lee M., 1809
Tana river, Kenya
  concessions, 770, 772–73
  fishes, 164 (10)
  water-supply, 1730 (20)
Tanga, Tanzania, cost and standard of living, 736
Tanganyika (general), 1, 6–9, 10, 18
  Committee of Inquiry Into the East African

Tanganyika (cont.)
Railways Road Services in Tanganyika, 635
Dept. of Education, 1295
Dept. of Lands and Mines, 1002
Dept. of Lands and Surveys, 1765
Geological Survey Dept., 1619, 1744–46
Government circular, 1503
Governor
1924–1931 (Cameron), 940, 1145, 1563
1931–1933 (Symes), 1564–65
1949–1958 (Twining), 14, 20
High Court, 974, 1326
Land Tenure Adviser, 1779
Laws, statutes, etc., 208
Legislative Council. *Sessional paper,* 90, 151, 336, 527, 608–9, 837, 940, 968, 1457, 1501–2, 1523–24, 1566
Mambo leo, 1198
Treaties, etc. Great Britain (on behalf of Kenya and Uganda) (Dec. 9, 1961), 1576–80
Tropical Pesticides Research Institute, 152–53
Tsetse Research Dept., 1602
Tanganyika Agricultural Corporation, 200, 208
Tanganyika Industrial Committee, 1118
Tanganyika Landing and Shipping Company, 458
Tanganyika National Parks, 675, 691
Tanning, 1121 (7)
See also Hides and skins
Tanzania
Community Development Division, 1280
Geological Survey Dept., 1719–20
Ministry of Agriculture. Agriculture Training Centre, Tengeru, 1298
Ministry of Information and Tourism, 1584
Ministry of Local Government and Rural Development, 1247
Ministry of National Education, 1277–78
Treaties, etc. (June 6, 1967), 914
Water Development and Irrigation Division, 1631
Wizara ya Elimu ya Taifa. *See* Tanzania. Ministry of National Education
Wizara ya Maendeleo na Utamaduni, 1240
Wizara ya Serikali za Mitaa na Maendeleo Vijijini. *See* Tanzania. Ministry of Local Government and Rural Development
Tariff, 282, 326, 329, 331–33, 337, 456–57, 489, 492, 499–500, 741
law, 284–86, 295–99, 307, 309, 329
Tariff (cont.)
See also Commerce and trade
Tax administration and procedure, 979
Taxation, 10, 952, 960–80
East Africa Protectorate, 1474
Kenya, 960
Treaties
Denmark, 975
Sweden, 977
Taylor, C. M., 1674 (v. 3, no. 6), 1730 (17)
Tea, 41, 722
Kenya, 1624 (7), 1674 (v. 2, no. 7)
Southwest Mau, 1624 (3)
Teacher education, 846–54
Teachers
handbook for literacy, 874
Kenya, salaries, pensions, etc., 1541–43
Teachers' colleges, 849
Teaching adults: a handbook for developing countries, 807
Technical and vocational education, 805, 855–62
Technical communications of the Commonwealth Bureau of Animal Breeding and Genetics, Edinburgh, 215
Technical conferences of the East African dependencies, 37, 86, 223, 230
Technology, periodicals, bibliography, 1601
Tejani, Bahadur, 272
Telecommunication, 384–86, 396, 404, 406
directories, 406a
Telephone directories
Kenya, 382, 390, 401, 406, 408, 422
Mombasa, Kenya, 382
Tanganyika, 390, 402
Tanzania, 402, 410
Uganda, 390, 403, 412
Telex directories, 406a
Temperature
Kenya, 1663, 1712, 1731
Nairobi, 1673, 1689, 1713
Seychelles, 1663
Tanganyika, 1663, 1712
Tanzania, 1731
Uganda, 1663, 1712, 1731
Zanzibar, 1663, 1712
Tephigram, 1674 (v. 2, no. 4)
Teuzi za nafsi, 1218
Text-books, 83–93
Theatricals, amateur. *See* Amateur theatricals
Theobald, Fred V., 1412 (3, pt. 7)
Thesiger, G., 1474
Thiong'o, Ngugi Wa, 269, 273

Thirteen offensives against our enemies, 260
This time tomorrow, 273
Thogo, S., 176 (29)
Thomas, D. P., 1018 (3, 5)
Thompson, B. W., 1686 (7–8)
Thorkil, Søe, 893
Thornthwaite's classification (meteorology), 1674 (v. 3, no. 2)
Thornton, R. S., 1795–96
Threadgold, Nesta, 1397–98
Tides, tables, 506
Tilapia, 160 (1), 163, 164 (1), 168 (2)
Tiles, 1121 (16)
  roofing, 1121 (12)
Timber, 41, 191, 193–94, 197, 777
Timms, Geoffrey L., 1350
Tin ores
  Tanganyika, northwestern Karagwe, 1620
  Uganda, southern Ankole, 1620
Tipoo Tib. *See* Hamid ibn Muhammad, called Tipoo Tib
Tobacco, 235
  Kenya, 235
  Tanganyika, 235
  Uganda, 235
Todd, C. T., 1242
Tomsett, J. E., 1730 (14)
Tonnoir, A. L., 1756 (v. 1, no. 4)
Tourist trade, 41, 338–46
  Kenya, 344–46
  statistics, 752, 761, 763
  Tanganyika, 344–36
  Uganda, 344–46
  Zanzibar, 344–46
  See also Description and travel
Townsend, A. L. H., 1752
Trade. *See* Commerce and trade
Trade and revenue report for Kenya, Uganda, and Tanganyika, 291, 303
Trade regulation, 700
Transport Advisory Council, 437–38, 443–44
Transportation, 11–12, 319, 347–81, 427–695, 1556, 1561
  See also Cargo handling; Communications and transportation
Trapnell, C. G., 767 (9)
Travel guide to Kenya and Uganda, 680–86
Treasury of East African history, 428, 1019, 1023
Treasury of East African literature, 1267, 1269, 1275, 1281
Treaties, etc.
  Denmark—Great Britain, 976
  East African Common Services Organization—Great Britain, 1545
  East African Community—Great Britain, 1551
  East African Community—International Bank for Reconstruction and Development, 450
  Ethiopia—Great Britain, 1091
  Germany—Great Britain, 1059, 1077, 1081, 1083, 1086, 1089, 1410
  Germany—Zanzibar, 1056, 1078
  Great Britain—Denmark, 976
  Great Britain—East African Common Services Organization, 1545
  Great Britain—East African Community, 1551
  Great Britain—Ethiopia, 1091
  Great Britain—Germany, 1059, 1077, 1081, 1083, 1086, 1089, 1410
  Great Britain—Italy, 1084
  Great Britain—Kenya, 1545
  Great Britain—Sweden, 977
  Great Britain—Tanganyika, 1322, 1545, 1576–80
  Great Britain—Uganda, 1545
  Great Britain—United States, 554
  Great Britain—Zanzibar, 1033, 1038, 1058–59, 1078, 1087–88, 1093
  Imperial British East Africa Company—Zanzibar, 1099–1100, 1103–6
  International Bank for Reconstruction and Development—East African Community, 450
  Italy—Great Britain, 1084
  Kenya—Great Britain, 1545
  Kenya—Tanganyika, 1576–80
  Kenya—Tanzania, 914, 1591, 1598
  Kenya—Uganda, 914, 1591, 1598
  Sweden—Great Britain, 977
  Tanganyika—Great Britain, 1322, 1545, 1576–80
  Tanganyika—Kenya, 1576–80
  Tanganyika—Uganda, 1576–80
  Tanzania—Kenya, 914, 1591, 1598
  Tanzania—Uganda, 913, 1591, 1598
  Uganda—Great Britain, 1545
  Uganda—Kenya, 914, 1591, 1598
  Uganda—Tanganyika, 1576–80
  Uganda—Tanzania, 914, 1591, 1598
  United States—Great Britain, 554
  Zanzibar—Germany, 1059, 1078

Treaties, etc. (cont.)
Zanzibar—Great Britain, 1033, 1038, 1058–59, 1078, 1087–88, 1093
Zanzibar—Imperial British East Africa Company, 1099–1100, 1103–6
See also Commercial treaties
Treaty for East African co-operation, 1591–92, 1598
Annex, 914
Tree breeding, 173, 176 (1–2, 15–18)
Trees, 174, 181
Tanganyika, 1602–3
See also Names of trees, e.g., Coniferae; Cypress; Eucalyptus
Triangulation, 999, 1005, 1013–14
Trichoptera. *See* Caddis-flies
Tropical Pesticides Research Institute, 132, 153–55
about, 69, 765
Troughton, J. F. C., 1497
Trypanosomiasis, 52, 69, 244, 1401–3, 1406–9, 1412 (1, pt. 1; 2, pt. 3; 3, pt. 5–6; 6, pt. 12, 14; 8, pt. 17, 21–22; 10, pt. 31, 34; 12, pt. 2, 4, 6–8, 10, 13–14; 13, pt. 1, 10, 14; 14, pt. 3)
East Africa Protectorate, 1407–8
German East Africa, 1407–8, 1410
Kenya, 1399–1400
Tanzania, Musoma District, 1405
treaties, 1410
Uganda, 1399–1400, 1407–8, 1412 (1, pt. 2; 4, pt. 8; 5, pt. 10; 6, pt. 11; 8, pt. 16, 18–19; 9, pt. 23–24; 10, pt. 35–36, 38–39; 11; 12, pt. 9, 15; 13, pt. 3–4, 8; 14, pt. 1–2)
Zanzibar, 1412 (10, pt. 30)
See also Mosquitoes; Parasites; Tsetse-flies
Tsetse-flies, 10, 1404, 1412 (8, pt. 20; 12, pt. 12; 17)
control, 134, 138–40, 1401–3, 1409
Kenya, maps, 1011
maps, 1009–11, 1411
Tanganyika, 134 (3–6)
See also East African Tsetse and Trypanosomiasis Organization; Trypanosomiasis Tsetse Fly and Trypanosomiasis Committee, 1401
Tsetse Fly Committee. *See* Great Britain. Economic Advisory Council. Tsetse Fly Committee
Tubbe, S. R., 1527
Tuberculosis, 1378
Tuberculosis research, 1360, 1362, 1596
Tubulidentata, fossil, 1018 (10)
Tulloch, F. M. G., 1412 (6, pt. 14; 8, pt. 16, 21)
Tumbian culture, 1020
Turkana (ethnic group), 1474
Turner, E. F., 1001
Turner, G. C., 806
Turrill, William B., 1604
Twende tusome, 1280
Twining, Edward F., 14, 20
Twining, Helen Mary Twining, Baroness, 822, 1379

U

UNDP/WHO hydrometeorological survey of the catchments of lakes Victoria, Kioga, and Albert, 1621
UNESCO. *See* United Nations Educational, Scientific and Cultural Organization
UNIDO Workshop on Financial Planning of Industrial Projects, 1117
Ubeberu utashindwa, 1191
Udoji, J. O., 1538
Uganda (general), 1, 6–9, 10, 22–23, 24, 26, 671–72
Agricultural Dept., 56, 84
Customs Dept., 332, 337
Dept. of Information, 677
Economic Committee Appointed To Consider and Report Upon the Most Productive Route To Be Followed by the Proposed Extension of the Uganda Railway Into the Protectorate, 613
Geological Survey, 1620, 1746
Governor
1925–1932 (Gowers), 1159, 1563, 1564–65
1935–1940 (Mitchell), 838
1952–1957 (Cohen), 14, 21
High Court, 974, 1326, 1333
Land and Survey Office, 998
Lands and Surveys Dept., 1002
Laws, statutes, etc., 1592
Legislative Council. *Sessional paper,* 324, 610–11, 969, 1458, 1504–5, 1525–26, 1535
Medical Dept. Laboratory Services Division, 1406
Treaties, etc. (June 6, 1967), 914
Uganda Development Corporation, 1124
Uganda Industrial Committee, 1118
Uganda National Parks, 675, 692
Uganda Railway, 614–23, 694–95, 1810
about, 79, 210, 321, 428–29, 533–53, 600, 770–71, 774, 779, 932, 1099–1100

Uganda Railway (cont.)
budget, 532, 615–16, 924–25, 929
cost of construction, 553
maps, 555–56, 1101
Uganda Railway Committee, 534
Uhud, battle of, 1222
Ulenge, Yussuf, 1281–82
The uniformed man, 261
Union Castle Main Steamship Company, 531
United Kingdom. *See* Great Britain
United Nations
Development Programme, 624, 1549, 1553, 1621, 1628a
about, 446
Economic and Social Council. Statistical Commission, 290
Treaty series, 1576
United Nations Educational, Scientific and Cultural Organization, 1253
United States
Agency for International Development, 1393
Kenya, 979
Army Map Service, 992, 1002–3
Internal Revenue Service, 979
United States Educational Commission in the United Kingdom, 82, 1610
Universities of Eastern Africa Conference on Teacher Education
9th, National Institute of Education (Uganda), (1970), 852
10th, University of Nairobi (1971), 853
11th, Dar es Salaam (1972), 854
University of East Africa, 839–41, 1751
about, 823–26, 839–40, 842, 844–45
Committe on Needs and Priorities, 842
dissolution, 845
entrance requirements, 844
Grants Committee, 843
University of East Africa Conference on New Directions in East African Teacher Education: Innovation, Implementation, and Evaluation, 7th, Mombasa (1968), 850
University of East Africa Conference on Permanent Staffing of Teacher Education Institutions, Dar es Salaam (1966), 849
University of East Africa Conference on Teacher Education, 8th, Dar es Salaam (1969), 851
University of Zambia. Institute of Education. *Progress report,* 851–53
Upper atmosphere. *See* Atmosphere, upper
Urinary organs, diseases, 1361
Urquhart, W., 50, 434
Ushirikina si mzuri, 1214
Utenzi wa Abdurrahmani na Sufiyani, 1171
Utenzi wa Al-Akida (a Swahili poem), 1183
Utenzi wa Enjili Takatifu, 1292–3
Utenzi wa Fumo Liongo, 1219
Utenzi wa Fumo Liyongo, 1192
Utenzi wa Jamhuri ya Tanzania, 1206
Utenzi wa jengo lenye itifaki: baiti 334, 1205
Utenzi wa Kadhi Kasim bin Jaafar, 1172
Utenzi wa Kutawafu Nabii, 1173
Utenzi wa Mkunumbi, 1220
Utenzi wa Nushur, 1221
Utenzi wa Seyyidna Huseni bin Ali, 1174
Utenzi wa Vita vya Maji-Maji, 1187
Utenzi wa Vita Vya Uhud, 1222
Utenzi wa vita vya Wadachi kutamalaki Mrima, 1307, A.H., 1175
Utenzi wa zinduko la ujamaa, 1197

V

Van Arkadie, Brian, 895
Van Deventer, J. L., 1420
Van Emden, F., 1756 (v. 2, no. 3–4, 6)
Van Rees, C. J., 351
Van Someren, Vernon D., 168 (14)
Vaughan, John H., 1304
Venereal diseases, 1365
Vere-Hodge, Edward R., 1102
Vesey-Fitzgerald, D. F., 120 (20)
Veterinary medicine, 95, 236–47
dictionaries, Swahili, 1297
Kenya, 243, 246
Tanganyika, 246, 755
Uganda, 243
See also Trypanosomiasis
Veterinary microbiology, 238
Veterinary research, 50–52, 69, 236–38, 241–42, 765
Victoria (ship), 482
Victoria, lake. *See* Lake Victoria
Virus research, 1354–55, 1363
Visibility, 1642
Visual education, bibliography, 787, 794
Vocational education, 805
See also specific types of vocational education, e.g., Agricultural education and extension; Medical education
Voltaire, François Marie Arouet de, 1283

W

WHO/Tanzania bilharziasis pilot control and training project, 1358
Waadhi wa ushairi, 1204
Wages
  Kenya, 753, 1127, 1129, 1134
  Tanganyika, 755
  Uganda, 756
  See also Civil service
Waimbaji wa juzi, 1199
Wakefield, A. J., 203
Walford, Arthur S., 1284
Waliaula, E., 97
Walker, J., 247
Waloff, Z., 120 (9, 26), 121 (1)
Walsh, G., 282
Walter, Albert, 725–26, 751, 894, 1336, 1644, 1648, 1650–52, 1657, 1674 (v. 1–2, no. 1)
Wananchi mashuhuri wa Tanzania, 1188
Wandera, Billy O., 274
Wangati, F. J., 1658
Wanjala, Chris, 275–77
Wasifu wa Siti binti Saad; mwimbaji wa Unguja, 1217
Water-power, 1629
  See also Evaporative power
Water-supply
  Kenya, 722–74, 779, 1623, 1730 (20)
  Tanganyika, 755, 1623
  Uganda, 1623
Watson, Robert, 220
Wavivu, 1212
Weather, 1637, 1639, 1659, 1674 (v. 2, no. 3), 1626 (7)
  influence of the moon on, 1677
  Uganda, 1733
Weather forecasting, 1646, 1674 (v. 3, no. 9), 1686 (7), 1691, 1711 (9), 1726 (6), 1736
The weather of East Africa, 1690, 1714
Weights and measures, 712, 714
Welbourn, Hebe, 1397–98
Welch, J. R., 1603
Weller, H. O., 1121 (5–6, 8, 12–14)
Weston, H. C., 805
Wheat, 47, 219
  Kenya, 71
Wheatcroft, Stephen, 365
Wheller, J. F. G., 168 (15)
Whitehead, Peter J., 168 (14)
Whitehouse, Capt., 1013
Whiteley, Wilfred H., 1139–42, 1160–61, 1181, 1199
Whitson, H. A., 425–26, 625–26
Whitworth, S. H., 247
Whitworth, T., 1018 (7, 15)
Wienk, J. F., 47
Wigram, J. M., 855
Wikondeji, 1212
Wildlife Conference for Eastern Africa, 1st, Nairobi (1969), 1811
Wildlife conservation, 767 (12), 1797–1812
  East Africa Protectorate, 1801–5
  German East Africa, 1801
  Kenya, 1798, 1812
  maps, 675, 766, 1806–7
  Tanganyika, 1798, 1808
  Uganda, 1798, 1801–5, 1812
  Zanzibar, 1801
  See also Game; National parks and reserves
Wildlife research, 1809
Wilkinson, R. Michael, 1333
Wilkinson, W., 187, 198
Williams, F., 168 (8)
Wiliams, F. H. P., 633
Willmore, P. L., 1615
Wills, 1302
Wilson, P. M., 1297–1300
Wilson, Sir Samuel, 1557
Wilson Airways, 414
Winds
  measurement, 1642, 1657, 1730 (12)
    Dar es Salaam, Tanzania, 1734
    Entebbe, Uganda, 1735
    Kenya, 1667, 1685
    Nairobi, Kenya, 1689, 1713
  observers' manuals, 1647 (5–7, 18)
  Seychelles, 1667
  Tanganyika, 1667
  Uganda, 1667
  Zanzibar, 1667
  See also Atmosphere, upper; Balloons—pilot; Cyclones
Witu, 1094, 1099
Wivu mwovu, 1214
Woman. *See* Marriage
Wood, 176 (22, 28)
  See also subdivision Concessions under names of forests, e.g., Budongo forest, Uganda—concessions
Wood borers, 194

Wood-pulp industry
Kenya, 1124
Uganda, 1124
Wood waste, 1121 (11)
See also Furnaces
Woodcock, K. E., 140, 143
Woodhead, Terence, 1630–31
Woods, Sir Wilfrid W., 980
Wool trade and industry, 1109
Word, Michael, 29
Working Party on Entrance Levels and Degree Structure of the University of East Africa, 844
Working Party on Higher Education in East Africa
(1955), 834–35
(1959), 832
(1969), 845
World Meteorological Organization, 1621, 1628a
World War (1914–1918). *See* European War (1914–1918)
World War (1939–45), 1417, 1456
art, 1421
campaigns, Africa, East
Ethiopia, 1148, 1423
Madagascar, 1419
manpower, 1432–33
periodicals, 1413, 1415, 1428, 1437
pictorial works, 1420–21
registers of dead
Tanganyika, 1431
Uganda, 1431
See also Askaris; Great Britain. Army. East Africa Command; King's African Rifles
Worthington, Edgar B., 34–35, 1812
Worthington, Frank, 1285
The wound in the heart, 273
Wright, Fergus C., 344–46
Writers in East Africa, 278
Writing, 263, 1258
Wurzel, P., 1721 (v. 4, no. 5)
Wynne, T. R., 779

Y

Yates, R. J., 146
Yellow fever, 1363
Yeo, D., 138, 144
Yoder, P., 1259
Young, E. Hilton, 1556
Young, T. R., 808

Z

Zani, Zacharish M. S., 1223–24
Zanzibar (general), 6–10, 22–26
British Resident, 1528, 1530
Grading Team Appointed To Examine Clerical Posts, 1527
High Court, 974, 1326
Laws, statutes, etc., 1060
Legislative Council. *Sessional paper,* 381, 1506–8, 1528–31
Sultan. *See* names of sultans, e.g., Bargash bin Said, Sultan of Zanzibar (1870–1888)
Treaties, etc.
1870–1888 (Barbash bin Said), 1033, 1038, 1078, 1103
1888–1890 (Khalifa bin Said), 1058, 1093, 1104
1890–1893 (Ali bin Said), 1059, 1105–6
1893–1896 (Hamed bin Thwain), 1087
1896–1902 (Hamoud bin Muhammad), 1088
Zetland, Lawrence John Lumley Dundas, 2d Marquis of, 350
Zoology, 1747–61

Index to Major Series

Colonial Office Library
East Africa pamphlet
folio
1: 1096
2: 923
14: 378
33: 1480
95: 613
106: 529
117: 1337
137: 999
138: 1012
171: 1740
183: 333
192: 282
203: 595
204: 596
214: 614
233: 1651
234: 1467
241: 1486
279: 838
295: 196
328: 1656
333: 589
367: 1399–1400
373: 237
374: 576
387: 1629
395: 804
402: 1341
414: 34
416: 917
419: 347
420: 361
425: 48

Colonial Office Library
East Africa pamphlet
octavo
7: 600
26: 1475
27: 1478
66: 1441
67: 1440
75: 936
103: 1301
115: 218
120: 110
141: 1373
142: 1487
147: 314
171: 676
199: 586
217: 349
227: 88
228: 41
244: 833
255: 316
286: 578
287: 246
316: 1432
324: 1121 (5)
325: 1121 (11)
339: 352
343: 590
349: 1418
351: 577
352: 962
381: 803
387: 1492
388: 1507
391: 1496
397: 587
399: 1495
403: 240
405: 239

Great Britain.
Colonial Office.
African no.
775: 1472
839: 1477
876: 1469
903: 1473
973: 1479
974: 1476

Great Britain.
Colonial Office.
African no. . . . , confidential
772: 770
777: 998
783: 1444
784: 1443
785: 1450
844: 771
855: 1451
862: 429
865: 924
869: 772
877: 416
895: 925
902: 1340
914: 773
919: 1446
921: 926
929: 774
944: 927
949: 1442
951: 775
953: 116
954: 1474
955: 1447
964: 928
965: 776
976: 919
983: 929
985: 777
993: 117
996: 930
998: 778
1016: 779
1018: 118
1025: 1378
1027: 931
1030: 530
1032: 780
1040: 932
1041: 933
1042: 781
1063: 934
1077: 1482
1084: 281
1089: 935

Great Britain.
Colonial Office.
African (East) no. . . . , confidential
1086: 1371
1090: 1076

Great Britain.
Colonial Office.
Colonial no.
33: 999
50: 60
51: 60
57: 1563
69: 60
78: 60
86: 60
96: 1321
100: 60
119: 60
142: 831
144: 60
151: 60
167: 60
180: 60
181: 60
183: 60
191: 1567
193: 1138
203: 60
208: 32
210: 1568
213: 60
223: 1491
235: 60
245: 1569
246: 220
258: 211
263: 1569
279: 1569
289: 1569
290: 15
297: 1569
305: 1569
316: 1569
326: 1569
331: 1569
352: 1812

Great Britain.
Foreign Office.
Africa no.
1887 (3): 1079
1888 (1): 1080
1888 (6): 1056
1888 (7): 1055
1890 (5): 1082
1890 (6): 1081

1890/91 (1): 1060
1891 (6): 1061
1892 (6): 1062
1893 (6): 1064
1893 (12): 1063
1895 (4): 1092
1895 (6): 1065
1896 (7): 1066
1897 (1): 1068
1897 (2): 1067
1898 (6): 1069
1899 (8): 1069
1900 (3): 1071
1901 (4): 1072
1902 (6): 1073
1903 (9): 1468
1904 (10): 1470
1904 (14): 1074
1905 (3): 1471
1909 (3): 1075

Great Britain.
Foreign Office.
Slave trade no.
1874 (2): 1033
1874 (5): 1035
1874 (7): 1036
1874 (8): 1034
1875 (1): 1037
1876 (3): 1039
1876 (4): 1040
1877 (2): 1042
1878 (3): 1044
1878 (4): 1043
1879 (1): 1045
1880 (5): 1046
1881 (1): 1047
1882 (1): 1048
1883 (1): 1049
1884 (1): 1050
1885 (1): 1051
1886 (1): 1052
1887 (1): 1053
1888 (1): 1054
1889 (1): 1057

Great Britain.
Parliament.
Papers by command, C.
141: 1025
209: 1027
340: 1026
385: 1028
598: 674
657: 1030
820: 1032
867–1: 1030
889: 1033
946: 1035
1062: 1036
1064: 1034
1168: 1037
1387: 1038
1521: 1039
1546: 1041
1588: 1040
1829: 1042
2139: 1044
2140: 1043
2422: 1045
2720: 1046
3052: 1047
3160: 1048
3547: 1049
3849: 1050
4523: 1051
4609: 1079
4776: 1052
5111: 1053
5315: 1080
5428: 1054
5559: 1056
5578: 1055
5821: 1057
6043: 1082
6046: 1081
6211: 1060
6373: 1061
6555: 538
6557: 1059
6560: 539
6702: 1062
7025: 545
7035: 1064
7203: 1086
7247: 1063
7646: 1092
7707: 1065
8049: 537
8275: 1066
8394: 1068
8433: 1067
8435: 547
8858: 1069

8942: 548
9331: 549
9333: 540
9502: 1070

Great Britain. Parliament.
Papers by command Cd.
96: 1071
97: 536
355: 541
430–6: 243
434: 552
593: 1072
670: 533
674: 542
787–13: 79
1009: 1089
1080: 543
1082: 535
1389: 1073
1625: 551
1628: 768
1635: 1468
1767–11: 321
1770: 544
2100: 769
2163: 1470
2164: 534
2165: 1627
2330: 1074
2332: 546
2378: 796
2408: 1471
2716: 550
3189: 1801
4319: 1410
4354: 553
4472: 1802
4732: 1075
5136: 1803
5215: 119
5775: 1804
6514: 1370
6671: 1805
7211: 1368
7349: 1408
7350: 1407
7792: 1369

Great Britain. Parliament.
Papers by command Cmd.
1311: 1790
1327: 322
2016: 350
2387: 10
2463: 319
2696: 937
2701: 938
2904: 1555
3234: 1556
3378: 1557
3494: 939
3573: 1488
3574: 1559
3848: 941
4141: 1565
4235: 525
4263: 1320
4921: 1409
5523: 415
5558: 323
5770: 372
5784: 1794a
6050: 1394
6051: 1394
6663: 32
7030: 203
7151: 32
7314: 201
7493: 32
7739: 32
7987: 5
8063: 32
8125: 202
8303: 32
8665: 32
8965: 554
8971: 32
8994: 744
9158: 200
9198: 208
9303: 32
9475: 11
9626: 32
9801: 14
9804: 13

Great Britain. Parliament.
Papers by command Cmnd.
52: 32
281: 1430
321: 32
418: 1434
591: 32

903: 976
938: 32
1215: 32
1433: 1575
1584: 32
2031: 1322
2244: 1545
5361: 1551

Great Britain. Public Record Office.
C. O. 879/–
87: 770, 998, 1472
88: 1443–44, 1450
92: 771, 1477
93: 429, 1451
94: 924
95: 772, 1469
96: 416
97: 925
98: 1340, 1473
99: 773, 1446
100: 926
101: 774
103: 927
104: 775, 1442
105: 116, 928, 1447, 1474
107: 776
108: 1476, 1470
109: 919, 929
110: 777
111: 117, 778, 930
115: 118, 779, 1378
116: 530, 780, 931
117: 781, 932–33
119: 934–35, 1482
120: 281, 936, 1076, 1371

Library of Congress Publications on Africa Since 1960

Africa, south of the Sahara; a selected, annotated list of writings. 1963. 354 p.
Ph (electrostatic print) $30
Ph (positive microfilm) $9

Africa south of the Sahara; index to periodical literature, 1900–1970. 1971. 4 v.
Available from G. K. Hall and Co., 70 Lincoln St., Boston, Mass. 02111; $325 in the U.S., $357 elsewhere

Africa south of the Sahara; index to periodical literature. First supplement. 1973. 521 p.
Available from G. K. Hall and Co.; $65 in the U.S., $71.50 elsewhere.

African libraries, book production, and archives; a list of references. 1962. 64 p.
Ph (electrostatic print) $9
Ph (positive microfilm) $7.50
Also available as electrostatic print (OP17109) from University Microfilms, 3300 North Zeeb Rd., Ann Arbor, Mich. 48106 for $6

African music; a briefly annotated bibliography. 1964. 55 p.
SuDocs (LC12.2:Af8) $1.10

African newspapers in selected American libraries. 3d ed. 1965. 135 p.
SuDocs (LC6.2:Af8/969) $1.60

African acquisitions; a report of a publication survey trip to Nigera, southern Africa, and Europe, 1972. 1973. 122 p.
SuDocs (LC2.2:Af8/12) $2.10

Agricultural development schemes in sub-Saharan Africa: a bibliography. 1963. 189 p.
Ph (electrostatic print) $20
Ph (positive microfilm) $9

American doctoral dissertations on the Arab world, 1883–1968. 1970. 102 p.
SuDocs (LC1.12/2:Arl/883–968) $1.20

Botswana, Lesotho, and Swaziland; a guide to official publications, 1868–1968. 1971. 84 p.
L

French-speaking Central Africa; a guide to official publications in American libraries. 1973. 314 p.
SuDocs (LC2.8.Af8/3) $3.70

French-speaking West Africa; a guide to official publications. 1967. 201 p.
L

Ghana; a guide to official publications, 1872/1968. 1969. 110 p.
SuDocs (LC2.8:G34/872–968) $1.50

A list of American doctoral dissertations on Africa. 1962. 69 p.
Ph (electrostatic print) $10
Ph (positive microfilm) $7.50

Madagascar and adjacent islands; a guide to official publications. 1965. 58 p.
L

Nigeria; a guide to official publications. 1966. 166 p.
L

Official publications of British East Africa
Part 1. The East Africa High Commission and other regional documents. 1960. 67 p.
Ph (electrostatic print) $10
Ph (positive microfilm) $7.50
Part 2. Tanganyika. 1962. 134 p.
Ph (electrostatic print) $16
Ph (positive microfilm) $9
Part 3. Kenya and Zanzibar. 1962. 162 p.
L
Part 4. Uganda. 1963. 100 p.
L
Official publications of French Equatorial Africa, French Cameroons, and Togo, 1946–1958; a guide. 1964. 78 p.
Electrostatic print (OP36430) available from University Microfilms, 300 North Zeeb Rd., Ann Arbor, Mich 48106 for $6
Official publications of Sierra Leone and Gambia. 1963. 92 p.
SuDocs (LC2.2:Sil/2) $1.40
Official publications of Somaliland, 1941–1959. 1960. 41 p.
Ph (electrostatic print) $10
Ph (positive microfilm) $7.50
Portuguese Africa; a guide to official publications. 1967. 217 p.
L
The Rhodesias and Nyasaland; a guide to official publications. 1965. 285 p.
L
Serials for African studies. 1961. 163 p.
Ph (electrostatic print) $18
Ph (positive microfilm) $9
Spanish-speaking Africa; a guide to official publications. 1973. 66 p.
SuDocs (LC2.8:Af8–4) $1
Sub-Sahara Africa; a guide to serials. 1970. 409 p.
SuDocs (LC2.8:Af 8/2) $7.05
United States and Canadian publications on Africa in 1960. 1962. 98 p.
SuDocs (LC2.2:Af8/7) $1.35

Ph For sale by the Photoduplication Service, Library of Congress, Washington, D.C. 20540. Checks should be made payable to the Chief, Photoduplication Service.

SuDocs For sale by the Superintendent of Documents, U.S. Government Printing Office, Washington, D.C. 20402. When ordering, cite the GPO catalog number; it appears in parentheses after the symbol "SuDocs." Add 25% for foreign postage. Increases in costs make it necessary for the Superintendent of Documents to increase the selling price of many publications offered. As it is not feasible for the Superintendent of Documents to correct the prices manually in all publications stocked, the prices charged on your order may differ from the prices printed in the publications.

L Available to U.S. libraries and institutions upon request to the Library of Congress, Central Services Division, Washington, D.C. 20540. Foreign libraries may apply to the Exchange and Gift Division.

Guides in Preparation or Under Consideration

Bibliographic guides on the following subjects are in preparation or under consideration in the Library's African Section; when published, each will be announced in the Library's *Information Bulletin*.

Arab-African relations, 1973–75
Eastern African university publications
Islam in sub-Saharan Africa
Kenya, official publications
Liberia, material in the Washington, D.C. area
Nigerian petroleum industry
Tanganyika African National Union (TANU)
Tanzania, official publications
Uganda, official publications
United States Government publications on Africa

☆ U.S. GOVERNMENT PRINTING OFFICE: 1976 O—587-874